Medieval Chiv

CU00927388

Emerging in the medieval period, chivalry
riors cherished and practices that formed their profession. In this major new
overview, Richard Kaeuper examines how chivalry made sense of violence
and war, making it tolerable for elite fighters rather than nonknightly or
subknightly populations. He discusses how chivalry buttressed status and
profession, shaped active piety, and fostered intense warrior attachments
and heterosexual relationships. Though showing regional and chronological
variations, chivalry at its core enshrined the practice of prowess in securing
honor, with this process significantly blessed by religion. Both kingship and
church authority sought to direct the great force of chivalry and, despite
tensions, finally came to terms with rising knightly status and a burgeoning
military role. Kaeuper engages with a wide range of evidence in his analysis,
drawing on the chivalric literature, manuscript illumination, and sermon
exempla and moral tales.

RICHARD W. KAEUPER is Professor of History at the University of Rochester,
NY. His previous publications include *Holy Warriors* (2009), *Chivalry and Violence
in Medieval Europe* (1999), *The Book of Chivalry of Geoffroi de Charny* (with Elspeth
Kennedy, 1996), and *War, Justice and Public Order* (1988).

Advance praise for *Medieval Chivalry*

"Professor Kaeuper is one of the foremost experts on medieval chivalry, equally at home with the evidence provided by literature and the sources normally used by historians. This new textbook draws together the important insights that he has offered on violence and religion within medieval chivalric culture, to provide a clear and exciting vision of this complex field."

Craig Taylor, University of York

"Richard Kaeuper's new book is a *tour de force*. It presents chivalry as one of the great defining forces of medieval culture. Anyone wishing to grasp medieval chivalry, and indeed the Middle Ages as a whole, will have to read this book or run the risk of seriously misunderstanding the topic."

Christoph T. Maier, University of Zurich

"*Medieval Chivalry* is a deeply erudite and multilayered analysis of a complicated and much misunderstood subject. Professor Kaeuper, the leading scholar in the field, examines chivalry in its political, social, economic, and literary contexts. It is a *tour de force* that will set the terms for future discussion."

William Caferro, Vanderbilt University

"In what is destined to become the standard work on the subject, Richard Kaeuper's *Medieval Chivalry* explores the historical evolution of this aristocratic military ethos from the ninth through the fifteenth century. Guided by his unrivaled mastery of chivalric literature, Kaeuper strips away the varnish of nineteenth-century romanticism to reveal a contested ideology that, at its heart, valorized the practice of violence by a social elite."

Richard Abels, United States Naval Academy

"In this masterly new study of the nature and development of European chivalry from the eleventh to the fifteenth century. Kaeuper takes us into the thought world of the medieval warrior aristocracy with verve and rare perception. He probes the essence of chivalric values and their expression in war and peace, elucidating with freshness and clarity chivalry's complex and subtly evolving interaction with religion, nobility, courtliness, and the state. Impressive in its range and skillful synthesis, this valuable and thought-provoking study will be essential reading for specialists and students alike."

Matthew Strickland, University of Glasgow

Cambridge Medieval Textbooks

This is a series of introductions to important topics in medieval history aimed primarily at advanced students and faculty, and is designed to complement the monograph series *Cambridge Studies in Medieval Life and Thought*. It includes both chronological and thematic approaches and addresses both British and European topics.

For a list of titles in the series, see www.cambridge.org/medievaltextbooks

MEDIEVAL CHIVALRY

RICHARD W. KAEUPER

University of Rochester

CAMBRIDGE
UNIVERSITY PRESS

CAMBRIDGE
UNIVERSITY PRESS

University Printing House, Cambridge CB2 8BS, United Kingdom

Cambridge University Press is part of the University of Cambridge.

It furthers the University's mission by disseminating knowledge in the pursuit of
education, learning and research at the highest international levels of excellence.

www.cambridge.org
Information on this title: www.cambridge.org/9780521761680

© Richard W. Kaeuper 2016

First published 2016

Printed in the United Kingdom by Clays, St Ives plc

A catalogue record for this publication is available from the British Library

Library of Congress Cataloging-in-Publication Data
Kaeuper, Richard W., author.
Medieval chivalry / Richard W. Kaeuper, University of Rochester.
pages cm. – (Cambridge medieval textbooks)
Includes bibliographical references and index.
ISBN 978-0-521-76168-0 (alk. paper)
1. Chivalry – Europe – History – To 1500. 2. Knights and knighthood – Europe –
History – To 1500. 3. Civilization, Medieval. I. Title.
CR4513.K36 2015
940.1–dc23

ISBN 978-0-521-76168-0 Hardback
ISBN 978-0-521-13795-9 Paperback

To the memory of Joseph R. Strayer
and Edmund B. Fryde

CONTENTS

FIGURES

—————— • ——————

ACKNOWLEDGMENTS

———— • ————

Since this book investigates a cluster of topics that has become almost unmanageable in scope in the past quarter century, much assistance was needed and is here noted with thanks, however inadequately. Margaret, to whom I am fortunately married, made the writing of this book possible and enhanced its approaches with her acute observations and penetrating questions; she merits more thanks than I can express.

My former and current students performed wonders. Christopher Guyol read a painfully early draft line by line and stubbornly insisted that I write clearly. Among the many forms of assistance Samuel Claussen provided was keeping me in touch with the instructive Iberian evidence on chivalry; he likewise cheerfully conducted word searches in the thickets of *Barbour's Bruce*. Peter Sposato generously and helpfully took me south of the Alps and especially into the tangled and easily misunderstood world of Florentine chivalry. Daniel Franke provided essential service by guiding me across the Rhine. Paul Dingman commented on issues raised in Part V. With heroic and tireless exactitude, Tristan Sharp transformed many of my initial and sketchy draft footnotes into the real thing, pointing out useful evidence in the process and also constructed the bibliography. Sebastian Bezerra scanned Malory's *Morte Darthur*, allowing numerous word searches, and offered helpful suggestions on the results. As the project came to a close, Sam Callis carefully aided in a variety of further word searches, as did Ben Einhouse. Courtney Hubbart, Andrew Rizzo,

Noah Bender, and Garrett Gay skillfully managed the last stages of proofreading and corrections.

A valiant cohort of professionals at Cambridge University Press managed this complex process elegantly. I am indebted to Michael Watson, who requested and encouraged me to undertake this project, to Elizabeth Friend-Smith for getting it launched, and to Rosalyn Scott, Rebecca Taylor, Emma Collison, Mary Bongiovi, Philip Alexander, and Sri Hari Kumar Sugumaran for their patience and unfailing assistance in shepherding the book into final form. I also thank Birgitte Necessary for creating the index.

Significant scholarly work, often in advance of publication, was collegially provided by Matthew Strickland, Max Lieberman, Richard Abels, Rory Cox, Ruth Karras, Helmut Pouff, and John Block Friedmans. Thomas Bisson threw a lifeline as I struggled through the stormy seas of the Carolingian era and its aftermath and Anthony J. Pollard offered helpful comments on specific points. The collegial assistance of Martin Jones gave me the courage to draw on German literature. In Rush Rhees Library and the Robbins Medieval Library within my home university, Alan Unsworth and Alan Lupack provided laudable and appreciated assistance in obtaining needed sources. Nicola Zamboni and Sara Bolzani supplied photographs of their marvelous life-sized sculptures of knights in action, which I reproduce on the book cover with gratitude; Donatella Stocchi-Perucchio and Federico Siniscalco enabled my contact with these artists.

As I wrote this study, I often found that my thought returned to basic humanistic instruction and to the enduring historical issues raised by my teachers decades ago. Though I should have thanked all of them more copiously and more often while I had opportunity, I can at least recall here with special gratitude my mentor, Joseph R. Strayer, and my unofficial mentor, Edmund B. Fryde. I have dedicated this book to their memory. That they proved inexhaustible sources of knowledge could be taken as a given; that they subtly and generously infused instruction with wisdom truly constituted a gift. That gift is acknowledged with humility as I conduct a scholarly life ever in search of meaning as a student continuing to learn.

Part I

AN APPROACH TO CHIVALRY: WAS IT REAL AND PRACTICAL?

·

Standing securely upon its spur of rock above the Charente River in south-central France, the castle of Verteuil seemed impregnable. A French force under the duke of Bourbon was besieging the castle in 1385 as part of a campaign to sweep away garrisons of *routiers* who, though formally aligned to the English crown, were simply robbing and devastating the countryside for their own profit.[1] To attack this formidable fortress, the duke relied on two classic siege techniques: he bashed parts of the defenses with stone-throwing machines (leaving several projectiles embedded in the fabric for later discovery by archaeologists), and he cut mines under the walls to topple them (and traces of these, too, have been found). The defenders had to endure the missiles, but knew how to respond more actively to the mines: they dug counter-mines, eventually intersecting the advancing tunnels of the besiegers. Armored men fought in these cramped tunnels as torches cast fantastic shadows of their hacking and thrusting figures on the chiseled rock walls. One chronicler, Jean Cabaret d'Orville (who wrote about the duke of Bourbon under the patronage of the ducal family), tells that the duke himself, wanting a share in the danger and glory, descended into the mine with a few close followers and, gripping ax and sword, battled a defender named Regnaud de Montferrand. The duke's identity remained deliberately hidden until, in the heat of combat, one of his excited followers suddenly

---

[1] Philippe Contamine provides a guide to various forms of military recruitment in *War in the Middle Ages*, trans. Michael Jones (Oxford: Blackwell, 1984), 150–165.

shouted out his lord's war cry, "Bourbon! Saint Mary!" Hearing these potent and revealing words, Regnaud, a nobleman who was an unknighted squire, dropped his sword, fell to his knees, and offered to hand over the castle if only the duke would knight him, for this would be the greatest honor that could come to him.[2] At least this is Jean Cabaret's account. Another chronicler, the famous Jean Froissart, says simply that the garrison surrendered after their leader was fatally struck by one of the massive stone projectiles flung at the fortress.

How can modern investigators understand these conflicting narratives of the capture of Verteuil and make sense of the chivalric culture they apparently reflect? Did Regnaud cheerfully surrender a strong base (from which plundering raids had sustained his band) in return for the honor of being knighted by a great lord? The modern conclusion might hold that the colorful narrative is merely an invention or that, if accurate, the actions it described remain puzzlingly impractical. Accustomed to thinking of leaders bent over maps far from the front lines, we may ask if the great duke was eager to risk his own life in a cramped underground passage for the sake of glory and adventure. Yet our sense of possibilities might be stretched by Geoffrey le Baker, a mid-fourteenth-century English chronicler who insisted that during the early phase of the Hundred Years War the duke of Lancaster acted in the very manner attributed to the duke of Bourbon.

[Lancaster] was often fighting in underground mines, dug to overthrow towers and walls. He met strong counter attacks from the brave defenders and fought hand to hand against the besieged and in these same mines he made both Gascons and Englishmen knights, a thing unheard of before.[3]

Some modern readers will maintain an unshaken belief that Froissart's plain version of events conveys more information about what happened at Verteuil, though he was assuredly capable of recording

[2] For Cabaret's account, see A. M. Chazaud, ed., Jean Cabaret d'Orville, *La Chronique de le bon duc Loys de Bourbon* (Paris, 1976), 149–154; for general information on this castle and the physical results of the siege, see the article by the Marquis de Amodio printed in *Memoires de la Société Archéologique et Historique de la Charente* (1985), available online at andre.j.balout.free.fr/charente(16)_pdf/verteuil_chateau003.pdf.

[3] *The Chronicle of Geoffrey le Baker*, David Preest, trans., introduction and notes by Richard Barber (Woodbridge: Boydell Press, 2012), 68.

colorful stories in his own chronicles.[4] Other modern romantics will be enthralled with accounts by Cabaret and Baker for their seeming irrationality, and will welcome colorful alterity as an antidote to gray modernity. Yet either view trivializes chivalry by declaring it fanciful and divorced from real life with its serious business of war and loot.

The central issue, of course, is not whether such particular combats by a French or an English duke took place but whether hardened medieval warriors in general acted on such chivalric motives (or believed they should do so). To argue the contrary, to make a case for the seriousness and practicality of chivalry, even when possibly embedded in storybook incidents, we need not – indeed, cannot – determine the factual accuracy of many hundreds of incidents, such as the conclusion of the siege of Verteuil, centuries in the past. Obtaining truth quotients from a vast roster of such incidents would be impossible and could, in any case, never calibrate a scale for the importance of chivalry as a historical force. We will come closer to success by seeking to understand why chivalry was so important to influential medieval people; for virtually every medieval voice we can hear accepts a chivalric *mentalité* and seems anxious to advance it (and often to reform it toward some desired goal) as a key buttress to society, even to civilization.

What quickly becomes apparent is the striking compulsion to read the world in chivalric terms; for Cabaret's and Baker's insistence on the presence and power of such motives and gestures is scarcely unique or even unusual. Portrayals of men similarly moved by chivalric ideals on campaign, in battle, and in courtly gatherings appear regularly throughout chronicles, biographies, handbooks, treatises, and the entire corpus of chivalric literature. This overwhelming mass

---

[4] Though in this instance Froissart's account may seem good factual reporting, his massive chronicle in general famously portrays men animated by chivalric motives to perform colorful gestures through bold feats. For scholarly analysis, see John Bell Henneman, "The Age of Charles V," in *Froissart: Historian*, ed. J. J. N. Palmer (Woodbridge: Boydell Press, 1981), 46–49; Craig Taylor, *Chivalry and the Ideals of Knighthood in France during the Hundred Years War* (New York: Cambridge University Press, 2013); C. T. Allmand, *Society at War: The Experience of England and France during the Hundred Years War* (Rochester: Boydell & Brewer, 1998), 185: "Froissart, the 'Chronicler of European Chivalry,' who was probably less interested in the military aims of the war than with recording the opportunities which war gave to individuals, especially to those nobly-born, to perform fine deeds, thereby bringing both honour to their ideal and reputation to themselves."

of evidence presents real or fictional incidents like the scene in the tunnel, each described in exuberant language. Moreover, the incidents may not all be invented. Grand chivalric actions are documented by what seems secure evidence. Even the grim battlefield could generate scenes and incidents that seem lifted from the pages of romance. To take only one classic example, the great Castilian knight Don Pero Niño sent to his lady love the twisted and bloodstained sword he had used in combat, its edge toothed like a saw from striking mighty blows.[5] This battle relic would have made a more suitable gift than the severed genitals of Simon de Montfort sent by one of his enemies to that victor's wife after Montfort was killed at the battle of Evesham in 1265.[6] Aspects of tournament from the very real world of the twelfth century made their way into description of that sport in romance literature, where they were splashed with even more color and adorned with symbolism that, in turn, affected historical tournament practice.[7]

The elite military function glorified in chivalry may sometimes have adopted fancy dress and embraced flashy gesture, but it was obviously recognized as crucial within its society; chivalry emerged and matured in a hard world well aware of dangers from enemies, some at a distance, some quite close at hand. The medieval lay aristocracy developed as a warrior caste in response to these conditions and opportunities for advancement. Though never the sole element of military force, and rarely even the most numerous body of fighters, knights were crucial to military success; and they knew that their military performance was likewise crucial to their social success. Any doubts will vanish upon reading the immensely practical

---

[5] The action took place near the city of Ronda in the kingdom of Granada, and his biographer says, "His sword was like a saw, toothed in great notches, the hilt twisted by dint of striking mighty blows, and all dyed in blood. Later Pero Niño sent this sword by a page to France, with other presents to my Lady of Serifontaine" (Evans, 196). The original language is: Gutierre Díaz de Gamez, *El victorial*, ed. Juan de Mata Carriazo (Madrid, 1940): "e la su espada toda mellada, e sacados grandes pedazos della, e la espiga torzida, de los grandes que avía fecho con ella, e toda bañada en sangre. Esta espada envió él después a Franzia, con otras joyas, por vn donzel, a madama el Almirallap" (292).

[6] *Metrical Chronicle of Robert of Gloucester*, vol. 2, ed. W. A. Wright (London: Eyre and Spottiswoode, 1887), 765.

[7] Larry D. Benson, "Tournament in the Romances of Chrétien de Troyes and L'Histoire de Guillaume le Marechal," in *Chivalric Literature*, eds. Benson and John Leyerle (Toronto: University of Toronto Press, 1976).

questions about the division of loot and the profitable matter of ransoming prisoners posed in the *Questions for the Joust, Tournaments and War* composed by the great fourteenth-century knight Geoffroi de Charny for the royal French Order of the Star.[8]

Yet we will need to look beyond combat and see in chivalry a wide and working set of ideals and ideas. Social markers essential to establishing status bore a clear chivalric stamp, a fact well known to all with ambitions to rise in the medieval world. Chivalry in fact provided the *esprit de corps* for the laity in this world; it framed not only war and peace, but status, acquisition and distribution of wealth, the practice of lay piety, the elevated and elevating nature of love, and ideal gender relationships, among much else. Its ideals and practices, in short, performed crucial societal work that was far from fanciful or merely silly, but rather was fundamental. The evidence and the argument of this book are meant to sustain such a case. Of course the color and exuberance of chivalry and even its hyperbolic spoken language and enacted gestures will surely strike us, but they cannot mask the consequential work being accomplished. To say so much is not to admire, nor to condemn; but understanding how chivalry functioned at the core of medieval society for half a millennium remains an important task of analysis. The first chapter of this section seeks to cut a path through the thickets of romanticism to reach authentically medieval chivalry, and then emphasizes the practical role of that chivalry within its society. The second chapter turns to the useful evidence that can be extracted from the careers and writings from several model knights.

---

[8] Michael Taylor, "A Critical Edition of Geoffroy de Charny's *Livre Charny* and the *Demandes pour la joute, les tournois et la guerre.*" (PhD dissertation, University of North Carolina, Chapel Hill, 1977); Steven Muhlberger, trans., *Charny and the Rules for Chivalric Sport in Fourteenth-Century France* (Union City: Chivalry Bookshelf, 2002).

THE REALITY OF MEDIEVAL CHIVALRY

Chivalry may sometimes seem to slip through our fingers and separate into discrete spheres. This quicksilver quality may tempt scholars to jettison use of the term altogether, considering it too fragmented to sustain meaning. This view, emerging from understandable impatience with sweeping generalization, resembles what medieval philosophers would have termed nominalism with its focus on specific phenomena alone as having meaning, while the general, classifying category is granted no genuine existence. Adopting this view, martial or honor culture might be granted existence in particular traits, attitudes, and acts, but an overarching idea of chivalry would be thought to fail to catch anything general for historical analysis.

Yet the very term *chivalry* was continually and confidently spoken and written throughout half a medieval millennium. Not all the terms we employ as modern scholars studying those centuries can make this claim to reality in the society they are meant to describe. Feudalism as an abstract noun is a modern construct intended to encapsulate basic aspects of medieval society; but it was not a word used in the Middle Ages and has caused seemingly unending debate among scholars.[1] Chivalry, however, was a term used reflexively by medieval people from the late eleventh century and the twelfth century through the

[1] See, for example, Elizabeth A. R. Brown, "The Tyranny of a Concept: Feudalism and Historians of Medieval Europe," *American Historical Review* 79, no. 4 (1974), and Thomas Bisson, *The Crisis of the Twelfth Century: Power, Lordship, and the Origins of European Government* (Princeton: Princeton University Press, 2009).

remainder of what we consider the medieval period and beyond. It was their term. They thought it could and should convey important meaning. Their reliance on the term sets our goal of understanding what it meant to them and why they used it.

If some scholars imitate nominalists and avoid the term as overly general, other scholars avoid the term for nearly opposite reasons. They would grant that the values we analyze in chivalry were real, but insist that in fact the ideas or behaviors we are observing in certain medieval centuries represented nothing more than the eternal warrior code. In this view, how warriors think and how they act remain at base a constant, and this enduring code represents what is truly important in scholarly analysis: doughboys in the First World War, Greek hoplites, Native American dog soldiers of the Plains, Carolingian *milites*, Japanese samurai, high and late medieval knights – all were a part of the grand procession of warriors whose essence is not dependent on specific social and cultural context of time and space.[2]

It does seem likely, of course, that classes of warriors in all ages necessarily shared certain qualities worth study. One theme of this book, however, builds on the crucial importance of context. We need to understand the fit of medieval European chivalry with other institutions and ideas of that time and to analyze its development as a response to specific problems and opportunities within its centuries. To reduce chivalry merely to one exhibit in the long museum case illustrating men at war is, for the medieval historian, an act of surrender; it gives up the vast importance of a chivalry inextricably interlinked with other formative and motive features of medieval civilization, and closes a wide and essential window on the medieval past. If chivalry can be read as a part of an eternal warrior code, it remains a specific and essential feature of medieval Europe. Analyzing some persistent warrior code over millennia may produce useful results, but it is a very different enterprise from that undertaken in this book.[3]

If the term must be allowed, can we define it? Medieval people who promoted and practiced chivalry did not regularly define it concisely. Apparently they thought it did not require definition.

[2] Steve Morillo discusses the issues in "Milites, Knights, and Samurai: Military Terminology, Comparative History, and the Problem of Translation." Available on the website Academia.edu.
[3] These themes are also discussed in R. W. Kaeuper, *War, Justice and Public Order* (Oxford, 1988) and *Chivalry and Violence in Medieval Europe* (Oxford, 1999).

Scholars have, however, long recognized three clusters of medieval meaning in surviving sources.[4] Chivalry could, first, denote deeds of great valor performed by arms bearers. The great fighter on some battlefield, historical or imagined, who carved his way through ranks of his foes, cracking helmeted skulls like walnuts, would be breath-lessly praised for the chivalry he has *done*. In a second meaning, the collective body of knights present for any action might themselves be termed chivalry. A lord who asked how much chivalry his enemies possessed would likely be inquiring about the number of armored and mounted warriors to be faced, rather than the degree to which they followed some code. Little controversy troubles these meanings of chivalry, though less attention has been paid to them than they deserve.

If these first two meanings are straightforward, the third meaning does turn attention, dauntingly, to formative concepts. A medieval speaker or writer can use the term *chivalry* to convey an accepted or desired set of ideas and practices. All writers assume that elite warriors, wherever their homelands or life spans, are joined in a great commu-nity, share common views, and act in ways understood to be appro-priate and praiseworthy – or at least have some idea that they should do so. Violating these standards, it is regularly claimed, will bring dreaded shame in all courts.[5] Significantly, such ways of thinking and being are often assumed to be clear, almost as if they were a part of the natural order; at other times principles are spelled out more explicitly in an attempt to encourage thought and behavior that will meet some societal, cultural, or religious imperative. Medieval commentators constantly sought to elevate elite practitioners and, at least among the more thoughtful, to delineate highly desired goals. Being a knight did not imply a military rank such as lieutenant or captain; rather, it – in time – placed an arms bearer within a vast body of men through time and space who were of elite status and admired fighting capacity

---

[4] Usefully discussed in Jeremy Duquesne Adams, "Modern Views of Medieval Chivalry," in *The Study of Chivalry: Resources and Approaches*, ed. Howell Chickering (Kalamazoo, MI: Medieval Institute Publications, 1988).

[5] E.g., *History of William Marshal*, ed. A. J. Holden, S. Gregory, and D. Crouch, trans. S. Gregory (Anglo-Norman Text Society, 2002–2006), 104–105, 130–131; Marjorie Chibnall, ed., trans., *The Ecclesiastical History of Orderic Vitalis*, bk. X, ch. 10 (Oxford: Clarendon Press, 1969–1980). The deterrent is likewise regularly common in imaginative chivalric literature.

and who (as we will see) shared at least a core of ideals and behaved in an accepted manner. Discussion, debate, and contention could only be expected to surround such a body of men and ideals. So powerful a social, cultural, and military force inevitably spurred concern and argument then as well as now; reform ideals stirred within their own ranks as well as among outsiders. Idealists and reformers were sufficiently realistic to recognize the need for strong sword arms to create and sustain the social order they ardently desired and that they thought was desired by God. Reform plans to direct and channel knightly force fill treatises and appear in works of imaginative literature that contribute no small part of our surviving evidence. Read carefully, these works can provide priceless evidence on knightly behavior and advice directed to practitioners.[6]

No known suit of armor included an ironclad pocket to accommodate a handy tome laying out "The Code and Settled Rules of Chivalry." We must avoid the notion of a rigid and singular code or detailed list of inalterable practices, set forth once and always and everywhere agreed upon and enacted. Rather, we will analyze a more nuanced social construct. Significant continuity across time and space can indeed be found; as we will see, an important core cluster of common values and agreed practices persisted widely. Yet these core notions were surrounded by cultural discussions and ideals advanced by advocates and reformers reacting to the exigencies of their age. Precisely how chivalric ideals applied to specific and complex situations in life inevitably varied by region, over time, and with pressing particular circumstances. As a formative force in a vibrant society, chivalry can scarcely be captured in a single sentence or paragraph of definition written by some medieval reformer or adept modern scholar; even the most valiant efforts would likely fail to

---

[6] R. W. Kaeuper, "The Social Meaning of Chivalry in Romance," in *Cambridge Companion to Medieval Romance*, ed. R. Krueger (Cambridge University Press, 2000); "Literature as the Key to Chivalric Ideology," *Journal of Medieval Military History* 4 (2006). The argument of these studies emerged from reading of Old and Middle French literature and Middle English literature. A similar case can be made for Middle High German literature, both for the seminal works of Wolfram von Eschenbach and Hartman von Aue and for the Nibelungenlied. As Francis G. Gentry says of all this German literature, "the poet forces his audience into a dialectic confrontation with its own ideals and their inadequacies." "Key Concepts in the Nibelungenlied," in *A Companion to the Nibelungenlied*, ed. Winder McConnell (Rochester, NY: Camden House/Boydell, 1998), 66.

satisfy all medieval audiences of every time and place and would only incite modern scholars to unceasing rounds of intellectual single or group combat.

Yet we can try to identify working codes of practicing knights, the clusters of general principles and practices that most knights accepted and could aspire to follow, and we can find enduring fundamental values within them. To achieve this goal requires more than reading prescriptive treatises, penned by hopeful clerical reformers; or perhaps, better, the goal requires reading them with care and understanding. Reform plans must be critically sifted and compared with general recorded behavior, ever in awareness that what was done at any time in the past does not always give full measure of what was intended. Vigorous martial deeds that help to define chivalry stand in fascinating dialogue with the hopes and worries of reformers; how knights acted on campaign, on the battlefield, on the tourney ground, in the court, and even in ladies' chambers can be as informative as any reform plan. The tendency to ask what chivalry was and turn conveniently to quote, say, an idealistic medieval exponent of chivalry, such as Ramon Llull, is obviously insufficient (useful though Llull's famous treatise and his other writing remain). That is, we cannot limit our investigation to idealizing passages in reformist treatises any more than we can narrow our focus to descriptions of individual historical actions. We must rather seek all available evidence and keep the distinction between ideals and descriptions in mind as we encounter their powerful mixture at work in accounts of knightly lives. If we think chivalry was only ideals, we will miss the rough texture of real life; if we think it meant only actions, we will deprive the knighthood of the ideals that were so important to them. Thankfully, this task becomes less arduous once voices of the knights, themselves, can be distinctly heard.

Yet we initially confront the problem that the medieval voices we can hear speaking for or about chivalry usually do not reach us unmediated from their own age; instead they come to us through the later and distorting filter of romanticism. That is, our medieval evidence on chivalry from roughly the tenth century through the fifteenth century reaches us highly colored by the views of scholars and popularizers from the late eighteenth century through the early twentieth century. The result is apparent in the muffling and profound alteration of reports from the medieval world that have created common modern views of what chivalry was and what it did.

THE VIEW THROUGH ROMANTIC SPECTACLES

Léon Gautier published his classic *La Chevalerie* in 1884,[7] the final book to emerge from a lifetime of study of the Middle Ages by a grand romantic interpreter. It must also be said that the book emerged from certain particulars in Gautier's worldview, especially his devout Catholicism and intense French patriotism, values that he saw embodied in ideal and unquestioned form in the knighthood of medieval France (but only until the death of Saint Louis in 1270, when drastic decline set in). The tone and interpretation of his massive book can be concisely caught in what he suggested as The Ten Commandments of Chivalry, laid out boldly in its early pages:

1. Thou shalt believe all that the Church teaches and shalt obey all her commandments.
2. Thou shalt defend the Church.
3. Thou shalt respect all weaknesses and shalt constitute thyself the defender of them.
4. Thou shalt love the country in which thou wast born.
5. Thou shalt not recoil before thine enemy.
6. Thou shalt make war against the infidel without cessation and without mercy.
7. Thou shalt perform scrupulously thy feudal duties, if they be not contrary to the laws of God.
8. Thou shalt never lie, and shalt remain faithful to thy pledged word.
9. Thou shalt be generous and give largesse to everyone.
10. Thou shalt be everywhere and always the champion of the Right and the Good against Injustice and Evil.

British and American writers of the same era could have added two further commandments, bringing the list up to a full dozen. Their first addition would insist that the game must be played by the rules with all combatants "fighting fair," a condition they would gladly see complementing Gautier's dictum about right causes. The influential writer Sir Walter Scott had characterized chivalry as founded on generosity and self-denial.[8] Those in shining armor should use

---

[7] *La Chevalerie, par Léon Gautier* (Paris, 1884), *Chivalry*, ed. Jacques Lavron, trans. D. C. Dunning (New York: Barnes & Noble, 1965).

[8] As quoted and discussed in Malcolm Vale, *War and Chivalry* (Athens, GA: University of Georgia Press, 1981), 4.

violence only when strictly necessary and then reluctantly, under the helpful aegis of religion. They would not start fights, but they surely finished them. In the process, the strong (the rightful elite in society) would beneficently protect the weak.

What was termed the "gentle sex" being regarded as the classic component of the weak, the twelfth commandment would mandate good behavior toward women in particular. In the popular modern view (as in some scholarship), this commandment, in fact, may threaten to overshadow or absorb all the others. Its absence from Gautier's list is a surprising omission from a gallant French writer of his day. Even today the cry "Chivalry is not dead" may greet almost any display of formal courtesy by a male. One female student reported to me that carrying a copy of Maurice Keen's grand book on the subject elicited from female friends an injunction to distribute it widely to – in their view – the insufficiently civilized lads all around them. Of course many thoughtful males would willingly subscribe to what they take to be a chivalric code of conduct.

With these two additional commandments, we could, in imagination, incise an impressive stone tablet, perhaps taking the shape of a great shield, as the emblem of our modern popular conception of chivalry: the strong (outfitted in splendid plate armor and plumes) protect the weak, and especially women. To the extent that they constitute an elite group in society, these men, distinguished by inherent virtue, provide muscular enforcement of proper morals and behavior; yet despite elite status, they present the ideal model toward which all males should at least strive. The entire structure in the Middle Ages stood on a religious foundation; the knights' minds were piously packed with ethical principles by clerics, and they unquestioningly and passively adhered to what was taught them.

Chapter by chapter, this book will argue a different conception of what chivalry was and how it worked in the Middle Ages. This is no claim that the popular notion is entirely off the mark. Not all of the Twelve Commandments we have incised need be thought utterly foreign to the original knighthood once they are placed within the context of medieval culture and are significantly qualified to fit. It would be possible, as indeed Gautier showed, to find prescriptive lines in medieval texts that at least superficially sound like many of these commandments. Faithfulness to one's word (chivalric *loyauté*) was truly a goal, and praise for largesse is undoubted. Never flinching in battle was regularly lauded, as was the killing of "infidels."

Yet the problem of common terminology applied in quite different contexts could scarcely be more apparent; even where specific words seem to coincide, the *mentalité* of the late nineteenth century cannot be superimposed onto a medieval world, not even onto prescriptive elements in medieval texts. We will, for example, encounter intense knightly piety, as enjoined in The Commandments, but will discover that it was significantly qualified by a pious sense of independence along lines crucial to the knights (Chapter 9). Fierce and unflinching delight in combat likewise fills countless medieval texts, but it was scarcely directed solely at "infidels" or against Wrong as both sides in a conflict defined Wrong. Fighting often pitted adherents of one idea of Right and Justice against another, though both sides claimed a common religion. Asking whether knights protected all the weak might generate bitter and ironic responses if the inquiry were addressed to villagers whose modest homes were still smoldering and whose families had been decimated, their crops ruined (Chapter 6). Chivalric protection of women in practice became protection of ladies; women socially below the elite level should take care, and even elite ladies might be wise to bolt their doors or set a clear-eyed guard on the walls (Chapter 10). Exactly what constituted fair fighting was less a matter of simple, common agreement than a subject for debate. Nineteenth-century nationalism is likewise out of place. In the Middle Ages, France and other countries hardly existed in the form that Gautier loved. Asking whether the medieval chivalric universe was moral, again by nineteenth-century standards, might generate animated discussion, then or now. Prowess was not a berserk quality or brutality without check;[9] nor was it merely a species of moral courage practiced without show of emotion or obvious bloodshed; we will see that to medieval knights it meant hands-on, exultant warrior violence, often carrying out hot-blooded vengeance.[10] Of

[9] Wolfram von Eschenbach has a character announce, "I never heard any man praised if his courage was without true courtesy, and many agree with me in this." Mustard and Passage, *Parzival*, 185. Formal courtesy, of course, need not be a check on prowess vigorously practiced. See R. W. Kaeuper, "Chivalry and the 'Civilizing Process,'" in *Violence in Medieval Society*, ed. R. W. Kaeuper (Woodbridge, Suffolk: Boydell, 2000).

[10] E.g., Perceforest asserts he killed a dread giant "with my own hands," in *Perceforest*, trans. Nigel Bryant, 86. Gawan in Wolfram's *Parzival* (trans. Mustard and Passage, 323) asserts that "anyone who has seen me fight must admit my knightly qualities." Examples in Malory's equally vast work are too numerous to cite.

an imagined classic battle, Wolfram von Eschenbach declared, "Whoever held a shield to his neck and carried it properly as he charged through the dust was doing justice to his knightly calling."[11] If loyalty in the world of the nineteenth century featured well-established and hierarchical institutions of governance in church and state, in the world of knighthood loyalty long found its center in personal reliability within a somewhat shaky hierarchy of lordships.

Our popular modern notions, embodying distortions and misunderstandings more than a century old, originated in the tidal wave of Romanticism that swept over Europe (and to a lesser extent over America) beginning in the late eighteenth century, and coming to a peak in the late nineteenth century.[12] Our debt to the great scholars of this era is immense. As we will see repeatedly, they edited and published texts without which modern medieval scholarship would have been impossible. Our gratitude for this vast and productive labor, however, need not commit us to their views on the medieval period in general or chivalry in particular. Romantic neo-medievalism bears responsibility for the persistent misconception among modern students that they already know what chivalry was, even before engaging in its close study. Does anyone not know what knights in shining armor were and what they did? Were they not the defenders of the gloriously impossible dream wistfully lauded in the lyrics of perennially popular musicals, splashed across the cinematic screen, or enacted on the small screens of video games?

[11] Gibbs and Johnson, *Willehalm*, 189.
[12] A daunting body of writing addresses neo-medievalism and Gothic Revival. Several volumes of *Studies in Medievalism* address aspects of these topics: *Medievalism in Europe* (V, 1993; VIII, 1996), *Medievalism in England* (IV, 1992; VII, 1995), *Medievalism in North America* (VI, 1994). A romantic approach is likewise often evident in Johan Huizinga's famous study, *The Autumn of the Middle Ages* (Chicago, 1006), originally published as *The Waning of the Middle Ages* (London, 1924), and is discussed in Malcolm Vale, *War and Chivalry* (Athens, GA: University of Georgia Press, 1981), 1–12. A variety of topics is treated in *Medievalism and the Modern World*, eds. Richard Utz and Tom Shippey (Turnhout: Brepols, 1998) and in Alice Chandler, *A Dream of Order: The Medieval Ideal in Nineteenth-Century English Literature* (Lincoln: University of Nebraska Press, 1970). A classic study on the Anglophone chivalric revivals is Mark Girouard, *The Return to Camelot: Chivalry and the English Gentleman* (New Haven: Yale University Press, 1981). Sidney Painter, near the opposite end of the spectrum of authorial stance, dismisses the religious element in chivalry as a "pleasant dream": *French Chivalry* (Ithaca, NY, 1957), 94.

This powerful neo-medievalism took root in a belief that foundations of national greatness or cultural identity lay, in some measure, in medieval ideas and forms. Problems marring perfection in modern society might find solutions through medieval revivals. Fresh growth could emerge from rediscovered old roots: disruptive male aggression could be channeled; excessive and soulless materialism might be purged. Far from dark, the medieval past was not only colorful and fascinating, but too important and too useful to be ignored. The romantic revivers did not and perhaps could not recognize that they were altering the original drastically and investing it with meanings that would have surprised its first practitioners.

In the Anglophone world, this "return to Camelot" can broadly be characterized as Victorian, yet it began earlier and took somewhat different form in the British Isles and the United States.[13] It should be clearly acknowledged that much of great value was achieved: publication of medieval records of government began as early as the opening years of the eighteenth century,[14] and efforts reached full flower after the mid-nineteenth century with the fundamental Rolls Series.[15] By that time, however, the popular conceptions were in flower. The rage for neo-medieval architecture was transforming public and private buildings with Romanesque and Gothic arches, colorful surface decoration, fanciful battlements, spires, and towers – as any look around any English town even today can attest. In the countryside, elite landowners cherished picturesque Gothic ruins on their estates, and some simply built them if they lacked originals. Bookish Victorians at least knew the neo-medieval views of John Ruskin, or adopted ideas of the Gothic Revival or Arts and Crafts movement. In the grand royal monument in Kensington Gardens, London (completed in stages in the early 1870s), the gilded statue of Prince Albert, beloved consort of Queen Victoria, sits beneath a gothic canopy culminating in a great spire. The reading public could scarcely get enough of the romantic novels of Sir Walter Scott (whose profits created Abbotsford, his great neo-medieval home) or the poetry of Alfred Lord Tennyson with its frequent

[13] Mark Girouard, *The Return to Camelot: Chivalry and the English Gentleman* (New Haven: Yale University Press, 1981).

[14] Thomas Rymer, *Foedera*, 17 vols. (London: A. and J. Churchill, 1704–1735).

[15] See the Rolls Series of Chronicles and Memorials edited by William Stubbs from 1858, with his *Introduction to the Rolls Series*, collected and edited by Arthur Hassall.

medieval themes. Pre-Raphaelite artists supplied paintings that drew inspiration from an era before the Renaissance. Tory peers commissioned painters to present their families on canvas in rich samite and glowing armor. The more physically vigorous males famously staged a tournament at Eglinton in 1839, and carried on bravely despite the rain, with the incongruous help of butlers bearing umbrellas.[16]

With a different and less distant period of national origins, Americans showed some predictable ambivalence about the Middle Ages in general and chivalry in particular, a fact evident to all readers of Mark Twain's classic *A Connecticut Yankee in King Arthur's Court* (1889) with its complex mixture of vitriol and admiration.[17] The men evocatively termed robber barons built neo-medieval mansions complete with stained glass, and some imported suits of armor. Similarly imposing neo-medieval piles housed governing agencies of many an American town. Even humbler dwellings aspired to gothic structure and decor; "steamboat gothic" was afloat on every river and inspired gingerbread ornamentation on many a middle-class home. Armed forces of the Confederacy in the American Civil War self-consciously claimed the designation of "the chivalry."[18] In memoirs written after the war, a Confederate naval officer fondly recalled passing an anxious evening before battle in 1862 eased by enthusiastically discussing one of Sir Walter Scott's novels with his commander.[19]

Such enthusiasm for the medieval world, scarcely limited to the British Isles and America, animated continental Europeans, taking forms that emerged from particular national histories. Here, too, scholars steadily produced new editions of medieval documents: French royal records were published;[20] records from medieval Germany went into print in the massive German *Monumenta*

---

[16] Girouard, *The Return to Camelot: Chivalry and the English Gentleman* (New Haven: Yale University Press, 1981), 100–102. Note the difference between the watercolors and the Punch drawings.

[17] R. W. Kaeuper, "Telling It Like It Was? Mark Twain's Rereading of Chivalry in Malory's *Morte Darthur*," in *Retelling Tales*, eds. T. Hahn and A. Lupak (Woodbridge: Brewer, 1997).

[18] A. Veitz, "Shoot Them All: Chivalry, Honour and the Confederate Army Officer Corps," in *The Chivalric Ethos and the Development of Military Professionalism*, ed. D. J. Trim (Leiden: Brill, 2003).

[19] William Harwood Parker, *Recollections of a Naval Officer* (Annapolis, MD: Naval Institute Press, 1985), 247.

[20] *Ordinances des Roys de France* from 1723, *Recueils des historiens des Gauls* from 1738, *Les Olim* ... 1839, Mignon, *Inventaire* from 1899 ...

Germaniae Historica (from 1826); Italian chronicles were edited (in the *Registrum Italicarum Scriptores*, 1900–1935).[21] In Spain, the publisher Manuel Rivadeneira spearheaded the publication of the *Biblioteca de Autores Españoles*, presenting works from medieval and early modern (Golden Age) Spanish archives beginning in 1846 and continuing through much of the nineteenth century. The effort was continued by the great Spanish historian Marcelino Menéndez Pelayo into the first years of the twentieth century.[22]

As many visitors to Carcassonne in southern France or the color-fully restored German towns of Rothenburg or Goslar could testify, the medieval past was important and brought back to life in stone and timber; the Imperial Palace at Goslar even added a remarkable series of murals linking the medieval past with the present of the early twentieth century, and, making the point even more unambiguous, the restorers placed dramatic equestrian statues of Frederick Barbarossa (d. 1190) and Kaiser Wilhelm I (d. 1888) before the heavily restored great hall (Figure 1). Likewise, the series of statues outside the royal palace in Madrid emphasizes the great medieval monarchs of Castile, León, and Aragon.[23]

The Great War (1914–1918), which erupted not many years later, provides perhaps the best evidence for the appropriation and distortion of medieval chivalry. Propaganda with a neo-medieval character flowed from all combatants in posters to boost morale and recruitment, on postcards and – after the war – memorials in stone and stained glass erected in cemeteries and chapels. All contenders linked modern technological warfare mired in the mud of Flanders with the idealized glories of knighthood, which they pictured in primary colors in the medieval past; each side likewise found heavenly blessing for its cause, and portrayed angels ministering to the suffering warriors conceived as pious fighters akin to crusaders; even the figure of Christ was boldly thrust into that valorizing role.

Though these media were thoroughly present-minded, their inescapable implication for a view of the medieval past must be clearly read: values of past and present fuse; medieval and modern warriors share the same ethos; no barriers arise between them as sociocultural,

---

[21] *Registrum Italicarum Scriptores*, ed. Nuova (Bologna: Nicola Zanichelli, 1900–1935).

[22] *Biblioteca de Autores Españoles* (Madrid: Ediciones Atlas, 1846–1880).

[23] The site was viewed by Samuel Claussen, who described the statues to me.

Figure 1 The Imperial Palace at Goslar, built in the eleventh century, was heavily restored in the second half of the nineteenth century. One modern equestrian statue represents Kaiser William I (1861–1888); the other, Frederick Barbarossa (1152–1190).

political, and religious contexts changed dramatically over centuries; men killed with high explosives, chlorine gas, and machine guns are remembered as peerless knights. Knights inspired modern fighters because they were essentially like those who fought in the Great War or they at least showed what warriors might best become. Practices and ideals that could inspire worthy struggle in the Great War must have been truly worthy themselves in their original setting; knighthood fought as "our troops" fought in the early twentieth century – only for Right and Justice, with God's bountiful blessing descending upon them.

Even so swift a walk through the broad fields of romantic revival serves to remind us how clearly our imagined tablet of chivalric commandments stands more fittingly on late nineteenth- or early twentieth-century soil than on any medieval field. Chivalric revivers obviously intended to shape their own society along lines they deeply valued. They were not pursuing tasks undertaken in this book, which tries to describe and understand ideas and practices in the medieval world. Revivals are always new movements, changing and adapting what they supposedly restore. No doubt later nineteenth-century males, and the women who improved them, took inspiration from the medieval past while they revived what they considered chivalry in their own day, but the knights were not early Boy Scouts or Victorian gentlemen who only lacked a good tailor to cut them proper frock coats. Whatever view we take of the enterprise of reviving chivalry (or any other medieval frame), the salient fact remains that chivalric ideals were originally responses to the rich mix of societal hopes and fears in their own time. Prescriptive medieval hopes for reform were real and important, but were we simply to link them with equally fervid postmedieval romanticism we would not explain the complexity of meaning and crucial societal role of chivalry in its birthplace and time. History is more profitably read forward than backward. Persistent romanticism does not merely provide colorful, harmless background; it matters a great deal. If we remain grateful for pioneering efforts in publishing medieval archives, editing a vast corpus of literary works, and preserving monuments, we must strive to cut through the lingering distortions in order to look afresh at evidence.

If the distortions of painting knighthood in pastel hues have been emphasized, the other extreme follows a tough and supposedly realistic view. Inappropriate modern cynicism ever stands as the reverse side of the debased coinage of the impossible dream. From this viewpoint, either chivalric ideas had no real existence or the hard men of war knew the ideals but simply disregarded them as fanciful notions. This makes the knights thickheaded or merely brutish. The key phrase in such discussions is often "true chivalry," which on inspection turns out to be a romantic conception slipping surreptitiously back into the analysis. To avoid such a superficial and judgmental line of thought entails no apology for the pretensions or behavior of socially elite warriors. It insists, rather, that the chivalric ideals knights actually accepted and strove to fulfill were indeed realistic and deeply rooted in medieval rather than postmedieval life and concerns. Undoubtedly knights fell short, even by standards they would have personally accepted; but discovering human imperfection once again can scarcely represent a surprising conclusion of historical analysis for any age. The temptation to hold medieval people to an impossible standard, to see them exclusively in primary colors – admirably bright or depressingly dark – is nowhere more out of place than in the study of chivalry.

Idealism and more contextual realism actually appear as issues in the medieval sources we will use, for much of our evidence has a reformative, idealistic character. That is, many treatises, much *chanson de geste*, and nearly all romance literature take prescriptive rather than merely descriptive form. Contemporary medieval authors wanted to shape so powerful a force as chivalry in particular directions, moral or social. Yet medieval idealism, carefully investigated, can aid analysis, for it was intended to serve as a reforming force for its own time and reveals problems perceived and hopes raised. If Chrétien de Troyes, Geoffroi de Charny, or Christine de Pizan proposes some best practice for knighthood, we recognize it as a goal for improving society, rather than as a description of universal social practice. This reformative aim of all such works makes them highly informative, even if they are not simply descriptive. The idealism of the nineteenth-century Romantic movement had a significantly different character; its advocates assumed medieval ideas of reform were descriptions of actual behavior from the golden past and wanted to infuse them into their own quite different societies. Thus if the medieval reforming effort informs, the later romantic program distorts, telling us vastly more about its own age than about the medieval past. As a result, we can draw on medieval romances and treatises carefully, but confidently, seeing in them forces pointing to problems and attempting to shape their own age.

The challenge is to determine what clusters of meaning most frequently animated chivalry conceived as a working code of actual warriors. In formulating principles to guide their lives and behavior, the arms bearers and their allies could draw upon idealistic treatises and imaginative works to learn what was valued, what was thought missing and necessary. We can construct a more complete picture of how chivalry functioned or failed. With minimal practice, students manage the process of separating the elements; they learn that conflating prescriptive and descriptive evidence is the cardinal error. Prescriptive texts propose glowing reform plans rather than quotidian reality. Of course both prescription and description appear in the same text, perhaps even in neighboring lines. What the good knight should ideally do (in the plan of a reformer) must be distinguished from what all knights habitually did and always knew they should do. If all available evidence is brought to bear, we can learn about standards and hopes beyond customary behavior in the world. This

book tries to chart where the paths of ideal and actual behavior
converge and where they diverge.

THE PRACTICALITY OF CHIVALRY

Despite the hearty praise and thanks owed to the cast of *Monty Python
and the Holy Grail*, we must recognize that Camelot was actually not
a silly place, or at least no more silly than other places historians study.
Chivalrous style and gesture were undoubtedly colorful; they could
become decidedly exotic at court, on the tourney field, even on the
battlefield; but it makes little sense to lose so complex and powerful
a fusion of ideas and practices relating to basic issues of real life in
swirling clouds of rosy mist. Chivalry was neither sublime nor silly; it
was not centered on inconsequential acts and attitudes or merely
quaint gestures and customs. Eminently practical, chivalry – as is
worth emphasizing – performed crucial social work, for it was largely
through a chivalric lens that the medieval lay, male elite viewed and
made sense of formative elements in their lives. Even a brief list of
these issues would include the valorizing of status and social dominance, the practice of licit violence, active lay piety, the demands of
loyalty, the need for openhanded generosity, and the framework for
heterosexual love and proper relations between the genders along
with intense friendship among elite warriors. In short, for those near
the top of the social pyramid (and for many trying to gain even
a foothold at such slippery levels), chivalry formed a veritable template for understanding the social world and for living within it.
Of course in all centuries characterized as chivalric, the intractable
contradictions and complexities of life proved to be messy beyond the
analytical and governing powers of any ideal code; yet serious
attempts to formulate meaning and to direct and justify practice
went into chivalry; the efforts left rich deposits of evidence.

Our sense of the practicality of chivalry is heightened by recognizing the role of the knights themselves in its creation. Actions and ideas
in their world, it is important to remember, did not neatly divide
along lines of knightly physicality and force versus clerical thought
and pacifism. The chivalry knights created in collaboration with
clerics close to them proposed ideas and ideals that met the needs of
their group. Any view that chivalry consisted of restraints that they
stubbornly resisted, or that they accepted with reluctance and gritted
teeth, seriously misconstrues these men and their world. This book

will argue, in fact, that chivalry was not something external to the knighthood, not essentially and exclusively a set of civilizing restraints imposed upon a body of merely glandular fighters.[24] Knights cannot be imagined as somehow immune from the necessity felt by most elite groups in most of time to form and (however imperfectly) follow guiding frameworks for life. That their sense of themselves and their place in the world was complex and sometimes self-contradictory can cause little surprise, for they lived within an intensely religious society as vigorous warriors enacting a profession always fraught with moral tensions.[25] If strong voices urged reform measures to direct their swords, we can picture practicing knights as well as clerics in the group. All such clarion calls are significant for our analysis, even if not all were fully incorporated in chivalry as practiced; the importance of chivalry was regularly demonstrated by efforts to reform it as a crucial force in society. As generally accepted by knighthood, chivalry represented a warrior code fiercely proud of its capacities, rather than diminution of a warrior code by restraints imposed upon the knights from outside the group.

In short, their working codes – the object of analysis throughout this book – were always, finally, their own codes, a set of beliefs that they wanted ideally to follow. Scholars have not always recognized the extent to which the knights themselves actively participated in the creation of chivalry. At the very least, the warriors functioned as co-creators. If they did not originate all the ideals, many of these norms emerged from their own concerns. They accepted none that were not compatible with their high sense of status, function, and mission. As we will see (in Chapter 9), the knights and clerics close to them were selective and creative in their selection and adaptation of religious and reformative ideas. They showed a remarkable sense of their innate right to accept or reject directives, without fearing any tarnishing of their intense piety.

---

[24] Norbert Elias, *The Civilizing Process: Sociogenetic and Psychogenetic Investigations*, trans. Edmund Jephcott (Malden: Blackwell, 2000), 194–195. Elias held that the social conditions and forces of the Middle Ages created a distinct temperament among the medieval knights, one prone to rages, excess cruelties, and a decidedly unstable mental constitution, yet were also part of a broader spectrum, namely, "one and the same structuring of the emotional life" common to all social orders. Cf. Aldo Scaglione, *Knights at Court: Courtliness, Chivalry and Courtesy from the Ottonian Court to the Italian Renaissance* (Berkeley: University of California Press, 1991).

[25] See Chapter 9.

Recognizing the practicality of chivalry, then, offers a broadly important goal of analysis, for we cannot understand the medieval male lay elite without a close understanding of what chivalry provided them as both justification and respectful guidance. Our approach to this dominant social layer through half a millennium of early European history will swiftly lose focus without the perspective this understanding provides. Gaining the needed perspective becomes more possible once we have identified and analyzed a group of knights who served as models to their own age. This will be the work of the following chapter.

2

MODELS OF MEDIEVAL CHIVALRY

•

The ideal process for reconstructing the working chivalric notions we seek would require the assistance of Merlin, with whose incomparable help we might assemble in one room a group of leading knights from various periods and regions. Prudently requiring these heroic if slightly touchy men to check their swords at the door, we could pose basic questions and surreptitiously record their eloquent answers, and perhaps even their grand gestures as they spoke with knowledge and feeling.

This chapter will argue that considerable agreement on basics would emerge from such a group, whatever the differences in point of view on some particulars. Since Merlin, sadly, is no longer available, we might best arrive at this understanding of working notions of chivalry – rather than abstract reform plans – by assembling information from and about a set of knights undoubtedly regarded as models in their lifetimes. They ideally should be drawn from various regions of Europe and various chronological points in the "age of chivalry." Finding suitable great knights is not difficult, though surviving evidence does not provide as fully satisfying a chronology and regional distribution as might be desired.

To be most useful, those chosen should represent men highly praised by contemporary practicing men-at-arms as well as by clerics or intellectuals. We seek figures who were, in fact, elevated as model knights suitable for emulation. Clearly their lives and views must be recoverable. This requires that they formed the subjects of extensive accounts by others who knew them well (or had access to such knowledge) or wrote serious discussions on chivalry themselves. In short, we are searching for knights with detailed evidence available on active historical careers and as much information as possible about motivating ideals.

Five figures come quickly to mind as amply meeting these criteria. The first must be the cross-Channel hero William Marshal (d. 1219), whose life is recounted in the *Histoire de Guillaume le Maréchal*, our earliest nonroyal, nonclerical biography (completed in 1226) by an anonymous writer employed by the Marshal's family.[1] Second, we can turn to the warrior-king Robert Bruce of Scotland (d. 1329), whose biography, *Barbour's Bruce*, was written in 1375–1377.[2] An obvious third choice is the great French knight and author Geoffroi de Charny (d. 1356), whose own ur-treatise, *Livre de Chevalerie (Book of Chivalry)*, was likely written in 1350 and who also wrote a shorter verse treatise, the *Livre Charny*, and a set of *Demandes pour la joute, les tournois et la guerre (Questions for the Joust, Tournaments and War)* for the French royal chivalric order.[3] A good fourth figure is the indomitable and roving Castilian warrior Don Pero Niño (d. 1453), whose biography – *El victorial* – by his standard-bearer, Gutierre Díaz de Gamez, was probably written between the early 1430s and 1443.[4] Finally, we can turn to the English knight/ author par excellence, Thomas Malory (d. 1471); his *Morte Darthur* was first printed in 1485.[5]

---

[1] A. J. Holden and D. Crouch, eds., *Histoire de Guillaume le Maréchal: History of William Marshal*, trans. S. Gregory (London: Anglo-Norman Text Society, 2002–2006).

[2] M. P. McDiarmid and J. A. C. Stevenson, eds., *Barbour's Bruce*, vols. 1–3 (Edinburgh: Scottish Text Society, 1980–1985).

[3] Kaeuper and Kennedy, *The Book of Chivalry of Geoffroi de Charny* (Philadelphia: University of Pennsylvania Press, 1996); cf. Kaeuper and Kennedy, *A Knight's Own Book of Chivalry* (Philadelphia: University of Pennsylvania Press, 2005); Michael Taylor, "A Critical Edition of Geoffroy de Charny's *Livre Charny* and the *Demandes pour la joute, les tournois et la guerre*" (PhD dissertation, University of North Carolina: Chapel Hill, 1977); Steven Muhlberger, trans., *Charny and the Rules for Chivalric Sport in Fourteenth-Century France* (Union City: Chivalry Bookshelf, 2002).

[4] Gutierre Díaz de Gamez, *El victorial, crónica de Don Pero Niño, conde de Buelna*, ed. Juan de Mata Carriazo (Madrid: Espasa-Calpe, S.A., 1940). An English translation of parts of this biography was edited by Joan Evans, *The Unconquered Knight: A Chronicle of the Deeds of Don Pero Niño, Count of Buelna* (New York, 1928; repr. in Cambridge Medieval Castilian Series, 2000; repr. Boydell & Brewer, 2004).

[5] Of the several editions of Malory's text, I will cite Eugène Vinaver, *Malory: Works* (Oxford, 1971).

If the list does not provide us with all we could desire – a suitably full eleventh-century biography, or a richly documented German or Eastern European knight to round out our set – we can be grateful for the wealth and range of evidence supplied by our five chosen figures.[6] They come from medieval centuries that all scholars would recognize as chivalric and thus show us developed qualities of special interest. Each was unquestionably a renowned and strenuous knight; three of the five (the Marshal, Robert Bruce, and Pero Niño) became the subjects of significant and extensive chivalric biographies. Charny wrote his own *Livre de Chevalerie* (*Book of Chivalry*) and his *Demandes pour la joute, les tournois et la guerre* (*Questions for the Joust, Tournaments and War*) for French knights of the royal Order of the Star near the end of his active career. Even if we cannot know Thomas Malory's career as fully as the others, his great summation of imaginative Arthurian chivalric literature in the *Morte Darthur* can be compared with the other, more classically historical accounts. These five martial, courtly, and politically active careers span the better part of four centuries and sweep over a considerable expanse of Europe, the action taking place on an arc from Ireland to the Mediterranean. What we can know of their lives and what they say about the practice and ideals of their profession can bring us close to what we are seeking in a working notion of chivalry. Each career will be brought briefly into the spotlight as a prelude to considering characteristics of the entire group. The goal is to discover chivalric elements that persisted through time and over space no less than important regional variations and change over time.

William Marshal, born into a world wracked by civil war, was the younger son of John Marshal, who could claim the title of royal marshal, but possessed little land.[7] At age 13 William was sent to the great Tancarville household in Normandy for an education that was predominantly, though not exclusively, military; some of his

---

[6] Some of the challenges presented by drafting Ulrich von Liechtenstein into service as a model knight appear in Albrecht Classen, "Self-Enactment of Late Medieval Chivalry: Performance and Self-Representation in Ulrich von Liechtenstein's *Frauendienst,*" *Seminar* 39 (2003), 93–113.

[7] This brief account draws on David Crouch, *William Marshal: Court, Career and Chivalry in the Angevin Empire* (Harlow, 1990); Georges Duby, *William Marshal: The Flower of Chivalry* (Toronto, 1985); and Sidney Painter, *William Marshal: Knight-Errant, Baron, and Regent of England* (Baltimore, 1935).

formative values were likely instilled in him through chivalric literature. Knighted in 1167 at age 20 in what seems to have been a modest
ceremony, he quickly joined an equally modest border war along the
fault line between Plantagenet and Capetian spheres of dominance.
Though he fought with distinction, one hard lesson he learned was
that honor was supported by loot: the Earl of Essex pointedly asked
him for a gift from loot he had collected, but William had garnered
none in his enthusiasm for the fighting. This lesson stuck, and
William soon began applying it in the honorable and profitable
tournaments that proved to be his means of ascending the social
pyramid.

When real warfare replaced tournament for a while, William
gained great credit and patronage by his determined defense of
Queen Eleanor of Aquitaine, wife of Henry II of England. In effect,
he was largely supported by royal patronage for the next decade and
a half, serving the Young King (Henry, son of Henry II) on the field
of the tournament and at court. The latter role may have been the
more dangerous: his biographer claims that enemies falsely accused
him of adultery with the wife of the Young King; some think it was
a romantic invention of his biographer. If an accusation was in fact
made, Marshal solved it as he did later when charges were brought
against him at the court of King John: by challenging his accusers to
fight, a challenge that they prudently avoided. It is fascinating to note
that Lancelot, with a roughly contemporary beginning to a career in
imaginative literature, would respond in just this fashion to charges
against him.[8] And the Young King, needing William's martial skills
(as Arthur needed those of Lancelot in romance), soon retained the
great warrior in his service again. When this patron died with
a crusade vow unfilled, William's biographer assures us, he loyally
spent several years in the Holy Land, redeeming this pledge. He
returned to take on rising responsibility and power and to garner
wealth, serving Henry II, Richard Lion-Heart, and the mercurial and
difficult John, as each held the throne. The vast rewards included
marriage to an heiress to an earldom, and sizable estates in England,
Wales, and Ireland.

A grand statesman in his final years, he stood loyally by King John
in the crisis of the Magna Carta, knighted John's son Henry (as he had

---

[8] R. W. Kaeuper, "William Marshal, Lancelot, and the Issue of Chivalric Identity,"
in *Essays in Medieval Studies* 22 (2005), ed. Anita Riedinger, 14.

earlier knighted Henry II's son Henry), played an instrumental role in repulsing French invasion, and became virtual head of the government when the young Henry became Henry III. In a protracted death scene worthy of the opera stage, William spoke his mind and received the highest praise from leading lay and clerical figures.

The *Histoire* is thankfully available in a splendid edition with Anglo-Norman French and modern English on facing pages, complete with scholarly apparatus and supportive studies.[9] The medieval text is an authorized biography, commissioned by the Marshal's son; its strategic omissions and hagiographic qualities are well known. Yet warts and all, it is priceless for the present study, for whatever its factual errors or sly omissions, the book gives us access to chivalric *mentalité* and sometimes even to chivalric speech.

If we can free our minds of the Hollywood film extolling William Wallace at the expense of Robert Bruce, we will see the king as the admired knightly figure (no less than national hero) that he appeared to contemporary eyes.[10] Our source, John Barbour's *Bruce*, was written in 1375–1377, a little more than a generation after the king's death; it narrates his fighting to become the accepted king of Scotland and then his fighting to defend his kingdom against English invasion (along with his own counter-invasions of the north of England), and the ill-fated invasion of Ireland led by his brother Edward. There is no shortage of discussion about warriors and campaigns, in other words; the qualities of a knight and the characteristics of chivalry appear frequently. Barbour seems to have relied heavily on oral sources, both testimony from the living and, for about half of the treatise (books 3 through 8), lays sung about the Bruce.[11] Barbour received patronage from Robert Bruce's son, but seems not to have been paid specifically for this chronicle (which he also terms a romance). As in the *Histoire* of the Marshal, the account's likely bias and provable omissions or errors within the detailed narrative do not reduce its usefulness for our inquiry into broad and crucial elements of thought about chivalry.

[9] *History of William Marshal*, 3 vols., ed. A. J. Holden, trans. S. Gregory, historical notes by David Crouch (London: Anglo-Norman Text Society, 2002–2006).

[10] M. P. McDiarmid, ed., *Barbour's Bruce*, Scottish Text Society, vols. 12 (1080), 13 (1981), 15 (1985) . . .

[11] Ibid., 15, 38–39.

Geoffroi de Charny was a younger son in a noble family without great estates.[12] An enthusiastic warrior, he could not (in the apt phrase of Raymond Cazelles) imagine living without an enemy to fight.[13] Since his adult life span coincided with the opening phase of the Hundred Years War, Charny had no difficulties on that score. He fought in Gascony, in the Low Countries, in Brittany, at Calais, and at Poitiers. Along with other virtuous and honored knights, Charny joined the king's council in 1347. By this time he had returned from a crusade in Anatolia undertaken when a temporary truce interrupted the Anglo-French fighting. No doubt he would have enthusiastically joined the planned invasion of England that was ruined by the onset of the Black Death in 1348.

Geoffroi de Charny was obviously an excellent practitioner of his profession: to contemporaries he represented the leading French knight of the age. Excellence did not always guarantee success, however; he was twice captured, and he died under enemy sword blows at Poitiers. Yet he was vastly admired; he carried into battle the Oriflamme, the sacred banner of the kings of France; he was chosen as a charter member of the royal order of chivalry founded by his king, Jean le Bon; and he wrote three works on chivalry. His *Book of Chivalry* sought to inspire its members and, by extension, French knighthood generally to greater prowess, especially against the English invaders; but it provides us with an even broader insight into the chivalric culture of his age. William Caferro has observed that a key passage in Charny's writing could serve as a summary of the career of the greatest fourteenth-century English mercenary, Sir John Hawkwood.[14] And Charny's *Questions for the Joust, Tournaments and War* proposed a wide range of militant topics to be debated by the royal chivalric order. The *Book of Chivalry* in particular shows his

---

[12] Kaeuper and Kennedy, *The Book of Chivalry of Geoffroi de Charny* (Philadelphia, 1996); Philippe Contamine, "Geoffroy de Charny (début du xɪvᵉ siècle–1356), 'Le plus prudhomme et le plus vaillant de tous les autres,'" in *Histoire et Société: Melanges Georges Duby, Vol. II: Le tenancier, le fidèle et le citoyen* (Aix-en-Provence: Publications de l'Université de Provence, 1992), 107–121.

[13] Raymond Cazelles, *Société politique, noblesse et couronne sous Jean le Bon et Charles V* (Paris: Librairie Droz, 1982), 13.

[14] William Caffero, *John Hawkwood: An English Mercenary in Fourteenth-Century Italy* (Baltimore: Johns Hopkins University Press, 2006), 553. He quotes Kaeuper and Kennedy, *Book of Chivalry*, 92–93.

intense piety no less than his sheer enthusiasm for knightly violence, the impression of his piety being strengthened by the likelihood that he was the first historically documented owner of the Shroud of Turin.

Charny wrote to revitalize French chivalry in a period of crisis and defeat. That high purpose undoubtedly infused a sense of urgency, sometimes even a strident tone, into his treatise. Undoubtedly the work shows its particularity in Charny's conservative denunciation of new form-fitting male clothing, adorned with gems, just then becoming popular. Yet he is writing broadly about chivalry and if, as we will see, these overarching views fit companionably with those of other writers we examine, the result will be significant, for we will recognize in the *Book of Chivalry* the unmediated voice of a practicing knight speaking about his profession.

We know the life of Don Pero Niño through the extensive and admiring biography of his standard-bearer, Gutierre Díaz de Gamez, under the revealing title *El victorial* (the *Unconquered Knight* in the Joan Evans partial translation). Gamez probably joined Pero Niño's service in 1402 and began writing an account of his hero's deeds several decades later, basing most of his book on personal observation.[15]

In boyhood Pero Niño was the close companion of the future king of Castile, Enrique III (1390–1406), whom his early military exploits served. After several rounds of combat against rebels and against the neighboring kingdom of Portugal, Pero Niño was commissioned in 1404 to take galleys into the western Mediterranean to clean out troublesome pirates there. Although the only actual corsairs he encountered seem to have been "pirates of the lord pope," who had to be left in peace, he raided the North African coast. Again using a force of galleys, he later raided English Gascony, the southwest English coast, and the island of Jersey in the English Channel,

---

[15] The modern English translation of a part of this work by Joan Evans has been used often in the present book because of its accessibility; but passages she omitted and her translation in general have been checked against the Castilian original, now available in critical scholarly editions that had not appeared at the time she wrote. For the original Spanish text, see Gutierre Díaz de Gamez, *El victorial, crónica de Don Pero Niño, conde de Buelna*, ed. Juan de Mata Carriazo (Madrid: Espasa-Calpe, S.A., 1940).

taking time out for sojourns in France during which he won great fame as a jouster and great joy in an affair with the young widow of the Admiral of France. On his return to Castile, he commanded the royal bodyguard and fought in campaigns against the Muslims of Granada. Forced into exile in France when his secret marriage to a lady within the royal family became known, he was pardoned (in the manner of William Marshal and Lancelot) when his military skills were once again needed by his king. Covered with honors, he died in his midseventies in 1453.

The identity of Sir Thomas Malory, long a matter of scholarly contention, now seems settled on the man by that name from Newbold Revell in Warwickshire.[16] No single definitive medieval work lays out his career, but we know that he served on military expeditions in the north of England and fought in the conflict with France; he may have been active in the civil war at home between Lancastrians and Yorkists. Legal records show an undoubtedly vigorous and violent man repeatedly charged with offenses ranging from cattle raids and extortion to breaking into and robbing an abbey and raping and abducting another man's wife. Imprisoned eight times, he proved difficult to confine and escaped twice. His great book, the *Morte Darthur*, likely was written during his final imprisonment.

It is this Arthurian book that mainly interests us, though the rough fabric of the author's career provides its own evidence. Malory's importance for us is basic: he provides another practicing knight's view of chivalry in his adaptation of great chunks of the early thirteenth-century Vulgate or Lancelot-Grail cycle of French romances, combined with sources closer to home such as the foundational Arthurian narrative going back through various medieval translators to Geoffrey of Monmouth's twelfth-century *History of the Kings of Britain*, as well as the anonymous fourteenth-century *Alliterative Morte Arthure*. As more than an editor or a translator, he puts his stamp on his entire book and apparently wrote at least one component tale. Though many in middling social orders may have read Caxton's printed edition of his book with the aim of social ascent, Malory was thinking as a knight and thinking of knights as he wrote. The world of chivalry imagined in Malory's writing

[16] Gweneth Whitteridge, "The Identity of Sir Thomas Malory, Knight-Prisoner," *Review of English Studies* 24, no. 95 (1973), 257–265.

adds wonderfully to our cast of characters and our list of issues of concern to them. We see Lancelot, Galahad, and a host of others as imagined by a practicing knight who is filled with admiration for them and who can only with melancholy tell the dolorous tale of their grand civilization going to pieces.

CORE VALUES IN FIVE MODEL KNIGHTS

Even brief overviews of these five careers point us toward an important generalization: although we will see that many traits made up chivalry, a core formed around prowess exercised in the pursuit and defense of honor. These linked goals or qualities formed the most potent bond at the heart of chivalry. There was also a chivalric soul. As is so often true in examining matters medieval, religion quickly enters discussion of issues that at first glance may seem beyond its immediate scope. Animated and valorized by a distinctive but intense species of lay piety, chivalry claimed the Lord of Hosts as its founder and sustainer (discussed in Chapter 9). Adding this capstone of piety secured the great chivalric arch, which came to be possessed of such resilient strength that it could stand for centuries, whatever changes of detail could transpire in the structure based on its solid presence, with inevitable changes over time and in varying regions.

Our five model knightly careers feature this structure of prowess securing honor and blessed by piety, and it appears in the great mass of evidence on chivalry that we will repeatedly encounter. Of course we must continually exercise caution in the use of terms that at first glance may appear clear and straightforward; they can easily fall classic victims of modern (or at least nineteenth-century) romanticization. Medieval prowess then becomes abstract moral courage, a nonphysical and bloodless notion of ethereal stoutness of heart, cleanly divorced from muscle and steel. Touchy medieval honor can be bowdlerized as timeless upright behavior, equally available to all. Piety can be transmuted into pacifistic self-restraint or utterly unwavering obedience to every clerical directive. If such transformation makes the triad of characteristics more palatable to modern sensibilities, it reduces the originals to a pale shadow of their medieval reality. Knightly motives become altruistic assistance to the weak rather than proud self-assertive dominance, joyful vengeance, or acquisition of glory and loot. Equally important, any tension between tough warrior values and demanding religious ideals fades.

The sheer physicality of prowess constantly demands recognition. Early in his great book, Malory tellingly speaks of "dedys [deeds] full actuall" which leave knights "wagging, stageryng, pantynge, blowynge, and bledyng."[17] Wolfram von Eschenbach writes more than once of "true manly combat."[18] Each of our five knights virtually worshiped prowess as the demanding practice of physical skill and capacity sustained by high resolve. The process of beating another man in heroic armed combat is lavishly praised as the great chivalric deed; each of its physical components cannot be esteemed too highly: our sources tirelessly laud skillful and powerful blows as a lance knocks an opponent from his great warhorse, and perhaps even splits his shield to reach a human target, or as swords slash through armor. The representation of this combat features not abstract moral courage, though that may be required, but intensely physical work – muscular and bloody work. It was assumed that the better or harder the stroke, the higher the status of the man delivering it.

Despite all talk of further chivalric qualities, good fighting is essential; prowess is often considered almost synonymous with chivalry itself. In the Marshal's *Histoire*, knights rushing upon enemies conducting a siege are said to be sallying forth literally "to *do* chivalry" (*por faire chevalerie*).[19] Barbour repeatedly describes knights on both the Scottish and English sides as "doing chivalry."[20] In fact, linked and often overlapping terms such as wycht, worthy, prowess, manhood, valor, and chivalry appear hundreds of times as unstinting praise in *Barbour's Bruce*. Geoffroi de Charny truly cherishes all heroic combat: individual jousting wins honor, and the enthusiastically communal fighting of melee wins even more honor; but real warfare is the grandest source of honor.[21] The greater the effort and physical danger willingly practiced, the greater the honor won. In the same mental frame, *El victorial* can refer to prowess as the "great labours of

---

[17] Vinaver, *Malory: Works*, 23, 198, respectively.

[18] See, for example, Helen M. Mustard and Charles E. Passage, *Parzival* (New York: Vintage, 1961), 245.

[19] *History of William Marshal*, line 176. Emphasis supplied. Wolfram von Eschenbach described Christian and Saracen heroes performing "such deeds of chivalry that God and the ladies too should give thanks for it." Gibbs and Johnson, *Willehalm*, 183.

[20] Among many examples, see *Barbour's Bruce*, bk. 2, lines 348, 370; bk. 6, line 12; bk. 9, line 589; bk. 10, line 817; bk. 11, line 532; bk. 12, line 496; bk. 13, line 750.

[21] Evans, *Unconquered Knight*, 88–91.

chivalry" and link it with well-doing and with early knowledge of love on the part of Pero Niño.[22] Díaz de Gamez is confident that women are moved to love simply by hearing reports of a knight's great prowess. He intones that Pero Niño's intense focus on prowess brought him the honor he craved:

He gave all his life to the calling of arms and to the art of chivalry, and from his childhood laboured at no other matter. And though he was not in rank so great. . .I judged that he was well deserving of honour and renown, and worthy to be set by the side of those who have won guerdon and honour through feats of arms and of chivalry, striving that they might attain the palm of victory.[23]

Malory could not have more fully agreed. In fact, sometimes he simply cannot contain himself. In the midst of a pastel passage on the pleasures of the glorious month of May, he suddenly exclaims, "And worshyp in armys may never be foyled!"[24] One pictures him writing this line left-handed, with the right arm uplifted, fist clenched.

At one point his hero Lancelot is seen to bear so many wounds on his body that observers deem him a man of worship.[25] Sir Thomas would have appreciated the heralds who on a battlefield in the Perceforest cry out, "On with your helmets, knights! Lace them well! Honour is on offer today – come and win it!"[26]

Striking moments of valor are not simply imagined; our heroes' accounts leave modern readers with images of historically enacted physicality that can scarcely be forgotten. All who know his *Histoire* will forever recall the Marshal, after a hard-fought tournament, bent double with his helmeted head resting on an anvil, while a prudently careful blacksmith tries to remove the battered helm.[27] Who could forget Pero Niño with a crossbow bolt lodged in his nose in an early fight, enemy blows inconveniently driving it deeper? The pain, his biographer assures, only redoubled his zeal.[28] More often, the damage reported was done by a hero to a worthy enemy. Díaz de Gamez tells that Pero Niño split not only the shield but also the skull of his enemy Gómez Domao, adding proudly, if redundantly, "And that was the

---

[22] Ibid., 18.   [23] Ibid., 6.   [24] Vinaver, *Malory: Works*, 649.
[25] These wounds can be healed only by the Holy Grail: Vinaver. *Malory: Works*, 499–500.
[26] Bryant, trans., *Perceforest*, 129.
[27] *History of William Marshal*, lines 3103–3112.
[28] Evans, *Unconquered Knight*, 37–38. Carriazo, 82–83.

end of Gómez Domao."[29] With equal pride, John Barbour shows Robert Bruce at the beginning of the battle of Bannockburn splitting the head of Sir Henry Bohun "till ye harnys" (that is, the ax blade penetrating all the way into the hauberk).[30] He is even more exultant after Robert Bruce defends a ford alone (or, as Bruce insisted, only with God's help) against pursuing enemies, leaving fourteen bloodied bodies eddying in the water:

> A der God quha had yen bene by
> & sene hove he sa hardyly
> Adressyt hym agane yaim all
> I wate weile yat yai suld him call
> Ye best yat levyt in his day...
> & giff I ye suth sall say
> I herd never in na tym gane
> Ane stynt sa mony him allane.[31]
> [Dear God, had you been there
> To see how so valorously he
> Stood alone against them all
> I know well you'd call him
> The best alive in his day
> And to tell you the truth
> I never heard ever
> Of one standing alone against so many.]

Geoffroi de Charny, urging improved martial behavior of French knighthood, rather than any description from historical battlefields, provides less in the way of anatomical detail or body counts, yet his unfettered praise for prowess is unceasing and his frank advice for young knights is not to think of what the enemy may do to them, but to concentrate thought on what they will do to the enemy. The doing will clearly involve well-sharpened blades and well-hardened muscles, "for it is from good battles that good honors arise."[32] The link is recurrently made in chivalric literature. In reading the *Morte Darthur*, as is true in reading all of our sources on model knighthood, we are almost listening to the active knights thinking about, worrying over, and praising their high profession.

The sheer toughness of the practice of knighthood is often emphasized in accounts about or by our model knights. Endurance and the

[29] Evans, *Unconquered Knight*, 37. Carriazo, 82: "e allí quedó Gómez Domao."
[30] *Barbour's Bruce* 12, 50–56.   [31] Ibid., vol. 2, bk. 6, 140, lines 173–180.
[32] Kaeuper and Kennedy, *Book of Chivalry*, 89–91.

acceptance of physical suffering stand behind all their great deeds, tirelessly lauded. The biographer of William Marshal has already been quoted along such lines, but Charny is an outstanding spokesman, describing the rigors and deprivations of a life at arms – poor food, uncomfortable beds, dangers of travel by land and even more by sea, constant alarms, even the intolerable waiting for the charge in battle. Such a life becomes a form of martyrdom. And the result, as Charny had good reason to know, might not always be victory; but really good combat won both honor and divine approval:

And does not God confer great honor when He allows you of His mercy to defeat your enemies without harm to yourself? And if you are defeated, does not God show you great mercy if you are taken prisoner honorably, praised by friends and enemies? And if you are in a state of grace and you die honorably does not God show you great mercy when He grants you such a glorious end to your life in this world and bears your soul away with Him into eternal bliss?[33]

Our model knights reject the soft life utterly. Though Charny does not seem to be a man for whom satire was a natural form, he turns to it with vigor as he bitterly denounces any form of self-indulgent softness, any reluctance to join the fray boldly and without regard for personal consequences. Pero Niño is not far behind. He can denounce any desire for the soft life with a vigor that parallels or possibly echoes Charny. He knows intimately the hard conditions of campaigning. At one point, as Díaz de Gamez tells, the stout young warrior had to wear at least a part of his chafing armor without a break for seventeen straight days.[34] Wearing armor could be intolerably debilitative: popular films err in showing shining armor as the daily sartorial choice for knighthood. Pero Niño demonstrated his bravery and endurance much more dramatically when a leg wound caused by an arrow refused to heal. He resolutely grasped the iron, heated red-hot at its tip, from the trembling hands of a surgeon, and thoroughly seared his own wound; amputation of his leg would have been the only alternative lifesaving cure, with the end of his career as consequence.[35]

---

[33] Ibid., 132–133.

[34] Evans, 35. Carriazo, 79. The Spanish reads "nunca Pero Niño dexó el arnés aquel que razonablemente puede el hombre traer de cada vn día."

[35] Evans, 100. Carriazo, 138.

If Pero Niño saved his leg with his own hands, our sources regularly specify that characteristic knightly labor means hands-on work against enemies. Such terminology is evocative and instructive. In his *Histoire*, William Marshal is praised for knowing how to use his hands, he fights hand-to-hand-battles, and he promises to kill enemies "with my own hands."[36] In one tough fight,

> He hit back and bludgeoned
> like a man who was one of the foremost
> and was not without the use of his hands:
> ...
> it seemed rather that he had four of them
> when you saw the way he overturned and knocked down
> those on the other side who came across his path.[37]

Significantly, when accused of an illicit relationship with the Young King's wife, he offered to fight to prove his innocence, dramatically offering to cut off one essential sword-gripping finger from his strong right hand.[38] Moreover, the author's praise for hands-on prowess extends to others; Sir John de Preaux, for example, is termed a man who was pure gold when it came to taking blows:

> but those who tangled with him did not get off lightly themselves,
> for he was well capable of showing them what he was made of,
> since he knew all about handling arms.[39]

This emphasis is scarcely unique to the *Histoire*. Charny intones the merits of hand-to-hand combat with zeal as when he advises the ambitious to:

> seek constantly and diligently opportunities to perform deeds of arms. And when God grants you the good fortune to find them, do your duty wisely and boldly, fearing nothing except shame, striving with the skill of your hand and the effort of your body to as great a degree as your powers can extend in order to inflict damage on your opponents, always being among the first in battle.[40]

John Barbour early in his chronicle lauds his heroes Robert Bruce and Sir James Douglas as hardy of both heart and hand,[41] but he similarly

---

[36] Paraphrase and quotation, respectively, from *History of William Marshal*, lines 3906 and 258.
[37] *History of William Marshal*, 1: 150–153, lines 2970–2975.
[38] Ibid., lines 2970–2975.   [39] Ibid., lines 4663–4665.
[40] Kaeuper and Kennedy, *Book of Chivalry*, 194–195.
[41] *Barbour's Bruce*, lines 227–229.

praises even a knight opposed to Robert Bruce as being "of his hands a worthy knight (off his hand a worthy knycht)."[42] In his first fight (at about age 15), Pero Niño, we are told, did more than any other "by his hands (*por sos manos*)"[43] to win honor in arms and chivalry; such language is repeated throughout the account of his victorious life. References to hands-on chivalric violence form a leitmotif in Malory's book. King Arthur himself is "off [of] his hondes a grete knight" and Lancelot's hands are decidedly deadly, as his many opponents learn to their cost.

Much of this action takes place on the tourney ground, which frequently provided a stage for such enacted prowess yielding honor. In many hundreds of lines of his verse biography, we are assured that William Marshal fought so well in this extreme sport and triumphed so regularly that the Young King, son of Henry II, wanted him constantly at his side in the perilous confusion of the melee. After one good day on the field the author exalts, "that day he captured with his hands ten knights in the tournament." Robert Bruce may not have played the tourneyer, being kept fully occupied by fighting his English and Anglo-Scottish enemies, but Pero Niño (who is said to have been the finest jouster at the Castilian court) later held the field in Paris for an entire day and night against all comers. Two honored ranks on Charny's scale of ascending martial virtue, as we have seen, came from the tourney field. Malory's great book would risk collapse if deprived of its steady presentation of one tournament after another. Perhaps to flatter the hardy self-conception of knighthood, these tournaments often seem little differentiated from war and certainly serve to "prove the worth" of major characters. Like John Barbour, Sir Thomas seems to keep a fresh scorecard always near at hand, to record the changing ranking of knights as settled by jousting.

Interpreting honor calls for particular caution, for the term remains durable in modern usage. We still label actions or people we admire as honorable and could easily, almost unconsciously, assume that the term simply implied our ideals in the past. The eminent social anthropologist Julian Pitt-Rivers provided a helpful corrective to such concepts in his classic analysis of codes of honor in early

---

[42] Ibid., lines 200–203; 34, line 264.   [43] Evans, 30. Carriazo, 74.

European history.[44] He argued persuasively that honor meant status and precedence (a desired place in the "pecking order"), vigorously asserted and even more vigorously defended against any perceived slight. Honor was given to those who could enforce their claim to possess it. Strenuously and stridently won, honor was cherished as a social rather than an ethical possession. He added that "on the field of honour, might is right."[45] In effect, medieval honor and prowess intertwined. Mervyn James, a Tudor/Stuart historian, has written convincingly in similarly uncompromising terms.[46]

It is important to acknowledge that medieval reformers sought changes in these formulations. Chrétien de Troyes, to take one eminent example, wanted a knighthood more concerned with service than vainglory. Yet such urgings toward a more beneficent motivation, of course, underscore Pitt-Rivers's point from a different direction: altruism being less common than medieval idealists would have wished, they spoke and wrote to encourage what was lacking or inadequately present. Wolfram von Eschenbach, as Marion Gibbs and Sidney Johnson (modern translators of his Middle High German *Willehalm*) astutely observe, "from time to time...addresses his audience, demanding a response, which may indeed have been forthcoming."[47] The same technique appears in Hartman von Aue's *Erec and Iwein*.[48] Chivalric literature was ever a debate form.

Yet recognizing such debate does nothing to reduce the centrality of medieval honor, which remained the great goal and unsurpassed good, regularly ranked as more valuable than life itself. For if death claims all warriors in the end, dread shame that tarnishes or obliterates precious honor can and must be avoided. John Barbour notes as a principle that, given the option, men should chose to die chivalrously rather than live as cowards.[49] Charny's admonition is

---

[44] J. A. Pitt-Rivers, "Honour and Social Status," in *Honour and Shame: The Values of Mediterranean Society*, ed. J. G. Peristiany (London: Weidenfeld and Nicolson, 1965).

[45] Ibid., 24–25.

[46] Mervyn James, *English Politics and the Concept of Honour 1485–1642* (Oxford: Past and Present Society, 1978).

[47] See their introduction to *Willehalm* (London: Penguin, 1984), 11. They say the audience was "listening to his tale and reacting as he went along." Ibid.

[48] A point made by Albrecht Classen, "Self-Enactment of Late Medieval Chivalry: Performance and Self-Representation in Ulrich von Liechtenstein's *Frauendienst*," *Seminar* 39 (2003), 93.

[49] *Barbour's Bruce*, 3, line 2646.

characteristically even more direct: he urges knights to "care less about death than about shame."[50] Adding amorous incentive and the link with prowess, he notes that a man without prowess will experience the shame that ends love affairs.[51] Pointedly, he further asks French knights to contemplate how shameful an old age they will face if they have failed to live up to their full potential for valorous acts.[52] In a proliferation of negative terms, he exhorts, "Surely, ill deeds are shameful, fearful, and dangerous to commit, and unworthy ways of life bring shame, blame and an increase of sin."[53] Religious language has joined the formulation and is emphasized as Charny advances a powerful and revealing paralleling of honor achieved and maintained in the world with the immortal soul. To take one example of many in his treatise, Charny denigrates the mere body, but exhorts the knights to "instead direct your love toward the preservation of your soul and your honor, which last longer than does the body, which dies just as soon, whether it be fat or lean."[54]

We can almost hear our other model knights shouting agreement in Anglo-Norman French, variants of Middle English, and Castilian. The Marshal's biographer denounces shameful behavior regularly, and even warns ominously against "eternal shame"[55] or at least "shame that lasts longer than destitution."[56] He even thinks the goal of crusaders is to avenge the shame inflicted on God by unbelievers.[57] At the quotidian level, he knows that "a man takes full revenge for the wrongs and shame done to him."[58] Fleeing a fight is clearly shameful in the eyes of Barbour, who generously recognizes the corrective not only among stout Scotsmen, but in occasional firm fighting by the English; his special admiration goes to the English knight Giles d'Argentine, who refused to flee shamefully at Bannockburn and died honorably on the points of Scots' spears.[59] Repeatedly, honor is said to have been physically won and maintained

---

[50] Kaeuper and Kennedy, *Book of Chivalry*, 132–133. [51] Ibid., 120–121.
[52] Ibid., 112–113. [53] Ibid., 146–147. [54] Ibid., 122–133.
[55] *History of William Marshal*, line 13522. [56] Ibid., line 13726.
[57] Ibid., lines 7339–7340. [58] Ibid., line 16195.
[59] *Barbour's Bruce*, vol. 3, bk. 13, 61, lines 305–307. A contemporary chronicle, *Vita Edwardi Secundi*, ed. N. Denholm-Young (1957), 53–54, described Giles as "very expert in the art of war," who chose to die trying to save the Earl of Gloucester, "thinking it more honourable to perish with so great a man than to escape death by flight."

in the valor of battle in his pages.[60] Pero Niño's biographer links honor with prowess with similar regularity. As a lad, his hero was taught to pay heed to all knights, Christian or non-Christian, who have endured so much to gain honor and renown.[61] God gave El Cid, he was taught, greatness and honor "and much was he feared by his neighbours."[62] Pero Niño learned his lessons well, and in his first fight, Díaz de Gamez insists,

[Pero Niño p]ressed forward before the rest so often that none did so much with their hands as he. He struck signal blows which drew blood. . .and he was twice wounded. So long as the siege lasted, he thrust himself forward so often and accomplished so many fine feats with his hands, that all spoke well of him and said that he had made a good beginning, and showed a will to gain great honour in arms and chivalry.[63]

Sir Thomas Malory uses the term "worshype" for honor and nearly fills his great book with instances of stout knights winning such worship through physical prowess. The flavor of his adulation appears when, in the midst of a passage rejoicing in the glories of a day in May he suddenly explains, "And worshyp in armys may never be foyled!"[64]

We need not deny that elements in the medieval concept of honor could be admired by many modern people: for example, our heroes and their many imitators and admirers showed steady fidelity to obligation and sworn word, maintained in the face of great danger, difficulty, or even death. The gravitas that often accompanies so steady a sense of self and purpose likewise may win admiration. Yet historical analysis is well served by keeping in mind the prickly and violent components of knightly honor. Any perceived threat must be resolutely countered, and, as Pitt-Rivers aptly observed, "the ultimate vindication of honour lies in physical violence."[65]

---

[60] E.g., bk. 2, 357; bk. 8, 250–253, 318; bk. 12, 162.

[61] Evans, *Unconquered Knight*, 3–4. Carriazo, 4–7.   [62] Ibid.

[63] Evans, 30. Carriazo, 74–75: "Allí peleó tanto este donzel, que se esmeró de los otros allende dellos tantas vezes, que non fué ninguno aquel día que tanto fiçiese por sus manos. E dió allí muchos golpes señalados. . .e él fué ferido de dos feridas. E en quanto duró aquella çerca, él se esmeró tantas vezes, e fizo tantos Buenos fechos por sus manos en armas, que quantos ende heran fablauan vien; e dezían que él començaua bien e mostraua que grand honrra auía de alcançar por arte de armas e ofiçio de cauallería."

[64] Vinaver, *Malory: Works*, 649.   [65] Pitt-Rivers, "Honour and Shame," 29.

Piety hovers over this potent bond of prowess and honor, as briefly noted before. Of course sources on our model knights are replete with predictable references to divine presence, heavenly will, and mercy in knightly careers; oaths are sworn by invoking God or a saint. Constant divine intervention in the world is assumed. Likewise, the orthodoxy of the knights is always assumed and sometimes stressed.

More significantly, our five knights found in piety the ultimate guide to the practice of a hard profession; it was through religious ideas and language that they finally framed their lives, as we will see more fully in Chapter 9. If the most thoughtful among knighthood struggled with issues of morality in killing and destruction, valorization was provided (intermixed with many critiques, of course) by their religion.[66] God had given demanding work to knights and had endowed them with great physical and mental capacity to carry it out in his created world. In the foundational medieval conception of social organization, the knight was designated a fighter: our model figures stood proudly in the *ordo* of *bellatores*, one of the socio-professional groups derived from the divine plan for the proper functioning of the world. Such men were not citizen soldiers who leave a peacetime profession temporarily for the exigency of war; their function defines them lifelong. They are answering a divine call, not a recruiting poster or a draft notice: God established chivalry; he loves the knights, generation by generation, and rewards their good work.[67]

Origins myths in chivalric writing stress this function. Before turning to detail his hero's many bold acts, Díaz de Gamez recounts such an imagined origin for knighthood: leaders of society in a mythical past gradually found the right males to serve as fighters. Men who practiced the mechanical arts (such as carpenters and stonemasons) could strike great blows, and butchers were thought inured to bloodshed, but all these men lacked the capacity to wear armor or to retain courage in the face of danger. Only fearless men would do. Identified initially by careful observation of behavior on the battlefield, their bravery, an inherent quality, was genetically passed on to male children who, like them, must be given generous support in recompense for their stout combat. Díaz de Gamez's book is dedicated to such men: "to noble knights who strive to win honour

---

[66] An argument of R. W. Kaeuper, *Holy Warriors*.
[67] Themes and questions that may have troubled the knights will be the concern of Chapter 9.

and renown in the art of arms and chivalry." He is adamant that he writes for such men "and not any others whatsoever." Of course other men such as the gluttonous, with no control over appetite, lose endurance and sink into dishonor; but the elite of later ages stemmed from men of sterner stuff.[68]

This explicit sense of mythic origins of good fighters hovers in other accounts of the model knights. Several centuries earlier, the anonymous author of William Marshal's *Histoire* tells no formal and elaborate creation myth, but advances similar ideas and uses some of the same language about the superiority and honor of the labor that characterizes knights.

> What is armed combat'? Is it the same
> as working with a sieve or winnow,
> with an axe or mallet?
> Not at all, it is much nobler work,
>
> for he who undertakes these tasks is able
>   to take a rest when he has worked for
>   a while.
> What, then, is chivalry?
> Such a difficult, tough,
> and very costly thing to learn
> that no coward ventures to take it on.[69]

John Barbour's chronicle of Robert Bruce likewise tells no formal origins myth, but sees the divine plan for knighthood – at least for Scottish knighthood – at work in the heavenly support provided; explicitly, he parallels Bruce and his men with the Macabees in the "bibill" (Bible and specifically the Old Testament) who won "gret worschip and valour" (honor and worthy prowess) by defending those who otherwise had no protection.[70] Barbour repeatedly shows the Bruce counseling men to have belief in God's help; it had come to men in worse straits even than theirs.[71]

Geoffroi de Charny continually lauds prowess as great martial achievement and admonishes all men-at-arms to acknowledge such a gift from God with humble thankfulness. He piously and formally grants that the clerical *ordo* stands at the apex of society, but he edges quickly toward a stirring defense of the claims of his own

---

[68] Evans, *Unconquered Knight*, 2–3.
[69] *History of William Marshal*, lines 16853–16862.
[70] *Barbour's Bruce*, bk. 1, lines 446–471.
[71] Ibid., bk. 3, 199–206; bk. 4, lines 525–530; bk. 6, lines 88–90.

knightly order. Of necessity they suffer more meritoriously on campaign and on the battlefield; more than any others, the knights must be good Christians, for death is always close to hand, transporting them suddenly before the judgment throne of the Almighty. Charny shows confidence in a highly positive divine verdict on knighthood. Sir Thomas Malory's view was, if anything, even more proud; his glowing references to the Hyghe Ordre of Chivalry are too numerous to cite.

Clearly in active minds beneath their helms, our heroes believed knighthood entered God's world as a body of ideal fighters and were confident that their good fighting merited heavenly reward. Did they not always fight in good causes even when fighting each other? Did they not suffer in these good causes?

CHIVALRIC BALANCE AND PRAGMATISM

Prowess and honor, adorned with religious blessing, were central to chivalry, but they were clearly surrounded, supported, and sometimes channeled by other qualities, emphasized both within individual texts and within the entire body of evidence available. The constant and ideal goal was to produce the worthy man (*prudhomme*) who achieved a balanced set of desirable traits.[72] This meant adding to the chivalric core we have been investigating; a list of significant characteristics includes loyalty, generosity, wisdom, courtliness, and the expression and practice of good love. The full list is not static or fixed, but represents a commentator's ideal knight. Both John Barbour and the chronicler Jean le Bel, for example, state that all loyal, sturdy fighters qualify as worthy men.[73] Charny's view does not

---

[72] The importance of the *prudhomme* is emphasized in David Crouch, *The Birth of Nobility: Constructing Aristocracy in England and France 900–1300* (New York: Pearson/Longman, 2005).

[73] Nigel Bryant, ed., trans., *True Chronicles of Jean le Bel*, 21–22; he names knights who have "been victorious and displayed such valour that they should be deemed worthy men indeed, supremely so." His French terms are *"proeuz et oultre proeuz."* And he continues, "truth to tell, all should be considered worthy who in such fierce and perilous battles...have had the courage to stand fast to the last, ably doing their duty." For the original French, see Jules Viard and Eugene Déprez, eds., *Chronique de Jean le Bel* (Paris: Renouard, 1904), 3. For *Barbour's Bruce*, see bk. 20, lines 428–432: "Thar mycht men felloun fechtyn se, / For thai war all wicht and worthi / That war on the Cristyn party / And faucht sa fast with all thar mayne / That Saryzynys war mony slayne." Cf. ibid.: Before the battle at

disagree, but takes a more elaborate form, as we will consider in a moment. In other words, a set of ancillary traits usually orbit around prowess and honor like satellites to these imposing planets; they complement the centrality of the primary bodies of thought and practice, but they may sometimes help to guide and guard against excess or wrongdoing that might easily lurk in the shadows cast by central and oversized chivalric qualities.

Loyalty provides a good case in point. A knight's sense of loyalty tended to be intensely personal and demanded faithfulness to obligation, being steady and reliable, never devious or untrustworthy. Such a conception must replace modern connotations, which mainly focus on hierarchy and major institutions. Good men, all medieval commentators would agree, are loyal men; disloyal men are traitors. In *Barbour's Bruce*, the worthy men are presented as free of treachery and fully trustworthy. The Scots loyally abide by treaties; the English cannot be trusted, as the Welsh should have learned from experience.[74] As always, this individual quality stands arm in arm with others; as Barbour describes him, the earl of Moray

> Loved loyalty above all else.
> Truly he stood particularly
> Against false treason and felony.
> Truly he loved honour and largesse.[75]

William Marshal's biographer never doubts that loyalty constituted a great buttress to the Marshal's career or to the worthiness of the Young King, whom William served so loyally. He quotes William's own assertion that he has never in his life acted disloyally,[76] and refers tirelessly to the Marshal as "worthy and loyal,"[77] "courtly, wise and loyal,"[78] "brave, devoted and loyal,"[79] or "brave, noble-hearted and loyal."[80]

Methven, the king addresses his troops saying: "Ye ar ilkan wycht and worthy / And full of gret chevalry, / And wate rycht weill quhat honour is." Cf. ibid., bk. 2, lines 337–339: "Thar mycht men felloun fechtyn se, / For thai war all wicht and worthi / That war on the Cristyn party / And faucht sa fast with all thar mayne / That Saryzynys war mony slayne."

[74] *Barbour's Bruce*, bk. 19, 192–196; bk. 1, 12, respectively.
[75] Ibid., bk. 10, 290–294. My translation. These lines come in a rush of fulsome praise for various chivalric qualities.
[76] *History of William Marshal*, line 1149.   [77] E.g., ibid., lines 15134, 15763.
[78] Ibid., line 14337.   [79] Ibid., lines 12123–12124.   [80] Ibid., line 17612.

Such loyalty seems almost to constitute an element of the war-riors' environment. Not only does it link together desirable quali-ties in heroes, but it even infuses the beloved animals who serve them. Pero Niño knows that a good warhorse could show loyalty, reflecting the knight he faithfully carried,[81] and his view paralleled that of crusading *exempla* in which knights speak earnestly about their motives to their *destriers*, and may find that while they are in devotions at a holy site the loyal horse has stood stalwartly across the door of an inn, thus reserving a room for its master.[82] In the biography of Robert Bruce, Barbour presents a hunting dog full of such loyalty that he constantly follows the Bruce. Ironically, this helps enemies track his master.[83]

What is more, a loyal man has a better chance for love. Both Pero Niño and Geoffroi de Charny closely associate loyalty with winning the best love (and both link such success with prowess). The Castilian biographer asserts that a woman's love seeks not great riches or a great estate, but "a man brave and bold, true and loyal,"[84] and quotes his hero's pledge to Doña Beatriz to "love her uprightly, loyally, and to the honour of them both."[85] Charny's agreement appears in a characteristically concise maxim: "Love loy-ally if you want to be loved."[86] The reward is to "live joyfully and honourably."[87] No surprise registers when we find him urging knights to "carry out all their undertakings loyally and with good judgment" and speaks of "true loyal prowess."[88] Of course a chief merit in love, Charny is convinced, lies in its capacity to increase a man's prowess.

Our model knights – reflecting an attitude found in chivalric litera-ture in general – often assume that great prowess is a sure indicator of the presence of other desired qualities. At the least, prowess is con-stantly paired with another quality such as generosity or loyalty; but multiple chivalric qualities are profligately linked to form flowery

---

[81] Evans, *Unconquered Knight*, 5, 79.

[82] E.g., British Library, Additional 18344 f 113b.

[83] One of the Bruce's hounds followed him wherever he went, for the hound loved him so. "He folowyt him quharever he yeid / Sa that the hund him lovit sua / That he wald part na wys him fra." Bk. 6, lines 492–494.

[84] Evans, *Unconquered Knight*, 19.   [85] Ibid., 85.

[86] Kaeuper and Kennedy, *Book of Chivalry*, 122–123.   [87] Ibid.

[88] Both in section 35, pp. 182–183 in Kaeuper and Kennedy, *Book of Chivalry*.

chains of words of praise to garland knighthood.[89] William Marshal's *Histoire*, for example, yokes prowess with wisdom and with good qualities and honorable conduct.[90] Even more broadly, he counsels, "Foresight, common sense and right are often the partners of physical prowess."[91] In a garland of personified qualities, he joins "Chivalry and Prowess, Nobility and Generosity,"[92] and later enthuses, "My God! what magnificent things are prowess, nobility of heart, generosity and wisdom, when they are gathered together."[93] Personifying again, he lauds the earl of Salisbury for having Generosity as his mother and "supreme, untarnished Prowess" as the symbolic banner carried before him.[94] Geoffroi de Charny's intense hymn to prowess likewise broadens to praise "the worth, the prowess, and the other strengths" in good men-at-arms or to laud "wisdom, beauty, worthiness, prowess or valor."[95] Men of rank and prowess naturally form a pair in his mind, as do "noble prowess and great understanding."[96]

Openhanded generosity, practiced and praised in sources on all five model knights, is similarly linked with other chivalric qualities. Pero Niño's first lady love knew he was "young, fair, generous, bold, courageous, gentle and in all things as he should be."[97] His biographer is equally comprehensive: "Pero Niño was at this time greatly renowned as a good knight, as well in battle as in jousts and tourneys, generous, enterprising, most brilliant in his equipment, distinguished at the palace and very courteous, which made him beloved of all the world."[98] Isolating the strand of largesse, his biographer admires the French as "generous and great givers of presents."[99] Ever the conservative voice, Charny admonished French knights to "be generous

[89] Barthélemy similarly notes "expressions… like so many petals euphorically arranged to compose an attractive rhetorical flower." *The Serf, the Knight, and the Historian*, 150.

[90] *History of William Marshal*; link with wisdom at lines 2668, 2676, 3601, 18148, 184743; link with good qualities and honorable conduct at line 5950.

[91] Ibid., lines 10841–10842.   [92] Ibid., lines 4315–4316.

[93] Ibid., lines 5105–5107.   [94] Ibid., lines 12124–12128.

[95] Kaeuper and Kennedy, *Book of Chivalry*, 156–157, 160–161.

[96] Ibid., 104–105. The title refers to this link.

[97] Evans, *Unconquered Knight*, 46. Carriazo, 95: "moço e fermoso e generoso, e ardid, esforzado, gentil e guarnido."

[98] Evans, *Unconquered Knight*, 203. Carriazo, 300: "E Pero Niño en aquel tiempo hera famoso cavallero, ansí en harmas como en juegos de armas, franco e ardid, e muy arreado, palançiano e muy cortés, tal que se fazía amar a las gentes."

[99] Evans, *Unconquered Knight*, 133. Carriazo, 217: "Son francos e dadivosos."

in giving where the gift will be the best used."[100] Turning to rulers, he warns against largesse to unworthy wastrels but urges giving "freely and generously" to men of worth.[101] The right kind of generosity takes its place in a characteristic string of virtue words: he wants "men of worth, wise, loyal, without arrogance, joyful, generous, courteous, expert, bold, and active, and of good conduct toward all others."[102] Pragmatically, the *Histoire* of the Marshal at one point praises generosity in sharing out loot won by battle prowess, as does the biographer of Robert Bruce.[103] The Marshal's biographer implies that prowess had likewise supplied largesse during William's three years while on crusade, for the Marshal "showed himself to be so generous, / he performed so many feats of bravery and valour, / so many fine deeds that no man before had performed so many, even if he had lived there for seven years."[104] Chivalric garlands appear to be ubiquitous: the young king is "so handsome, fair and noble, so courtly, generous and valiant [si proz]."[105] Though Malory seems less prone to long chains of linked terms, he can without strain join prowess with other desired qualities. No knight recognized an herb that is a sign of the Holy Grail, he writes, "but he were a goodly lyver and a man of prouesse."[106]

It is impressive to find this overlapping of multiple terms in the late twelfth-century cross-Channel world, in early fourteenth-century Scotland, in mid-fourteenth-century France, in the Mediterranean, Spain, and the Channel at the very end of the fourteenth century, and in late fifteenth-century England. Why was so wide a range of terms so evidently useful in valorizing and praising chivalry? Our writers' fondness for such chivalric garlands of praise reveals more than a tendency to prolix style. Clearly these concepts interlocked in the minds of authors who found a shifting variety of terms and combinations essential to the proper praise of chivalry, even though a core set of values appears in them all. So elevated is their conception of chivalry that they can only, in effect, toss terms of praise over it as if they were handfuls of celebratory confetti.

[100] Kaeuper and Kennedy, *Book of Chivalry*, 128–129.
[101] Ibid., *Book of Chivalry*, 25.   [102] Ibid., 192–193.
[103] *History of William Marshal*, line 351; *Barbour's Bruce*, bk. 15, lines 540–550: Douglas's men are stronger and more worthy when he distributes spoils to them.
[104] *History of William Marshal*, lines 7277–7280.   [105] Ibid., lines 7168–7169.
[106] Vinaver, *Malory: Works*, 81.

Yet the relative weights attributed to any particular chivalric value could shift within the set, and this might reflect hard necessity rather than permanent change in ideals. Circumstances could require emphasis on one quality while another value was rather quietly diminished for the time being. Laudatory accounts by or about our model knights reveal the process at work. Observing this phenomenon need evoke no shallow cynicism. Few sets of guiding ideals known to historians escape the iron frame of such necessity. In a fascinating case, Barbour tells how Robert Bruce explained his plans to attack an unsuspecting enemy garrison at Turnberry: the Scots may be able, he says, to kill all the Englishmen while they are sleeping.[107] Perhaps Bruce felt some compulsion to justify such an attack; his nephew had once reproached him for using cunning tactics ("slycht") against the English rather than engaging in straightforward combat ("playne fechting").[108] Barbour said he assured his men that no one will reprove them for "werrayour na fors suld ma / Quheyer he mycht overcum his fa / Throw strenth or throw sutelte. / Bot yar gud faith ay halden be."[109] Exactly how good faith is maintained while eviscerating sleeping enemies remains a bit murky. Yet the evidence and even the specific language are priceless; an ideological affirmation of one prized quality is being employed to paper over a deep crack in another. And the garrison was, in fact, overwhelmed in the manner proposed. To Barbour, Robert Bruce's chivalry remains beyond question: "mycht" and "slycht" are not stark alternatives, but two trump cards in a winning chivalric hand well played by his hero.[110] This same issue is similarly resolved as the Scots face the daunting task of capturing the castle at Edinburgh, seemingly impregnably perched upon its great rock. Randolph, Earl of Moray, decides he must find

---

[107] David Preest, trans., *Chronicle of Geoffrey le Baker*, 101, gives a parallel case of a night attack on a sleeping garrison and a stealthy attack on Guines during the Hundred Years War.

[108] *Barbour's Bruce*, bk. 9, lines 749–752.

[109] Ibid., bk. 5; speech begins at line 71, quotation at lines 85–88.

[110] See the comments of Matthew McDiarmid, *Scottish Text Society* 15, p. 45, and Sonja Cameron, "Chivalry and Warfare in Barbour's Bruce," in *Armies, Chivalry and Warfare in Medieval Britain and France*, ed. Matthew Strickland (Harlaxton Medieval Studies 7; Stamford: Paul Watkins, 1998), 13–29. Cameron considers *Barbour's Bruce* essentially a romance and sees the tensions within it regarding chivalry and pragmatic warfare a reflection of the *Fierabras*, with the English regime in Scotland standing in for pagans who need not be fought with what she considers chivalric fairness.

some cunning means, a "slycht," which in combination with "hey chevalry" could win the fortress. He found it: local guidance led his force to a path up the rock reaching a back wall. With this crafty approach and the bold chivalry of his force, Moray gained entry to the castle and, after a sharp engagement, took it.[111] Again a great warrior did what was required and the claim was made that his victory was no violation of chivalric ideals. Perhaps in both cases an early form of Scots nationalism became a sufficient justifying mechanism, substituting for – or perhaps better fusing with – religious valorization of a sort more readily called upon.

Geoffroi de Charny confronted a comparable military problem in a similar manner. He tried to recover the great port of Calais held by the English against his master, the king of France, by resorting to bribery. Amery de Pavia, a captain of a key gate, actually took the money offered, but had prudently informed his English masters of the plan. Undoubtedly Charny expected a satisfying fight once his force penetrated the imposing defenses, but he was caught completely by surprise as the trap was suddenly sprung; characteristically, he fought stoutly and urged the same of his force, but he was wounded and captured. Messire Geoffroi stoically endured the shaming rebuke delivered face-to-face by Edward III at the festive banquet that followed his capture. Of course once ransomed, Charny caught Amery and soon displayed the man's quartered body, a fate befitting a vile traitor. Nothing indicates that his chivalric reputation was tarnished among French knighthood by an effort to secure entry into Calais by mere money. Charny had stocked his personal treasury of merit with glowing deeds of prowess. Could he only have gotten through the walls and into the city, he planned to enact more of the same.[112]

Tension and compromise even appear in the life of the Marshal. We have seen that loyalty was the chivalric virtue often paired with prowess to characterize William; yet as the cross-Channel realm under Plantagenet control came apart along its watery centerline, William found ways to remain the faithful vassal of both his sovereign

[111] See bk. 10, lines 514–707.
[112] Kaeuper and Kennedy, *Book of Chivalry*, 14; Jean Froissart, *Oeuvres de Froissart*, vol. 5, ed. Kervyn de Lettenhove (Paris: Academie royale des sciences, 1867–1877), 271–274; *Chronique normande du xive siècle*, ed. Auguste Molinier and Émile Molinier (Paris: Librairie Renouard, 1882), 103–104; *Chroniques des quatre premiers Valois*, ed. Simeon Luce (Paris: V.J. Renouard, 1862), 29–30.

lords, the contending kings of England and France. During the civil war in England following the death of King John and the French invasion, he stood by the king of England, but it seems he encouraged his son to join the opposition. It costs his medieval biographer some effort to retain all the gold leaf on William's image, but (if the *Histoire* is accurate) he died with lavish praise from great knights and high clerics alike ringing in his ears.

Pero Niño, we might recall, likewise faced difficult tensions of principle on several occasions. He troubled his loyal relationship with his overlord in Castile by a secret marriage that ruined royal plans for the noble lady in question. For a time their resulting relationship became so fraught that he had to slip across the border to find a safe haven from his lord's wrath. All ended well, especially when his great prowess was urgently needed for the next war. Likewise, we have seen that both William Marshal and Lancelot could have appreciated military need overwhelming other feelings. Yet even Pero Niño's admiring biographer records the wrestling with moral tensions when the hero was ravaging the English Channel island of Jersey (as a part of his raiding on behalf of the French); he was plainly asked why one Christian should threaten other Christians with death and destruction in their own land. Discussions became complex as the tenurial history and consequent obligations of loyalty of the inhabitants of the isle were debated. A ransom payment was finally set and accepted.[113]

Of course, Thomas Malory provides the most famous exploration of significant tensions within knightly values, drawing on a central paradox in chivalric romance that was centuries old by the time he wrote. His admiration for Lancelot is legendary. If some of his French sources countered admiration for Lancelot by promoting Galahad as the ideal knight who transcended worldly chivalry to ascend to the spiritual, Sir Thomas seems to have preferred the more realistic human imperfection of Lancelot. Yet adultery with one's lord's wife was not a widely recognized chivalric virtue, and the combined sin and disloyalty prevent Lancelot from success in the Grail quest. Malory inherited this story of failure, did his best for his hero in the search for the Holy Grail, and then creatively rehabilitated him in a tale of his own composition ("The Tale of Sir Urry") in which

---

[113] Evans, *Unconquered Knight*, 79–80, 180–185.

divine forgiveness infuses Lancelot, even as he remains stained by his chivalric no less than his religious default. Lancelot perhaps represented a figure Sir Thomas could aspire to emulate, perhaps someone his readers could admire. In Malory's *Morte Darthur*, Lancelot, finally fully reformed and transformed into a pious hermit, is carried off to heaven by angels, as he had been in the French romance two centuries before Malory borrowed and adapted it. Sometimes the weights in the balance pans of chivalric virtues simply required shifting, in literature as in life. Like Charny, Lancelot had well stocked his chivalric treasury of merit by great deeds, fully admired. Malory had no final doubts that general adherence to the "moste kynge and noblyst knyght of the worlde" would sustain what was most needed: "the felyshyp of noble knyghtes."[114]

That working codes of chivalry as practiced in the world (and as revealed and shaped in imaginative literature) showed malleability is significant. All the satellite values – and even at times their relationship to core values – would periodically come under debate or circumstantial pressure. Far from monolithic, chivalry incorporated a volatile dimension. Historians are constitutionally inclined to anticipate and accept changes over time: undoubtedly chivalry as a whole evolved between the eleventh and the sixteenth century; the medieval world was far from static, and changing context would likely affect chivalric ideals. Chronological change will be especially apparent in the evidence offered in the chapters of Part II. Yet obvious variations also existed within Europe at any particular time; we cannot imagine that in any generation or century all chivalric ideals and their relative weights were set and uniformly accepted everywhere, or that in some later age all had changed, again uniformly. Variation was situational as well as chronological or regional. Yet, as argued before, against multiple forces for change we must set remarkable elements of stability, as will appear repeatedly in the pages that follow. An analytical balancing act is required, walking the thin high wire stretched between these elements of change and continuity.

In fact, the practitioners and advocates of chivalry were constantly engaged in a tightrope act of their own. Highly desired balance among qualities or restraint among impulses required what they termed *mesure* in Old French and Middle English, *mezura*

---

in Occitan, and *Mâze* in Middle High German; the preferred term in Castilian was *tenperença*. This balancing gyroscope is praised in more than one *chanson de geste* or troubadour lyric; the folly of disregarding it – and losing balance or direction – is writ large in more than one romance. We return full circle to the ideal goal, praised by chivalric authors in their day (and usefully studied by David Crouch in our day): to be a *prudhomme*, a worthy man. In his *Book of Chivalry*, Charny builds this ideal knight on the foundation of admired prowess, adding other needed qualities. If becoming a *prudhomme* implies more than vigorous prowess, a knight does not become a worthy man in opposition to prowess or by steadily diminishing its role in his life. He is always considered worthy in his fine, physical practice of prowess, as in the additional qualities he displays. Charny insists (as does much chivalric literature in general) that prowess must be guided toward certain goals; it must not be merely disorderly or selfish, enacted for individual glory at the expense of fellow men-at-arms. Charny wanted the Order of the Star to debate the question whether prowess or wisdom was more desirable. Without much difficulty, one can sense from the *Book of Chivalry* and from Charny's own life how he would have approached the question when his turn to speak came: the man of supreme worth in fact combines the best exercise of prowess with the finest wisdom.[115]

This discussion is continued in *Barbour's Bruce*, written less than a generation later. After breathless praise for Bruce's defense of the strategic ford, discussed earlier, Barbour agonizes over the possibility that the king's feat might have been considered brash or even showy. Honor, which he terms worship, is a wonderful goal, Barbour repeats: it is hard-won, and leads to love for the hero; but the great man must be guided by "wyt" in his exercise of his astonishing prowess. He must steer between extremes: foolhardiness is wrong;[116] so is its opposite, cowardice[117]. Robert Bruce found the mean through his "wyt" or "mesure"; he knew the ford was so narrow that only two enemies could attack at once, and he also knew that he could beat such pairs as they attacked. The point

---

[115] Craig Taylor devotes a chapter of his *Chivalry and the Ideals of Knighthood in France during the Hundred Years War* (Cambridge University Press, 2013) to prudence and wisdom; see pages 231–275 in Taylor's book.
[116] Barbour's term is *Fule-hardymen*: See *Barbour's Bruce*, bk. 6, 339.
[117] Barbour's term is *cowartys*: ibid., bk. 6, 340.

is emphasized when, fairly or not, Barbour finds the king's brother Edward Bruce lacking in such mesure:[118]

> Had he had mesure in his deid
> I trowe yat worthyar yen he
> Mycht nocht in his tym fundyn be
> Owtakyn his broder anerly,
> To quham in-to chewalry
> Lyk wes nane in his day.
> For he [i.e., Robert] led him with mesur ay,
> And with wyt his chewalry
> He gouerneyt sa worthily
> Yat he oft full wnlikly thing
> Broucht rycht weill to gud ending.[119]

Perhaps an only slightly different sense of balance appears in a story recounted a century and a half earlier in the Marshal's *Histoire*, if not in many modern histories. William's valuable warhorse was stolen from the grasp of his young page while the hero attended a pre-tournament party. The luckless thief was caught, despite the darkness of night and the narrowness of the meandering streets of the town, because that horse whinnied enough to guide William and his friends to the hiding spot where the man must have been trying with increasing desperation to quiet the great beast. Using the baton he was carrying, William struck the man's head with sufficient force to propel an eye out of its socket. When his friends enthusiastically suggested they proceed to hang the thief, William demurred. The punishment has been enough. Is this not *mesure* finding the mean between warrior vengeance and pious mercy? Might not this virtuous balance be one of the salient points in telling the story in this idealizing biography? For his part, even Malory, speaking through the voice of his Tristram, granted that "manhode is nat worthe but yf hit be meddled [suffused] with wysdome."[120] The great gift of prowess must ideally be used well.

---

[118] If, as the modern editor of the *Bruce* argues, it is simply too facile for Barbour to attribute proper wisdom and restraint ("wyt" and "mesure") to some characters and merely reckless courage to others (McDiarmid, Scottish Text Society 15, 42), we can take notice that such a tension in chivalry is openly discussed in this source. Our goal, happily, is to analyze chivalric *mentalité* rather than to ascribe particular qualities to one historical actor or another, the reasonable objective of a different study.

[119] *Barbour's Bruce*, bk. 9, 666–676.   [120] Vinaver, *Malory: Works*, 428.

As the revered body of practices and ideas that animated the lay elite for centuries, chivalry and its practitioners were bound to show more complexity than modern popular images suggest. That complexity does not make of them either fakes or cads, but adherents of a chivalry that could retain its core values only by being flexible and finding balance. Our quest to understand knighthood will be successful only if we can set chivalry firmly in its original context, rather than romantic haze or modern contempt. Of course the challenge is intensified by surviving investments in romantic conceptions of chivalry; these investments may even be nourished by a tendency to consider the elite in the Middle Ages – as perhaps in any age – to be owed steady deference as naturally dominant and correct in views and behavior. Analyzing chivalry in its medieval setting, the present study insists that chivalry be taken seriously, for it shaped values about justifiable status, licit violence, hypermasculinity, gender relations, and lay piety that lasted for centuries and still sometimes surface in the modern world. Yet it contests gauzy idealization or any notion that the lay elite should command reverence and the turning of a blind eye on their behavior and its societal effects. We cannot improve the present or increase hope for the future by falsifying the past. Understanding the force of chivalry in a formative period of European history is well worth the effort, even if – perhaps especially if – we realize that chivalry was not the broadly protective and altruistic force of romantic dreams.

---------- Part II ----------

THREE BROAD CHRONOLOGICAL PHASES

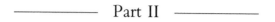

Insight into chivalric continuity and change can be found in what might seem a minor incident described in one of our finest sources, the *History of William Marshal*.[1] As the great rebellion broke out against Henry II in 1173, his eldest son, Henry the Young King, turned against his father and prepared to fight for a degree of autonomy he had never been granted, Henry being a prudent father. The Young King's entourage reminded him that he had never been knighted and argued that taking this formal step in the crisis "would make the whole of your company more valorous and more respected, and would increase the joy in their hearts." According to Marshal's biographer, the Young King accepted their advice and declared he would be knighted by "the best knight who ever was or will be, or has done more or who is to do more..." This was, of course, William Marshal, his biographer tells us. Stepping up to the Marshal with sword in hand, the Young King says, "From God and from yourself, My lord, I wish to receive this honour." William girded him with the sword and "asked that God keep him most valorous, honoured and exalted..." The entourage viewing this short and simple ceremony is studded with counts and barons (you may be sure!), but the poet proudly says of the Marshal, "And yet he had not one strip of land to his name or anything else, just his chivalry."

Strong ideas about chivalric function, status, and ideology animate this narrative of an affecting ceremony. The function of the warrior

---

[1] The quotations that follow all appear in *History of William Marshal*, lines 2071–2096.

stands out clearly. The Marshal is chosen to knight the Young King because he is the best, and this evaluation comes from a celebrated patron of valorous deeds in tournament on the eve of a civil war in which even more intense fighting could be expected and enacted for higher stakes. In short, the Young King was considered a good judge of the knightly function of prowess; the poet/biographer assures his audience that the Young King, through his generosity to masterful warriors, even those who were landless, will revive chivalry. And chivalry commands enough esteem to be considered ever in steep decline by its practitioners, with – one imagines – downcast eyes and shaking of heads. So honorable and so vital a compound of ideals and behaviors must always be preserved in ideal form and so would always fall just short of the impossibly high standard set for it. William Marshal stands before them as the poster boy of martial excellence, a point the poet emphasizes by proudly insisting it is his prowess rather than extensive landed wealth that qualifies the Marshal to knight a king.

The social status associated with chivalry by this time could not be more evident. Powerful men of the later twelfth century proudly wear chivalry's mantle in company with valiant but land-less newcomers such as William Marshal, as they were unlikely to have done several generations earlier. Even a great king's crowned son accepts collective advice that he should formally be knighted, that this honored status in a lord gives his men joy and encourages their own martial vigor. And it is an entourage of counts and barons that presents such a high view of chivalric status.

A recognizable ideology of chivalry suffuses the scene. This is a group of courtly men, practitioners of the sport of tournament and as fashionable as any set of men in their world, as could be observed in their style and warrior fellow feeling, even in their pious confidence, which appears in the easy certainty of divine approval and blessing. Both the Young King and the Marshal speak reflexively of God as author and guardian of chivalry. Ultimately, this honored status descends on a knight from God, though it is bestowed on earth by the broad hand of a truly strenuous knight, and, in the Young King's dubbing, the man claimed to be the greatest contem-porary knight. However simple the ceremony, it embodies a set of ideas that inform and enact a lay parallel to a sacred rite of initiation into a recognized status. Potent ideological elements are here embedded in a quasi-sacrament of formal entrance into – or more likely formal recognition of standing within – the order of chivalry.[2]

These key Issues of function, status, and ideology can help us navigate the centuries-long history of chivalry, which – never static – was always engaged in the complex process of fitting itself into its environment (military, social, cultural, religious, and political). Investigating changing function, status, and ideology will allow us to find within the flow of centuries several broad eras with patterns that enable analysis. Marshal's biography catches a period recognized by more than one historian as a crucial time of change in chivalric history.[3] It was written in 1224 and retrospectively presented a chivalric life vigorously lived in the cross-Channel world from the later twelfth century. It captures an era when, as emphasized by Georges Duby, Jean Flori, Maurice Keen, David Crouch, and Dominique Barthélemy, chivalry has definitely taken mature form; secure anchors steadied it within turbulent seas of change. Its military function is undoubted and draws strength from a long procession of fighting men, both historically real and imaginatively created. Its practitioners' status has risen with dizzying speed. Its sustaining ideology is forming both courtly polish and a sacred glow through socially defining practices of speech and behavior, sport, and formal attitudes about love, and by acquiring spiritual blessings for the hard labor of fighting that is always assumed to further just causes.

This dramatic era of classic chivalry, caught in the spotlight of a single incident from 1173, occupies a middle ground in the long chronology of chivalry. From this elevated vantage point we can conveniently look both backward and forward in time. Looking backward, we can see that this classic phase emerged from an earlier phase characterized by Jean Flori as the prehistory of chivalry, the time when the "ideology of the sword" had yet to mature into classic chivalry of higher status and more developed ideology. This same early phase Matthew Strickland and John Gillingham consider the authentic era of the birth of chivalry.[4] Looking forward in time from our twelfth-century vantage point, we

---

[2] Max Lieberman, "A New Approach to the Knighting Ritual." I am grateful to Dr. Lieberman for a copy of this study in advance of publication.

[3] Jean Flori, *L'idéologie du glaive: préhistoire de la chevalerie* (Geneva: Droz, 1983); Flori, *L'essor de la chevalerie: 11ème et 12ème siècles* (Geneva: Droz, 1986); and David Crouch, *The English Aristocracy, 1070–1272: A Social Transformation* (New Haven: Yale University Press, 2010).

[4] Discussed, with citations, in Chapter 3.

can see that as the medieval world changed, chivalry entered a third phase. If we are willing to extend our vision beyond the lifetime of the Marshal and his companions into the later Middle Ages, roughly the fourteenth and fifteenth centuries, we can again find both continuities and significant new dimensions as social and cultural change animated these centuries associated especially with the Hundred Years War, and with socio-demographic and economic crisis.

In quite broad terms we will thus analyze a first phase in roughly the period before the mid-eleventh century, a second extending through the thirteenth century, and a third during the fourteenth and fifteenth centuries. Recognizing these phases requires use of the telescope, not the microscope, and yields an important sense of broad processes of change, rather than strict chronological delimitations. With the widest focal setting of the lens, we may say that in the initial phase militant function dominated over status and ideology (for status remained uncertain at best, and the ideology we associate with chivalry was yet to emerge). Heavy emphasis on the military function never excluded other functions (such as the judicial work of a court-holder or the economic function of a landlord), but the warrior function was crucial, it was emphasized, and it persisted through later phases. In a second-phase function, status and ideology stoutly intertwined, creating the classic age of chivalry evident in the biography of William Marshal. Chivalry as many historians in the modern world tend to think of it is on display. The third phase brings seemingly contradictory developments: both contraction and expansion of knighthood and chivalry seem to occur, for aristocrats (attempting to safeguard status) sought to restrict entry into knighthood, but lesser (if still relatively elite) fighters, lawyer-administrators, and merchant-bankers laid claim to chivalric status and claimed the valorizing ideology of chivalry for themselves as they enacted its traditionally strenuous work or provided essential administrative support, or cash, to the elite families they served.

If generalization at this level entails risks (that many will be swift to point out), it also offers benefits, especially for the initial and final periods, which have sparked much discussion. Precise dating for chivalric origins (a particularly troublesome issue) need not derail analysis once we sense the considerable evolutionary arc under observation and the many components needed for the construction of medieval chivalry; we need not repeat for chivalric history the sorts of quarrels over exact dating that (to take one example) long ensnarled study of the emergence of parliament in England. For our third period, we can likewise comprehend aristocratic closing of ranks (reducing the numbers of dubbed knights) occurring simultaneously with a stretching of the coveted chivalric mantle and look to the uncompromising need for even more men to fulfill elite military functions and the needs of growing governing structures in an era of expanded warfare. The triumph of the early European state, sanctioned by religious blessings, gradually transformed chivalry. Watching this lengthy process, which extended through the later Middle Ages and into the early sixteenth century, we might adapt the famous phrase of Mark Twain and note that reports of the death of chivalry have been greatly exaggerated.

Each broad phase informs one of the three chapters that follow. Each chapter will investigate the many components of chivalric function, status, and ideology within chronological borders kept quite flexible. Obviously, behind all broad analysis stands the immense particularity of the evidence. The determined positivist will see only particularity in all this evidence and insist that each decade in every era of "the age of chivalry" was unique, making generalization impossible. The contrary approach of these chapters argues that chivalry emerged gradually and like a flexible steel cable that intertwined individual strands into a seemingly unbreakable whole. New elements wound around undoubtedly older strands. Some core elements persisted, even if others frayed or snapped; yet a recognizable cable endured for centuries.

3

PHASE ONE: KNIGHTHOOD BECOMING CHIVALRY

———————— • ————————

A thick European mist obscures the origins of chivalry, making close investigation difficult and hope of certainty doubtful. An analysis seeking general patterns may even prove perilous, for the landscape beneath the mist is crisscrossed by deep furrows of scholarly controversy, and contested ground, still heavily mined, is periodically swept by erudite gunfire.[1] If this chapter attempts some generalizations, it

---

[1] Jean-Pierre Poly and Eric Bournazel, *The Feudal Transformation, 900–1200*, trans. Caroline Higgitt (New York: Holmes & Meier, 1983). Dominique Barthélemy, *The Serf, the Knight, and the Historian* (Ithaca: Cornell University Press, 2009). For the prolonged debate between Poly and Bournazel and Barthélemy, see Poly and Bournazel, "Que faut-il preferer au 'mutationnisme'? Ou le probleme du changement social," *Revue historique de droit francais et etranger* 72 (1994), 401–412; Dominique Barthélemy, "Encore le debat sur l'an mil!," *Revue historique de droit francais et etranger* 73 (1995). For the debate within *Past & Present*, see T. N. Bisson, "The 'Feudal Revolution,'" *Past & Present* 142 (1994), 6–42; Dominique Barthélemy and Stephen D. White, "The 'Feudal Revolution,'" *Past & Present* 152 (1996), 196–223; Timothy Reuter and Chris Wickham, "The 'Feudal Revolution,'" *Past & Present*, 155 (1997), 177–208; Bisson, "The 'Feudal Revolution': Reply," *Past & Present* 155 (1997), 208–225. Bisson, *The Crisis of the Twelfth Century: Power, Lordship, and the Origins of European Government* (Princeton: Princeton University Press, 2009); Philippe Contamine, *War in the Middle Ages*, trans. Michael Jones (Oxford: Blackwell, 1984), 3–65; Jones, *La Noblesse au royaume de France* (Paris: Presses Universitaires de France, 1997), 17–21; Jean Flori, *Chevaliers et chevalerie au moyen âge* (Paris: Hachette, 1998); *L'idéologie du glaive: Préhistoire de la chevalerie* (Geneva: Droz, 1983); *L'essor de la chevalerie, 11ème et 12ème siècles* (Geneva: Droz, 1986); Charles West, *Reframing the Feudal Revolution: Political and Social Transformation between Marne and Moselle, c.800–c.1100* (New York: Cambridge University Press, 2013).

recognizes that many questions await further investigation or at least scholarly willingness to observe truce.

Reasons for this degree of contention are not far to seek. The seedbed of chivalry must be sought in the Carolingian and immediately post-Carolingian era, a time abounding with unresolved interpretive issues. If scholars could agree on social, political, and cultural continuity from the ninth century through the eleventh century, or agree, instead, on the rise of transformative forces as the Carolingian regnum collapsed, historians of the origins of chivalry might plan extended holidays. Lacking such agreement, they find problems stubbornly clustering around such basic issues as the efficacy of centralized rule by Charlemagne and his successors. Did royal/ imperial authority constitute a public governmental capacity with armies built on universal male service? Did this authority for a time effectively and closely rule this vast Carolingian land mass, only to see it fracture into privatized local rule by military strongmen, or does such a view perpetuate what R. I. Moore termed "the fantasy of a revived Roman empire with which clerical courtiers flattered their masters and themselves"?[2] One or another approach to such issues could determine whether early knighthood arose during Carolingian rule, even at the Carolingian court, or only emerged from the rubble as this world fractured, leading to a rise of the knights.

To ask when and how chivalry emerged is thus to pose no simple question that can be settled with a precise birth date. Finding formative chivalric ideals and assessing their importance become crucial issues. So does discerning the early appearance of men who will be instantly recognizable as knights in both popular and scholarly views. Did these warriors constitute an emerging aristocracy with a distinctive style of living? Were they already features of a Carolingian world or rather a new group emerging from the mist? Did military function define them and slowly bind together fighting men at a variety of social levels? Or were they being more formally defined through juridical status? Even to hope for answers would mean following separate, twisting analytical tracks and finding their crucially important intersections. Historians have found it so difficult to proclaim a convergence of these tracks leading toward chivalry, let alone a precise occasion of birth, that they may be willing to recognize an evolutionary process.

---

[2] *Times Literary Supplement*, October 18, 2013.

This chapter at least briefly examines that process through a focus on early evidence of elements that are in process of becoming chivalric function, status, and ideology. It sweeps chronologically toward about the mid-eleventh century (sometimes necessarily reaching a bit beyond), without making a fetish of dating. Of course these analytical elements of function, status, and ideology will often overlap and blend in this discussion.

CHIVALRIC FUNCTION — MILITARY TECHNIQUE AND
TECHNOLOGY

If military function is crucial to the earliest chivalry, its purely technical aspects might seem the most direct path through the mist-shrouded interpretive landscape. In fact, for a time some historians thought this approach would prove the key to understanding early chivalry. Obscuring doubts might be swept aside, it seemed, by emphasis on changes in military technique and technology. Such prime movers possessed seductive charms; an analysis of chivalric origins focused on technology obviously appealed to modern investigators and students in whose lives technological change has played a crucial role. And the case would likewise be appealingly clear-cut. Even if a baseline warrior code throughout the centuries were posited, it would necessarily accommodate changes over time in weaponry and tactics. To the extent that medieval armed force revolved around armored horsemen – a topic that can bring military historians themselves close to personal combat – and to the extent that such horsemen constituted the chivalrous, all would go smoothly for scholars keen on seeing knighthood as a subset of the endless procession of warriors through time. Discussion could turn on discrete and answerable questions – about the dominance of cavalry in combat, the breeding of great warhorses, the utilization of platform stirrups by the riders atop these horses, reliance on striking with stout lances, and progressive advances in protective armor. With problems solved, chivalric origins would be explained and even dated.

The humble stirrup claimed a central role in these discussions. To any rational person it may seem that vigorous combat conducted atop a tall and swiftly moving horse without benefit of the firm balance provided by stirrups would be an act of madness. Of course the history of warfare provides many examples to the contrary, especially involving warriors employing bows at a distance from the enemy. But vigorous physical fighting at close quarters between mounted medieval warriors, tellingly termed "mounted shock combat," was enabled by the adoption of stirrups and a high-backed saddle; these gave the warrior enough stability to swing a sword and seated him firmly enough on his powerful warhorse to strike an opponent with a sturdy lance grasped in his hand and firmly clasped between arm and body. The blow struck by that lance had the full impact of both the charging horse and its rider. The formula taught in classes on elementary physics – force equals mass times acceleration – applied even in the Early Middle Ages.

Yet even with this focus on precise technical issues interpretive problems quickly surfaced. What the introduction of stirrups did for warriors generated more scholarly agreement than the equally important question of when these benefits became widespread and effective. Scholarly controversy over sociocultural effects from technological changes in modes of fighting has first raged and then simmered since the mid-twentieth century when Lynn White Jr. extended the older theories of Heinrich Brunner about a supposed dramatic shift to cavalry in Carolingian warfare. Though the consequences of changing military technology were first debated in terms of the emergence of feudalism, their implications for its cousin chivalry are important. White dated the introduction of the stirrup into Europe to the era of Charles Martel in the eighth century and posited profound cultural as well as martial effects: Charles Martel (718–741) seized church property to finance the more expensive mounted fighters required to stop Muslim invaders moving northward into Frankish land. This military innovation could easily be taken to mark the effective beginnings of a crucially important force of armored and mounted warriors.[3]

Critics of White's imaginative and provocative theory, Bernard S. Bachrach to the fore, have altered the picture considerably.[4] What

---

[3] Lynn White Jr., *Medieval Technology and Social Change* (Oxford, 1962).

[4] Bernard Bachrach, "Charles Martel, Mounted Shock Combat, the Stirrup and Feudalism," *Studies in Medieval and Renaissance History* 7 (1970), 49–75. Cf. Philippe Contamine, *War in the Middle Ages*, trans. Michael Jones (New York, 1990), 179–184, and Kelly DeVries, *Medieval Military Technology* (Lewiston, 1992), 95–122. Review articles summarizing the debate and providing abundant citations include John Sloan, "The Stirrup Controversy," medieval@ukanym.cc.ukans.edu (October 1994); Alex Roland, "Once More into the Stirrups: Lynn White Jr., *Medieval Technology and Social Change*," *Technology and Culture* 44 (2003), 574–585;

Figure 2 The Bayeux Tapestry (1070s) shows Norman warriors at Hastings (1066) using lances with overhead strokes as well as couched under arm to strike with the combined force of man and mount.

seems most important for our inquiry is the case that has been made for a remarkably slow adoption of the stirrup. Far from any lightning stroke transforming the mode of combat, general realization of martial benefits within medieval society seems to have required several centuries. General, transformative Carolingian adoption seems unlikely,[5] and notably, as seen in Figure 2, Norman fighters pictured at the battle of Hastings in the famous Bayeaux Tapestry (c. 1070) often jab with their lances held overhead or even throw them at the enemy; only some of the horsemen couch their lances to charge in the manner that technological change would permit.[6] Evidence of this sort suggests a remarkably gradual adoption of new techniques that remained incomplete into the second half of the eleventh century. Such

and Bert Hall, "Lynn White's *Medieval Technology and Social Change* after Thirty Years," in *Technological Change; Methods and Themes in the History of Technology*, ed. Robert Fox (Amsterdam: 1996), 85–101.

[5] Philippe Contamine, *War in the Middle Ages*, 179–181; J. F. Verbruggen, "The Role of the Cavalry in Medieval Warfare," trans. Kelly DeVries in *Journal of Medieval Military History* vol. III, ed. Clifford J. Rogers, Kelly DeVries (Rochester: Boydell & Brewer, 2005), 46–71; White's thesis has been challenged successfully in a series of articles by D. J. A. Ross, "Pleine sa hanste," *Medium Aevum* 20 (1951), 1–10; P. H. Sawyer, "Technical Determinism: The Stirrup and the Plough," *Past & Present* 24 (1963), 90–100; D. A. Bullough, "Europae Pater: Charlemagne and His Achievement in the Light of Recent Scholarship," *English Historical Review* 85, no. 334 (1970), 59–105; Bernard S. Bachrach, "Charles Martel, Mounted Shock Combat, the Stirrup, and Feudalism," *Studies in Medieval and Renaissance History* 7 (1970), 49–75.

[6] E.g., Lucien Musset, *The Bayeaux Tapestry*, trans. Richard Rex (Rochester: Boydell & Brewer, 2005), scene 51, 236–237.

a chronology intersects with significant evidence of the undoubted appearance of tournament, which David Crouch assigns to early decades of the twelfth century.[7] A war game featuring mounted shock combat with lances, followed by vigorous hacking with swords, would require a stable seat for fighters atop charging warhorses. As individual jousting became the sporting norm, the case is even clearer.[8]

These changes in military technique and technology seem indisputably important. Our conception of chivalry would change dramatically if deprived of this classic image of the knights in action, securely seated in deep saddles, with feet firmly planted on effective stirrups, thick lances tucked under the arm, and elongated shields raised for the shock of combat. Joust, tournament, and war featuring cavalry charges, characteristic knightly pursuits, would vanish or at least show modification almost out of recognition without these specific innovations in martial combat. The chronology of these changes, however, points us more clearly toward the second half of the eleventh century – and thus toward our second chivalric phase (to be considered in Chapter 4) – rather than to the age of Charlemagne and his heirs. To the extent that they can be causative, these matters of military technique might help to explain not the origins of chivalry, but the transition into its second phase. Our present concern with the initial phase requires a different set of questions. The following section of this chapter examines the social implications of an elite military profession. That is, we turn away from technique and technology to the emerging tie between early chivalric function and status.

FUNCTION AND STATUS: GREAT LORDS

Concentrating first on the upper levels of society puts us on relatively solid ground, for military service was one of the functions exercised by the powerful lay elite. In fact, historians can agree that these lords added this function to others that had long elevated status.[9] As Karl Leyser wrote of them in the ninth and tenth centuries, "There were

---

[7] Dominique Barthélemy, "Les chroniques de la mutation chevaleresques"; David Crouch, *Tournament* (New York: Bloomsbury Academic Group, 2006), 6–8.

[8] Discussed in Chapter 8.

[9] As Maurice Keen concisely noted, "To judge men and to fight were the original functions of nobility." *Chivalry*, 152.

no civilians in this lay nobility." He drove home the point by adding that the aristocracy constituted a "military caste," in which a nonmilitary nobleman would seem a "monster."[10] This military role obviously reached to the very peak of the hierarchy of lords. Dominique Barthélemy observes that when Charles the Bald was given a sword along with the crown by his father in 888, it marked "a triple accession to the kingship, to manhood, and to the status of warriors."[11]

The exact composition, nature, and recruitment of military force in the ninth and tenth centuries remain troublingly murky. Carolingian rulers had tried to field sufficient armies through a broad system of obligations. Charlemagne (imitated by his heirs) had expected military service from all freemen of a certain landed status (with lesser free-holders expected to join together to provide a serving soldier). The effectiveness and breadth of such recruitment, however, remain uncertain, and later civil conflicts in the splintering Frankish realm were fought by what Guy Halsall tellingly terms "aristocrats and their loosely defined followings of vassals and other clients."[12] Any historian of chivalry would give much to be able to arrange a conversation between such a group and William Marshal, watching and listening closely to see how much understanding was evident. How fully would the Carolingian aristocrat identify himself as a warrior? Would his status depend to a significant degree on his warrior qualities? Would his vassals and clients think that they elevated their status by their military service, bringing themselves one step closer to their lord? Regretfully, we cannot hear the voices speaking to such questions.[13]

Scholars debate whether periods of intense warfare generate closer bonds between lords and followers who serve together on campaigns. If the link is valid, it may be significant that large military forces were

---

[10] "Early Canon Law and the Beginnings of Knighthood," repr. in *Communications and Power in Medieval Europe: The Carolingian and Ottonian Centuries*, ed. Timothy Reuter (London: Hambledon Press, 1994), 67.

[11] Barthélemy, *The Serf, the Knight, and the Historian*, 161.

[12] Halsall, *Warfare and Society in the Barbarian West*, 69–110, quotation at 96. He thinks that by 900 "in most of western Europe landowning had become the basis of military service." Ibid., 109.

[13] David Bachrach comments that "much ink has been spilled to justify the claim that milites of the Ottonian period were early members of a juridical-social caste that would ultimately evolve into the dominant warrior nobility of medieval Europe." *Warfare in Tenth-Century Germany* (Woodbridge, Suffolk: Boydell, 2013), 85–86.

required for constant campaigning throughout much of Europe in the age of chivalric origins. In broad terms, the warfare that had expanded Frankish Christianity was followed by efforts to secure local defense against swift Viking and Saracen incursions and by internal warfare breaking up the Frankish regnum.[14] The investigation need not be limited to the Carolingian Empire but can usefully draw as well on distinctly post-Carolingian chronology and from regions never under Carolingian rule. Anglo-Saxon England, as James Campbell has argued, probably represented the best-functioning and best-documented exemplar of a Carolingian style of governance.[15] Extra-Carolingian areas, too, knew almost constant warfare. The Anglo-Saxons struggled with Scandinavian invaders who triumphed first as conquerors and then for a time even as rulers before their Norman descendants arrived decisively in 1066. In the Iberian Peninsula, Kings of León and Castile had long gathered force against Muslim kingdoms, drawing on various types and social ranks of *caballeros*, some of whom were recruited by municipal obligation to service, others as vassals of *señores*.[16] And by this time the Norman diaspora was sending its armed and ambitious sons across Europe and into the Mediterranean no less than into Anglo-Saxon England. By the close of that century the first crusading expedition had reached and taken Jerusalem. In all these regions many men were required to fight by broad public obligations, but private arrangements and the sheer draw of opportunity for social and economic advancement also fueled military service. Anglo-Saxon rulers and great lords stood in a battle line with their select retainers by their sides. Such men are celebrated in surviving epics both on the battlefield, where their loyalty is unshakable, and in lofty halls where their drinking horns are never empty and golden bracelets come to them from the soft hands of a lord's wife.

That extended and intense warfare encouraged bonds between great lords and those who stood by them in the ranks has been doubted. This contrary view holds that the great were remarkably slow to show such warrior fellow feeling and to identify with lesser

---

[14] Note that this paragraph draws generally on Guy Halsall, as cited in a previous note.

[15] James Campbell, *Essays in Anglo-Saxon History* (New York: Bloomsbury Publishing, 1995), 161–170.

[16] James F. Powell, *A Society Organized for War* (Berkeley: University of California Press, 1988), 14–17.

men as brothers under a warrior mantle. Jean Flori has emphasized that they actually emphasized superiority and social distance by the designations they adopted, calling themselves *dominus* (lord) or some term indicating a great fighter, such as *pugnator* or *bellator*.[17] They were, in short, significantly unlikely for a long time to term themselves *milites* (singular *miles*). This terminology is revealing, for *miles* was the term that came to designate the knight.

We are thus left with evidence that shows the warrior quality of the elite in our first chivalric phase, and what seems to be a select layer of particularly adept and reliable fighters below them, differentiated from a mass levy of adult males. But this evidence is thin and spotty, and it leaves us in uncertainty over the exact status of fighters below the level of the nobility and likewise unsure of the relationship between the great and these lesser fighters. Function is clear, but status is not. We must turn to the *milites*, recognizing that surviving evidence on the warriors is even less copious than that for the lords.

FUNCTION AND STATUS: MILITES

The noun *miles* had long existed. Its original and general meaning in the Carolingian world suggested a servitor holding some office. As a specialized group, monks thought of themselves as *milites Christi*, the servitors of Christ.[18] Yet the term came to be claimed especially by fighting men essential in an age of much warfare. These men formed at least a key important element in armed forces and would form the largest part of the knighthood; their numbers could not have been supplied by great lords and their progeny only. Unsurprisingly, these men, so hard to see clearly in the shadowed evidence from their world, have occupied the central place in scholarly debate.[19] Their origins, their degree of social diversity, the chronology of their appearance and rising status in society, no less

---

[17] Jean Flori, "Knightly Society," *New Cambridge Medieval History*, ed. Daniel Luscombe, Jonathan Riley-Smith; IV, Part 1 (Cambridge, 2004), 148–184; cf. his *Idéologie du glaive*, passim.

[18] Andre Vauchez provides a historical survey of the changes in use of this term in "La notion de Miles Christi dans la spiritualité occidentale aux xiie et xiiie siècles," in *Chevalerie et christianisme aux xiie et xiiie siècles*, ed. Martin Aurell (Rennes, 2011), 67–77.

[19] See, e.g., Bernard Bachrach, "The Milites and the Millennium."

than their relationship with the great lords they served, have in particular resisted analytical consensus.

Above all, throughout our first chivalric phase we must recognize the uncertain social status of the men coming to be called *milites*. This status could vary with particular conditions occurring regionally as well as chronologically, but often many of these men appear to be struggling to distance themselves from unfree status. They take pains, that is, to assert that they bear nothing of the stain that marked dependent agriculturalists; they stand resolutely apart from and above those lesser beings who tilled the soil with their own hands and suffered concomitant social, legal, and economic consequences.[20]

Uncertainties of status may appear most clearly – especially over the course of the eleventh century – in the extensive German Empire. There a significant and illuminating contrast emerged between juridical and social status. In law the group coming to be known as *ministeriales* (service-men) remained legally unfree, even though in many instances their power and prestige in society as functioning knights and able administrators rose significantly.[21] Formally, they

---

[20] Constance Bouchard, *Those of My Blood: Creating Noble Families in Medieval Francia* (Philadelphia: University of Pennsylvania Press, 2001), 14–15. Bouchard argues for a relative degree of social mobility in which lesser families, often recipients of delegated power, managed to climb their way upward through service, alliance, and marriage; Regine La Jan, "Continuity and Change in Tenth-Century Nobility," in *Nobles and Nobility in Medieval Europe: Concepts, Origins, Transformations*, ed. Anne Duggan (Rochester: Boydell & Brewer, 2000), 53–69.

[21] Classic studies include Karl Bosl, *Die Reichsministerialität der Salier und Staufer: ein Beitrag zur Geschichte des hochmittelalterlichen deutschen Volkes, Staates und Reiches*, 2 vols. (Stuttgart: Hiersemann, 1950); Joachim Bumke, *The Concept of Knighthood in the Middle Ages*, trans. W. T. H. Jackson (New York: AMS Press, 1982), 46–71; and Jan Keupp, *Dienst und Verdienst: Die Ministerialen Friedrich Barbarossas und Heinrichs VI*. Mono graphien zur Geschichte des Mittelalters 48 (Stuttgart: Hiersemann, 2002); John B. Freed, *Noble Bondsmen: Ministerial Marriages in the Archdiocese of Salzburg, 1100–1343* (Ithaca: Cornell University Press, 1995); Benjamin Arnold, *German Knighthood 1050–1300* (Oxford: Clarendon Press, 1985). Arnold states that "it is clear that the type of German knight regularly called *ministerialis* in the Latin sources was being enfeoffed on a large scale in the eleventh century. No doubt the War of Investitures and its ramifications demanded an accelerated rate of enforcement, and the sources reveal larger war-retinues produced in those troubled times." *German Knighthood 1050–1300* (Oxford University Press, 1985), 17. He concludes (22) that "Committed to military valour and living in fortified houses and castles, the *ministeriales* were themselves a noble landowning class with interests to defend, and were, for the purpose, imbued with the German political mentality of conflict. They took it for granted, like their masters, and it made them dangerous. Not only were

were serfs (who were legally disadvantaged) as well as knights; but their service won them enviable estates, and many soon built impress-ive stone castles. They filled significant positions at the court of the king and of great lords lay and ecclesiastical. A well-known document called "The Rights of the Ministerials of Bamberg" from 1061/1062 shows something of the status achieved and duties owed by the service-men in the service of the bishop of Bamberg:

The son of a ministerial is entitled to his father's fief. If there is no son, the closest arms-bearing relative shall turn over the dead kin's armor and a horse – the best that he had owned – to his lord; the fief of the deceased, however, he may keep for himself. If a ministerial participates in a campaign, he shall join his lord's host at his own expense. After that, he shall be maintained by the lord.[22]

Despite their subordinate legal status, these ministerials held heritable fiefs and gave mounted military service in armor. Clearly, they exercised the function of knighthood and must have enjoyed some-thing of its social status, though they lacked its formal rank in the eyes of the law.

Within the broad area influenced by German custom, the king and the great lords viewed the nonfree condition of the *ministeriales* as an attraction, making them – in theory – more malleable and subject to control; their service could be a counterbalance to any aristocratic inclination to much greater independence.[23] Of course, tensions could be generated by the disparity between juridical and social standing or by any blocking of ministerial ambition. Attempts to curtail the actions of ministerials led to the murder of Count Sighard of Burghausen in 1104.[24] Perhaps even more famously, the Erembald clan in Bruges, administrators serving Count Charles the Good of Flanders, became outraged by opponents who brought up their legally unfree status; fearful that Count Charles would use this status against them (as a response to their violent treatment of

they required to perpetuate violence in the service of their lords, but were also habituated to using force for their own purposes."

[22] Philipp Jaffé, *Bibliotheca rerum Germanicarum*, 5, 50–52, quoted and translated by Stefan Weinfurter, *The Salian Century*, trans. Barbara M. Bowlus (Philadelphia: University of Pennsylvania Press, 1999), 73.

[23] Timothy Reuter, *Germany in the Early Middle Ages* (New York: Longman, 1991), 36–37.

[24] Stefan Weinfurter, *The Salian Century* (Philadelphia: University of Pennsylvania Press, 1999), 73.

enemies), they brutally murdered their lord while he was at prayer in church on Good Friday in 1127.[25] German historians continue to debate the exact nature and functioning of the ministerials, but the continuing rise of these unfree *milites* well beyond the early period of chivalry reminds us that over much of medieval Europe early knightly juridical status could stand at odds with emerging social power and prestige.

This German pattern predominated in a part of the Low Countries, which divided between regions culturally and politically linked either with the Empire or with France. Function and status in the Low Countries thus provide an instructive societal microcosm, clearly analyzed by Johanna Maria Van Winter. Regions close to France followed the social evolution that we will see shortly in France itself. In the imperial Dutch territories, however, a number of legal statuses divided people into categories ranging from the unfree to the free and noble rank.[26] Service-men in the provinces politically and culturally linked with the empire did not escape servile juridical status in this period; yet they contributed an important component of emerging knighthood. They performed the military function sorely needed and carried out significant administrative duties as well. Many of them also acquired elevated social status, though technically unfree, and, in time (the chronology varying with the region) held considerable property and power.

Some of this uncertainty clinging to early knightly standing can be found within the kingdom of France and the broader French cultural zones as well, even though the societal movement in this entire region, in contrast to that within the Empire, finally produced legally free as well as socially elite status for the *milites*. Normandy seems to have been important in the changes taking place, and Norman evidence provides good cases in point. Norman *milites* appear in grants made to monastic houses, either as a part of the gift or to be excluded from it, in either case suggesting uncertain legal status. Sometime between 1051 and 1066, Duke William the Bastard granted to the monastery of Saint-Florent de Saumur carefully

---

[25] The story is told unforgettably in English translation as *The Murder of Charles the Good*, ed. and tr. James Bruce Ross (New York: Columbia University Press, 1960).

[26] This distinction is drawn classically in Johanna Maria Van Winter, "The Ministerial and Knightly Classes in Guelders and Zutphen," *Acta Historica Neerlandica* (Leiden: Brill, 1966), 171–187.

specified possession of lands and rights over people; the list includes "five free knights and one mill (*V libros milites, et unum molendinum*)."[27] Another grant by one of his men in 1060, confirmed by Duke William, carefully excludes the knights associated with the land given (*exceptis milites*).[28] That the second of these grants explicitly excluded some dependent *milites* is significant; that the first grant specified that the knights involved were free ("*libros milites*") is likewise important: not all men covered by this designation of *milites* enjoyed unambiguously free status. Other such cases have been helpfully examined by Max Lieberman.[29] And Marjorie Chibnall, the editor/translator of the great Norman chronicler Orderic Vitalis (d. 1142), notes her agreement with Philippe Contamine, the eminent historian of medieval warfare and nobility, that knightly function is clearer than knightly status and that even in Orderic's early twelfth-century Normandy not all knights were equal. "Qualifying adjectives crept in," Chibnall writes, so that distinctions were drawn between *gregarii milites*, *pagenses milites*, and *legitimi milites*.[30] Orderic records that the term *gregarii milites* became a taunt hurled by a haughty noble at royal household troops; but the chronicler used the term *legitimus miles* to describe a knight with distinguished lineage. Of course, lowly birth might be remedied by such prowess in battle that a lord would provide a marriage that elevated status; this proved to be the ladder of mobility climbed by Ingelmar, a Norman knight thus rewarded for military service provided to the Norman adventurer Count Roger of Sicily in the late eleventh century.[31] Function could guarantee status, if well enacted.

In the Anglo-Norman kingdom ruled by other Norman adventurers, the status of *milites* in the eleventh century appears to have been equally mixed. Rich stores of evidence were embedded in the great Domesday Book commissioned in 1086, though it has proved

[27] *Recueil des actes des ducs de Normandie de 911 a 1066*, ed. Lucien Musset (Caen, 1961), 199.
[28] Ibid. 147. [29] Max Lieberman, "A Practical Guide to Knightings," passim.
[30] Chibnall, *World of Orderic Vitalis*, 141. She notes that the evidence for knights of unfree origin outside of Germany is scarce, but cites some legal and literary sources suggesting the possibility. See Sergio Boffa, who has some interesting information on *ministeriales* in Francophone regions of the Low Countries in *Warfare in Medieval Brabant, 1356–1406*, 94, and Philippe Contamine, *War in the Middle Ages*, 161.
[31] Chibnall, *The World of Orderic Vitalis*, 142; Ingelmar married the daughter of the Count of Boiano. She complained, to no avail.

difficult to interpret. One analysis that seems compelling argues that the term *milites* (appearing frequently in the great survey) covers a wide range of men with varying military functions. At the lower end of this range, these men may have served as infantry; some at a somewhat higher status may have been light cavalry; the greatest men covered by this term were heavy cavalrymen of more social and economic status.[32] For some *milites*, fears of losing status persisted through the twelfth century.[33]

This broad and nonspecific sense of the meaning of *milites* found in the Anglo-Norman world might apply more generally in medieval society. Jean Flori points to chroniclers such as Fulcher of Chartres, who could describe an army of soldiers (*milites*) as consisting both of mounted men (*equites*) and footmen (*pedites*). In the eleventh century, these soldiers, Flori says, did not constitute "a particular social status, still less a privileged rank, or even a specific way of fighting," although the beginnings of the fusion of the terms *equites* and *milites* can be discerned.[34] In post-Conquest England, many *milites* were still living as dependents within households of powerful men and held no land, or perhaps, to use the evidence from the Domesday Book, combined a small holding with subsistence provided by their lord. As Donald Fleming argues, the social scale extended downward "without any evident break to men who were, by aristocratic standards, humble, yet still possessed estates which honorial surveys reveal were ... considerably larger than the prosperous peasant's holding."[35]

Other regions within the French cultural sphere likewise give signs of lingering uncertainty of status. In 1037, the priory of Saint-Cyr-Rennes in Brittany was given some land, the grant significantly including its *milites*, sharecroppers, and villeins. As Barthélemy notes, such gifts are couched "in servile terms."[36] In the county of Maine, the status of lordship in relation to land tenure seems to have

---

[32] Donald Fleming, "Landholding by *Milites* in Domesday Book: A Revision," *Anglo-Norman Studies* 13 (1990), ed. Marjorie Chibnall, passim.

[33] Jean Scammel, "The Formation of the English Social Structure: Freedom, Knioghts, and Gentry," *Speculum* 68 (1993), 591–618.

[34] Jean Flori, "Knightly Society," 149.

[35] Fleming, "Landholding by *Milites* in Domesday Book: A Revision," 83–94, with full citations on previous scholarship. The quotation comes from p. 87.

[36] Discussed and source cited in Barthélemy, *The Serf, the Knight, and the Historian*, 120 and note 189.

remained fluid into the mid-twelfth century.[37] Yet in a famous study of the Macconais region of Burgundy, Georges Duby found many witnesses to charters increasingly identified as *milites* during the eleventh century.[38] Clearly the term carried a significantly wide variety of meanings, implying a range of social standings, not yet established by function. Clarity will be evident only in our second chivalric phase.

EARLY CHIVALRIC IDEOLOGY?

Evidence on early chivalric function and status has produced a mixed impression of knightly practice and social standing by about the mid-eleventh century. Yet significant steps toward an identifiable chivalric group are apparent, even if they seem far from complete or decisive. Does existing evidence also suggest the early emergence of what we can recognize as chivalric ideology? Any signs of chivalric self-consciousness that might to some degree bind all *milites* together could claim genuine significance. As noted earlier, the most important and relevant case has long been advanced by the work of Matthew Strickland and John Gillingham, with recent support from Dominique Barthélemy.[39] In an Early Medieval heroic age of

---

[37] Richard E. Barton, *Lordship in the County of Main, c. 890–1160* (Rochester: Boydell & Brewer, 2004), 197–219.

[38] Georges Duby, *The Chivalrous Society*, trans. Cynthia Postan (Berkeley: University of California Press, 1980), 159–161. He does not claim this as a general pattern, recognizing that some regions showed a slower development.

[39] This discussion draws on the following studies: Dominique Barthélemy, "Les chroniques de la mutation chevaleresque en France (du xe au xiie Siécle)," *Comptes rendus de l'Academie des inscriptions et Belles-Lettres* (2007), 1643–1665; John Gillingham, "'Holding to the Rules of War (Bellica Jura Tenentes)'; Right Conduct before, during, and after Battle in North-Western Europe in the Eleventh Century," *Anglo-Norman Studies* 29 (2006), ed. C. P. Lewis, 1–15; Matthew Strickland, "*Mise à mort ou clémence? La rançon, la chevalerie et la transformation de l'attitude à l'égard des ennemis vaincus dans les îles Britanniques et dans la France du nord,*" in *Guerre et société au Moyen Âge Byzance – Occident (viiie–xiiie siècle)*, eds. D. Barthélemy and J.-C. Cheynet. Series: Monographies (Centre de recherche d'histoire et civilisation de Byzance) (31). l'Université de Paris IV–Sorbonne, Paris, France (2008); "The Vanquished Body: Some Comparisons and Conclusions," in *El Cuerpo Derrotado: Cómo Trataban Musulmanes y Cristianos a los Enemigos Vencidos: Península Ibérica, ss. VIII–XIII*, eds. M. I. Fierro and F. García Fitz. Series: Estudios árabes e islámicos: monografías (15). Consejo Superior de Investigaciones Científicas, Madrid, Spain, 531–570 (2008) (2001); "Killing or Clemency? Changing Attitudes to Conduct in War in Eleventh and

combat, they hold, defeated warriors could be killed or enslaved, and many military expeditions essentially functioned as slave raids. The early age of chivalry brought a remarkable change: combat became less relentlessly bloody, and surrender could be negotiated, at least for elite warriors.

Victors ceased to slaughter opponents and became more interested in ransoming them. Except on the shifting borders of its relentless expansion, medieval Europe, whatever the regional variations, witnessed seismic changes in warrior combat. The slave trade slowly disappeared, though vestiges of it lasted through the eleventh century and even later. In Wales, Scotland, and Scandinavia, slavery persisted into the twelfth or even thirteenth centuries.[40]

It would be difficult to imagine the emergence of what all scholars easily recognize as chivalry in, say, the later twelfth century, in the absence of this significant shift a century or more earlier. Gillingham, in fact, sees in the change the very definition of chivalry, although granting that this is "not what twelfth-century authors meant by 'chevalerie.'"[41] Causation for change on this scale remains distressingly murky. As Matthew Strickland writes,

There may well have been a developed body of custom relating to surrender, ransom and the treatment of captives in France and the Anglo-Norman kingdom of England by at least the end of the eleventh century, but this preserve was largely secular and its transmission was predominantly oral, making it difficult to recover its workings until at least the thirteenth century.[42]

Twelfth-Century Britain and France," in *Krieg im Mittelalter*, ed. H. H. Kortüm (Berlin: Akademie Verlag, 93–122).

[40] David Wyatt, *Slaves and Warriors in Medieval Britain and Ireland: 800–1200* (Leiden: Brill, 2009); Eljas Orrman, "Rural Conditions," in *The Cambridge History of Scandinavia*, ed. Knut Helle (New York: Cambridge University Press, 2003), 310–311. Slavery in Denmark did not formally end until the first half of the thirteenth century, whereas it would last another hundred years in Sweden, only officially abolished by royal decree in 1335. Norway, if the continued presence of thirteenth-century legislation regarding freed slaves (*leysingjar*) is an accurate indicator, like neighboring Sweden and Norway, also went through a very drawn-out process of abolishing slavery that lasted throughout the high Middle Ages.

[41] Gillingham, "1066 and the Introduction of Chivalry into England," in *Law and Government in Medieval England and Normandy*, eds. George Garret and John Hudson (Cambridge, 1994), 31–55 at 32. In the killing and devastation of the Hundred Years War he finds a late medieval decline of chivalry.

[42] Strickland, "The Vanquished Body: Some Comparisons and Conclusions," in *El Cuerpo Defforado*, eds. Maribel Fierro and Francisco Garcia Fitz (Madrid, 2008),

As a working hypothesis, both Gillingham and Strickland see Carolingian political disintegration, local and regional warfare, and the proliferation of castles – and their sieges – as spurs to negotiated surrenders; they are less certain of the influence of the Peace and Truce of God or of an increasingly monetized economy as agents supporting ransom.[43] The motivation may well have come from the practice of warfare, rather than from exterior sources. As Matthew Strickland observes, "The choice between death, ransom or captivity seems to have depended less on preconceived mores than circumstances and the volition of individual commanders."[44]

The new sense of warrior forbearance toward worthy foes seems established; it indicates that opponents were evidently seen as equals, as fellow fighters in the great enterprise of combat; and this suggests at least a self-consciousness emerging by the close of our first period. Both Strickland and Gillingham see the transition beginning as early as the ninth- and tenth-century Carolingian and post-Carolingian warfare.[45] Some warriors were coming to think of themselves as part of an elite group. If ordinary foot soldiers might still be killed more easily, indiscriminate slaughter of civilians in general seems to have lessened. We will see that plunder, arson, and fiscal exaction, of course, continued unabated. The treatment of what we might pardonably term noncombatants in general will be a concern later (in Chapter 6).

Religious ideals, however we estimate their role in the shift toward negotiated surrender and ransom,[46] contributed to other dimensions of chivalric ideology. The blessing of God was fervently sought for campaigns throughout the Carolingian era. As David Bachrach has amply shown, processions and prayers implored divine valorization of

---

531–570, quotation from 533. The process was then spurred by political disintegration and increase in construction of castles (539–540).

[43] Gillingham, "Fontenoy and After: Pursuing Enemies to Death in France between the Ninth and Eleventh Centuries," in *Frankland: The Franks and the World of the Early Middle Ages* (Manchester, 2008), 242–265.

[44] "Rules of War or War without Rules?" in *Transcultural Wars from the Middle Ages to the 21st Century*, ed. Hans-Henning Kortum (Berlin, 2006), 107–140, quotation at 137.

[45] Strickland, "The Vanquished Body," 539; Gillingham, "Fontenoy and After," 242.

[46] Gillingham is certain that religion played no role in chivalry: he sees chivalry as a secular code; "1066 and the Introduction of Chivalry into England," 32. In the killing and devastation of the Hundred Years War he finds a late medieval decline of chivalry.

combat and success for armed force; platoons of priests accompanied each army, especially charged to fortify the fighters with the rites of confession and penance. These rites, he argues, significantly aided morale and discipline within the fighting force.[47] These prayers and supplications for armies touched all fighters and were not specific to an emerging elite of *milites*. They do, however, indicate a valorization of warfare as a religious foundation on which more specific structures will be built on behalf of these elite warriors.

Was there more specific ideological content in the well-known formulation of tri-functionalism? This concept envisioned society composed, by divine plan, of three *ordines* (orders in society): those who pray, those who fight, and those who work – that is, the clerics, the most elite warriors, and all others (principally peasants at this time, though town populations would swell). It seems likely that this set of ideas applied especially to truly elevated warriors. If prayers were applicable to more than the *milites*, the concepts of tri-functionalism may have applied, at this early stage, to only a subset of elite warriors. As Jean Flori has argued, the designation of *bellatores*, the warriors within the order, did not encompass all fighters – not even, that is, the entire range of *milites*, whose mixed status we have been examining – but was focused on the very grand lay figures, kings and princes in particular. He suggests that around 1100, when Adalbero, Bishop of Laon, formulated the tri-functional conception, there was as yet "no warrior order."[48] "In the eleventh century," Flori writes, "the warriors were emerging from obscurity."[49] In time the military *ordo* would encompass the *milites* generally, though Flori's dating suggests this generalization unfolded as our second phase opened. Trying to understand exactly how religion intersected with chivalry will concern us more closely later (in Chapter 9); but the early signs of religious valorization stand like a signpost to the future. When the knighthood takes clearer form, ideas already in circulation will be of great import for the *milites*.

What of the process by which a man formally became a knight? Such ceremonies, with an importance long emphasized by Jean Flori and Maurice Keen, and more recently by Max Lieberman, provide

---

[47] David Bachrach, *Religion and the Conduct of War, c. 300–1215* (Woodbridge, Suffolk: Boydell, 2003).
[48] Jean Flori, "Knightly Society," 148.   [49] Ibid., 149.

highly useful insights into both status and nascent ideology.[50] Of course, once again historians confront scattered evidence and slippery terminology in an era of change. The granting of arms to mark the transition of a young man into the status of an adult and a warrior had been a feature of ancient Germanic society even before the medieval period.[51] Yet analysis cannot be simplified by an assumption of continuity, tracing the evolution of this act into what scholars take to be chivalric "knighting" or "dubbing." Considerable scholarly effort has generated divergent views, suggesting the need for closer analysis.[52] Formally giving arms seems in our first phase to have characterized only the top social levels. We can recall Barthélemy's suggestion that Charles the Bald was given arms along with a crown in 888 to mark "a triple accession to the kingship, to manhood, and to the status of warriors."[53]

As so often, the eleventh century seems to represent a time of significant transformation. In a case study of "deliveries of arms" from the eleventh century, Max Lieberman analyzed six instances from around midcentury and two from late in the century, all of them clearly involving great men (William II of Normandy; Fulk IV of Anjou; Harold Godwineson; Philip, son of Henry I of France; Henry, the future Henry I of England; and Louis, the future Louis VI of France).[54] His nuanced argument ponders whether all such acts were the same or produced the same results, whether they created or identified knights, whether at this point such acts implied the existence of a recognized group, such as an *ordo* (which was clearly the case by the thirteenth century, as the pontifical of William Durandus makes clear).[55] These ceremonies favored Whitsun as the date and a royal or comital "capital" for the site; usually a senior man performed the act of granting arms to a junior; if churchmen were

---

[50] Flori, *L'essor de chevalerie*; Keen, *Chivalry*, 64–82; Max Lieberman, "A Practical Guide."

[51] Dominique Barthélemy, *Le chevalerie: de la Germanie antique a la France du* XIIe *siècle* (Fayard, 2007), 9–75.

[52] As noted by Max Lieberman.

[53] Barthélemy, *The Serf, the Knight, and the Historian*, 160–161.

[54] Max Lieberman, "A New Approach to the Knighting Ritual."

[55] For Durandus, see *Guillelmus Duranti, Rationale divinorum officiorum I–IV, V–VI, VII–VIII*. Corpus Christianorum, Continuatio Mediaevalis 140, 140A, 140B, ed. Anselme Davril, O.S.B., and Timothy M. Thibodeau (Turnhout: Brepols, 1995, 1998, 2000).

involved, they seem not to have been required.[56] Lieberman sees significant common features in these cases, though the granting of arms to Harold by his future conqueror shows particularities. The most wealthy and powerful young men (or those close to them at court) were being recognized as expert adult mounted warriors; the Latin term *miles* may justly be the equivalent of the French *chevalier*. In short, a constitutive ritual existed, although the precise implications and social extent remain elusive. Once again we can see chivalric markers associated with elite *milites* on the border between our first and second chivalric phases. And once again the view below these eminent figures is obscured in shadows.

If the process of making a knight is at least informative, some further insight appears in the action to unmake a knight, though such steps occurred much more rarely. Canon law of the Carolingian and post-Carolingian period provided what were, in effect, demotions declared against great noble warriors whose actions were deemed especially dreadful; church councils on occasion formally stripped these sinners of the right to wear the *cingulum militaris*, the sword belt adorned with precious metal that symbolized their elevated lay status as noble fighters and officials. In theory, and sometimes in practice, the offenders were deprived not only of the distinct honor their military status represented, but also of their marriage and the right to take communion; other severe penances might be imposed. Clearly the standard and expected valorization of noble warrior status, adorned with religious blessings and social eminence, was highlighted when both were lost.[57] In the early twelfth century, Abbot Suger of Saint Denis happily notes in his history of the righteous kingly and knightly deeds of Louis the Fat that the process continued – or more likely was revived – in his own time. The target was Thomas of Marle, a leading villain in his account, "the vilest of

---

[56] Maurice Keen recognized that such rites may have combined clerical and secular ideas, but he argued that they were essentially secular and noted that, unlike royal coronations, these arming or dubbing rituals never came under ecclesiastical control. *Chivalry*, 74–77.

[57] Leyser, "Early Canon Law and the Beginning of Knighthood," points to the ninth century as the period in which the *cingulum militare* "became emblematic and summed up aristocratic military status" (55); he notes that "multiple Carolingian councils, synods, decretals, capitula, and ordinances all laid down sanctions against aristocratic/warrior misconduct in which the loss of the *cingulum militare* was a central facet in penance."

men and a plague on God and men alike."[58] A general church council meeting at Beauvais in 1114 issued the declaration that Thomas, who was not present, was deprived of the *cingulem militarem*. Suger claimed that this clerical denunciation sparked King Louis into action against Thomas.[59] We need not think that Carolingian warriors were regularly policed and deprived of status in any numbers, or that Thomas changed his life after the council declared against him, to recognize the importance of this evidence. In this critical time of transition, ecclesiastics recognized high warrior status, wanted it to carry responsibility, and were willing – at least in scattered and high-profile cases – to issue formal acts against notorious offenders. In their view, great warriors possessed high status linked to their essential military function; the link was so important that malfeasance could lead to formal demotion.

A constant theme in this book holds that chivalry, while presenting a core of values and practices, emerged gradually through a considerable span of time. If we wish to speak of Carolingian or immediately post-Carolingian chivalry, we can see this core emerging in the elite warrior function, in rising status for the *milites*, and the beginnings of a guiding and valorizing ideology; but we must recognize that chivalry in these centuries could not anticipate important elements of chivalry that developed in what historians like to call the long twelfth century (roughly 1050 to 1215) or throughout the thirteenth century since chivalry then was, in significant measure, shaped by decidedly post-Carolingian forces.[60] Along some lines, this is a matter of scale or clarity coming to an aspect previously seen only shrouded in mist, rather than a completely new phenomenon; in other cases, elements seem to be completely fresh and to be recognized as such by both medieval contemporaries and medieval historians. Early and fascinating forms

---

[58] Richard C. Cusimano and John C. Moorhead, eds., trans., *The Deeds of Louis the Fat* (Washington, DC: Catholic University of America Press, 1992), 37.

[59] Ibid., 107. In endnote 1 for this chapter (194–195), the editors note that Orderic Vitallis corroborates Suger. The process against Thomas included an anathema and possibly a statement that he was deprived of all fiefs.

[60] Dominique Barthélemy, who has long emphasized continuity from the Carolingian period, has more recently suggested a chivalric transformation of the year 1100, gathering force across the second half of the eleventh century: "Les chroniques de la mutation chevaleresque en France," *Comptes rendus de l'Academie des inscriptions et Belles-Lettres* (2007), 1643–1665.

of dubbing or knighting exist as we cross the mid-eleventh-century line, but cases must be hunted down, leaving us to wonder about their exact meaning and societal spread. Knighthood has yet to come together within an *ordo* spanning all differences of juridical status and social class. The great literary vehicles that will motivate so much in chivalry, both *chanson de geste* and romance, have yet to begin their crucial work of opening topics of debate, providing guidance, and offering almost worshipful valorization of the chivalrous. Even mounted shock combat as the chosen fighting technique seems uncertain in its spread and triumph. Successive tidal waves of crusade are only gathering force beyond the horizon and, though armies of Charlemagne and his heirs have long been blessed, the later individual and almost contractual link between one who has taken the cross and the sacred will carry a different charge of piety by the twelfth century. Religious ideas that will be selectively adapted by the knights to shape and bless their vigorous lives, valorize their hard profession, and bolster envied status have yet to appear: changing ecclesiastical ideas on the morality of killing in battle, and the conception that suffering incurred by warriors within their professional labors counted as meritorious and penitential, reducing the time spent enduring dreaded cleansing in purgatory, had yet to enhance their piety; indeed, a clear formulation of purgatory itself lay in the future. Tournament, even if we might think it lurking under the guise of quasi-war, has yet to take firm shape and to seduce nearly all knights with its charms and opportunities. What will become the increasingly complex science of heraldry lies in the future, as does the courtliness practiced with ever more elaborations at hundreds of lordly courts. The many blossoms of the flower of love – hothouse creation though it may have been – have not even sprouted to become an emblem of chivalric life and a staple of chivalric literature.

Of course it seems equally unlikely that chivalry emerged suddenly and without precedent, instantly generating its classic phase in the long twelfth century. In previous centuries, important initial steps were undoubtedly taken, so that the centuries of our first phase retain a fascination and significance as obvious as the interpretive difficulties with which we have wrestled. Changes heralding the new stage – such as knightly forbearance with regard to fellow warriors – lead us easily toward the later eleventh century and beyond, to a whole new phase in which chivalric function, knightly status, and a satisfying ideology develop new forms and strengths.

4

PHASE TWO: KNIGHTHOOD AND CHIVALRY FUSE

·

That the earliest of our set of model knights (discussed in Chapter 2) date from this second phase of chivalric history can cause little surprise. More surviving evidence does not always prove new social phenomena, yet some correlation between evidence and historical change likely exists and is, as we will see, especially likely in a second chivalric phase. We have no trouble picturing a figure such as Richard Lion-Heart and his armored contemporaries as knights, and quickly form mental images of Arthurian heroes such as Lancelot. We can even assign the knightly label with confidence to William the Conqueror or any of the Normans of his generation active across Europe more than a century earlier. Building on the undoubted changes from the ninth and tenth centuries, this second phase (c. 1050–c. 1300) brings classic chivalry fully to life. Elite social status for knights became a given and a valorizing and inclusive ideology, expanding and extending earlier developments, fused with an older military function. The results both reflected and shaped structural dimensions as chivalric ideals and practices interacted powerfully with the vibrant socioeconomic, religious, and political changes of this central period of medieval history.[1]

---

[1] With a focus on formative ideology, Jean Flori argued in *L'essor de chevalerie* (Geneva: Droz, 1988) that at about the midpoint of this period (specifically in 1175–1180, in fact), the protective functions long attributed to kingship – protecting the church, the weak, securing internal order – blended with the rising valorization of warriors to form a group spanning elite lay society from great lords to local knights, and supplied them with an overarching ideology replete

Crucial new strands intertwined, adding strength to an existing older core.

Of course the chronology often remains approximate, varying region by region; blurred demarcation lines persist. Some changes that will fully appear in the third phase of chivalric development (to be considered in the following chapter) began to come tellingly to the surface by the end of the thirteenth century. Each line of inquiry we follow could justly demand its own monograph (which some have truly received), but the goal here remains thematic overview rather than encyclopedic particularity. Viewing the forest can reasonably hold our attention as much as any individual stand of trees. As before, discussion is intended to set powerful and in some cases well-known phenomena within a developing chivalric function, ideology, and status, rather than to adumbrate topics as freestanding subjects. Relying on useful clusters of evidence, a first section will serve as a brief reminder that function retained its military core – never exclusive, but ever central. A second section will explore how chivalry now came to characterize a broader social range; lay aristocrats accepted the designation of knighthood and were joined by men rising in status so that chivalry came to comprehend the entire lay male elite (if we exclude, as they did, a thin upper layer of thriving merchants). The remaining sections analyze the developing link between status and ideology. If the exterior lines of chivalry constantly reflected a society far from static, in this period core elements (foreseen in an earlier era) came into their own; we will see their continuing life in a third period (in Chapter 5).

CONTINUING WARRIOR FUNCTION

First we must simply and briefly register the mass of evidence that shows continuation and adaptation of an ethos and practice of the warrior prowess that had flourished in earlier centuries. Little space and effort are required, for throughout this entire period, chronicles and biographies fulsomely report knights active in raid, war, and tournament, and imaginative literature is animated by lance strokes

with ethical content. With no lessening of admiration for the immense scholarly achievement of this analysis of originating elements in chivalric ideology emerging from clerical intellectuals, we might continue with the framework established earlier in this part.

and sword blows breathlessly admired. By the mid-twelfth century *chansons de geste* had begun to appear, and later in the century seemingly countless romances won a wide readership. If these works ideally tempered vigorous masculine combat with wisdom, they continued to praise knightly prowess as the very heart of masculine virtue and the means for achieving good in the world.[2]

Reflectively, the poet/biographer who wrote the *History of William Marshal* (1224) mused over the special significance of the hard profession of knighthood:

> What is armed combat? Is it the same
> as working with a sieve or winnow,
> with an axe or mallet?
> Not at all, it is much nobler work,
> For he who undertakes these tasks is able to take a rest
> When he has worked for a while.
> What, then, is chivalry?
> Such a difficult, tough,
> And very costly thing to learn
> That no coward ventures to take it on.[3]

The poet hymns prowess unceasingly and sometimes equates it with chivalry per se. Standing shoulder to shoulder with epic and romance writers, the author speaks of deeds of prowess as the essence of chivalry – as feats or acts of chivalry, literally as enacted *"chevaleries,"* as they are tellingly termed in Old French.[4] In narrating William's first fight after being knighted, the poet exults, "What a deadly companion they found him to be / as he cut a swathe through the throng" of his enemies.[5] When he narrates William's victory at the battle at Lincoln, much later in his hero's career (1217), the author again warmly praises the winning of high honor through deeds of arms. He recognizes that not all knights achieved great deeds with their weaponry, though he notes that all surely boasted of it! He assures readers that the heroes at Lincoln had been well schooled in chivalry.[6] The fighting might be especially fierce, bloody, and fatal, especially when the stakes were high, as in the quarrel between

[2] R. W. Kaeuper, *Chivalry and Violence*, 121–160, provides copious evidence.
[3] Holden, Gregory, and Crouch, *History of William Marshal*, lines 16853–16863.
[4] E.g., ibid., line 5584 (a tournament marked by great feats of chivalry), and lines 5595, 6232, and 7898 (chivalry performed). That chivalry can be performed is regularly expressed in imaginative chivalric literature.
[5] Ibid., lines 920–921.   [6] Ibid., lines 16853–16870.

Stephen and Matilda for the English throne or during the French
invasion of England in the minority of Henry III.[7] The civil war
during Stephen's reign, which William's father enthusiastically
joined, involved ambushes and battles in which

> many a shield was smashed in pieces, many a
> hauberk drenched with blood,
> many a soul was made to part from its body
> many a prized and valiant knight
> was wounded, killed, or taken prisoner;
> many a lady was left a hapless widow,
> many a maiden orphaned...[8]

At times the poet seems to be writing in the mode of *chanson de geste*:

> There were losses, there were gains,
> Many a man killed and maimed,
> Many a brain spilled from skull
> And many a gut trailing on the ground.[9]

During the French invasion, fatalities on the enemy side seem to be
emphasized; at one point, the poet reports that he saw dogs eating the
bodies of a hundred enemies who had been killed by the English
between Winchester and Romsey.[10] At another point he proudly
notes that the Marshal's apt military tactics resulted in the killing of
a thousand of the "rabble of footsoldiers" on the French side.[11] His
general comment on the battle at Lincoln is that "there was no
question there of offering pledges, for the sole price to pay would
be their heads and their lives."[12]

Sometimes the poet can give individual thrusts the attention they
merit. He relates that Reginald Croc killed the Count of Perche "by
a cruel straight thrust of the sword ... with the point of the sword
straight through the eye."[13] One of the limitations of what at least
claims to be reportage of historical combat was that in general

---

[7] Richard Abels, "Cultural Representations of Warfare in the High Middle Ages:
The Morgan Picture Bible," notes the likelihood that such combat will be intense
and costly in a forthcoming study in a Festschrift for John France, which he kindly
sent me in advance of publication.

[8] *History of William Marshal*, lines 141–167, with quotation from lines 158–164.

[9] Ibid., lines 325–328.   [10] Ibid., lines 1510–1512.

[11] Ibid., lines 15779–15783. He contentedly notes that Louis lost a thousand men
who died "who never received confession; all they received were the spears and
swords and these they had in abundance." Ibid., 15812–15814.

[12] Ibid., lines 16834–16835.   [13] Ibid., lines 16738–16742.

individual sword strokes could not actually be followed in the confusion and clouds of dust so that they could be reported in detail, specifying the damage done to bodies. More imaginative literature could meet that need, likely magnifying the effectiveness of weaponry on armored bodies as a glorification of the hard profession of chivalry. The twelfth-century chronicler who wrote *The Crusade of Richard Lion-Heart* enthusiastically glorified the knightly valor of his hero in more precise terms, likely to satisfy an audience:

> Never did man such mighty deeds;
> He charged among the miscreant breed
> So deep that he was hid from sight.
> Forward and back he hewed a swath
> About him, cutting deadly path
> With his good sword, whose might was such
> That everything that it could touch,
> Or man or horse, was overthrown
> And to the earth was battered down.
> I think 'twas there he severed
> At one stroke both the arm and head
> Of an emir, an infidel
> Steel-clad, whom he sent straight to hell,
> And when the Turks perceived this blow,
> They made broad path before him.[14]

The author of the *Perceforest* frankly boasts of his capacity to give his audience what they want; he has elaborated the Latin chronicle source he claims to have, giving more of the specifics of combat:

Without altering the facts, I do embellish some incidents and describe them in more detail than I find in the Latin to make it more enjoyable to hear; for if I just said "So-and-so killed So-and-so and someone else wounded someone else and this army beat that other" and skimmed over it as briefly as the Latin does, you'd soon have heard the whole story and it wouldn't have been much fun![15]

But *chansons de geste* were the great source for physical combat almost lovingly described. Combat and individual lance or sword blows could be followed almost as if filmed in slow motion with the ideal lens on the camera. Champions seem to live (and often to die) on the battlefield, with their performance fully presented. In that early and

[14] M. J. Hubert, trans., ed. John L. La Monte, *Ambroise: The Crusade of Richard Lion-Heart* (New York: Columbia University Press, 1941), lines 605–626.
[15] Bryant, trans., *Perceforest*, 97.

foundational *chanson, Song of Roland,* the warrior function is repeatedly praised, and embodied in the eponymous hero, even as Oliver
represents a corrective for its excesses. The fighting Archbishop
Turpin in the first great fight sings out,

> You! Roland! What a fighter!
> Now that's what every knight must have in him
> Who carries arms and rides on a fine horse;
> He must be strong, a savage, when he's in battle;
> For otherwise, what's he worth? Not four cents!
> Let that four-cent man be a monk in some minster,
> And he can pray all day long for our sins.[16]

Perhaps a century later, the theme is still being sung. *Girart de Vienne*
opens with a promise to its audience:

> Lords, will you hear a worthy tale I'll tell,
> Of lofty theme and deeds of great prowess?
> My song is not of pride or foolishness,
> Neither of treason nor of deceitfulness,
> But of a breed whom my Lord Jesus bless,
> As fierce as any who ever yet drew breath...[17]

This promise is amply fulfilled in the *chanson* that follows. At one
point Garin de Monglane declares his guiding principle:

> I do believe if I had peace for once,
> I would be struck by sickness within a month,
> Or leprosy or some great plague or such!
> But when I see the whinnying war-steeds plunge
> With worthy knights into a battle's crush,
> And see their spears and cutting blades well struck,
> There is nothing on earth I love so much![18]

Romance writing continued the valorization of prowess so resolutely presented in epic. We sometimes forget that romance pictures
and praises active prowess as well as investigating love; and now and
again even these works narrate battlefields with an intensity that
would do epic authors proud. Reform efforts directed at modifying
or channeling warrior prowess make the same point from another
direction; that is, they acknowledge the violent actions of warriors in
society, often praising skill, force, and victory, even though they may

[16] *Song of Roland,* trans. Frederick Golden, lines 1876–1882.
[17] Quoted in the vigorous translation of Michael A. Newth, *The Song of Girart de
Vienne by Bertrand de Bar-Sur Aube* (Tempe, AZ, 1999), lines 1–7.
[18] Ibid., lines 2106–2111.

seek to direct the action against targets they select. Chrétien's *Yvain, the Knight with the Lion* (c. 1173–1176) provides a splendid case in point with its attempt not to reduce knightly ardor but to direct it into protective service and away from merely self-centered aggressive paths. Several of the sprightly *lais* of Marie de France, written in the same period, recognize the primacy of prowess even as they etch in acidic verse the deleterious effects of such obsession.[19] She faced an uphill climb in making such critiques, for knightly valor can be praised in almost sensual, nearly idolatrous terms. Even the Christ-like Galahad is shown exercising impossibly impressive sword strokes. When Bors confronts him in the *Post-Vulgate Quest* he is swiftly deprived of his lance in the combat. The sword fight comes next in chivalric choreography, and Bors welcomes it, calling out, "Come test me with the sword, and then I will see that you are a knight." The test is far more convincing than he had anticipated.

[Galahad's] blow cut through his shield, the pommel of his saddle, and the horse's withers, so that half the horse fell one way and half the other in the middle of the road, and Bors was left on foot, holding his naked sword, and half his shield, the other half having fallen in the road.

Stunned, Bors can only cry out, "I see by this blow you're the best knight I ever saw."[20] Galahad is the best, but a newcomer in this game; his father Lancelot has long commanded similar reactions. After witnessing Lancelot's marvels of prowess (including the skewering of three knights on a single lance), a knight stammers out glowing praise: "If it were up to me, he'd never leave me. I'd keep him with me always, because I couldn't hold a richer treasure."[21] Similar themes are voiced south of the Pyrenees in the *Poem of the Cid*. One of the warriors fighting against the Moors says he will not take a penny of booty until he proves himself "struggling with the Moors on the field, making use of the lance and the sword in my hand and glinting with blood down to the elbow." As El Cid is besieged, he asks for advice from one his companions, Minaya, who counsels fighting instead of waiting, saying, "In the name of the Creator, it should not happen [that we don't fight the Moors]. We must go and

[19] Glyn S. Burgess, Keith Busby, trans., *The Lais of Marie de France* (New York: Penguin, 1999), 97–108. The *lais* are *Milun* and *Chaitivel*.
[20] *Post-Vulgate Quest for the Holy Grail*, in *Lancelot-Grail*, V, 17.
[21] *Lancelot-Grail*, III, 162.

smite them tomorrow." El Cid replies: "You speak wisely to me, and honor yourself, Minaya. I expect such from you."[22]

EXPANDING CHIVALRIC RANKS

A telling scene opening *The Wagon-Train of Nimes* (a *chanson* in the cycle of William of Orange, likely written in the first half of the twelfth century) illustrates issues intertwined with elite knightly status and self-conception.[23] On a fine day in May, William of Orange is returning from hunting and rides with a sizable retinue. He is accompanied by "forty youths, sons of counts and of enfeoffed princes who had recently been dubbed knights. They held falcons for their entertainment and had packs of hounds with them."[24] Markers of elite status stand out clearly: these young men come from families of rank, headed by fief-holders; the lads have all been dubbed knights themselves; and they are wealthy enough to afford and display high fashion, as their hooded falcons and braying hounds attest. With such details, the author has presented an idealized group portrait; full details such as dress and courtly demeanor could easily be assumed by any contemporary audience or readership.

Yet all is not well even here, for tensions quickly erupt into the idealized scene, and these tears in the social fabric, too, are informative. Though the fickle king has been distributing rich estates, William's nephew tells him, "You and I, uncle, are overlooked."[25] The serious nature of the slight is heightened because William has given the king so much valiant armed service replete with toil and suffering. Disingenuously, the great William rushes to court and loudly tells the king he does not know how he will even feed his warhorse, a statement through which the author may intend to link the imagined William's plight to that of even the simplest knight in the audience. Had each not given good service with the sword? Was there ever any adequate reward on offer to set against mounting expenses of service, let alone of the trappings required for courtly self-presentation? The very prominence in this vast literature of issues

---

[22] *Cantar de Mio Cid*, ed. R. Menéndez Pidal (Madrid: Espasa-Calpe, S.A., 1956), 1044, 1051. I follow the translation suggested by Samuel Claussen.

[23] Glanville Price, trans., "The Waggon-Train," in *William, Count of Orange: Four Old French Epics*, ed. Glanville Price (London: Dent, 1973), 61.

[24] Ibid.   [25] Ibid.

stemming from difficulties in obtaining fiefs provides significant insights into *mentalité* of *milites*.

Similar questions are raised by Bernier in the rambling, violent, and revealing epic *Raoul de Cambrai* (a late twelfth-century work from the cycle of the barons in revolt). Conflict with his lord Raoul centers on rights that Bernier claims to a great estate and outrage over ill-treatment unbefitting a man of his status and service. Bernier's concern over status is intensified by his illegitimate birth, his father having raped his unmarried mother, who has become an abbess. If this poem offers a remarkable catalog of issues for debate – reciprocal loyalty, righteous vengeance and astonishing forgiveness, sacrilege, a sheer delight in bloody combat – its engagement with matters of status speaks powerfully to our analysis. Repeatedly, its author assures hearers or readers that the major cast of characters (though swiftly declining through battlefield mortality) is composed of men and women of high status and even noble rank.[26] Two social issues, in short, drive the action in *Raoul*: landed endowments badly and unfairly distributed spark the action, and the intensifying catalyst comes from honor impugned through personal, degrading assault.[27] In such epics, high birth, public display of wealth used to create the right effect, and landed possessions all show the status that the *milites* – at least those not great lords – longed for. The young William Marshal, as David Crouch, one of his modern biographers, has pointed out, was raised on such stories and might have memorized some.[28] Having already noted similarities between the *Histoire* and epic narrative, we can sense the common spirit in both.

Establishing desired social status depended, as it usually does, on powers of exclusion and clear markers of inclusion. Over time, the defining social forms became increasingly elaborate and costly (as we will see more clearly in our third phase); those within the charmed circle attempted to erect high walls around its periphery in order to exclude, or at least limit, the entry of eager newcomers. Yet in the middle phase under discussion here the currents moved with different effect. Near the top of the social heap, inclusiveness was enabled not only by wealth and power, but by the importance of specialized

[26] In more than a third of the laisses (stanzas) of the early version of *Raoul de Cambrai* the term "noble" appears in an elevating social sense.
[27] See the text and discussion in Sarah Kay, *Raoul de Cambrai*, and the discussion in R. W. Kaeuper, *Chivalry and Violence*, 244–252.
[28] David Crouch, *William Marshal*, 23.

military function and capacity; further down the social slopes even
the simplest among those who could claim knighthood disdainfully
distanced themselves from lesser beings below knightly status. Thus
elite warrior status, broadly conceived, arched over social or juridical
ranks within the group that remained recognizable. Chivalry became
a satisfying and honorable designation for men without – at least until
the late thirteenth century in most of Europe – eliminating the social
or legal ranks into which they could also be slotted.[29] Great lords and
even kings were coming to represent themselves as knights, as did
men of little land or wealth who served them. Such lesser men cast
a broad shadow only under a local sun and likely glanced anxiously at
a competitive world from within dwellings only recently crenelated
to resemble castles. Yet all knights were a part of an elite group and
even the small fry in these enchanted waters, as we have seen, had
come to assert that they were free, specialized warriors; they were
absolutely certain that their status associated with their military function elevated them above cultivators of the land whose hands were
stained by the soil they personally worked, and they stood even well
above successful merchants whose hands were soiled by filthy lucre
(accumulated in greed and seldom dispensed in shows of largesse).
This sense of shared, honorable function and elite status obviously did
not make all knights socially equal; but all knights could claim – and
strive to display – an enviable status without asserting parity with the
great and powerful. They could all at least claim a place beneath the
broad and boldly striped pavilion of chivalry, even if some could only
stand in the back rows and gaze in awe and envy at those prominently
occupying the center.

[29] See the classic medieval law books. *The Coutomes de Beauvaisis of Philippe de
Beaumanoir*, trans. F. R. P. Akehurst (Philadelphia: University of Pennsylvania
Press, 1992), s.1496–s.1509, 536–539. Cf. Robert H. Lucas, "Ennoblement in Late
Medieval France," *Medieval Studies* 39 (1977), 240–260; *The Saxon Mirror:
A Sachsenspiegel of the Fourteenth Century*, trans. Maria Dobozy (Philadelphia:
University of Pennsylvania Press, 1999), bk. iv, 143–180. For the *Siete Partidas,
Medieval Government: The World of Kings and Warriors* (Partida II), trans. Samuel
Parsons Scott, ed. Robert I. Burns, S.J. (Philadelphia: University of Pennsylvania
Press, 2001), nobility, 314–315; knighthood, 417–432; the *Siete Partidas* (Part II,
Title XXI) excludes women, members of religious orders, the insane, those under
age, the very poor, the physically defective, a merchant, a traitor, a man guilty of
perfidy, a man under a death sentence, a man who has received the order of
knighthood in jest, and those who would purchase knighthood.

Some less obvious means proclaimed specifically chivalric status to the world. Self-representation appeared in several forms, each informative. The knights literally sought to make a good impression by imposing their claims onto wax seals used to authenticate important documents.[30] They likewise shaped their images by means of three-dimensional tomb effigies and etched ideal portraits (of status and function if not usually of individual features) onto two-dimensional memorial brasses set into stone slabs atop their graves. They elaborated what Maurice Keen considered a secular science of heraldry, and adopted ceremonies of dubbing as rites of entry into the chivalric order. Some of these social and functional assertions are well known, but others have been less fully investigated and all need to be brought into conjuncture in order to understand classic chivalry. Caution requires that we recognize that the broad reach of such practices did not erase distinctions of rank, for lords standing on upper rungs of the social ladder reaching toward the clouds never doubted that they were more powerful, and more feared, envied, and respected than those below them; but the common use of such chivalric markers across this social spectrum commands attention. This widespread and convincing corpus of evidence suggests important social developments and helps to provide its chronology.

Knightly seals

Significant images and assertive words stamped into wax seals authenticating formal acts clearly allow us to see public self-presentations. They reveal claims to knighthood as elite status, often linked with a distinctly military function. By adopting a vigorous and even aggressive armored image on a seal, a man was, in the words of John McEwan, "claiming membership in the ruling group."[31] In the course of our second chivalric phase, a range of men joined the very grand in this practice of sealing documents. Simply to adopt the practice constituted a social claim. It had once been a prerogative limited to kings and emperors and then to the very greatest ecclesiastical lords as well; vigorous use of seals was a "symptom of the Carolingian renaissance,"

---

[30] The pun is borrowed from *Good Impressions: Image and Authority in Medieval Seals*, eds. Noel Adams, John Cherry, and James Robinson (London: British Museum, 2008).

[31] *Seliau/Seals in Context: Medieval Wales and the Welsh Marches*, eds. John McEwan and Elisabeth A. New (Aberystwyth, 2012), 42.

and, from the tenth century on, monarchs, bishops, and great barons proudly affixed seals to their documents in Germany, France, and Anglo-Saxon England.[32] Coming into more general use through the eleventh and twelfth centuries, the practice of sealing began its steady glide down the slopes of the social pyramid. Keeping a leading role in the practice, kings adopted great seals showing themselves majestically enthroned, holding symbols of power. German emperors adopted such a great seal in the early eleventh century, with the French kings close behind.[33] Late Anglo-Saxon kings, too, created great seals, but Edward the Confessor used a double-sided pendant seal that was secured around a strip of parchment or cording threaded through a slit in the document. It bore an image on each side showing King Edward enthroned.[34] A double-sided pendant seal would generate many imitators, but they significantly came to display a mounted warrior on one of the sides.

This key change emerged in the practice of some lords of principalities; by the mid-eleventh century, just at the beginning of our second phase, they were coming to represent themselves on single-sided seals as armed, armored, and mounted warriors. Counts of Anjou, Fulk Nerra (d. 1040), and Geoffrey Maretl (d. 1060) provide good examples, but many other provincial lords also show the trend.[35] David Bates has declared that there is no clear evidence that William used a seal as duke of Normandy; but once he became William I of England (r. 1066–1087), he adopted a double-sided pendant seal, on one side of which (drawing on the style of Edward the Confessor) he was pictured crowned and seated in majesty; this was an image of William as king, a conception the inscription makes clear. He significantly changed the other face of the royal seal, however; it had formerly showed another seated image, but was now

---

[32] See the wide-ranging discussion in T. F. Tout, *Chapters in the Administrative History of Medieval England*, 6 vols. (University of Manchester Press, 1920–1933), I, 123–127.

[33] For German seals, see Otto Posse, *Das Siegelwesen der deutschen Kaiser und Könige von 751 bis 1913* (Dresden: Wilhelm und Bertha v. Baensch Stiftung, 1913); knightly representations do not generally figure until the mid-thirteenth century.

[34] David Bates, *William the Conqueror* (Gloucestershire: Stroud, 2001), 138–140. Numerous online sites also provide illustrations or photographs of this seal.

[35] See the wealth of illustrations in Georges de Manteyer, *Memoires de la société nationale des antiquaires* (1899), and Walter de Gray Birch, *Catalogue of Seals in the Department of Manuscripts in the British Museum*, 6 vols. (London, 1892–1900).

altered to show the king as an armed and mounted knight; on this side he is represented as Norman duke and warrior, the inscription again doubling the visual statement.[36] This fusion of images depicting ruling status and military function in the wax of the English great seal would prove fruitful.[37] This military, equestrian image was soon widely adopted, both in the British Isles and beyond; frequently it was combined with an image of ruling capacity. Granted, continental kings retained conservative traditions. French kings, with only an uncharacteristic shift to a double-sided seal with one military image under Louis VII, kept their tradition of a single face to their seals, showing a crowned and enthroned monarch; but they sometimes later impressed a small counter-seal (featuring a fleur-de-lis) on the back of the larger face of their great seal.[38] German kings/emperors likewise retained the image of monarch seated on a throne.[39]

But the military equestrian style triumphed on many other elite seals. English lords regularly presented themselves as knights. Those on the marches of Wales quickly adopted the style, as did Welsh

---

[36] Images of the seals of Edward and William and a useful discussion appear in David Bates, *William the Conqueror* (Gloucestershire: Stroud, 2001), 138–140. Before 1066, those leading Norman individuals and institutions wishing to receive ducal grants often presented documents they had drawn up in advance; some received signature crosses in authentication: Tout, *Chapters*, I, 125–126; and see G. R. C. Davis, "A Norman Charter," *British Museum Quarterly* 25 (1962), 75–79.

[37] Harvey and McGuinness, *A Guide to British Medieval Seals*, 43, make the point clearly: "Certainly until the late twelfth century the almost universal design of upper-class men's seals was a mounted knight, a design that stemmed directly from the seal of William I. Like the king's great seal, these equestrian seals were a personification of the owners, a powerful image of their social standing and military skill. Alternative designs were few. . . The pattern was set in England by the 1090s. . . by the accession of Henry II in 1154 probably any knight might have one." Ibid., 43. They find similar seals in Scotland and Wales about mid-twelfth century, but think that lost documents may cause this seeming later.

[38] As R. H. C. Davis noted, "The Norman practice of validating charters with autograph crosses, or signa, did not secure any solid foothold in England after the Norman Conquest. . ." See "A Norman Charter," *British Museum Quarterly* 25 (1962), 75–79, at 75.

[39] Birch, *Catalogue of Seals in the Department of Manuscripts in the British Museum*. For French royal seals, see vol. 5, numbers 18,052–18,086, Charlemagne to Philip the Fair. The Louis VII double-sided seal is number 18,073, the reverse side of which shows the king, as duke of Aquitaine, mounted and in armor. Later double-sided seals, as under Philip II, show an enthroned king plus a small counterseal, but no knightly representations.

princes, as can be seen in the earliest of their seals to survive.[40] Llywellen ap Iorwerth, Prince of North Wales, for example, used such a seal in the early thirteenth century.[41] English lords in Ireland imitated their king. Richard de Clare, earl of Pembroke ("Strongbow"), used a seal of the royal English type and when later in the twelfth century Prince John, son of Henry II, was sent to rule the island he adopted a single-foiled military equestrian type.[42] The earliest surviving seal of a Scottish king (Duncan II, r. 1093–1094), though single-sided, presents that king as a mounted knight.[43] Many lords in Scotland adopted the same image.[44] Later, Robert Bruce as King of Scotland (r. 1306–1329) used a two-foiled seal with one military equestrian image.[45] Karl Sverkerssohn, King of Sweden, used such a seal in 1164–1167, as did several Swedish jarls.[46]

Almost without exception, great French lords from roughly the eleventh century (such as the counts of Anjou, Champagne, Flanders, Maine, and Nevers) significantly portrayed themselves as mounted and armored warriors.[47] These lords are often shown carrying a lance with a war banner attached as a sign of leadership, power, and position, though the drawn sword became more popular in the second half of the twelfth century. In her study of 108 French

[40] Examples in John McEwan and Elizabeth New, eds., *Seals in Context: Medieval Wales and the Welsh Marches Ages* (Aberystwyth, 2012): see 42–43, 68–69 (native Welsh) and 70–72, 90–91, 98–99 (English lords in Wales).

[41] An image is provided by McEwan and New, *Seals in Context*, 42–43. Cf. ibid., 68–69 for the seal of Caradoc Uerbeis from the late twelfth century.

[42] Illustration of the Strongbow seal provided in R. F. Foster, ed., *Oxford Illustrated History of Ireland* (Oxford, 1989), 56. For Lord John's seal, see online image from the National Archives, "Uniting the Kingdom, 1066–1603," catalog number C 109/87 (seal date 1185–1199).

[43] This seal is reproduced in P. D. A. Harvey and Andrew McGuinness, *A Guide to British Medieval Seals* (Toronto, 1996), 6.

[44] Scottish equestrian seals appear in Walter de Gray Birch, *Catalogue of Seals in the Department of Manuscripts in the British Museum*, 6 vols. (London, 1887–1900). vol. IV, which describes seals dating between 1120 and the fourteenth century.

[45] The Robert Bruce Birthplace Museum (National Trust for Scotland) provides a copy of this seal on its website.

[46] Gören Tegnér, "The Oldest Equestrian Seals in Sweden," in *Good Impressions*, eds. Adams, Cherry, and Robinson, 66–70.

[47] Brigitte Bedos-Rezak provides general discussion in *Form and Order in Medieval France: Essays in Social and Quantitative Sigillography* (Great Yarmouth, 1993). Birch, *Catalogue of Seals*, also provides seals for these counts and others. Cf. the series of examples for the counts of Flanders in Germain Demoy, *Inventaire des sceaux de la Flandre* (Paris, 1873), seals numbers 134–167.

seals from 1050 to 1180, Bedos-Rezak found that "The theme emphasized is that of the lord as a warrior, specifically a mounted warrior."[48] Even if, through early decades of the twelfth century, such a lord may have considered himself as a leader of warriors more than simply as one of the knights, this visual link shows significant conceptions. Such warrior self-presentations would become the proud image of many lords for centuries to come, emphasizing the continuity of a core military function and a link to status in emerging chivalry.

Some lesser men within broadly lay elite ranks were more cautious than those contemporaries who adopted aggressively military equestrian seals. Publicly adopting such an assertive image may have seemed too brazen a step for warriors who could claim only modest power and wealth. Though these less grand men adopted the practice of sealing their documents, they generally chose to represent simply a coat of arms on their seals;[49] their rising family could thus at least assert what it saw as a rightful status in the world, without provoking the ire of those more securely in position. Prudently, the identifying personal titles stamped into the legends on the seals of simple French castellans usually linked them to the castle they held, in theory on behalf of one in a higher place on the chain of lordship. Even some brothers, cousins, and uncles of undoubtedly great men used these armorial seals, rather than the militant depictions favored by their powerful relatives. If the rising social status of knights below the top level was undoubted, the improvement may not have at once convinced great lords to see themselves as fully united with them by comradeship in arms.

Yet the spreading use of even armorial seals retains significance. An armorial seal presented a heraldic statement through its coat of arms, using symbols with an importance to which we will soon turn. The words they inscribed on seals can also tell us much; some men began after mid-twelfth century to term themselves *domini* no less than *milites* in the legends carved around the circumference of their seals, thus publicly claiming both lordship and knighthood. By the second half of the thirteenth century, French ducal, comital,

---

[48] Brigitte Bedos-Rezak, "The Social Implications of the Art of Chivalry: The Sigillographic Evidence (France 1050–1250)," in *Form and Order in Medieval France*, VI, 15.

[49] Adrian Ailes, "The Knight's Alter Ego: From Equestrian to Armorial Seal," in *Good Impressions*, eds. Adams, Cherry, and Robinson.

and vice-comital seal legends could include *miles* among the honorific words of self-description.[50] These dukes, counts, and *vicomtes* were proudly declaring themselves to be knights, using technical terminology no less than equestrian, military imagery. As the social pyramid broadened in this period, the sheer number of armorial seals increased, though near the top of the heap great lords continued to represent themselves in person, in armor, and on horseback, galloping across battlefield or tourney ground.[51] Military function (or at least its leadership) has acquired genuinely elite status. Likewise, it seems obviously significant that even kings and great lords accepted this knightly self-representation.

Although increasing numbers of armorial seals provide valuable evidence of social change,[52] interpretation of this evidence need not hurry us into imagining an imminent demilitarization of the medieval lay elite. Undoubtedly, some of those newly claiming knightly status were not strenuous knights, eager for battle and tourney, always within easy reach of well-fitting, finely polished armor and sharpened weaponry. Men who saw themselves primarily as administrators and courtiers, and who were beginning to claim knighthood, will concern us even more in our third chivalric phase. But as we have already noted, a military function was in no danger of waning and there was no dearth of active, strenuous knights. Men ready and willing to use swords would be required for quarrels between Plantagenet and Capetian rulers, crusades (in Spain, southern France, and the Holy Land), revolts against kings and great lords, open civil wars, seigneurial wars, interurban and intraurban rivalries, English conquests in Wales and Ireland (along with attempts in Scotland), German expansion to the east, and contests for control in Scandinavia. If genuine war was lacking at any point – or while it was progressing – tournament continued as extreme sport. To a significant degree this fighting

---

[50] Bedos-Rezak, "Social Implications of the Art of Chivalry," 18.

[51] A helpful sample of seals from across Europe, preserved in Flemish archives, appears in Germain Demay, *Inventaire des sceaux de la Flandre* (Paris, 1873). The collection is not limited to seals of Flemish origin. I am grateful to the International Museum of Photography, Rochester, NY, for providing access to this book.

[52] Use of seals in general spread to townsmen, the lower clergy, and even some peasants. Adrian Ailes speculates that some of these men did not have active military careers, did not tourney or go on crusade, and may have been reluctant to show themselves as active knights: comments in Adams, Cherry, and Robinson, *Good Impressions*, 9.

would continue to employ knights, though many companies of their social inferiors would be employed, armed with bows, spears, or the humble shovels of sappers and miners. Everywhere, local violence, almost beyond formal labels, erupted to forestall or punish pesky neighbors. Dress rehearsals for the Hundred Years War, so to speak, appeared in the Anglo-French war for Aquitaine in the late thirteenth century and the war of Saint-Sardos in the early fourteenth century. The function of fighting continually recruited elite males. Whenever and wherever the trumpet sounded, it regularly generated ample responses.

Representation on tomb monuments

The spreading network of men representing themselves as knights likewise appeared in the vast numbers of tomb monuments – both three-dimensional effigies carved in stone or cast in metal, and representations depicted on sheets of incised brass set into stone slabs or on etched stone slabs placed as tomb covers.[53] Though no longer extant in the thousands originally created, surviving examples document the social rise of men who continued to represent themselves as armored knights. Some examples speak to lives of military vigor; others may simply point to the social cachet of armor. The very fact of interment within the walls of a cathedral, a parish church, or the precincts of a monastery provides significant social insight, for the knights were the first nonroyal lay burials permitted within a church (rather than in the surrounding graveyard). If we could observe the funeral pomp that ushered their bodies to the grave, we would be witness to great warhorses loaded with colorful armor led snorting down church aisles, all (or their money equivalent) to be donated to the church as a burial tax.[54] If some effigies and memorial brasses remain in situ, others are known only from drawings that antiquarians made early enough to record monuments later ravaged by wars and revolution, or those ruined merely by centuries of accident or wear.[55] Significantly, elite male effigies constructed from the early thirteenth

[53] Examples can be viewed at http://effigiesandbrasses.com, where searches by time and region are possible.
[54] M. G. A. Vale, *Piety, Charity and Literacy among the Yorkshire Gentry* (York: Borthwick Papers, 50, 1976), 11–12.
[55] Judith Hurtig, *The Armored Gisant* (New York: Gerland, 1979), utilized 2,000 drawings of French tomb effigies begun in 1695; François-Roger de Gaignières,

century through the remainder of the traditional Middle Ages (and beyond) regularly appear in armor. Judith Hurtig notes that the workmanship on French tombs shows considerable variation in artistic quality; much of the work, in fact, was mediocre, suggesting that many patrons were of no great wealth or position.[56] Nigel Saul comments that by the end of the thirteenth century the surge in secular effigies in England "attests the extension of patronage to the increasingly self-conscious knightly or gentry class."[57] By the time English arms were triumphing in the Hundred Years War, the effigies, in Saul's words, "became a medium for the expression of the collective glory of the military elite."[58]

Monumental brasses gained popularity somewhat later in the thirteenth century, but may have been even more popular (and affordable): many thousands once graced the interiors of churches across Europe, but they have survived in quantity only in England. An inquisitive visitor who lifts a rug in many an English parish church will fortunately find a stunning brass inset into the stone slab covering a tomb.[59] If the surviving sample from England can be taken as representative, the evidence from memorial brasses reinforces that from three-dimensional effigies: through the thirteenth century and beyond, they overwhelmingly represent elite lay males in increasingly elaborate armor. Many of these brasses also display family coats of arms, sometimes, in the case of a double burial, providing the arms of both husband and wife. Whether on flat brass plates or on raised monuments, those enjoying or claiming knighthood wanted to be seen in armor as a clear indication of status.

Heraldry

All these streams of evidence on self-presentation of status (often linked with function) lead easily into a consideration of heraldry,

---

"Les Tombeaux de la collection Gaignières: Desains d'archéologie du xviie siècle," ed. Jean Adhemar, *Gazette des Beaux Arts* 84 (1974), 1–192.

[56] Hurtig, *The Armored Gisant* (New York: Gerland, 1979). She provides hundreds of photographs and drawings of effigies. I am indebted to her for a useful telephone conversation about this topic.

[57] Nigel Saul, *English Church Memorials in the Middle Ages* (Oxford, 2009), 208.

[58] Ibid., 225.

[59] A splendid source of images and scholarship appears in the regularly series *Bulletin of the Monumental Brass Society*.

which began its long life in this same period of chivalric history and flourished for many generations.[60] From the early decades of the twelfth century, purely decorative patterns on shields began to take on specific roles in identifying and glorifying particular knights and, in time, their families. The maturing – or at least increasing self-consciousness – of tournament in these same decades can be no mere coincidence.[61] Knowing who delivered the shattering blow, who unhorsed whom, became hugely important to the participants and, as they became a part of this hard sport, to spectators. And if prize-winning and potential patronage depended on easy identification of individuals clashing in a confused melee and swirling clouds of dust, distinguishing friends from enemies on the battlefield, of course, could be a matter of life and death – or at least of sacred honor – for the participants.

Of course, motivations involving social status reinforced – and in time overwhelmed – sheer military need for identifying insignia. Soon these insignia came to identify a family line as increased emphasis fell on the male line of descent (which the French term *lignage*). Displaying a coat of arms on shield, surcoat, and even horse trappings represented an assertion of status. As Keen noted, "there was a direct connection between the right to arms and the ancestral possession of fiefs and castles."[62] Showing distinctive arms in tourney or battle was a parallel to impressing these devices into the wax of armorial seals authenticating a document. Both practices involving armorial display were taken up by a wide range within the social elite, from simple knights on the make to the families of great lords (although at the top, as we have seen, specifically military equestrian representations also continued on seal designs).

Unsurprisingly, given its usefulness as a social marker, heraldry flowed swiftly down through the social hierarchy in the course of

---

[60] Examples of heraldic rolls for England can be found at http://www.bl.uk/manu scripts/FullDisplay.aspxef-Add Roll 77720 (Dering Roll, c. 1270–1280) and http:// bodley30.bodley.ox.ac.uk:8180/luna/servlet/detail/ODLodl~1~1~31396~108860: Roll-of-arms–Powell-s-Roll (Powell's roll, MS Ashmole 804 pt. IV, from mid-fourteenth century). For numerous German examples, see http://www.s-gabriel .org/heraldry/german.shtml.

[61] Crouch, *Tournament*, 2–12; Barthélemy, "L"Eglise et le premier tournois," in *Christianisme et chevalerie*, ed. Aurell, 139–149, on issues regarding dating. Tournament will be examined in detail in Chapter 7.

[62] Keen, *Chivalry*, 127.

the twelfth century; it also began the elaboration and intensification that transformed it into a species of medieval learning. Each heraldic device, its positioning of constituent elements, and all colors employed conveyed specific value or meaning. To quote Keen, this "sign language" of a "secular cult" unsurprisingly generated a sort of lay priesthood to act as a "registrars of prowess" and, in general, to manage the arcane discourse of heraldry and to settle the issues inevitably arising from its widespread and assertive use by the proud and the prickly.[63] Heralds played this essential role, though they emerge from shadowy origins only by the late thirteenth century and flourished more grandly in the following century, maintaining a close relationship with the literary culture that sustained chivalry, earning salaries and wearing distinctive livery granted by the masters who employed them. Even in our second chivalric phase, however, a science of signs transmitting elite personal and familial status provides evidence of use.

Entry into chivalry

The same group consciousness and individual claim to status appears in the acts by which knights were made, or at least confirmed, within chivalry (see Figure 3). In the modern popular imagination, all who became knights in the medieval world were dubbed in a standard ceremony outlined in some supposedly universal rulebook known to every knight. The historian's task would be much less arduous were such a view valid. Warrior societies traditionally mark a young man's entry into the group of adult male fighters by some more or less formal ceremony of initiation, as noted in analyzing our first chivalric phase. We saw in that earlier phase the beginnings and transformations of granting of arms. Even in the second chivalric phase the process was not uniform, nor omnipresent. As close studies by Georges Duby, Jean Flori, Maurice Keen, and Max Lieberman have amply shown, however, the mercurial appearance and alterations in knighting ceremonies make them good barometers of transformations of chivalric status in this second broad phase of its development and, as we will see, in the third phase as well. Only a simple ceremony might take place as this second chivalric phase began. The knighting of the Young King by William Marshal comes

[63] Ibid., 139, 142.

Figure 3 Dubbing could take place in any setting – battlefield, camp (as here), palace hall, or church. A hint of its growing cost and complexity appears in this illustration showing a special platform and musicians.

to mind, and it could be reproduced in many battlefield knightings, which could scarcely have involved ritual baths, elaborate and lengthy ecclesiastical blessings, and incense. Yet by the end of the period the occasion became increasingly elaborate and expensive. It might be set at a great court banquet, with scores or even hundreds of young men being knighted along with a king's son.[64] Whatever the setting, a significant feature, insisted upon by Maurice Keen, deserves emphasis: the making of a knight remained essentially a lay ceremony. Popular modern picture books on knighthood may feature idealistic texts or illustrations of ceremonies that give priests the key role within clouds of swirling incense and the sound of sacred

---

[64] For the case of the knighting of the young Edward II, see *Annales Londonienses* in "*Chronicles of the Reigns of Edward I and Edward II*," vol. I, ed. William Stubbs (London: Longman and Co., 1882), 146. Cf. Adam Murimuth, *Adae Murimuth Continuatio Chronicarum; Robertus de Avesbury de Gestis Mirabilibus Regis Edwardi Tertii*, ed. Edward Maunde Thompson (New York: Cambridge University Press, 1889), 9.

chant.[65] Clerics might indeed participate, and some high clerics might on occasion perform the ceremony with their own hands; however, the historical record in general shows the variety of lay settings and occasions and underscores the lack of clerical control; this form of laying on of hands – or a swipe with the flat side of a sword blade, or investiture with a sword, or affixing of gilded spurs – may have paralleled the ordination of a priest, but the officiating hands were almost always those of a layman.

Issues concerning dubbing were prominent in the Iberian kingdoms. Some kings used the knighting ceremony to emphasize their preeminence. In June 1188, Alfonso VIII of Castile knighted the young King Alfonso IX of León as a conclusion to a peace sworn between the two kingdoms. When their relationship soured, however, Alfonso IX emphatically had himself newly knighted; but in this ceremony he girded the belt on himself, insisting that a king could not be knighted by someone less than himself.[66] Fernando III (San Fernando), Alfonso IX's successor as King of León (who was also King of Castile, uniting the two realms), also knighted himself in 1219, his mother taking part in the ceremony.[67] A need to provide clear guidelines about dubbing generated statements in the *Siete Partidas* toward the end of the thirteenth century. Endorsing what is announced as an ancient rule, the law code insists that no man should be crowned king or emperor who has not already been knighted, insists that no man can knight himself, denies women (even a queen or an empress) from knighthood and from dubbing knights.

---

[65] Keen, *Chivalry*, 74. The contrast with the role of ecclesiastics in rites of coronation is striking. Though kings could barely keep a crown on their heads without securing sanctifying chrism from the hands of great bishops at their coronations, men-at-arms could become knights without a priest in sight. Yet the pull of piety and the glorification of formal and elaborate ceremony as an indication of the importance of dubbing appear even in Geoffroi de Charny's idealized description of dubbing; he borrows his description of the knighting ceremony from the *Prose Lancelot*, which presents a thoroughly pious ceremony with confession and Mass and knighting in a church. Even so, all the direction is in the hands of knights who see to the ceremonial bath, the clean bed, and the actual ceremony of dubbing. Though clerical agency must be assumed in the Mass, no priest is actually mentioned, and the clerical role is functionary rather than directive, despite the religious atmosphere. See Kaeuper and Kennedy, *Book of Chivalry*, section 36, 166–171.

[66] Miriam Shadis, *The Queen's Hand: Power and Authority in the Reign of Berenguela of Castile* (Philadelphia: University of Pennsylvania Press, 2012), 33.

[67] Ibid., 106.

Moreover, a man who could not qualify for knighthood himself was barred from creating a knight (including priests, men in religious orders, or the insane).[68]

Yet wherever and precisely however it was conducted, an entry ceremony suggests a clear consciousness of an important and separate group in society for whom status is assured and in whom function is elaborately praised. Even when some men come to think they are simply born into knighthood, the formal investiture of many elite men as knights continues to signify both function and status. It is full of meaning and intense emotion, however elaborate or streamlined the ceremony; the day and the doer are always remembered; and the act takes place in armor and almost always involves a sword guided by the hand of a veteran fighter.

MATURING IDEOLOGY

We will see that chivalric ideology will draw deeply on religious ideas and valorization; yet what we can broadly term courtliness provides another framework that aids in understanding ideas of chivalry. Though it may be more readily recognized in action than abstractly described, courtliness involved ways of thinking, speaking, dressing, and interacting with others (depending on their status). It secured membership in a courtly world. Even – or especially – attitudes about love characterized the elite.[69] In looking at these attributes, we witness what might be termed the secondary characteristics of a complex ideological structure justifying superiority and privilege and requiring deference. If these attitudes and actions seem merely quotidian and in themselves minute, they were endlessly repeated and tirelessly asserted in imaginative literature as crucial to desired elite identity.

The learning needed to establish and perpetuate desired and distinguishing social forms took place in the routine instruction of households to which young elite males were often sent. The process in detail may lie largely beyond our line of sight; but the lively work of Ruth Karras can be joined to close scrutiny of chivalric literature, one major function of which was precisely to purvey lessons on

---

[68] *Siete Partidas*, Part II, Title XI, 422–423.
[69] A topic examined in more detail in Chapter 10.

proper attitudes, speech, and behavior.[70] *Chansons de geste*, as we have
seen, lay out basic warrior values; they served as massive platforms for
household discussions about such issues as loyalty and independence,
piety and anticlericalism, and the proper distribution of revenue-
producing estates on the part of lords (and of appropriate responses
when the process went radically wrong).

A didactic role may be even clearer in romance; at least the
instruction took on new dimensions or addressed new themes on
courtliness. The didactic conversation by which the Lady of the Lake
explains ideal chivalry to the young Lancelot provides only the most
famous and most extensive case in point.[71] Its style of teacher and
pupil, of question and answer, recalls straightforward medieval treatises for basic teaching. Though romances are sometimes denigrated
as "escapist," they actually conveyed to the young and ambitious the
ideals and desirable practices that served as crucial social markers they
would have been eager to acquire. Even undoubted elements of
fantasy served; for what was fondly imagined in superlatives, or
vilified as ignoble in terms larger than life, surely enacted an educational role, even as it provides us with a window on values, however
tinted the glass. Reading any sample of this literature reveals, for
example, the importance of hospitality, with formally polite behavior
and correct conversation; it lays out crucially important greetings and
leave-takings, and shows heroes expressing gratitude with grace and
responding to threats with equal grace. The faulty and the villainous
trip and fall instructively. Piety is rewarded, even if rough-edged
anticlericalism puts in an appearance.

Of course, the picture expands beyond simple didacticism to
vision. The wealth and power of great knights are lovingly described
and exaggerated in a manner that shows their importance and the
absence of any excuse for failing to provide handsome largesse.
An imagined world is spread before the reader like a rich tapestry:
impregnable castle walls and towers soar into the cloudless sky;
sumptuous banquets await witty, beautiful, and stunningly dressed
knights and ladies; rich pavilions grace every forest clearing; armor
glows with gold and gems, while shields with brightly painted

---

[70] See the analysis of Ruth Mazo Karras, *From Boys to Men: Formations of Masculinity in
Late Medieval Europe* (Philadelphia: University of Pennsylvania Press, 2003),
20–67.

[71] *Lancelot-Grail*, II, 57–62.

heraldic devices catch sunlight. There is no rain, not even light drizzle; yet roses are always in full bloom. Each lady encountered is the most beautiful and each new knight introduced is the bravest and possessed of almost unimaginable prowess. Clerics baptize, bless, marry, and bury, but do not seriously interfere with courtly life. If all such hyperbole troubles the literal-minded modern reader (inclined to ask, "Is every lady the fairest?"), does it not parade the ideal world desired by the lay elite? In such details, the fundamental ideals of an *ordo* appear, miniaturized into such details as an ivory chessboard, or a pennant snapping in the breeze while a grotesque dwarf emerges from a pavilion, his very ugliness emphasizing the beauty of the chivalric elect awaiting the next plot twist under canvas.

The lessons and the vision were readily absorbed. Although some exceptional villains lurk and add their own inverse instruction, most of the imagined young elite males hurry to a glittering court, seeking ideal knighthood and beautiful and rich ladies through service to those more powerful and, they hoped, committed to generosity. Perhaps they nearly drooled over the prospect of wealth dispensed in showy displays of the great virtue of generosity. Their worthiness is soon tested on quests that try body and spirit, but their prowess in chance combat, tournament, or war wins luscious ladies and the rolling estates that come with them. Modern realists may claim that the estates attracted them most, but any hint of mere greed is swept under a rich carpet in these stories in which love and honor triumph.

If basic values were purveyed, not all issues were easily resolved; on many points of conduct, epic poets and writers of romance seem deliberately to offer choices or to pose dilemmas or paradoxes – much remains open to debate. The formulas of *sic et non*, pro and contra so common in schooling provided a great mechanism for much medieval instruction in general, and seem to be in play on the pages of literature no less than in the schoolrooms. The texts that knights heard or read presented not simply set templates for behavior, but topics that would animate an evening of earnest conversation. Loyalty can have many objects – is there a clear chivalric hierarchy? What if one must decide between helping a brother or a lady in danger? Combat involves hundreds of scenarios – must sides be equal? Can mounted men attack unhorsed opponents?[72] The list of

---

[72] Numerous specific examples are provided and discussed in R. W. Kaeuper, *Chivalry and Violence*, passim.

topics could easily run on. What constituted proper behavior cannot always have been obvious, and many voices, both from clerics and from fellow knights, could defend one choice or another. Across Europe, many questions of the type that filled Charny's *Demandes* (intended to be debated by the royal French chivalric Order of the Star) appear in works of literature read in courts great and small.[73]

We can also be fairly certain that elite young males were absorbing lessons from experience as they advanced on the upward path to success. That vigor yielded patronage, marriage, and securing of property could scarcely have been lost on them. Nor could they doubt that the process might be uncertain and unfair. We have seen that *chansons de geste* worried over the unfair distribution of lands to worthy arms bearers by those vested with great power. Romance shows a greater sense of security in lay elite property holding, bolstered by a conviction of undoubted cultural superiority. Generally in the pages of romance a legitimate heir is simply assumed to hold his father's estate, and the rise of such men above common life is tirelessly celebrated in acts of love, war, and courtesy. That vigorous exercise of martial virtues brings assured status provides the firm ground on which romance rests.

CHANGING LEGAL STATUS

The self-representation and self-assertion we have been examining – by means of seals, tomb monuments, heraldry, dubbing, and imaginative literature – can be confirmed and extended by other sources. Administrative documents and law codes expand our understanding of the importance of both chivalric status and function through a line of sight that has been less frequently employed. This new evidence can point us toward the increasing association of knighthood, lordship, and noble lineage that will be of considerable import in the transition into our final chivalric phase. Growing governing power, especially that of royal administrations, left deposits of records that show not only the elite social status recognized in knighthood, but

---

[73] Steven Muhlberger provides English translation in *Charny's Men-at-Arms* (Wheaton, IL: Freelance, 2014). For the original French, see Michael Taylor, "A Critical Edition of Geoffroy de Charny's *Livre Charny* and the *Demandes pour la joute, les tournois et la guerre*" (PhD dissertation, University of North Carolina, Chapel Hill, 1977).

also the growing tendency for recognized chivalric status to imply noble rank in legal terms.[74] Royal administrative and legal documents thus provide excellent evidence on another dimension of social position achieved by knighthood.

Although England remains an exception in its lack of a noble rank rooted in law, evidence from English royal documents is particularly clear on knightly social status. The precocity of royal government in England produced massive deposits of parchment records that happily survive, and these documents catch some phenomena we are seeking. The "Constitutio Domus Regis," probably written in 1136, provides a good example, though its author's purpose was to explain the organization of the household of Henry I (1100–1135) just after the king's death. In the midst of mundane details about wages, food rations, which favored men received candles, and who got clear (rather than ordinary) wine or beer (heroically measured in gallons), we learn that officials who ranked as knights received eight pence each day, the hefty going daily rate for knights hired for campaigning, while similar officials who were not knights had to be satisfied with lower pay.[75] Clearly, these knights could claim a distinct status and did not merely exercise a function, though their warrior capacity hovers in the background.

That the claims of knighthood recognized both function and status is clear from lines in the *Dialogus de Scaccario*, written in 1170, for in its explanation of the workings of the English exchequer. The author (who adopts the scholastic form of a written dialogue between master and student) notes the good rate of pay for knights employed in this nerve center of royal administration, and he adds, "for they say that they must needs be equipped with horses and armour, to perform their duties when sent out with treasure."[76] If a note of early bureaucratic competitiveness surfaces, more than once this treatise emphasizes the special consideration owed those possessing the status of knighthood. As the master instructs,

---

[74] In strict terms, nobility is often considered a matter of legal rank, while more amorphous terms such as aristocracy reflect social status not necessarily embedded in law.

[75] The document is printed in translation in Carl Stephenson and Frederick George Marcham, *Sources of English Constitutional History* (New York: Harper & Brothers, 1937), 65–70.

[76] Charles Johnson, ed., trans., *Dialogus de Scaccario* (Oxford, 1955), li.

Note that if the insolvent debtor has ever been knighted, when the other chattels are sold, a horse shall be kept for him, and it must be a made horse, lest a man who is entitled by his rank to ride, should be compelled to go on foot.[77]

Yet we learn that not all of knightly rank are truly vigorous warriors (a topic that will take on even more importance by the later Middle Ages) and that the status of such truly strenuous knighthood counts as superior. Once again, function is not forgotten in the rush to consider status. As the text insists,

But if he is the kind of knight who keeps his armour bright and loves to use it and who has earned the right to be considered a "mighty man of valour," the whole of his personal armour and the necessary horses shall be exempted from distraint [legal seizure], so that when need arises he can be employed on the business of the King and the realm, fully equipped with arms and horses.[78]

If the knight has not managed to clear his debt by the time the exchequer rises, he is to be kept not in the prison awaiting ordinary men, but in some "safe place" to await action on his case by the king or high officials, though sterner measurers are in order if he breaks his pledged word. The king's interests must be served, yet the master exults,

[O]ur glorious king, with memorable nobility, has decreed that a man who has the honour of knighthood and is held by the Sheriff and by his neighbours to be poor, shall not be thrust into prison for his own debt, but kept in free custody.[79]

What was expected of knights in the legal apparatus being created especially during this reign is as important as the privileges they were granted. The English government never commanded a large bureaucracy, but instead relied on participation of locals in administration and law; those of knightly rank were specified for carrying out certain tasks, such as that of the Grand Assize (1179) used to determine the rightful holder of an estate.[80] In mid-thirteenth century, the famous law treatise of Henry of Bracton assumes that men of knightly status will be called on to certify the validity of certain delays (*essoins*) that defendants used as excuses for not

---

[77] Ibid., 111.   [78] Ibid.   [79] Ibid., 117.
[80] This legal measure is discussed in W. L. Warren, *Henry II* (Berkeley: University of California Press, 1977), 352–353.

keeping court appointments.[81] Such important legal and administrative roles would, of course, only increase in the next generations as "knights of the shires" came to represent their county communities in the gradual emergence of parliament. That story is well known, but adds to a sense of the rising status of knighthood.[82] From the reign of Henry III (1216–1272), landowners with a certain income could be required by the crown to take on knighthood and serve the crown in local administration.[83]

Similar evidence appears when we turn to French legal sources. The later chronology of their appearance may result from the slower emergence of such records in France, rather than any slower evolution of chivalric status there. The collection of customary law entitled *Etablissements de Saint Louis* written in 1270 can speak easily of "barons and other knights," suggesting that common attributes of knighthood had spread across elite social levels.[84] The fine for unlawful entry into another's lands, for example, is set at the same level for both barons and knights.[85] One principle in this treatise holds that gentlemen are likely to be of knightly status, though they may not yet have formally taken on that honorable rank; a gentleman not yet knighted can legitimately counter a case brought into court by an opponent by requesting a delay of a year and a day to arrange for the ceremony of dubbing.[86] This famous law book, in fact, displays much sensitivity to issues of distinguishing knightly from common status. Careful rules are set forth for judicial duels (the knight can be mounted if he is the accused; the commoner must fight on foot); and these rules apply to "a knight or other gentleman who could be a knight."[87] In effect, the status and its advantages do not depend on having been formally dubbed, an issue that we will examine more closely in our third chivalric phase. The status of a man's father, however, is considered crucial, for the sons of a knight can become knights, "if they

---

[81] Samuel Thorne, ed., trans., *On the Laws and Customs of England*, 4 vols., vol. IV, 42, 57, 115–130.

[82] John Maddicott, *Origins of the English Parliament, 924–1327* (Oxford University Press, 2010); Peter Coss, *Lordship, Knighthood and Locality: A Study in English Society* (Cambridge University Press, 1991).

[83] Michael R. Powicke, "Distraint of Knighthood and Military Obligation under Henry III," *Speculum* 25 (1950), 457–470.

[84] E. R. P. Akehurst, trans. *The Etablissements de Saint Louis* (Philadelphia: University of Pennsylvania Press, 1996), section 76.

[85] Ibid., bk. II, section 38. [86] Ibid., section 77. [87] Ibid., section 87.

wanted to," even if their mother is a peasant, though the reverse is not true, "for a man ennobles a woman." Solemnly, the text intones that a man making false claim to knighthood should have his emblematic spurs cut off over a dung heap and his property seized.[88] Even the more abstract and ideal attributes of knighthood put in an appearance: knights must deal with excommunicates whose faith is sadly in doubt, "for Holy Church can do no more, it must depend on the help of knights and the secular arm and force."[89] A little poem opening the second book of this treatise calls upon knights to "speak ill of no one ... be an honest counselor ... an honest judge," and it warns that "a knight's honor is diminished in his jurisdiction when he does wrong for a fee."[90] Like imaginative literature, the law books can take on a reforming, didactic tone.

Little more than a decade later, the equally famous treatise of Philippe de Beaumanoir, the "Coutumes de Beauvaisis" (1283), again explicates regional French customary law and reinforces the sense of high knightly social and legal status. Wage scales continue to show relative status: mounted commoners received eight deniers per day (twelve deniers making a sous, twenty sous a livre) and mounted squires could claim two sous, but a knight "with one shield" got five sous, while a more substantial knight banneret could negotiate for five sous for each of the men in his household and ten sous for himself.[91]

Issues of parentage in Beaumanoir are again revealing, with servitude passing from mother to son, though here even a knightly father does not wipe away the sociolegal disability imposed by a peasant mother: "all the children he had by her would be serfs ... refused the rank of gentlemen in that they could not be knights, even though the gentle blood which allows you to be a knight passed from the father." A father whose wife was a commoner but not a serf could produce knightly sons, but this was not true for a gentlewoman and a husband who is not a gentleman; these sons retain some of their gentle status, but cannot hold fiefs, tenure of which, the text claims, is beyond the bounds of commoners.[92] Beaumanoir even recalls (or imagines) a case of a knight marrying a woman he mistakenly thinks is free;

---

[88] Ibid., bk. I, section 134.   [89] Ibid., section 127.   [90] Ibid., p. 114.

[91] E. R. P. Akehurst, trans., *The Coutumes de Beauvaisis of Philippe de Beaumanoir* (Philadelphia: University of Pennsylvania Press, 1992), section 1342.

[92] Ibid., section 1434. Elaborate language in this section reveals the crucial importance of sorting out status.

the lord who knighted one son from that union accused the lad of being unfree, once the mother's status became known. Resourcefully, the new knight claimed that his mother was a serf of the lord who knighted him and who did not at the time know the mother's status. When the case reached the king's court, the ruling held that the lad had been given "the freedom of knighthood" by his lord, who could actually have sued him as a serf illegally freed. Later the text reiterates the absolute opposition between serfdom and knighthood and the principle that fathers confer knightly status, even when their wives are daughters of townsmen or commoners, but never when the wife is servile.[93] Detailed discussion of complexities arising out of inheritance and dower rights when more than one marriage is involved, or when fiefs have been purchased, fill many sections of the book. Such concerns emphasize how thoroughly knights were embedded in noble landholding and the transmission of real property.[94] Of course a knight would hold a court himself, no less than litigate in superior jurisdictions.[95] Knights judged others, whether, for serious offenses, they acted as agents of the crown in England or as possessors of justice elsewhere.

Across the Rhine, strong ideas about knighthood were set forth in the *Saxon Mirror* (*Sachsenspiegel*) written in 1225–1235 by Eike von Repgow. This significant text not only spread its influence throughout German lands, but served "as the most important legal text for all of late medieval Central Europe."[96] The knighthood appears under the book devoted to feudal law, which emphasizes an elevated status. This feudal law does not, the text specifies, apply to "priests, merchants, villagers, women, all who are encumbered in their rights or born illegitimately, as well as those who cannot trace their knightly status to their fathers and grandfathers."[97] Yet when such a person is granted a fief, stake in feudal law comes from the land, even though the possessor cannot pass the fief to heirs or have it renewed by a lord who succeeds the lord who granted it. In fact, those who lack knightly status can be excluded from testifying or adjudicating in a feudal court.[98] Where two men claim an estate, if one litigant enjoys

---

[93] Ibid., sections 1449–1450.   [94] E.g., sections 373, 375, 450–451, 477, 487.

[95] Ibid., section 227, which notes that he may use trial by battle in his court unless the king prohibits this practice.

[96] Maria Dobozy, *The Saxon Mirror: A Sachsenspiegel of the Fourteenth Century* (Philadelphia: University of Pennsylvania Press, 1999).

[97] Dobsozy, *Saxon Mirror*, 143 (bk. IV, 1).   [98] Ibid.

knightly status the case of his opponent is dismissed.[99] Only those within knightly status have the right to refuse to enfeoff someone who lacks such status.[100] Eike von Repgow has already specified what constitutes the military equipment (in dealing with the distribution of goods to a knight's heirs by his widow):

> her husband's sword, his best charger or riding horse with saddle, his best coat of mail and tent, and also the field gear, which consists of an army cot, a pillow, linen sheet, tablecloth, two washbasins, and a towel.[101]

In the case of multiple sons, the oldest gets the sword and then the rest of the gear is to be divided equally; when the sons are under age, "the nearest agnatic relative of equal birth" takes over the gear and the responsibility of acting as guardian until the sons mature.[102]

The *Saxon Mirror* is not solitary evidence. Legislation of the emperor Frederick Barbarossa in 1152 had shown a similar concern for the status given by wearing a sword. Farmers and Jews were prohibited from carrying them. And the desire to project status on the part of lords and knights appears, as John Freed has shown, in such literary productions as the *Codex Falkensteinensis* (prepared between 1164 and 1170), as a set of family documents that included a family portrait, a list of fiefs held, and the family claim to free status, plus a notice about the three chapels in Upper Bavarian castles held by the family. Freed suspects that the head of the family was roughly familiar with Latin.[103]

Across the Pyrenees similar ideas emerged in the great Castilian law code, *Las Siete Partidas*. Written under the direction of Alfonso the Learned (d. 1284), this work addresses most issues that occupied the French texts. Preserving the honor of chivalry through what is termed "excellence of descent"[104] forms a recurring refrain. A "son of quality" (*fijodalgo*, an appellation that later becomes the more familiar

[99] Ibid.
[100] Ibid., 143 (bk. IV, 2). Special sensitivity is shown concerning fiefs that owe military service.
[101] Ibid., 76 (bk. I, 22). The widow is excused if she swears she does not possess these items.
[102] Ibid. (bk. I, 23).
[103] John B. Freed, "The Creation of the *Codex Falkensteinensis* (1166): Self-Representation and Reality," in *Representations of Power in Medieval Germany 800–1500*, ed. Björn Weiler (Turnhout: Brepols, 2006), 189–210.
[104] *Las Siete Partidas*, trans. Samuel Parsons Scott, ed. Robert I. Burns, 5 vols. (Philadelphia: University of Pennsylvania Press, 2001), vol. 2, 418.

term *hildago*) can only descend, through many generations (the more the better), from noble males, "in the direct line from father and grandfather as far as the fourth degree, which is that of the great-grandfather."[105] Chivalric qualities are considered genetic (as they are in romance), for the right male bloodline produces those who naturally avoid shame and strive for honor. Since, as the code insists, "[m]en ... obtain the greater part of their excellence of descent through the honors of their father,"[106] the son of a *fijodalgo* born to a woman "of inferior rank" will still be considered a *fijodalgo*, but not a nobleman. To be a nobleman requires a *fijodalgo* and a *fijodalga* as parents, "for the greatest contempt that can befall anything that is honorable is when it is so mingled with what is vile that it loses its own name and acquires that of the other."[107] Engaging in mercantile activity could impart the vile stain: "We also decree that a man should not be created a knight who travels for the purpose of engaging in trade."[108] In fact, open trading constituted a cause for degradation from the honor of knighthood.[109]

The text also applies praise to the order of knighthood with a trowel: they possess energy, honor, and power; they embody the cardinal virtues of prudence, fortitude, temperance, and justice; their habits and manners are superior to commoners; though powerful and brave, they are said to be gentle and humble; their loyalty is displayed both in personal reliability and in hierarchical deference.[110] Who could ask for more? The flow of praise carries function, status, and ideology forward in its rush.

The right to make war could complicate relationships with kings climbing toward sovereignty. Throughout continental lands (in contrast, once again, with England), knights legally made war, a right claimed and often exercised. If this right seems to modern sensibilities the opposite of legal procedure, such a view would have surprised the privileged men we are studying. This right carried knights legitimately into action in what is often loosely termed private war, or what Justine Firnhaber-Baker terms seigneurial war. In medieval France, the use of armed force could be considered simply an extension of a knight's right to jurisdiction. The *Etablissements de Saint Louis* helpfully provides exact legal language to be used when making such an expedition. Royalism appears also, as the text prudently insists that

---

[105] Ibid. [106] Ibid., 419. [107] Ibid. [108] Ibid., 423. [109] Ibid., 432.
[110] Ibid., 518–521.

before he joins any superior's fight against the king, a vassal must carefully determine the truth of his lord's claim that he has been denied justice by the crown.[111]

Beaumanoir supplies an entire chapter on "private" war. In clear language he outlines the principle: "gentlemen can make war according to our customs";[112] but he drops these potent words into a subordinate clause and, showing the love of order characteristic of legists, hurries on to suggest that a judge should try to settle the matter before the fighting begins. He largely fills this chapter with means of containing the violence and ending the licit war through agreements or truces, even suggesting that the fight be condensed into a judicial duel between the principal lords. This emphasis on remedial action, of course, emphasizes the problem represented by a martial right, vigorously asserted. Insistently he intones that "no one but gentlemen can make war. Therefore we say that war cannot be made between commoners and gentlemen."[113] In fact, in order to achieve their desires, gentlemen seem to have managed simultaneously to hold their noses and to fight against townsmen and even clerics in cathedral chapters.[114] But the idea of their exclusive right is emphasized by the insistence that war can only involve gentlemen. Indeed, the impulse to take violent steps was fueled by the powerful engine of honor, and it is useful to recall Pitt-Rivers's stern dictum that "the ultimate vindication of honour lies in physical violence." We are confronted not simply by abstract legal right, but by a social and even a psychological impulse of immense force.[115]

The most striking evidence on such issues to come from German imperial authority appears in the *Liber Augustalis* (or *Constitutions of Melfi*) promulgated for the kingdom of Sicily (including the territory on the Italian peninsula below the papal states) in 1231 by Frederick II. These laws (extending previous Norman legislation) promulgated

[111] Akehurst, trans., *Etablissements*, bk. I, sections 52–53, and bk. II, section 38.
[112] Akehurst, *Coutumes*, 612; his chapter includes sections 1667–1688 and is followed by a chapter on truces and *asseurements*.
[113] Ibid., 612.
[114] A classic case appears in the long-standing conflict between Giles de Busigny and the clerics of St-Géry, Cambrai, studied by Robert Fossier, "Fortunes et infortunes paysanes au Cambrésis a la fin du XIIIe siecles," *Economies et sociétés au moyen âge* (Paris, 1973).
[115] Pitt-Rivers, "Honour and Social Status," in *Honour and Shame in Mediterranean Society*, ed. Peristiany.

a high sense of royal authority. The aim, as James Powell interprets this legislation, was "born of the need to show the king as the alternative to a violent society in which the privileged groups were free of restraint."[116] In a fundamental declaration, the *Constitutions* specify

that no one ought to vindicate himself in the future on his own authority for injuries and excesses already done or to be done and that no one should make attacks or reprisals or cause war in the kingdom, but he should prosecute his case before the master justiciar and the justiciars of the provinces.[117]

Obviously, all was not as neat as the law books might suggest, useful though their evidence has been. As even their language reveals, function, status, and ideology were in some cases drifting in slightly different directions. By the later thirteenth century new social levels were incorporated within the elite of old and established ranks. Above the peasantry in France strode (with increasingly bold steps) gentlemen, knights not yet formally dubbed, those who had been dubbed, barons, counts, and dukes. All might call themselves knights with some pride; some at the lower end of the chain might consider knighthood more a desired social status than a functioning profession of arms. In England this shift may have been especially evident. Though royal service there often required active governing roles to be played by knights, the crown accepted men of elite status who were not strenuous or dubbed knights for its many administrative and judicial tasks. And across Europe, armies were assuredly not formed exclusively of men who had formally entered into chivalry. Large numbers of footmen were required, and mercenaries – mounted or not, knighted or not – were enthusiastically recruited by all ambitious lords and kings. The degree of slippage among function, status, and ideology by the late thirteenth century varied region by region, and each case could be studied intensely.

---

[116] James M. Powell, *The Liber Augustalis; or, Constitutions of Melfi Promulgated by the Emperor Frederick II for the Kingdom of Sicily in 1231* (Syracuse, NY: Syracuse University Press, 1970), xxv.

[117] Ibid., 14. Powell argues in his Introduction to these laws that superior noble rights in law were accepted where they did not increase violence or impinge on crown prerogatives. Although the nobility were permitted to bear arms within the kingdom, severe restrictions were placed on the bearing of arms by nobles who were not members of the royal curia (xxxii). Once brought under its control, the nobility were considered a pillar of the crown (xxxi).

Yet if such undertakings must await the heroic efforts of specialists in every corner of Europe, an attempt to understand the general pattern remains important. Chivalric components came together more coherently in the twelfth and thirteenth centuries than at any other time; yet by the end of this phase new movements can already be sensed.

In the age of growth represented by the High Middle Ages, chivalry implanted its ideals and practices within the lay elite. As the social pyramid continually broadened in these centuries, all the socially ambitious among the laity felt the irresistible draw of chivalry, a process that would continue throughout our third period. Courtiers more interested in parchment records than in tournament records longed to be termed knights; bustling merchants in towns across Europe read romance and admired knightly trappings; some actually donned armor and fought or proudly jousted; even church-men who never quite managed to condemn the world adopted secondary characteristics of chivalry and sometimes even rode in the front ranks.[118] The social status and even the degree of common-ality achieved by the chivalrous in this central period of medieval history were real. Witnesses to this significant process appear plenti-fully in their meticulous seal images, in tomb effigies and memorial brasses, in the science of heraldry, in legal and administrative texts, and in a corpus of imaginative literature vast beyond measure.

---

[118] Craig Nakashian, "A New Kind of Monster ... Part-Monk, Part-Knight: The Paradox of Clerical Militarism in the Middle Ages" (PhD dissertation, University of Rochester, 2009). Note also the classic case of Bishop Gaudry of Laon and the urban population of that town as discussed by Guibert of Nogent: John Benton, ed., *Serf and Society in Medieval France.*

5

PHASE THREE: CHIVALRY BEYOND FORMAL KNIGHTHOOD

•

Chivalry did not suddenly wither and die in the final, traditional medieval centuries. Strenuous combat involving knights in full battle armor could be attested by the classic account of Philippe de Commynes (d. 1511).[1] It could be even more personally attested by the Burgundian lord Louis de la Tremoille in 1525, if we could interview him before the fatal shot on the battlefield of Pavia ended his intensely chivalric life, at that point devoted to the ill-fated French campaign in northern Italy. He died in a full suit of armor and with a full sense of religious no less than royal blessing upon his life's work.[2]

The ideas and ideals of chivalry so evident in Louis's life still permeated the general cultural atmosphere. Christine de Pizan wrote a much-appreciated work, *The Book of Deeds of Arms and of Chivalry*, in the vernacular in the early fifteenth century. Romances, likely reaching an even broader audience than ever, blossomed in such late – and very large – blooms as Matteo Maria Boiardo's *Orlando Innamorato* (1495), Ludovico Ariosto's *Orlando Furioso* (1532), and Edmund Spenser's *Faerie Queene* (1590, 1596).[3] Formal dubbing to

---

[1] *The Memoirs of Philippe de Commynes*, ed. Samuel Kinser, trans. Isabelle Cazeaux (Columbia: University of South Carolina Press, 1969).

[2] *Le Panegyric du chevalier sans reproche, ou Memoires de la Tremoille, par Jean Bouchet*, in *Collection complete des mémoires relatifs a l'histoire de France*, ed. M. Petitot, XIV (Paris: Foucault, 1820). I intend to devote a short study to this text and the career of Louis.

[3] The continuing popularity of romance form is apparent in – though not limited to – such massive works as *Orlando Furioso* of Ludovico Ariosto, *Orlando Innamorato* of Matteo Maria Boiardo, and *The Faerie Queene* of Edmund Spenser.

knighthood lasted throughout the fourteenth and fifteenth centuries and beyond, as could be attested by witnesses who stood on the crowded deck of the *Golden Hind* when a kneeling Francis Drake was knighted by Queen Elizabeth I in 1581.[4]

Yet during its final phase – as was true in earlier phases – if important elements of chivalry persisted, significant changes affected the fit of chivalry within its changing social context. That these centuries could generate changes in chivalry can come as no surprise. The age experienced seemingly endless war funded by effective systems of taxation; these conflicts occurred during a time of economic and demographic contraction. Royal power underwent severe modulations, and even when it was doing well faced problems of public order that persisted and seemed beyond its control, if not a by-product of its actions; beyond any scale of human agency, terrifying and destructive plague ravaged Europe. On the brighter side, new intellectual currents swirled around thinkers as winds of neoclassicism swept through the quiet nooks where scholars and writers pondered issues of sovereignty, war and peace, theology, and canon and civil law, and wrote both learned and more popular treatises, often with clear messages for the chivalrous.[5]

Although generalization remains as difficult as ever, two basic changes within the cosmos of chivalry will be the focus of the first two sections of this chapter. These changes seem obviously important, yet also seem to move in contradictory directions. On one hand, we can follow indications of constriction in the numbers of those unquestionably considered by elite members of their society to constitute the chivalrous. The portals giving entry to formal knightly status, that is, narrowed under the close guard of aristocrats who were fully conscious of the increasing link between chivalry and noble legal standing. The gatekeepers, at least those on the continent, strove to restrict so prized a status; gate-crashers or wall climbers had to be kept from forcing their way into the club unbidden.

Yet, in a second major direction of change, our evidence shows a significant expansion of a less formal knighthood; chivalric ideals

---

[4] Harry Kelsey, *Sir Francis Drake: The Queen's Pirate* (New Haven: Yale University Press, 1998), 218.
[5] Analyzed in Craig Taylor, *Chivalry and the Ideals of Knighthood* (Cambridge University Press, 2014), passim.

and valorization were reaching even beyond knighthood defined in a formal sense as a badge of nobility acquired by dubbing or simply possessed by noble birthright. Late in the thirteenth century, Ramon Lull proclaimed that "nobility is nothing less than a continuation of ancient honour," and saw nobility and chivalry as inextricably bound together: "if you make a man who is not noble a knight, you are making nobility and Chivalry opposites by what you are doing."[6] Yet he grants that "the Order of Chivalry permits that through many noble habits and deeds and through the nobility of some prince, any man of a new, honourable lineage may attain Chivalry."[7] He was recognizing social reality and princely practice; and some men who had never knelt to be dubbed and who could not claim to view the world from atop a tall family tree nevertheless considered themselves members of the great order of chivalry. Arguably, they found inspiration in aspects of its ethos and saw themselves and their professional labor of arms illuminated by its glow, even valorized by its religious blessings. Other men, who offered services to the powerful as desirable agents of administration, law, or finance, ardently wanted and thought they deserved chivalric status.

Another major factor, the role of the state and its powers, increased in influence though they did not suddenly originate in this era. Revived classical ideas strengthened the abstract case that could be made for sovereign power and bolstered its claims to discipline military force through its agents. A third section of the chapter is devoted to understanding these important developments in governing power and ideals unfolding throughout the fourteenth and fifteenth centuries.

A final section of the chapter brings the themes together. It briefly argues for closing the study not at some sudden decade marking chivalric death and not even as supposed waning and vaporous irrelevancies show the disappearance of chivalry as a force in the European world. The end comes rather by transformation and virtual absorption by rising state power. Many of the forms we associate with

---

[6] Fallows, trans., Llull, *Book of the Order of Chivalry*, 58.
[7] Ibid. Llull justifies this degree of openness by arguing, "And if this was not the case, it would follow that Chivalry would be more suited to the nature of the body than the virtue of the soul, and that is not true, for the nobility of courage that is suited to Chivalry is suited better to the soul than to the body."

chivalry lasted beyond the traditional confines of the medieval world, but their meaning had become significantly redirected.

NARROWING OF FORMAL KNIGHTLY RANKS

Individuals and families interested in an exclusive and narrowed chivalry ideally preferred to admit only those recognized as noble and especially those of nobility old enough to require regular dusting. The ideal qualifying family tree would be old, tall, and well-fruited. Of course, those who now wanted exclusive right to chivalry to be reserved in this manner for themselves and similar families deeply revered ancestors of several centuries past who, as we have seen in looking at the earliest phase of chivalry, had been doubtful that the designation *miles* provided a sufficient marker of their societal rank and superiority. History is at times a study in irony slowly unfolding.

If the aristocratic effort was not startlingly new in the fourteenth and fifteenth centuries, it did then take on renewed vigor. Dubbing continued to usher some young men into chivalric status and career; yet it had become a complex and costly ceremony, more easily managed by the great and satisfyingly rich, who could afford its lavish display. We have noted that the thirteenth-century French law book the *Etablissements de Saint Louis* insisted that a man of status be given a year of respite from lawsuit in order to arrange this formal entry into knighthood.[8] For many with clear title to nobility, however, the male family line itself, the *lignage*, gave sufficient license for an easy assertion of knighthood, with formal dubbing only an option, rather than a requirement. At mid-fourteenth century, Geoffroi de Charny noted that men might be formally knighted at the beginning or end of a chivalric career.[9] Don Pero Niño was knighted when he was well into his career and had already put many a nick in the trusty sword he sent as a gift to his lady.[10] Maurice

---

[8]   *The Etablissements de Saint Louis*, trans. A. R. P. Akehurst (Philadelphia: University of Pennsylvania Press, 1996), 51, section 77.
[9]   Kaeuper and Kennedy, *Book of Chivalry*, 170–171. He worries that some will seek knighthood for the wrong reasons, but grants "ancient" men a role as guides for the young.
[10] He was knighted by the King of Castile after returning from his adventures in the north. Evans, 190–191; Carriazo, 288–289.

Keen argued the optional quality of formal dubbing, noting that there was

a tendency to lay rather less emphasis upon the ceremony of initiation into knighthood and rather more upon eligibility to take knighthood, this coming to be regarded as principally dependent upon noble lineage. No man who cannot point to knights in his ancestry should be considered eligible to be made a knight.[11]

Even if great men conservatively followed tradition and saw their sons elaborately dubbed, they were sure a knight was born even more than he was made. By this time nobility, in the uncompromisingly direct words of Keen, "boasted no right of initiation beyond the childbirth pangs of a noblewoman."[12]

This proud aristocratic emphasis gave a general tonality to later medieval society, as is well known.[13] Cultural markers and signs of exclusivity appear throughout the upper layers of the social pyramid. Among elite arms bearers an effort was made to limit participation in tournament to those with suitable family background; four generations of nobility were sometimes stipulated. In his celebrated *pas d'armes* Jacques de Lalang (d. 1453) offered to joust against all who could claim four aristocratic grandparents. Proudly he displayed banners proving such antiquity within his own lineage.[14] Legal regulations on possession of fiefs as a qualifier for knighthood continued in force. Sumptuary laws tried to regulate the clothing that publicly identified each social rank.[15] Viewed from the apex of society, chivalry seemed to be passing through a social funnel fitted with a strong filter; only a pure remnant would pass through and remain.

---

[11] Keen, *Chivalry*, 143. The principle had appeared in the first half of the thirteenth century in an ordinance of Frederick II.

[12] Keen, *Chivalry*, 146, drawing upon the German historical idea of *Berufstand*.

[13] On the importance of later medieval signs of status, see William Blockmans and Antheun Janse, eds., *Showing Status: Representations of Social Position in the Later Middle Ages* (Turnhout: Brepols, 1999) for the Low Countries; for Iberia, see John Edwards, *Christian Córdoba: The City and Its Regions in the Late Middle Ages* (Cambridge University Press, 1982), 131–164.

[14] Georges Chastellain, "Le livre des faits du bon chevalier Messire Jacques de Lalang," in *Oeuvres de Georges Chastellain*, ed. Dervyn de Lettenhove (Brussels: Heussner, 1866), 189–197, 201–237, discussed in Ruth Karras, *From Boys to Men* (Philadelphia: University of Pennsylvania Press, 2003), 31.

[15] Catherine Kovessi Killarby, *Sumptuary Laws in Italy 1200–1500* (Oxford University Press, 2002); Alan Hunt, *Governance of the Consuming Passion* (New York: St. Martin's Press, 1996).

TOWARD AN EXPANDED AND MORE INFORMAL CHIVALRY

Civilian recruits

Of course the aristocratic effort to close ranks and exclude interlopers, however vigorously it was conducted, could not succeed. Plentiful evidence records the lack of desired results. In fact, the very effort at exclusivity likely whetted appetites among those who longed for higher status and labored ceaselessly to achieve it. The higher the restrictive wall rose, the longer the ladders brought by swelling numbers of those eager to surmount the wall and enter into the Promised Land. Some of these hopefuls were active fighters in the warfare of the period; others were essentially civilians rather than warriors.

Civilians among the climbers may have received the most attention as a relatively new or increasingly visible force in this world and one that may appeal to the sensibility of scholars. If the most direct approach to achieving the status of knighthood would be to exercise military virtue in service to a lord or the lord king (a path we will explore later), these lords and kings had need of many types of services, not all of them military. Men with appropriate talents earned the blessing of princes and received patronage from superiors glad for their service and sometimes eager for their loans. Geoffroi de Charny, however, deliberately ignored their potential for service and considered these men disreputable, for they

want to have the order of knighthood so that people will say that they are knights and so that they will receive greater attention and honor than they did before; but they do not want to fulfill the true conditions and services of knighthood. For that reason it might be said of these men that they may well have the order of knighthood but not the reputation of being a knight, for men may have the order who are not real knights.[16]

The scorn in his voice comes through almost as clearly as the importance of the phenomenon being slightingly addressed. He complained that such men sought a comfortable life, eating the best food, sleeping in soft beds, wearing elaborate clothing, stylishly playing real tennis. Thought of their timidity curls his lips as he writes of their lack of bold aggression. Such men, we might imagine, opted readily for demonstrating at least second-tier chivalric characteristics,

[16] Kaeuper and Kennedy, *Book of Chivalry*, 170–171.

such as maintaining household display, dispensing largesse in an effectively showy manner, avidly reading the latest romance and knowing how to speak of love, displaying formal courtesy, dressing in the right fashion, and attending – even if not directly participating in – grand tournaments.

Some of them could scale the restrictive wall by climbing up stacked legal tomes or plentiful piles of accounts compiled for their lords; others would have found that this excluding wall was simply crumbling or could be readily toppled by swinging a hefty bag of coin. Sadly, from the nobles' perspective, the best status did not always coincide with the means to support its costly style of life at full display. Despite their desires for exclusivity, the grand needed much clerical help; and when they ran low on sustaining funds, they might succumb to a good marriage alliance with a family of commoners who did not use the right fork (as soon as forks came into use), but who possessed plentiful cash and keenly felt a drive to rise in status. Rich social and psychological complications would result and provide grist for the mills of novelists and playwrights for centuries to come.

The administrators had a long record of success to back their hopes. Medieval England had known "barons of the exchequer" and "knights of the shire" for several centuries. Michael de la Pole offers a good fourteenth-century English case of a successful climber: his father, Sir William de la Pole, was a merchant and an important financier for Edward III; Michael became Chancellor (1383) and was soon made first Earl of Stafford (1385).[17] South of the Pyrenees and Alps, the claims of such men were much older and often closer to social and military reality.

Producing and managing complex administrative and legal systems, of course, represented no radically new phenomenon. Courtiers of multiple talents – adept not only at law, but at finance and administrative structures, their conversation garnished with wit and lubricated with shameless flattery – were certainly not new in the fourteenth and fifteenth centuries; they had already been targets of unmerciful satire in the twelfth century.[18] Walter Map wrote scathingly of the men of ambition and greed who made the court of Henry II resemble hell;

[17] E. B. Fryde, *Michael de la Pole, Merchant and King's Banker* (Hambledon, 1988).
[18] C. Stephen Jaeger, *Scholars and Courtiers* (Burlington, VT: Ashgate, 2002).

Orderic Vitalis had spoken with curled lip of "men raised from the dust" to serve kings in the twelfth century.[19] But able men of this sort represented a growing requirement of governance expanding its reach in society.[20] Famously, lawyers met the need resolutely and happily rested, at the end of busy and lucrative careers, beneath tomb monuments in brass or stone that portrayed them gloriously clad in plate armor. This plate may have been, as Nigel Saul suggests, the first and only suit of armor that many of them had known.[21] They were delighted to become holders of fiefs, to be addressed deferentially with a chivalric "Sir." We are witnessing a world beginning to move toward separation between what French scholars term the nobility of the sword and that of the robe. The old guard of aristocrats may have used simpler and more judgmental terms for the new men. As early as the mid-fourteenth century Charny, as we have seen, growled that "men may have the order who are not real knights."[22] If, at the English court of Elizabeth I, more than two centuries later, one sharp-tongued observer divided that competitive world between the warriors and the civilians, *milites* and *togati*, a bitter conservative labeled the latter *reptilia*, assuring all that he would never crawl to gain favor and patronage as they did.[23] In some early societies, a gap between courtiers and warriors is simply assumed – the early Chinese and Japanese cases come readily to mind, with fighters clearly distinct from a civil service of men trained in Confucian philosophy; but this separation developed more slowly and less completely in medieval Europe. Such a delay likely stemmed from the chivalric brotherhood that had to a significant degree spanned the entire lay, elite spectrum for so long.[24]

---

[19] Discussed in Ralph V. Turner, *Men Raised from the Dust: Administrative Service and Mobility in Angevin England* (Philadelphia: University of Pennsylvania Press, 1988).

[20] James A. Brundage, *The Medieval Origins of the Legal Profession* (Chicago: University of Chicago Press, 2008); Michael T. Clanchy, *From Memory to Written Record* (London: Arnold, 1979).

[21] Nigel Saul, *English Church Monuments*, 237.

[22] Kaeuper and Kennedy, *Book of Chivalry*, 170–171.

[23] Quoted in Richard C. McCoy, *Rites of Knighthood: The Literature and Politics of Elizabethan Chivalry* (Berkeley: University of California Press, 1989), 76.

[24] See, for example, *Courtiers and Warriors: Comparative Historical Perspectives on Ruling Authority and Civliization*, ed. Kasaya Kazuhiko (Kyoto: International Research Center for Japanese Studies, 2004), published in Japanese and English.

In short, if social change in general worked against aristocratic knightly exclusivity, our evidence shows some governmental policies encouraging the same result. At the end of the Middle Ages, in the ideal royalist vision of the world, kings were the prime movers of chivalry and nobility; they drew the ceremonial sword and dubbed knights.[25] Malcolm Vale speaks of the creation of "national chivalry" and argues that by 1520 dubbing was restricted to the crown in France.[26] Old noble families, of course, had long viewed the world differently, but in a portentous move, sovereigns began to issue documents creating nobility, providing official letters formally elevating into that rank those they wished to favor even if they and their progeny ranked as commoners. Of course, once again the process had important precedents; kings had long created nobles; but the favored ones of earlier eras were usually within at least the charmed elite circle; a few men of standing elevated to even higher and more formal rank could be grudgingly accepted by the old guard. Elevating those who were not obvious candidates sometimes generated active hostility and attempts to bring the newcomers down; radically raising the status of mere favorites could be costly, as Edward II, Piers Gaveston, and Hugh Despenser the Younger learned in England. Similar lessons were taught in Castile where Álvaro de Luna, a favorite of Juan II who served as constable and effectively ruled for the king, was arrested and executed.[27] During the later Middle Ages more numerous creations of nobility spanning a wider social gap could generate political opposition. Rulers were setting foot on the path that would broaden into a veritable highway over time, leading to what has been termed "the inflation of honours."[28] Early modern kings actually sold nobility outright. Other governing bodies were already on this path or at least were creating nobles and knights by official fiat. By the early fourteenth century, northern Italian urban governments were elevating "knights of the commune" (mainly honorific and for nonmilitary

---

[25] Usefully discussed in Keen, *Chivalry*, 145–146.

[26] Vale, *War and Chivalry*, 168.

[27] Nicholas Round, *The Greatest Man Uncrowned: A Study of the Fall of Don Alvaro de Luna* (London: Tamesis Books, 1986).

[28] Lawrence Stone, "The Inflation of Honours," *Past & Present* 14 (1958).

service). Florentine evidence, for example, shows that knighthood and nobility were matters of concern and even of regulation by the city government.[29] In Spain, a category of *caballeros villanos*, or municipal knights, had long existed and has sparked debate over the goals of these men and the nature of their service. Were they truly vigorous military men, or did they merely seek the legal and social benefits of knighthood?[30]

It seems that in general well-established aristocrats resisted intrusions and intruders for generations to come, but could not block a rising social tide. New groups within the broadly elite layers of society were edging into the honored status of knighthood.

Military aspirants to chivalry

An expanded and more informal knightliness did not depend solely on the nonmilitary men whose climb we have been observing, the men Charny hated, the lawyer-administrators and merchant-bankers who longed for chivalric status without undertaking the classic chivalric function of fighting, with all its dangers. Many fighting men who were active and successful but who could claim to be only marginally elite in origins wanted to stand among chivalrous ranks; they took on the coloration of chivalry as fully as they could, drawn by its radiant glow and hopeful of bolstering wealth and social status. John Hawkwood (Figure 4) provides only the most famous and most successful such career, rising from modest

---

[29] Peter Sposato, "Nobility, Honor and Violence: Knighthood and Chivalry in Florentine Tuscany, 1200–1450" (PhD dissertation, University of Rochester, 2014).

[30] See Jesús Rodríguez-Velasco, *Order and Chivalry*, trans. Eunice Rodríguez Ferguson (Philadelphia: University of Pennsylvania Press, 2010), 49–53, for a case that these men did keep arms and horses because they were legally required to, "but their defensive role had given way to a role in production, generally in commerce and agriculture." Rodríguez-Velasco is taking issue with this. Teofilo Ruiz is willing to blur the lines of urban and rural, in society at large as well as for divisions of knights. Ruiz, *From Heaven to Earth* (Princeton: Princeton University Press, 2004) and *Sociedad y poder real en Castilla: Burgos en la baja Edad Media* (Barcelona: Ariel, 1981). Another viewpoint is that the divisions of late medieval knights based on class were not fundamentally different in their function but that all of them, from the high nobility through the *caballeros villanos* and down to the men-at-arms, rarely manifested their martial calling, the only real exception being in the war against Granada. See María Concepción Quintanilla Raso, *Nobleza y caballería en la Edad Media* (Madrid: Arcos Libros, S.A., 1996).

Figure 4 The English mercenary John Hawkwood (d. 1394) was so valued by the city
of Florence that he was provided a prominent memorial in the Florentine Duomo.
Hawkwood (Acuto to the Italians) represents a classic late medieval case of social
climbing through warrior capacity.

beginnings in England through successful combat in the Hundred
Years War and then transferring his talents to Italy, where city-states
bid for his services. He had been knighted, though when, where,
and under what circumstances remain unknown, and he received
the unusual honor of being made a citizen of Florence. Hawkwood

charts a stunning rise.[31] If a count and a calibration of all other
mercenary careers is impossible, a clear impression of the number of
at least lesser men on the rise remains impressive; it stands out in
relation to the civilian recruits.[32] Constant warfare opened doors,
and a significant body of tough and able men could see a path to
success as willing fighters for the lord king, or for a local lord (or
a series of lords, individual or collective); they would fight for pay
on campaign or garrison duty. Anglo-French warfare encouraged
considerable numbers of such men. Nicholas Wright has estimated
that only 10 percent of the combatants in the Hundred Years War
were formally knighted fighters.[33] The rest of the men-at-arms
either considered their knighthood self-evident, given their eminent families, or assumed – with whatever degree of thrusting
ambition they possessed – that since they were carrying out knightly
functions they formed a part of the knighthood.

An expansion of warfare that drove the expansion of chivalry fed
on maturing state finance. The symbiosis was apparent by the late
thirteenth century, and the persistence and scale of combat increased
as the Hundred Years War swept as fitfully as a tornado across France,
the largest European kingdom for nearly two centuries. It readily
spread into neighboring lands as well. Fighting continued even during formal periods of truce, for war benefited warriors who needed
pay from someone – or who simply paid themselves – whenever it
was necessary or convenient. And the Hundred Years War hardly
exhausts the roster of combat available. Further conflicts troubled
France over issues of succession to the crown; struggles with the
Muslim powers in the Iberian Peninsula continued and intensified
by the second half of the fifteenth century expelled Muslim power;

---

[31] His life is related and analyzed splendidly in William Caferro, *John Hawkwood:
An English Mercenary in Fourteenth-Century Italy* (Philadelphia: University of
Pennsylvania Press, 2004); for his knighting see the discussion at 9.

[32] Kenneth Fowler, *Medieval Mercenaries* (Oxford: Blackwell, 2001); Janin Hunt with
Ursula Carson, *Mercenaries in Medieval and Renaissance Europe* (Jefferson, NC:
McFarland, 2013); David Murphy, *Condottiere 1300–1500: Infamous Medieval
Mercenaries* (Oxford: Osprey Publishing, 2007).

[33] Wright, *Knights and Peasants*, 9. "Of the soldiers who fought during the Hundred
Years War, only a very tiny and declining proportion were knights. Even among
the ranks of soldiers who were called men-at-arms – that is to say, those who
normally fought on horseback with the accoutrements and according to the rules
of chivalric warfare – only about one in every ten had been through some form of
initiation into the ranks of knighthood."

and here, too, internal struggles often opposed competing claims to a crown; fierce urban rivalries troubled the kaleidoscopic political patterns of the Italian peninsula, and urban and regional struggles drew arms bearers into action in German lands. If crusade to the Holy Land was no longer available, German crusaders and their friends rode militantly into Slavic lands. Hope for a new grand crusade to the Holy Land could neither die nor be ignored, even if it could never be implemented.[34] As the Hundred Years War waned, the Wars of the Roses broke out in England. Medieval warfare, we must also recall, was never limited to quarrels between sovereigns or great lords; seemingly perpetual local conflicts became cellular units in wider warfare or ran on their own energies; many local quarrels, we may suspect, were vigorously pursued, even if they left few enduring traces in records of governing agencies or chronicles.

Few historians would doubt that armies grew in size or that campaigns increased in duration; but an objection might hold that larger armies simply meant less chivalry, and that the chivalrous were actually dinosaurs in a changing world of warfare. Were not men armed with longbows, pikes, and early gunpowder weapons the wave of modernity sweeping the knights from battlefields? The best response may be that few people thought so in this period. In fact, knights represented no outdated and irrelevant element of military force in the later Middle Ages. Unceasing warfare still called for their services, even in armies employing growing units of socially inferior footmen. Heavy cavalry forces persisted. Sometimes the humbler men on foot put paid to proud, heavily armored horsemen, as the Flemings proved possible at Courtrai in 1302, the Scots at Bannockburn in 1314, or the English on several famous fields of the Hundred Years War. Yet the "age of chivalry" did not close with the twang of a bowstring or the sulfurous blast of a gun. Chivalry had flourished even when its armor was pierced with crossbow bolts in the twelfth century, as it did despite the pikes and cloth-yard shafts of the fourteenth century, and leaden shot of the fifteenth century. If the English longbow is famous, in other armies other weaponry was esteemed, and most armies included a significant armored and mounted contingent into the Early Modern era. Heavily armored cavalry had a long last inning. Large numbers of

---

[34] See the vain effort to establish Anglo-French peace in the interest of crusade, for example: *Letter to King Richard II*, ed. G. W. Coopland (New York: Barnes and Noble, 1976).

mounted men (with a range of quality in their armor and horses) still rode as one key element whenever armed force responded to trumpet calls.

What is more, the powerful set of ideas and ideals within chivalry continued and even expanded their reach not only among ambitious civilians, but also in the large body of fighting men roughly defined as the military elite. It can occasion no surprise that all men who were even moderately well mounted and armored wanted to assume knightly status and to adorn themselves with aspects of the valorizing ideology of chivalry. They were quite willing to be glorified (and sometimes guided or challenged) by chivalric ideals featured in treatises and works of literature. Any contemporary openly doubting the claim to esquires or dubious gentlemen who had never been dubbed and who lacked a lofty family tree might have experienced dangerous personal consequences. Of course the best-equipped and best-armored cavalrymen could claim noble descent or formal dubbing. Yet all – even the lesser imitators of the great – counted as "lances" when toting up needed and useful military force.[35] The key strategy for a climber was to assume knightly status coming from function. The hope was to hear no mocking laughter from someone already secure in the desired role and powerful enough to laugh publicly.

Men who conducted all this warfare knew that they carried out the central labor of the elite lay order in society, whether or not all aristocratic gatekeepers welcomed them; they wanted a share in the full range of benefits associated with that order, even if they had not been set on this path from birth. Many men, that is, claimed knighthood by acting the part of elite fighters in the seemingly omnipresent warfare of the later Middle Ages. Even those who might be tempted to classify them as mercenaries or *routiers* knew their value on campaign, in battle, or in garrison, and employed them whenever they could scrape up the money. William Caferro has shown how Siena, for example, caught as it was between the military powerhouses of Florence and the papal states (both avid employers of mercenary troops), took every financial measure possible to hire companies of

---

[35] The common usage of the term appears, for example, throughout *The Memoires of Philippe de Commynes*, ed. Samuel Kinser, trans. Isabel Cazeaux (Columbia: University of South Carolina Press, 1969).

mercenaries.[36] The large bands that swept through France in the 1360s, after the Treaty of Bretigny had in theory ended hostilities between the French and the English, gave themselves such grand terms as "*les gens de la Grant Compaigne*" and "*companies d'aventure*," both of which could come from a romance. Captains holding particular fortresses might adopt similarly grand titles.[37] Moreover, these useful forces arrived on the scene in mixed sets as to status: some of those taking pay from almost any source were, in fact, dubbed knights or could claim descent from noble lines, making a general claim to knightly status by others in the group all the more readily advanced since they were likely all taking pay for their work. Caferro has underscored the socially integrative function of the mercenary phenomenon, arguing that it provided "perhaps the most egalitarian spaces in all of fourteenth-century Europe." For the mercenaries coming to the continent, "Service overseas," he notes, "blurred traditional societal markers and distinctions and bound soldiers into the unique position of re-creating themselves."[38] He has presented the career of John Hawkwood as the most outstanding case in point.[39] A body of mercenaries or *routiers* might claim legitimacy by asserting a shaky allegiance to prince or king, though that degree of loyalty might easily shift or largely be imagined. Such men were feared and denounced, and might tellingly be denigrated as merely upstarts who only looked like the true knights of higher status; but they were paid and used by a range of employers from seigneurs at war with neighbors to kings at war with crowned rivals.[40] Even Bertrand du Guesclin, though he might be imagined a knight errant, had actually risen as a highly successful mercenary; Rodrigo de Villandrando, a Spanish mercenary, served as a captain in the French royal army, but was also hired by other powerful men, including the pope; his ravaging of villages was limited by no political

---

[36] William Caferro, *Mercenary Companies and the Decline of Siena* (Baltimore: Johns Hopkins University Press, 1998), passim. He argues that these measures helped to end Sienese independence.

[37] See the discussion and sources cited in Craig Taylor, *Chivalry and the Ideals of Knighthood in France*, 24–25.

[38] Caferro, *John Hawkwood*, 334.   [39] Ibid.

[40] Philippe de Mezieres, *Le songe du viel pelerine*, I, 530–531, cited in Craig Taylor, *Chivalry and the Ideals of Knighthood*, 118. Taylor comments that "of course the line between true knight and mercenary was profoundly unclear in practice." Cf. his similar view at 223.

allegiance, and his conduct did not dim his reputation or tarnish the titles awarded him.[41] The success of the most famous mercenary, John Hawkwood, is to this day memorialized in a mosaic in the Florentine *duomo*.[42]

All such facts might be easily forgotten in our hurry to recognize nonmilitary entrants into the chivalric order or at least its fringes. Complex social change is sometimes taken to indicate that chivalry was being drained of military content and that a warrior core in knighthood had atrophied. Were this line of thought accurate, we could only conclude that a fundamental dimension of chivalry disappeared in the later Middle Ages and that this tough warrior ethos, standing for centuries near the center of the chivalric enterprise, had disappeared. In fact, far from exorcizing the fierce warrior ethos it enshrined, chivalry actually expanded its number of practitioners and broadened the reach of its ideology.

Core concepts for sustaining belief as well as practical guides to behavior reached practicing warriors even on the rough lower edges of elite society. Martial values could join powerfully with cultural and religious values among recruits to this more diffused and less formal knighthood. They could quickly realize that certain attitudes and behaviors constituted a claim to status and merit, valorizing men-at-arms and lavishing praise on their dangerous and destructive work, while justifying it in religious as well as political terms. The entire group of late medieval warriors, ranging from grand princes to captains raiding the countryside from rude hilltop citadels, likely represent the largest body of men claiming to stand within – or at least to edge into – the orbit of chivalry in medieval European history.

Testimony from model knights and their friends

Telling evidence for this continuing vitality of knights in combat and for the social spread of later medieval chivalry could be garnered from those of our model knights active in this period (and from any number of their friends who might willingly join the discussion). Barbour's account of the career of Robert Bruce shows the trend clearly. The Bruce needed all the fighting strength he could gather to overcome Scottish enemies and the massive armed power arrayed

[41] Taylor, *Chivalry and the Ideals of Knighthood in France*, 26, 118–119.
[42] Caferro, *John Hawkwood*, passim.

against him by the kingdom of England. We have seen that broadly chivalric ideals about prowess, loyalty, and honor thus fuse with proto-nationalism in this account, with a distinctly generalizing effect; great lords such as Robert and Edward Bruce and James Douglas lead in raid and battle, but all fighters, from a variety of social ranks, are joined in the labors of campaign and combat; and all are blessed by an approving divinity that rewards hard efforts to secure liberty. Uncompromising demands of a war of independence thus generalize the sense of warrior fellowship and common effort that inevitably takes on important chivalric tonality. Perhaps the most concise statement on this theme is quoted by Barbour from Ingram de Umbraville, a Scots nobleman who is speaking to Edward II, whom he served, after previously serving the cause of independence. Umbraville declares of the men surrounding Robert Bruce,

> His men all worthy ar sa wicht
> For lang usage of fechting
> That has bene nursyt in swilk thing
> That ilk yowman is sa wicht
> Off his that he is worth a knycht.[43]
> [His men are all so valorously worthy
> By their long practice of combat,
> Trained in such practice
> That every man is quite tough.]

Geoffroi de Charny would willingly speak as a second prime witness both for a continuing martial code and for chivalry reaching, with his full approval, a broader swath of lesser, if still elite, fighting men. For a continuing martial function, we need only recall that his *Book of Chivalry*, written at mid-fourteenth century, sets forth an ascending scale of worth based on deeds of greater and more demanding prowess.[44] Equally significant, it comfortably addresses all good men-at-arms, whether or not they are formally knighted or highly born. He finds all such men worthy to hear and heed his message; indeed, he knows they are needed in the great struggle; their honorable careers and meritorious labors at arms are all praiseworthy. No hint of social exclusivity or snobbery about rank limits Charny's heartfelt appeal to take up arms and armor, win honor, and defend France. Only the cowardly, lazy, or misguided fail and must be

---

[43] *Barbour's Bruce*, bk. 19, lines 162–166.
[44] Kaeuper and Kennedy, *Book of Chivalry*, 84–85; he expresses such sentiments throughout his book.

excluded from the worthy circle that includes all the valiant. Charny enthusiastically assures good warriors that they receive divine blessing for their just and demanding labors. In effect, he thinks God looks at their deeds rather than their family trees.

As a great hero and model for emulation, Charny's personal views carry weight; but the evidence he provides is even broader, for he was writing for the French royal chivalric order and was speaking to themes approved by the French crown, which seems to have intended a pragmatically inclusive membership. King Jean's Order of the Star was to include not only the very great but significant numbers of simple knights bachelor. "Clearly," as Jonathan Boulton comments, "he did not want to abandon the advantages of size in favour of those of exclusiveness," and knew that his company "would include knights of several classes."[45] Chivalric reform was to be achieved on a wide scale in order to save the kingdom in its crisis. The ideals Charny elaborated were to guide them all.

Christine de Pizan took a similarly pragmatic and inclusive approach in her *Book of Deeds of Arms and of Chivalry* written in about 1410.[46] She suggests, for example, that in choosing a constable "greater attention should be given to perfection of skill in arms, along with the virtues and the character and good bearing that should accompany this, than to exalted lineage or noble blood," though she adds that a combination of skill and lineage would be ideal. This constable's casual talk should ever be focused on arms and chivalry.[47] Agreeing with Charny again (though she likely did not read his work), Christine reminds readers that chivalry entails pain and suffering, for which the warrior must be prepared.[48] She devotes many pages to questions of licit behavior in war, but shows no inclination to distinguish social status among men who will read or hear her words; dubbing is not an issue discussed.

At about the same time, but hundreds of miles distant, Don Pero Niño, like Charny, undoubtedly lived chivalry as an active martial profession. His biographer details an ideally heroic early career, that of a truly vigorous knight, a naval captain in the Mediterranean and a devastating raider along the English Channel, a highly successful

---

[45] D'Arcy Jonathan Dacre Boulton, *The Knights of the Crown* (New York: St. Martin's Press, 1987), 190.

[46] The modern editor of this text agrees: *The Book of Deeds of Arms and of Chivalry*, ed. Charity Willard, 5, says Christine wrote for military men in general.

[47] Ibid., 24, 26.   [48] Ibid., 37.

courtly lover both in France and in Castile, and a superb jouster, even by the high standards of Paris. Pero Niño models muscular and militant chivalric ideals. Significantly, he did not wait for a formal dubbing ceremony (which actually came much later in life) before entering as joyously as Charny or even Malory could have wished into his colorful militant career. From his first fight, his biographer gushes praise and reports that his society treated him in every sense as a knight and, indeed, a paragon of the entire range of chivalric virtues. If there is little specific discussion about lesser fighting men in relation to those classic knights, the emphasis in the biography, as in Charny's writing, falls on bold and effective fighting, with no obvious comment on differences in status between grand and obviously noble knights, dubbed men of lesser standing, and the ordinary fighting man. Pero Niño's family of origin was noble, but had experienced difficulties likely linked to his grandfather backing the losing side in the mid-fourteenth-century Castilian civil war.[49]

Was Thomas Malory, however, not a middle-class writer? From the late fifteenth century he can prominently take the witness stand, both as a historical figure and as a major chivalric author. His great book was indeed read by a social range that included merchants, lawyers, and ladies, and some in these ranks had been reading Middle English romances for several generations; they would never play Lancelot in life or claim to have settled with their enemies personally and vigorously, as Malory's heroes never tire of claiming – "with mine own handes." While the claim that chivalry has somehow gone mercantile or lost all military content is sometimes voiced, the opposite seems more likely. That Malory was read by the middle class of his day does not mean he wrote for the middle class or to advance middle-class values. Nothing we know about Sir Thomas suggests he longed for a quietly acquisitive life in a corner of some counting house, a lawyer's study, or some ancestral embodiment of a pub with a group of estate agents, with only the welcomed pouring of beer, the clink of coins, or the soft crackle of parchment documents to animate the peace. Basic facts of his life and basic values in the stories he tells unforgettably purvey and esteem a tough warrior code as the nucleus of chivalric life. Equally of interest, his view of knighthood is comprehensive; the idealized world he creates is populated by an entire range of figures from great lords to simple

---

[49] Carriazo, *El victorial*, 61–62.

knights often starting from scratch; and it is their common knightly practice that moves him, not the particulars of individual status. His imagined world is one of knightly deeds and not merely courtly settings; battlefields, tourney grounds, and fierce individual fights beyond numeration move action, not merely *courtois* scenes under striped pavilions or within private chambers. No less than Froissart, he wants to write regularly and in glowing detail about deeds of arms done by honored warriors, regardless of whether we know their family background.

However idealized, the lives of these heroes and the books associated with them reinforce the theme: knightly fighters came from various shadings of elite social ranks and (to the extent that we can recover their framework of thought) conceived of themselves as performing the militant function of knighthood. In so doing they gained at least some of the satisfying aura, social elevation, and even religious blessings that descended on chivalry, along with its sustaining profits.

Thinking of a much earlier period, Karl Leyser noted the tendency for shared military experience through expanded warfare to create warrior fellow feeling in the generations in which chivalry emerged; a similar case can be made for the intense warfare of the later medieval period, even though it had to move upstream against an aristocratic current of exclusiveness. A wide net – or perhaps a separate study – would be required to investigate this theme in detail, but tantalizing evidence is worth noting. In a remarkable sartorial change, those firmly possessing elite chivalric status, despite their strong desire for exclusivity, adopted clothing styles of those in merely would-be chivalric social layers. Elite men, it seems, were fascinated by new styles of these lesser men; by roughly the mid-fourteenth century they had given up the traditional long and loose garments in favor of short jackets and tight-fitting hose. The change was certainly noticed in its own time: clerical moralists denounced the new style, and the popular view (that of distinctly ordinary people) was simply derisory. The shift was happening in Geoffroi de Charny's lifetime and, conservative in this as in other ways, he uncompromisingly denounced form-fitting clothing as a deplorable innovation, however radically chic his contemporaries found the new style.[50] This fashion that

---

[50] See the historical study by Kaeuper in Kaeuper and Kennedy, *The Book of Chivalry*, where the censorious views of Jean de Venette are also quoted and discussed.

would last for centuries had moved up the social ladder and into courtly society; there it was domesticated by frequently attaching costly jewels to the fabric. Disgusted with this showy addition, too, Charny fumed that only women would so adorn their clothing.[51]

Since aping one's superiors has usually been the path to joining them, this adoption by the grand of a clothing style from those less than grand is striking. The more usual situation appears in a particular case in point in the confraternities of archers in the German Empire, France, the Low Countries, and England. John Block Friedman notes the important marks of status they adopted: wearing livery, carrying special weapons, and training with them in public spaces, even endowing hospitals and chapels.[52] Writing about such groups in Ghent, Peter Arnade sees "an attention . . . to the world of aristocratic chivalry."[53] Despite subknightly membership of merchants and even artisans, they attempted to bolster social status by imitating elite behavior. Through the practice of archery (with both crossbows and longbows) they could claim a form of prowess.[54] Among fighting men, the improved status could be gained by a conscious process of social osmosis at least to some degree elevating those aping the knights in all ways possible.

Even the famous Robin Hood, as portrayed in his early tales (and thus before he acquires genuinely elite status after the Middle Ages), shows decidedly knightly and even Arthurian concerns, despite sub-knightly social status.[55] In a central incident in the late fifteenth-century

---

[51] Kaeuper and Kennedy, *The Book of Chivalry*, 188–189. Díaz de Gamez, in his biography of Don Pero Niño, is less direct and vociferous, but he denounces *"ropas delicadas"* – what Evans translates as "soft garments" but which could also refer to delicate, refined, or exquisite clothes. Evans, 12. Carriazo, 42. He says, *"Ca los de los ofiçios comunes comen el pan folgando, çisten ropas delicadas, manjares bien adovados, camas blandas, safumadas. . ."* Carriazo, 61–66. My thanks, as so often regarding Castilian evidence, go to Samuel Claussen.

[52] "Robin Hood and the Social Context of Late Medieval Archery," in *Robin Hood in Greenwood Stood*, ed. Stephen White (Turnhout, 2011), 68–85.

[53] *Realms of Ritual: Burgundian Ceremony and Civil Life in Late Medieval Ghent* (Ithaca, 1996), 68, with general discussion 64–94.

[54] Such confraternities might remind an ecclesiastical historian of the lay confraternities that by this time had long associated themselves with the practitioners of piety in established and more formal religious orders.

[55] He became the Earl of Locksley only in much later storytelling. On the evolution of the character and story, see J. C. Holt, *Robin Hood* (New York: Thames and Hudson, 1982); and Stephen Knight and Thomas Ohlgren, eds., *Robin Hood and Other Outlaw Tales* (Kalamazoo, MI: Medieval Institute, 1997).

Geste his largesse and his prowess (utilizing both sword and bow) vigorously support an impoverished but truly vigorous knight, Sir Richard atte Lee. Robin likewise shows chivalric devotion to the Blessed Virgin when, formally dining in style, he delays his meal until, like Arthur, he experiences some splendid event.[56] Middle English romances were avidly read by those of subknightly status, the stories themselves, of course, purveying key chivalric values among knights from a range of social positions.

Chroniclers add to the store of fascinating evidence. Jean Froissart (d. 1405), whose famous chronicles understandably pay homage to men of grand status, also recounts the great deeds of all men-at-arms as part of the ennobling drama of chivalric action. The very words that introduce his account of Anglo-French warfare intone his goal, for he explains:

> To the intent that the honourable and noble adventures of feats of arms, done and achieved by the wars of France and England, should notably be enregistered and put in perpetual memory, whereby the prewe and hardy may have ensample to encourage them in their well-doing, I, sir John Froissart, will treat and record an history of great louage and praise.

However brief, this passage offers telling evidence: deeds of arms are the prime subject, rather than any focus on the rank of those doing them; these deeds are ever to be held in memory, always an inspiration to more chivalries; and these deeds and their doers are all honorable and noble, ever to be praised. Later in his life Froissart's view of chivalric exploits darkened somewhat as the effects of continual violence in society registered; yet his initial strong tendency to praise remains important.[57] Equally striking, some of the author's copyists, in effect, dub him to knighthood by adopting the title of "sir," though he was never formally granted knighthood and came from a non-noble family.[58]

---

[56] See "A Gest of Robyn Hod," in *Robin Hood and Other Outlaw Tales*, eds. Stephen Knight and Thomas Ohlgren (Kalamazoo, MI: Medieval Institute, 1997), 80–168; A. J. Pollard provides historical insights in *Imagining Robin Hood* (Abingdon, Oxfordshire: Routledge, 2004). See the discussion in John Block Friedman, "Robin Hood and the Social Context of Late Medieval Archery," in *Robin Hood in Greenwood Stood*, ed. Stephen Knight (Turnhout: Brepols, 2011).

[57] M. Zink, *Froissart et le temps* (Paris, 1998), and K. Fowler, in *History Today* 36, no. 5 (1986), 54.

[58] E.g., British Library Arundel 67, where he is termed *seigneur* in the prologue to his chronicle, and Paris BN fr 20356, where he begins his chronicle, "je sire Jan Froissart commence a parler..." Jean le Bel, on whose earlier chronicle Froissart

His source for the early years of the great Anglo-French conflict, Jean le Bel, carefully noted the social changes taking place among the fighters of his day (he covers the period 1290–1360):

At that time [the opening of the Hundred Years War] the great lords took no account of men-at-arms unless they had crested helms, whereas now we count any with lances, cuirasses, hauberks and iron caps. In my own time [Jean le Bel died in 1370] things have changed a lot, it seems to me[;] the splendid caparisoned horses and crested helms of old, and the shining plate and heraldic coats, are gone, replaced by cuirasses, gambesons and iron caps. These days a humble page is as well and as finely armed as a noble knight.[59]

The mantle of chivalry was being stretched well beyond the tight group of those formally dubbed or richly born and the glow of chivalry reflected on all grades of armor worn by elite fighters in general. Like heroes with whom they could identify in *chansons de geste* or romances, even the less grand among these men could manage to dress and act in some style, affect an occasional grand gesture (even if it strained the budget), and spend with at least apparent carelessness; they could practice elaborate courtesy, perhaps with a bit of pardonable awkwardness. And they fought so usefully in raid, skirmish, siege, and occasional pitched battle; they let none forget how much they suffered, even as they won patronage and (so they hoped) the love of alluring ladies. Might they not also hope that their good service and meritorious suffering counted when sin had finally to be balanced by merit?

Many passages from romance literature reinforce such a sense of knighthood, worthy of praise, whatever the status of the practitioner. In the *Lancelot do Lac* a speech of advice given to Arthur by a worthy man (interestingly, at a time of military crisis, when the king needs support) provides this point of view:

And when you see the poor *bacheler* whom poverty has in bondage and who has not neglected physical prowess, in his place amongst other poor men, do not forget him because of his poverty or his lowly lineage, for beneath poverty of the body often lies great riches of the heart.[60]

drew, is also sometimes termed "nonseigneur" – see British Library Royal D II.
I owe these references to Sebastian Rider-Bezerra, with thanks.

[59] *True Chronicles of Jean le Bel*, trans. Bryant, 68. At ibid., 78, Jean le Bel writes of such new pieces of armor as bascinets.

[60] See Elspeth Kennedy, "The Quest for Identity and the Importance of Lineage in Thirteenth-Century Prose Romance," in *The Ideals and Practices of Medieval Knighthood* II, eds. Christopher Harper-Bill and Ruth Harvey (Woodbridge,

Even knights who fall short of worldly greatness have their role to play, carrying forward the honorable function of arms. The message would not have been lost on many an aspirant for knighthood who heard or read this passage.

THE STATE AND THE NEW LEARNING

We have seen repeatedly that state power channeled into warfare acted as a catalyst for the upward movement of aspirants into knighthood. If this growing state power stimulated the social expansion of informal chivalric status, it likewise encouraged the incorporation of new ideals within chivalry. These important roles deserve emphasis.

The importance of the machinery of taxation cannot be missed, for it produced an almost audible suction as money was extracted from townsmen and country folk to fund broader, more ambitious warfare. The phenomena of taxation and war were in fact mutually stimulating, for the state grew as it collected tax revenues for war, always a legitimate case of necessity justifying such exactions. Royal, princely, and urban administrations could regularly siphon wealth from subjects to advance conquest or provide defense against it. This capacity, growing for generations, enabled a new scale and a longer timetable for campaigns. By the outbreak of major Anglo-French warfare, surprisingly large sums could be collected. On either side of the Channel just before the turn of the fourteenth century, in what proved to be only a prelude to the traditional Hundred Years War, the small but efficiently governed kingdom of England raised roughly 360,000 pounds sterling, which was roughly the sum the French government at least planned to collect for its own forces from a much larger realm (440,000 *livres tournois*).[61] This striking pattern was regularly repeated: invading forces went from England into France, perhaps at least in part because they could be fueled by the greater taxing efficiency of royal government in the smaller kingdom; French forces had to concentrate on resistance (though they at least planned a major invasion of their own, only to have it disrupted by the outbreak of plague, which possessed more devastating power than

---

Suffolk: Boydell, 1988), 70–86. Kennedy notes that this imaginative work was influential in Beaumanoir's legal treatise.

[61] J. R. Strayer, "The Costs and Profits of War," in *The Medieval City*, ed. H. A. Miskimin et al. (New Haven: Yale University Press, 1977), 271.

the most ardent human effort).[62] As France struggled with invasion and finally with civil war, the need for better-functioning royal governance was made clear; and if need was obvious in France, across the Channel the fact of efficient governance backing militant chivalric ambition was equally clear.

Yet through these generations of war, governmental weakness no less than its strength produced results of crucial importance. If more efficient government funded larger armies for longer periods of time, a weakened French government made other possibilities evident to vigorous arms bearers: in France bodies of irregular troops fought for any paymaster or simply eliminated the middleman represented by royal or princely government; the ruthless monetary collections carried out by these bands quickly shaded into brigandage and plain robbery.[63] Large portions of the kingdom were dotted with fortresses ranging from rough citadels to impressive castles.[64] If the political allegiance of ambitious warriors commanding these fortified centers was uncertain, we might nonetheless expect that their own self-estimate rose with each sweep into the countryside to collect funds that they might legitimize as one or another legal exaction. The captain in one fortress, as we saw in the incident used to open this book, was only a squire, but is represented as eager to be knighted.

This crisis of effective power and governance helped to guarantee a welcome for new conceptions that bolstered state action. Their impact would be important for chivalry. Discussions of ideal warrior qualities directed by effective governing power attracted much attention in the later Middle Ages. The need was obvious, and the intellectual atmosphere was stirred. So vital and venerable a force as chivalry was bound to take a central place as classical writings about political society and military discipline and command were revived and discussed. The king's sovereignty was emphasized, and his role

---

[62] Charny likely played a role in the planning: Kaeuper and Kennedy, *Book of Chivalry*, 9–10.

[63] While England escaped such disasters, it remains an open question whether the relentless focus on war and equally relentless taxation exacerbated problems of order in that country also, Fears of a rising similar to the Jacquerie in France increased after the Great Rising of 1381.

[64] Nicholas Wright points to a kingdom of France "studded with tens of thousands of castles, fortified churches, fortified farm houses, walled towns, and villages." *Knights and Peasants*, 3.

gradually came to be considered that of a lodestone for vigorous loyalty rather than a battlefield champion – especially in the French case and particularly after the capture of the king at Poitiers in 1356. *El victorial* makes the same point on the other side of the Alps, repeatedly stressing loyalty to the king as the correct motive for action.

Of course, views rooted in the classical past had always possessed special cachet in medieval society. Strands of neoclassical thought that foreshadowed the full flow of later humanism can be detected in the history of chivalry from at least the twelfth century, but the more influential wave began to roll ashore from roughly the mid-fourteenth century. If neoclassical borrowings appear throughout Europe, they were especially welcomed in beleaguered France; there such lines of thought could underscore efforts to establish military discipline and an effective hierarchical command structure worthy of idealized ancient Roman armies. Both goals would obviously enhance the effort to expel English invaders and maintain the unity of the kingdom. As Craig Taylor notes in his close and convincing study of this evidence, a royal interest in effective reform involved intellectual as well as structural military measures. In fact, he writes:

[T]he late Capetian and Valois monarchs sponsored an extraordinary pro-gramme of vernacular translation of classical works, that gave royal and aristo-cratic audiences access to many books that provided guidance and commentary on warfare by such authors as Aristotle, Vegetius and Valerius Maximus, as well as more recent writings by John of Salisbury and Giles of Rome.[65]

Over this time contemporary authors were likewise at work under the patronage of the crown or the great princes of the blood. The list serving one or another king includes Honoré Bonet, Philippe de Mézieres, Nichole Oresme, Christine de Pizan, Jean de Montreuil, and Alain Chartier. Taylor suggests that under Charles V (1364–1380) the crown maintained two think tanks, one at the College of Navarre, headed by Nichole Oresme, a translator of Aristotle (among much other work), and the second in the royal chancery (with a full scholarly staff).[66]

The usefulness of such thinkers readily appears in themes from the writing of Christine de Pizan and Honoré Bonet as examples. In her

---

[65] Taylor, *Chivalry and the Ideals of Knighthood*, 3.   [66] Ibid., 30.

Livre de Paix Christine wrote of chivalry in service to a knowledgeable prince who maintains perfect justice for all his subjects,[67] and maintains a well-paid and orderly army.[68] He thus suppresses the misbehavior of extortionate officials prone to robbery and pillage.[69] Bonet read in the history of the great ancient kingdoms, and Rome in particular, an assurance of the necessity of directive lordship, granted by God to avoid the dissensions that have troubled even great kingdoms.[70] Rationality on a battlefield was to be determined by the knights' lord and commander, whose orders set objectives.[71] In Bonet's words, "he is no true knight who, for fear of death, or of what might befall, fails to defend the land of his lord, but in truth he is a traitor and forsworn."[72] Duty and obedience become the font of knightly virtue for Bonet, eclipsing any desire for personal riches.[73] Commanders become responsible for ensuring that knights remain focused on their duties and disciplined in their behavior, lest in their eagerness to demonstrate personal courage they forget their purpose within a wider military organization.[74] Bonet's emphasis on obedience over any recourse to personal fortitude, which he does not even consider a virtue,[75] again reflects his consistent desire to emphasize the necessity of selfless obedience over personal honor as the only means through which the evils associated with war can be healed, and the righteous potential of violence channeled to a good end.

In addition to these intellectuals, some active military figures contributed basically similar ideals. We have seen that Geoffroi de Charny wrote for the royal chivalric Order of the Star in the mid-fourteenth century. Though perhaps not as completely royalist as Pizan or Bonet, he was second to none in his desire to defend the French kingdom and to stimulate loyal and vigorous service in arms, whatever the personal cost. Another active knight, Jean de Bueil, a century later composed a semiautobiographical work, *Le Jouvencel*, full of advice intended to direct young knights toward attitudes and behaviors that his intellectual colleagues were advocating.[76]

---

[67] *The Book of Peace by Christine de Pizan*, ed., trans., Karen Green et al. (University Park: Pennsylvania State University Press, 2008), 70, 72.
[68] Ibid., 76.   [69] Ibid., 86, 104.   [70] Bonet, *Tree of Battles*, 114 (ii.xvii).
[71] Ibid., 122 (iii.vii–viii on whether or not death is preferable to flight).
[72] Ibid., 131 (iv.viii).   [73] Ibid., 131 (iv.viii).   [74] Ibid., 131–132 (iv.ix–x).
[75] Ibid., 133 (iv.xi–xii).
[76] *Le Jouvencel par Jean le Bueil*, eds. Camille Favre and Léon Lecestre, 2 vols. (Paris: Renouard, 1887).

If these grand ideas could be implemented, the sociopolitical bonus would be a step toward ending the grim and divisive war and establishing royal supremacy over military force; and in longer-range perspective, such steps might alleviate the breakdown of public order in a realm wracked by contending forces, even by brigandage and banditry. Genuine royal capacity might suppress the companies of dangerously unpaid soldiers (known as *routiers*), who were traversing the realm or dominating their own bits of it, and might bring an end to the local tyrannies that too often centered on the hundreds of fortresses held by fighters of uncertain loyalties and unceasing appetites.[77]

Though a classic case, the French example was not solitary. New emphasis on measures to support sovereign power and the public good appeared widely, whether the political unit was a realm, princely territory, or city-state. Arguments in support of the res publica or commonweal proliferated. Diego de Valera (1412–1488) famously wrote to the Castilian king Juan II in 1441 describing the state as a body with the prince as head and the subjects as members. The two must achieve concord. His task was challenging because he was highly critical of Enrique IV, but Valera managed to assert that the prince is clearly the head in the body politic. It is worth noting that Valera was an active knight who had fought across Europe, including in the Hussite Wars.[78] Iñigo López de Mendoza (1398–1458; more often called in Spanish the Marqués de Santillana) wrote the *Doctrinal de Privados* on the career of Álvaro de Luna, the favorite of Juan II, warning readers not to attempt to accumulate wealth and power and usurp the authority of the king.

Idealized governing power was to be the directive force behind an equally idealized chivalry. Far from seeking to eliminate chivalry as some inconvenient relic of the past, late medieval scholars urged their

[77] Craig Taylor, *Chivalry and Ideals of Knighthood in France*, 19–54, and Justine Firnhaber-Baker, *Violence and the State in Languedoc, 1250–1400* (Cambridge University Press, 2014), 150–178, provide overviews of the civil, political, and financial problems of fourteenth-century France.

[78] Fernan Perez de Guzman, "Crónica del serenísimo príncipe Don Juan, segundo rey deste nombre en castilla y en leon," in *Biblioteca de Autores Españoles*, ed. M. Rivadeneyra, vol. 68 (Madrid: Impresores de Camara de S.M., 1877), 573. For an examination of Diego de Valera's works on chivalry, see Jesús D. Rodríguez-Velasco, *El debate sobre la caballería en el siglo XV* (Salamanca: Junta de Castilla y León, 1996).

prince to co-opt chivalric ideology and direct its energy with a strong guiding hand. Idealistic texts of the time regularly refer to the *"discipline de chevalerie"* as a desired reform goal, sometimes implying the supposed existence of clear rules of restraint, sometimes urging knightly self-control, and directly arguing for basic obedience to the prince or his military captain on the scene. The ancient Romans were thought to have been ideally chivalric – that is, the embodiment of ideal chivalry rather than its alternative. The influential treatise of Vegetius, *De re militari*, could thus be read almost as if he were a contemporary commentator on knighthood.[79] Since many other relevant classical treatises had found vernacular translators as well, a sturdy shelf of texts on military practice preached loyalty (meant now in a hierarchical sense) and strict discipline in service to an idea of public good.[80] The aim was always to restore and redirect military effort, producing a transformation of chivalry, not its suppression as a morally or militarily dubious enterprise.

Reform plans had always featured moral no less than structural elements. They wanted to infuse knighthood with the personal moral responsibility being stressed at this time in religious thought. Perhaps the spirit of the saintly Louis IX (more than a century after his death) flitted through the minds of writers of at least the French treatises: he had famously legislated general moral reform throughout his kingdom in pious hope that clearing corruption from governance and reducing detestably common sins from social life would bring needed divine favor on France and on its king, who hoped for a successful second crusade after the disastrous failure of his first expedition.[81] More certainly it was thought – or at least hoped and publicly asserted by Louis's political descendants – that nobility was the font of virtue. The chivalrous elite should lead in morality, just as they lead in war.

It was a hard sell. Pious hopes for a vast redirection and moral transformation of aristocratic attitudes were no less striking than their faint possibility of successful accomplishment. In the troubled border-lands between the Late Medieval and the Early Modern eras, the

---

[79] C. T. Allmand, *The De re militari of Vegetius: The Reception, Transmission and Legacy of a Roman Text in the Middle Ages* (Cambridge University Press, 2011).

[80] Taylor, *Chivalry and the Ideals of Knighthood*, 34–46.

[81] On Saint Louis's moral reform, see William Chester Jordan, *Louis IX and the Challenge of Crusade*. On moral reform in later medieval France, see Taylor, *Chivalry and the Ideals of Knighthood*, 42–44.

record of aristocrats and of those hoping to be taken for aristocrats does not fall easily under the heading of selfless advocacy of common good and leadership in broad moral uplift. Even before religious division added its potent catalyst, political rivalry, assassination, and civil conflict prevailed.

Learned commentators were certain that getting back to traditions of chivalry would restore the moral fiber of aristocrats gone soft and woefully inadequate as traditional defense of the kingdom. Stout martial vigor was the recognized need, almost shouted out by Charny and reinforced in revived classical works and early humanist treatises a century later.[82] Stalwart men in armor, undoubtedly recognized as essential in an imperfect world, received lavish praise from intellectuals for their labors and their nobility; ideally, these authors write, fingers crossed on the hand not holding the pen, such men ride into action on behalf of their sovereign and defend the public good of which the king is symbol and agent.

The impact of reform ideas must clearly not be exaggerated. These idealizing currents of thought were obviously neither suddenly causative nor unique in chivalric history. A centuries-old tradition of reform, in fact, marks the history of chivalry with repeated attempts to address perceived needs by reforming the great force of elite warriors. These earlier efforts are worth bearing in mind, even if they moved only part way along the later medieval scale. Chrétien de Troyes had urged knighthood to act in service, rather than in merely destructive and self-referential pride, though his plan was not royalist or statist; John of Salisbury had wanted knights to show the discipline as well as the valor of the Roman soldiers he read about in his (limited) library of classical works. The list of reformers could be extended to include Etienne de Fougeres and Ramon Lull, with massive additions in the vast corpus of imaginative chivalric literature. Later medieval development stands as the significantly intensified and expanded last phase of this long history of cutting the cloth of chivalry to fit the changing shape of social needs as perceived by clerical intellectuals and even some practicing knights.

---

[82] Early humanist writers scarcely attempted to waft peace across the landscape. Perhaps the intensely peaceable view in the crafted prose of Erasmus misguides us to consider humanist scholars quasi-pacifists. Most French intellectuals urged elite warriors to exercise public power in expelling invaders and suppressing widespread rapacious localism.

This late medieval intellectual current, like earlier writing that conveyed repeated reform efforts in the twelfth and thirteenth centuries, was prescriptive, urging ideal behavior, rather than providing descriptions of the world as it was. Craig Taylor notes the distortive modern tendency to read Honoré Bonet's *Tree of Battles* as accepted medieval military doctrine, rather than as a reform text.[83] Warriors did not hear or read a classical work rendered in their vernacular or a humanist treatise retailing its ideas and on the spot give up the pursuit of prowess to increase personal glory. These writings were no less prescriptive than reform ideals advanced by writers on chivalry in the twelfth and thirteenth centuries. Yet they are important in exactly the same ways; given time and continuing experience of contextual exigencies, their force was felt. We know that translations of classical works and treatises elaborating their themes were popular among the lay elite; the number of copies produced and the numerous contemporary citations from them reveal an awareness of problems and a vision of ideal motivations that at least should direct men of force and power; desired reforms, it was ardently hoped, might achieve goals they sought. Knightly careers could steer along new directions almost without open awareness of altering course, for much of the traditional language of chivalry continued to resound. A core of warrior values – and especially prowess exercised in defense of honor – remained current, accompanied by all the forms of courtliness, largesse, and attitudes about ideal love that we would expect. Significant changes and shaping of some values and qualities would be demanded.

If these reforms appear to be – and truly were – striking, it is useful to recall that merely personal glory had long been denounced by clerics as vainglory and might be contrasted to some larger benefit sought, such as victory over an enemy or defense of a kingdom; and such goals had long been acknowledged by knights themselves. As his career matured, William Marshal constrained young enthusiasts who wanted to delay an important mission by capturing some valuable horses; the Marshal knew in the late twelfth century that larger strategic considerations mattered beyond personal aggrandizement.[84] Charny denounced those men-at-arms more

---

[83] Taylor, *Chivalry and the Ideals of Knighthood*, 41.
[84] This theme is developed in Painter, *William Marshal*, and in Crouch, *William Marshal*.

interested in loot than in winning the battle. Moving the warriors
away from instant gratification had always been a challenge. Yet the
new line of neoclassical thought vigorously sought to suppress such
personal glory more decisively than earlier efforts, relegating personal glory to second place, and broadening the larger enterprise into a
general claim to promote public good. The dangers faced in France
acted as a catalyst to such efforts.

Certainly these reforming ideals were attributed to great knights
and would have been seen as outlining conduct to be emulated by
admirers of these heroes. A panegyric on the great Burgundian knight
Louis de la Tremoille (d. 1525; the text written in 1527), for example,
repeatedly extols knightly prowess in service to the sovereign and the
public good, adding religious valorization and claims of French
military action as just war to the thick layers of praise lavished on
this hero and his young son, both of whom died of battlefield wounds
in royal service.[85] Pierre Terrail, better known as the Chevalier
Bayard (d. 1524), appears as the model knight in the biography
written by the humanist Symphorien Champier. In these pages,
ideal knighthood combines prowess worthy of Lancelot with bound-
less love for the public good of the French nation. In the heat of
battle, Bayard shouted not his family name as war cry, which was
Geoffroi de Charny's practice, but "France! France!" And over all his
deeds hovers the approving hand of God, who seems in this text to be
decidedly French.

Such reforming goals need not be considered utterly foreign to the
chivalrous, for they had zealously fought for kings and great princes
over centuries. Yet the shift in a center of gravity of their interests is
apparent, for personal display and competitive acquisition of honor
had also long characterized the thinking and action of knighthood.
The new emphasis would require all fighting men to direct their lives
toward truly common effort, rather than dissipate their energies in
endless and particular strife. The strong element of personal independence in classical chivalry would have to be diminished in order for
common good to prevail as an overriding aim. The honor won by
prowess would have to be directed to the res publica as much as to the

---

[85] Jean Bucher, *Panegyric de Louis de la Tremoille*, passim, in *Collection complete
des mémoires relatifs à l'histoire de France depuis le règne de Philippe Auguste, jusqu'au
commencement du dix-septième siècle avec des notices sur chaque auteur et des observations
sur chaques ouvrage*, vol. xiv, ed. M. Petitot (Paris: Foucault, 1820).

valiant individual. Nothing short of a general reform working through discipline and devoted following of a hierarchy of leaders culminating in the crown (or regional prince or city-state) could achieve such a transformation. The goal was high and the road long.

CHIVALRIC TRANSFORMATION

Yet by the end of our third chivalric phase (and in what we might term its vigorous afterlife) some changes that these intellectuals might have recognized as important to their goals were appearing. Growth of sovereign governing power registered clearly in important dimensions of public life; as this sovereign power emerged, the seemingly eternal and balanced dynamics within the complex triad of chivalry, religion, and kingship changed.

The swift overview of chivalric chronology undertaken in the three chapters of this part ends not in sudden death but gradual transformation. Growing state power was the chief agency of this transformation, assisted by religious personnel and institutions. In simplest terms, if the institutional church came to be overshadowed by state power, it continued to transmit spiritual blessings not only on the sovereign but on the chivalrous; at the highest level these knights would retain much power for centuries; and in all constituent chivalric ranks they would continue to be much needed.[86]

Religious valorization continued to descend on elite warriors within their kingdom, principality, or city-state. Militant lay elite ranks readily accommodated chivalric profession and status within this changing pattern of the church universal. Long certain that divine blessing descended on their warfare even when it was directed at fellow Christians in another political unit, they remained certain of blessings even as their world changed. After the shattering blow of the Reformation, much of the thinking that had animated crusade even took a new lease on life as Catholic and Protestant forces fought each other with something of the old spirit of doing away with those they were certain were God's enemies.

It required more basic alterations for chivalry to come to terms with rising royal power. Understanding complex feelings about the

---

[86] Although the church operated through its own administrative map of provinces and parishes covering all of Europe, princes ruling over increasingly powerful political units tended to stress each res publica as a religious unit over which they had a greater measure of control and direction than in the past.

state on the part of the chivalrous becomes easier once we avoid a lingering, distortive myth. Far from suddenly appearing to finish off a decayed world of feudalism, the state had been emerging for centuries.[87] Chivalric adjustment proceeded gradually, with the process of absorption aided by the continuance of much traditional language about prowess, loyalty, and honorable service. For centuries the chivalrous had bristled with fierce independence when their asserted rights were constrained. Yet they had likewise shown willingness to be led into glorious war by kings and had always been willing to accept generous royal patronage. Whatever competitiveness they might show regarding kings and their ministers, "raised from the dust," the warriors had, over time, accepted a role as faithful knights of the crown and as its faithful agents, especially in England where the role of monarchy was writ large in society.

Scholars of the medieval state can point to well-documented moves toward sovereignty on both sides of the Channel in the generations (and in the English case even centuries) leading up to 1300. In England the long process had roots in Anglo-Saxon, Anglo-Norman, and Angevin work. The French case shows a shorter chronology, but the process took on particular clarity under Philip Augustus, Louis IX, and Philip the Fair. Serious efforts to increase French royal power had been halted by failure of male heirs in the Capetian line, followed by terrible and destabilizing warfare. Yet on both sides of the Channel royalism found new life and new sources of support by the late fifteenth and early sixteenth century. At the end of our third phase of chivalric life, the chivalrous were being integrated within a framework increasingly dominated by royal power, blessed by religion.

---

[87] A classic account is provided in J. R. Strayer, *On the Medieval Origins of the Modern State* (Princeton: Princeton University Press, 1970).

Part III

THE PRIVILEGED PRACTICE OF VIOLENCE

・

Steeped as we are in images of heroes as knights in shining armor, it is easy to lose sight of the essential function of the elaborate armor and even more elaborate sharp-edged and spiked weaponry that adorn the walls of museums with a wing devoted to the Middle Ages. In one of my own classes designed to make this stark function clear, one student suddenly exclaimed, "I get it! All that weaponry was not merely accessorizing!" Indeed, these armaments were not simply a statement of high fashion, though they undoubtedly fulfilled that function as well. How well such weaponry effected its purpose on the human body, even on the armored human body, could be patiently explained by archaeologists who have investigated military burials.[1] Moreover, the museums will present no remnant of that other great tool of war, the torch, which proved so effective even where the sword could not reach. The two chapters of this part investigate knightly violence, first in actual warfare and then as a form of extreme sport that was a close relative of war. To set the stage for this investigation, we need to focus on chivalric attitudes about the use of violence, including any sense of restraint on its usefulness.

Over centuries, most discussions of chivalry tirelessly projected an ideal image of the elite lay male as a vigorous warrior, proud of

---

[1] Numerous websites discuss the Battle of Visby and the effect of weaponry on the hastily buried and relatively poorly armored bodies found there. Cf. John Keegan, *The Face of Battle* (New York: Penguin, 1978), which includes, as its medieval chapter, a discussion of the battle of Agincourt.

his capacity to achieve his twin chief goals of honor and material gain through expert, personal violence. Seldom unqualified, the view shows complexities, for the sources will suggest a great variety of reform plans and ideal models for building a better knighthood (with greater or lesser degrees of subtlety). Even a cycle of *chansons de geste* or romance texts may carry reform significance through its structure, within and between texts justifying war or warning about excesses.[2] In individual works, these warnings may come with a roll of thunder or may speak only in a stage whisper. The mother of the eponymous antihero in *Raoul de Cambrai*, for example, gives her son stern admonitions against despoiling the poor or looting or burning churches; his stubborn insistence that he will commit these very acts in his determined fighting – clear violations of the *mesure* or wise restraint much praised in this and other literary works – leads to her potent cursing of her son. When Raoul is as good as his word and burns the town of Origny, despoiling its church and murdering its nuns in the great fire, he earns dubious distinction as the most infamous antihero of the Middle Ages (if we can write off Ganelon as a straight-out traitor).[3] Without any taint of pacifism, this epic at least raises questions about limits. With his usual subtlety, the great founding figure of romance writing, Chrétien de Troyes, shows war as virtually a natural force in his fine romance, *Yvain, the Knight with the Lion*. It can achieve good or evil results; but Chrétien, too, proposes a framework of reform of chivalric prowess; service in just causes is to motivate the knights, rather than mere lust or vainglory. Two centuries later, Honoré Bonet, in his learned treatise *The Tree of Battles*, assures readers that war is not evil in itself, that God instituted and practiced it, and that only bad usage spoils it.[4]

Valorization of violence (in causes championed by a writer) appears most prominently.[5] In the world created in chivalric

---

[2] See, for example, the various points of view on war in the classic three cycles of epic – the Cycle of the King, that of the Barons in Revolt, and that of William of Orange. A comparison of *The Quest for the Holy Grail* with the *Lancelot* in the *Lancelot-Grail* Vulgate Cycle is equally interesting.

[3] Sarah Kay, ed., trans., *Raoul de Cambrai*. Another good example appears in the changing nature of the great hero Lancelot from the first written component of the Vulgate Cycle of Old French romance, the *Lancelot*, to the last major romance, *The Death of King Arthur*.

[4] Coopland, ed., trans., *The Tree of Battles*.

[5] Kaeuper, *Chivalry and Violence*, 121–189.

literature, jousting resolves nearly every personal disagreement as men prove on other men's bodies whatever case they want to make (my property claim or religious views are better, my lady is the most beautiful, etc.); they likewise regularly win control over women's bodies through violence against competing males (and sometimes against resisting women – even against ladies).[6] Collective goals, or at least the goals of great lords and rulers who can marshal large forces, are regularly achieved by war, whether the actors are historical or are vividly imagined.

In fact, exuberant praise for such martial action pours out of almost every text we use, whether imaginative chivalric stories, manuals of knighthood, biographies of noted knights, or chronicles. Even pagan knights are elevated by their show of great prowess. The romance *Story of Merlin* pictures the young Gawain (affectionately called by a nickname) awestruck by the Saxon King Brandon on a field of battle:

And when Sir Gawainet saw what he was doing and the great slaughter of his people, he was certain that he was a highborn man of mighty stock, and he showed by the way he fought that he was a king or a prince; Sir Gawainet highly esteemed him, and would have been very glad if he had been a Christian.[7]

Virtually all medieval sources agree that violence in approved causes is righteous and that war is the highest expression of knightly manliness. Great blows delivered prove the high status of the man wielding the sword. The ascending scale of praiseworthy categories of fighting set forth by Geoffroi de Charny has become widely recognized in scholarly analysis.[8] In his *Book of Chivalry* he repeatedly intones that "he who does more is more worthy" and he leaves no doubt that the doing involves combat.[9] Individual jousting is good, the yet more demanding and dangerous group combat of the tourney is even better, but war is best. A century earlier, Bertrand de Born had anticipated Charny's zeal:

---

[6] Discussed in Chapter 10.

[7] Pickens, trans., "Story of Merlin," in *Lancelot-Grail* ed., Lacey, gen. 385; OF in Sommer, ed., *Vulgate Version*, II, 394.

[8] Kaeuper and Kennedy, *Book of Chivalry*, 84–91.

[9] E.g. ibid., 86: "qui plus fait miex vault." His English contemporary Thomas of Lancaster is said in a royal grant to be a man "who delights in acts of war." *Calendar of Patent Rolls, 1343–1345*, 196.

It pleases me ... when a lord is first to the attack on his horse, armed, without fear; for thus he inspires his men with valiant courage. When the battle is joined, each man must be ready to follow him with pleasure, for no one is respected until he has taken and given many blows.

I tell you, eating or drinking or sleeping hasn't such savour for me as the moment I hear both sides shouting "Get 'em!" and I hear riderless horses crashing through the shadows, and I hear men shouting "Help! Help!" and I see the small and the great falling in the grassy ditches, and I see the dead with splintered lances, decked with pennons, through their sides.[10]

Nearly a century after Charny, Jean de Beuil in *Le Jouvencel* creates a character who sings out in a similar strain: "War! What a joyful thing it is! One hears and sees so many fine things, and learns so much that is good."[11] Informing Charny's scale of martial virtue and the joy of *Le Jouvencel* and Bertrand de Born is a mental framework we might term worship of the demigod prowess, for to *gens d'armes* prowess ranked a near-deity whose hard service requires great effort and intense physical suffering, willingly and even joyfully endured for the great rewards on offer. All the model knights whose careers we especially follow in this book – and not merely Charny – could join the chorus. They all show significantly complex views of chivalry that include courtliness, largesse, and love; occasionally they show complications of thought about war and religion, recognizing moral ambiguities, or lamenting the loss of companions and the disruption of life in war.[12] Yet with laser-like intensity all focus on truly impressive fighting, which (in company with Charny) they may admire in forms of extreme chivalric sport, but which they find most fully exercised in war. Prowess often appears a virtual synonym for chivalry itself, for chivalry represents a performance of prowess as well as a set of ideals. Great chivalry is often said to be performed in deeds that are tellingly termed *chevaleries*. In the *Life of William Mashal*[13] chivalry is explicitly said to drive men on to just such great feats.[14] At one point his biographer enthuses that the Marshal "led

---

[10] Paden et al., *Poems of the Troubadour*, 338–343.

[11] *Le Jouvencel*, ii, 20, quoted in Wright, *Knights and Peasants*, 26.

[12] This frame of mind and many examples are provided in R. W. Kaeuper, *Chivalry and Violence*, 129–160. The tension between this mental framework and religious views is discussed in Kaeuper, *Holy Warriors*, and in Chapter 9 of this book.

[13] See, e.g., *Histoire*, lines 4750, 5584, 5595, 6232, 7898, 8716. The author fears that lesser exploits such as hunting with hounds or formal jousting will render chivalry helpless (4305–4307).

[14] *Histoire*, 2686–2692.

such a very fine life / that many were jealous of him. / He spent his life in tournaments and at war / and travelled through all the lands / where a knight should think of winning renown."[15] Pero Niño's biographer assures readers that on his first day of battle his hero at last got the combat he had long craved.[16] The sentiment parallels his assertion that noble renown is a matter "befitting knights and those who pursue the calling of War and the art of Chivalry."[17] He speaks easily of feats or deeds of chivalry, and refers to its great physical labors.[18] Robert Bruce, his biographer tells us, performed great deeds of chivalry;[19] some of his better sword or ax blows would, in fact, put him in a league with the romance hero Lancelot. Likely, one reason for the popularity of epic or romance literature for knights is that authors can follow individual sword or lance blows into and through the bodies of opponents, details so often lost in a chronicle's unsatisfyingly broad assertion that many great deeds of arms were performed.[20]

In fact, the massive corpus of *chansons de geste* stands like a towering war memorial. If most epics portray the harrowing nature of war, specifying its bloody anatomical results for warriors in detail, it never casts doubt on war's necessity, the heroism it embodies, or the glory it ensures. These are truly songs of great deeds, and the doing is starkly martial. The vast admiration in which martial deeds are cloaked is actually heightened by the unremitting portrayal of the struggle, the likelihood of dark periods of constant combat or even darker endings. Glory, eternal remembrance by other fighting men, and merit in the eyes of God are the glowing rewards.

Much the same can be said of works of romance, for they often further the valorization. We may be inclined to consider romance as less violent and certainly less focused on bloody battles than are epics, but in fact these texts regularly exult muscular feats of prowess and often glowingly portray war on an ambitious scale; many pages of most romances resound with the clash of armies and are soon littered with the human detritus of battles; jousting on individual quests is endlessly repeated. Audiences apparently could not get enough of it.

---

[15] Ibid., 1512–1517.   [16] Evans, 16.   [17] Ibid., 7.

[18] Ibid., 4, 6, 7, 9, 17, 18. In company with Charny and unlike the Marshal biographer, he is willing to include martial sport alongside war among the great labors of chivalry (18).

[19] *Barbour's Bruce*, bk. 6, line 12.

[20] The chronicles of Jean le Bel and Froissart provide ample evidence on this point.

A new emphasis on love is surely significant, but not because it drives out war and violence; often it provides a new stimulus, for love inspired prowess and prowess inspired love. Any reading of, say, most of the component romances in the vast Vulgate Cycle of romance or even the elegant stories of Chrétien de Troyes can provide sufficient confirmation.

That such attitudes would help to stimulate and sustain war should cause little surprise. Perhaps only our unshakable commitment to an idea of chivalry as essentially an agency of restraint has sometimes masked this obvious connection between a chivalric mentality centered on prowess and ceaseless medieval warfare. In the medieval social scheme, knights were indeed "those who fight." We must, however, add an element of motivation that is present but less emphasized than individual prowess. Chronicles will clearly show us the great importance of vast loads of loot carted off while on campaign. And they will show as well the mind-numbing destruction left in the path of campaigns. The torch may be missing from the museum wall, but it cannot be forgotten in analysis of knighthood and war.

6

CHIVALRY AND WAR

In the modern world we feel confident that we know exactly what war is. Thankfully, for most this sense derives only from awareness of conflicts remote in time or space, miniaturized on the screen of some electronic device, or splashed with brutal color on the vast cinema screen within overwhelming darkness; and both cases present technological vistas of sweeping, thunderous destruction in which grimy men and women heroically or at least stoically "get the job done" so that the rest of us can sleep peacefully in our beds and the fighters can soon return to restored civilian life and the degree of peace we take as normal.

In the medieval world, however, war edged closer to representing the normal and acceptable state of things. Whereas many modern people consider war a tragic mistake, most medieval people knew that the first war took place in heaven (God and his angels throwing out Satan and his rebels). As Honoré Bonet wrote in the late fourteenth century in his *Tree of Battles* (summing up much previous discussion), it would not be natural for the world to be at peace, for war came from God who awards victory and could be evil only in its use rather than its basic nature. If the innocent suffer, divine will may be allowing them to do penance for their sins even before death sends them to final judgment.[1] Moreover, medieval warfare took a greater

---

[1] Coopland, ed., trans., Honoré Bonet, *The Tree of Battles* (Cambridge, MA: Harvard University Press, 1949), 81, 118, 125, 158. Suffering as penance performed before death and judgment was a feature of knightly pious belief. See Chapter 9.

variety of forms and investments of personnel and resources. Two
lords quarreling over possession of a village and its revenues could
without hearing a contradictory voice characterize their conflict as
war; precursors of the Montagues and Capulets could seize arms and
rush into narrow Florentine streets shouting for war; the followers
of sovereigns disputing a province or a crown made war financed by
increasingly effective systems of taxation. Conducting licit violence
on any manageable scale represented the exercise of a right, a sign
and possession of sufficiently high status to be entitled to make war.
Those who possessed such authority the French termed *chevetaines
de guerre*, but there were many such "war chiefs" occupying upper
ranges of the social pyramid and more who longed to possess and
exercise the coveted right to use violence to secure goals. Only
slowly could this right to make war be restricted to sovereigns.
States were just forming at the beginning of the age of chivalry,
and though they pressed for sovereign rights with some success over
the chivalric centuries, the chaotic and shifting conditions of
Anglo-French warfare in the later Middle Ages increased the effective number of combatants across a wide swath of Europe from
Scotland to the Mediterranean.

Fitting chivalric ideas and practices into the swirl of this warfare
over centuries may be possible if we concentrate first on the
warriors themselves (a courtesy they would appreciate and might,
in fact, demand), and then turn to the impact of war on the
nonchivalric or subchivalric population at large – that is, to those
who often receive considerably less attention in analysis of medieval warfare. Each of these broad subjects will be subdivided, and
some overlap is inevitable. A first approach asks if chivalry shaped
warfare as a game of gentlemen who played by clear and even
humane rules. After dispensing with romantic conceptions, the
emphasis will fall on rules of war created and accepted by the
warrior elite. Within the second broad section, knightly treatment
of what we can loosely term "civilians" will first be analyzed,
followed by investigation of the responsibility of the elite warriors
for actions such as ravaging, looting, pillaging, arson, rape, and
ransom of noncombatant captives (Figure 5). Warfare and chivalry,
however, constitute so vast a topic that discussion focuses in
Chapter 7 on the mock war of tournament, and continues in the
following set of chapters (Part IV), which investigate chivalry in

Figure 5 If men-at-arms tried to protect their home territory, they also inflicted much damage in lands of others through standard practices of ravaging and looting. Armies looted for profit, to show the incapacity of an enemy lord, and to reduce his financial base.

relationship with governing ideals of major institutions that we loosely term church and state.

WAS CHIVALRIC WARFARE A GAME OF GENTLEMEN?

War free from deception and greed?

Some ideas about warfare of the Middle Ages have been a long time in dying. One notion still active in popular culture holds that medieval warfare was a grand game played by athletic gentlemen who knew and kept its rules.[2] This may have been close to the view of elite medieval warriors. As Nigel Bryant says of the chronicler Jean le Bel, who graphically narrated the opening phase of the Hundred Years War, "there is an overwhelming sense that the world is the fighting class's playing field, a place for a man to enforce his rights and prove his prowess."[3] But he concludes that devastation caused by war was to these men "merely a regrettable consequence."[4] We might pardonably wonder how much regret they felt as they triumphed and collected wagonloads of loot. In short, whatever game elements

---

[2] See the discussion in Mark Girouard, *The Return to Camelot: The English Gentleman and Chivalry*, 231–249.
[3] Bryant, ed., trans., *The True Chronicles of Jean le Bel*, 8.   [4] Ibid.

knights may have found in war, the reality for others was frequently devastating. As Bryant says, the devastations wrought by Edward III's armies are narrated "on a breathtaking and chilling scale."[5]

Avoiding a breezy conception of ideal warfare does not prevent us from recognizing the strong case Matthew Strickland and John Gillingham have made for certain basic changes in the nature of war at the dawn of chivalry. This scholarly case, closely attuned to the hard nature of medieval war (and contesting any line of sight through rose-tinted spectacles), underscores significant moderations as the heroic age of early Germanic and Viking warfare ended. In the heyday of such early warfare, warriors defeated and captured in battle had often been slaughtered as the final act of carnage on a field already soaked with blood.[6] The era was also characterized by widespread raiding to acquire slaves. The shift away from these practices by roughly the eleventh century was significant. Widespread slave-raiding gradually disappeared in most of Western Europe, and medieval instances of what the modern world has come to label "ethnic cleansing" likewise declined. John Gillingham has emphasized the reduced likelihood of women being dragged off and degraded by victors. It is worth emphasizing that both Strickland and Gillingham would be quick to point out the need for a realistic approach to

---

[5] Ibid.

[6] Matthew Strickland, *War and Chivalry* (New York: Cambridge University Press, 1996), 1–30; "Killing or Clemency? Changing Attitudes to Conduct in War in Eleventh and Twelfth-Century Britain and France," in *Krieg im Mittelalter*, ed. H. H. Kortüm (Berlin: Akademie Verlag, 2001), 93–122; "Rules of War and War without Rules, with Special Regard to the Relationship of Combatants and Noncombatants in the Middle Ages," in *Transcultural Wars from the Middle Ages to the Twenty-First Century*, ed. H. H. Kortüm (Berlin: Academie Verlag, 2006), 107–140; John Gillingham, "Women, Children and the Profits of War," in *Gender and Historiography: Studies in the Earlier Middle Ages in Honour of Pauline Stafford*, eds. Janet L. Nelson, Susan Reynolds, and Susan M. Johns (London: Institute of Historical Research, 2012), 61–74; "1066 and the Introduction of Chivalry," in *Law and Government in Medieval England and Normandy: Essays in Honour of Sir James Holt*, eds. G. Garnett and J. Hudson (Cambridge: Cambridge University of Press, 1994), 21–55; "Conquering the Barbarians: War and Chivalry in Twelfth-Century Britain and Ireland," ch. 3 in *The English in the Twelfth Century: Imperialism, National Identity, and Political Values* (Rochester: Boydell & Brewer, 2000), 41–58; and "Christian Warriors and the Enslavement of Fellow Christians," in *Chevalerie et christianisme aux XIIe et XIIIe siècles*, eds. M. Aurell and C. Girbea (Rennes: Presses Universitaires de Rennes, 2011), 237–256.

medieval warfare generally – even after these changes – and they stand far apart from any romanticizing of a warrior elite. Causation for the changes that interest them, they argue, should likely be sought in broad societal alterations, such as the decline of the very institution of slavery in the heartland of chivalry, rather than in any abstract elite benevolence. Moreover, they insist that the reduction of slaughter and slavery in warfare did not mean the utter disappearance of ravaging or civilian loss. Such horrors of war as looting, arson, capture of civilians for ransom, and rape continued to be inflicted almost casually upon civilian populations throughout the Middle Ages and beyond.[7] Plentiful instances of such conduct will appear in the analysis of this chapter and can readily be encountered elsewhere. Yet the remarkable change toward regular if not inevitable ransoming of prisoners that these historians have emphasized retains its importance. These changes, they assert, ushered in what they would identify as the age of chivalry and what Jean Flori and others would label the prehistory of chivalry.[8]

By contrast, the popular and romantic vision continues to shape opinions. Beginning students often bring glossy ideals to the subject, imagining that chivalry rendered medieval warfare totally different from the warfare practiced in nearly all other known ages. High medieval war as conducted by high-minded gentlemen supposedly guided this dangerous sporting enterprise by a strict and universal ethical code of honor featuring self-regulating and even self-denying norms. Common good (including even that of common people) was deliberately assured by those who had an inherent right to fight no

---

[7] Strickland, *Chivalry and Warfare*, 258–290; Laurence R. Marvin, "Atrocity and Massacre in the High and Late Middle Ages," in *Theatres of Violence: Massacre, Mass Killing and Atrocity throughout History* (New York: Berghahn Books, 2012), 50–62; Clifford J. Rogers, "Bellum Hostile and 'Civilians' in the Hundred Years' War," in *Civilians in the Path of War*, eds. Mark Grimsely and Clifford J. Rogers (Lincoln: University of Nebraska Press, 2002), 33–77; Craig Taylor, *Chivalry and the Ideals of Knighthood during the Hundred Years War*, 208–230. L. J. Andrew Villalon, "'Cut Off Their Heads, or I'll Cut Off Yours': Castilian Strategy and Tactics in the War of the Two Pedros and the Supporting Evidence from Murcia," in *The Hundred Years War, pt. II*, eds. L. J. A. Villalon and Donald J. Kagay (Leiden: Brill, 2008), 153–184; N. Wright, *Knights and Peasants: The Hundred Years War in the French Countryside* (Rochester: Boydell & Brewer, 2000), passim. H. J. Hewitt, *Organization of War under Edward III: 1338–62* (Manchester: Manchester University Press, 1966), 93–139.
[8] Flori, *Idéologie du glaive: préhistoire du chevalerie* (Geneva: Droz, 1983).

less than to rule. As a sporting affair, chivalric warfare is claimed to have emphasized fairness of combat, which apparently means that individual warriors or entire armies took no advantage of each other and practiced no deception. Sheer mental commitment and muscular capacity determined outcomes on a carefully leveled playing field. The knights' keen sense of honor is thought to have animated not only self-restraint but also control over the sadly common, if deplorable, proclivities of lesser mortals who always to some extent, and increasingly, filled out the ranks of medieval armies. Men of honor, the interpretation holds, turned instinctively away from any dreary desire for profit in war as from a dread stain. Playing well was the key; winning was secondary. Such pure motives are sometimes claimed for the knighthood outright, but they may merely hover as unspoken yet powerful assumptions over narratives of campaign and combat. Scholars may express disapproval at any sign of failure. The natural elite should have absorbed "true chivalry" in early training or, more likely, had begun life with these norms inscribed in their genetic code. The argument of this chapter holds that even if such views were believed by the medieval elite and were later revived by romantics, scholars need not be fooled.

The virtual absence of such "true chivalry" in the evidence cannot be denied. As already argued, the chivalry that knights cherished and practiced was of an entirely different sort.[9] Yet questioning such romantic interpretations requires an uphill climb, for positing an age of more humane warfare may be one of those hopeful concepts we simply feel compelled to preserve. Johan Huizenga suggested a parallel case about persistent belief in a single, lightning-stroke Renaissance that remade the world.[10] In the case of warfare, too, we may feel better simply thinking it possible: such restraint is within human nature; the impossible dream could happen again.

Of course no such reductive and romantic views can be sustained once any significant part of the vast body of evidence has been

---

[9] Chapter 2.

[10] See "The Problem of the Renaissance," in *Johan Huizinga, Men and Ideas: History, the Middle Ages, the Renaissance,* trans. James S. Holmes and Hans van Marle (New York: Meridian Books, 1959), 243–287. "The Renaissance cannot be considered as a pure contrast to medieval culture, nor even as a frontier territory between medieval and modern times... The picture displayed by the Renaissance is one of transformation and hesitation, one of transition and of intermixture of cultural elements" (286).

considered. Recognizing complexity in motivations and practices is no less necessary for understanding chivalric warfare than for discerning long chronological arcs of change that make a lightning-stroke Renaissance unlikely. The mass of evidence available in this book and many others contradicts any comforting notion that once upon a time warfare rose free from messy moral questions about tactics or widespread destruction, killing, arson, looting, and rape.

The issue of honor is crucial in this analysis. Acting honorably in a modern sense conveys quite different qualities from those at the heart of the concept of honor within medieval knighthood. Knights who were considered thoroughly honorable carried out warfare using the very tactics that romantics think "true chivalry" avoided and condemned. Such warriors were not considered failures or miscreants because they did not subscribe to the glossy ideal retrospectively imposed upon them by modern wishes. Although most scholars fully acknowledge the significant influence of medieval concepts of honor on the conduct of arms bearers, they realize that honor, so conceived, need not be set in opposition to pragmatic use of military stratagems nor to winning welcomed material gain, both secured by prowess. The young William Marshal after his first battle found himself covered in glory but empty of pocket, unable to provide the gift requested of him by his lord who was intent on teaching him the basic, pragmatic lesson that warfare produces wealth for able warriors.[11] William's full embrace of the lesson was manifest in his subsequent career as he acquired status and wealth on the tourney circuit and on the battlefield.[12] Wolfram von Eschenbach frankly declares, "Anyone who has engaged in battle knows how great is the need to win rich booty."[13] Honor was crucial, but it was no stranger to profit; indeed, profit buttressed honor quite nicely. A lord's collection of great estates in England, in fact, was termed his "honour." Many of the issues of Geoffroi de Charny's *Demandes*, his book of questions for elite knightly discussion on chivalric practice, concern the proper distribution of loot and ransoming of prisoners, as we will see. He knew that increase of profit through chivalric violence was scarcely a diminution of honor. In his *True Chronicles* Jean le

---

[11] *History of William Marshal*, lines 1142–1163.
[12] The full career is detailed in biographies by Sidney Painter, Georges Duby, and David Crouch.
[13] Mustard and Passage, *Parzival*, 195.

Bel, an almost fawning admirer of chivalric military triumph, can scarcely contain his delight over the vast amount of loot continually acquired by the English and their allies sweeping through the French countryside in the early phases of the Hundred Years War. Writing of one such expedition setting out from the Gironde into a region "so wealthy that they didn't know what to do with all they found," he enthuses,

No greater or finer campaign was ever heard of, truly, than that conducted by the worthy Earl of Derby, capturing so many well fortified towns and impregnable castles. It involved some great and notable feats of prowess and remarkable adventures – it would be tiresome to recount them all: there'd be no end in it! And no man alive could count the vast wealth and incalculable riches that were won either from looting or by ransoming towns and captives.[14]

Recognizing this truth in no way diminishes our attention to the active pursuit of honor via prowess. Before the Battle of Methven, the Bruce says to his men, "Ye ar ilkan yycht and worthy / And full of gret chevalry, / And wate rycht weill quhat honour is."[15] During this battle Barbour says of the Scots, "For the best and the worthiest / That wilfull war to wyn honour / Plungyt in the stalwart stour / And routis ruyd about thaim dang."[16] There are, indeed, cases of even terminal displays of spectacular gamesmanship related to honor. Trapped on an Egyptian village lane by Muslim foes during the first crusade of Louis IX (1250), Gautier de Chatillon, as Joinville narrates, stood tall in his stirrups and with upraised sword arm repeatedly and defiantly shouted his family name. Joinville later saw his great warhorse splattered with blood and heard a man boast that he had slit Gautier's throat.[17]

Unsurprisingly, however, in most cases winning and carting off wagonloads of loot and a cohort of profit-yielding prisoners seemed more important than merely playing the game whatever the outcome; the evidence is clearly documented in narrative sources, in formal treatises on deeds of arms, or even in scenes imagined in

---

[14] Bryant, *True Chronicles of Jean le Bel*, 159–160.

[15] *Barbour's Bruce*, bk. 2, lines 337–340.   [16] Ibid., lines 356–357.

[17] Shaw, ed., trans., *Joinville and Villehardouin: Chronicles of the Crusade*, 261. At Bannockburn (1314), Giles d'Argentin's refusal to retreat with Edward II's routed army and his determination, instead, to ride in style against fatal Scots' spears quickly comes to mind, as does the blind king of Bohemia advancing with a mounted squire on either side touching armored elbows to guide him to a similar death at the hands of the English during the battle of Crécy (1346).

chivalric literature. The attitude is concisely summed up in the telling reference of the mid-fourteenth-century chronicler Geoffrey le Baker, who refers to "the principal honour of victory."[18] Of course honor could be won by fighting well even while losing, as the Black Prince graciously said to the defeated Jean II after the battle of Poitiers in 1356;[19] but how much better to have fought and won. Losing could be fatal (even if capture of live enemies worth ransoming remained a goal); hand-to-hand fighting with edged weaponry amid flights of bolts and arrows did indeed produce casualties, even among those well cased in armor; and defeat easily became rout, a disaster in which the death toll climbed steeply off the scale of any game board. Even Geoffroi de Charny in his set of chivalric questions for the Order of the Star asked with perfect frankness when one could flee a lost field without loss of honor.[20] Excising such evidence from our conception of this warfare obliterates the warriors' pressing need for locating pragmatism within a complex and practical working code.

This code scarcely shied away from deception and trickery as an aid to victory. William of Orange, loyally coming to the rescue of King Louis in the "Crowning of Louis," "wanted to operate wisely; he left a thousand knights in four ambush parties and led on two hundred, all very well equipped."[21] Throughout all periods we might call chivalric, in fact, winning often required use of the full repertoire of timeless military stratagems and tactics, including ambush, deception, and nighttime assaults on unsuspecting castles or town garrisons; as we will see shortly, it also required what a modern view might consider nonheroic ravaging of noncombatant fields and homes. All these actions were carried out with minimal worry about whether they were truly chivalric. At one point in the ceaseless twelfth-century combat between Capetian and Plantagenet forces, William Marshal,

---

[18] Preest, *Chronicle of Geoffrey le Baker*, 132.

[19] Jean le Bel, *True Chronicles*, 228, quotes the words of the prince.

[20] See Question 7 in Charny's *Demandes* in Michael Taylor, "A Critical Edition of Geoffroy de Charny's *Livre Charny* and the *Demandes pour la joute, les tournois et la guerre*." (PhD dissertation, University of North Carolina, Chapel Hill, 1977). Steven Muhlberger published an English translation of these questions in *Charny's Men-at-Arms* (Wheaton, IL, 2014). See also Kaeuper and Kennedy, *Book of Chivalry*, 102–103, where Charny suggests a young knight must know when "to make a safe and honorable withdrawal, when it is time to do so."

[21] David Hoggan, trans., *Crowning of Louis*, laisse 36, in Glanville Price, ed., *William of Orange: Four Old French Epics*, correcting the term "ambushed" to "ambush."

having learned that the French king was dispersing his armed force, advised Henry II to do the same, but then to issue a secret order to reassemble and suddenly attack, ravaging undefended Capetian territory. King Henry enthusiastically responded, "By God's eyes, Marshal, you are highly courtly (*molt estes corteis*) and have advised me very well."[22] The view was not limited to one side in this conflict. The chronicler Jordan Fantosme records that Philip of Flanders, "that noble warrior," counseled ravaging as a major strategy of war to Louis VII, who welcomed and approved the advice.[23]

Even the mock war of the early tournament, the sport par excellence of the chivalric elite, utilized tactics that a romantic view would consider unfair. Such tricks were, in fact, praised by the Marshal's biographer. Count Philip of Flanders, he says, would announce that he would not take part in a tournament, but then would suddenly rush into the fray when the opposing sides had become tired and scattered across the field. Such a stratagem was adopted by the Young King Henry (son of Henry II), an admired patron of chivalry, who had suffered from its use on his own tourney team.[24]

It is not impossible to find evidence even of bribery and assassination. In 1369 Pedro I was challenged for the throne of Castile by his half-brother, Enrique de Trastámara, who was besieging him in one of his castles. When the rivals decided on a parley, Enrique sent as his negotiator the famous knight Bertrand du Guesclin. King Pedro offered him a large bribe to betray Enrique, but Bertrand told Enrique of Pedro's offer and asked Enrique to make it worth his while to behave differently. Since Enrique outbid King Pedro, Bertrand falsely informed the king that a peace had been negotiated and led Pedro to Enrique's tent. There Enrique stabbed his half-brother in the face, killed him in ensuing fight, and became Enrique II, the founder of the new Trastámara dynasty.[25]

These stratagems of war, moreover, were accepted by a full range of authorities in civil and canon law and in theology, so long as sworn

---

[22] *History of William Marshal*, lines 7779–7802, with my translation of words in parentheses.

[23] Cited and quoted in Strickland, *War and Chivalry*, 285.

[24] Crouch, *Tournament*, 85.

[25] Pero López de Ayala, "Crónica del Rey don Pedro," in *Biblioteca de Autores Españoles*, ed. M. Rivadeneyra (Madrid: Impresores de Camara de S.M., 1877), vol. 68, 554–556.

word was not broken in the process.[26] One section of the great Castilian law code, *Siete Partidas* (begun after the mid-thirteenth century), grasps the nettle and asserts that knights must combine dexterity in the use of weapons with cunning, for "shrewdness causes them to seek ways to accomplish better and more safely what they desire." This law code adds that astuteness "enables them to overcome many with few, and to escape from dangers when they encounter them."[27] In her popular late fourteenth-century treatise, *The Book of Deeds of Arms and of Chivalry*, Christine de Pizan summarizes pragmatic views on military deviousness stretching back into antiquity.[28] "Wiles and the subtle chivalric devices that the ancients have discussed" get her full attention and admiration, comprising nearly 10 percent of her book. "Reading these," she plainly exhorts, "can set a good example for similar action, if deemed desirable by those who find themselves in similar situations through fortunes of war."[29]

Many knights needed no convincing. When warriors self-consciously invoked fairness in fighting they might be employing a tactic of their own to throw an enemy off balance or gain an advantage.[30] Philip VI tried to get the English army closely besieging Calais to come out of their encircling fortifications and fight on open terrain, only to be told that he would have to come to them.[31] Moving against invading Scots early in his reign, the young Edward III requested their agreement for him to cross an inconveniently intervening river in order to fight them on open ground; this request was similarly rebuffed, as the Scots said that they would stay where they were, twisting the knife by adding that they had happily been burning and wasting that part of Edward's realm.[32] We have already observed Robert Bruce successfully shaming three would-be assassins armed with bows into coming within fatal reach of his sword (and his faithful hound's jaws); yet this same Bruce justified a night assault in which enemies were to be slain in their beds while asleep; he and his subordinates regularly led their forces

---

[26] See Craig Taylor, *Chivalry and the Ideals of Knighthood*, 231–275, who notes the theme and some qualifications.

[27] Both quotations from *Siete Partidas*, Law VIII, 421.

[28] *Book of Deeds of Arms and of Chivalry*, 81–104. The two quotations that follow appear at 81.

[29] Ibid., 81.   [30] Discussion in Strickland, *War and Chivalry*.

[31] Bryant, *True Chronicles of Jean le Bel*, 199–200.   [32] Ibid., 45–46.

in surprises and ambushes. Could he have read it, the Bruce might
well have appreciated a classical case cited by Christine de Pizan
in which a sleeping enemy sentry was killed, the action being
justified by a claim that the slayer "considered a sleeping man
dead."[33]

A full account of ambush and ruse in the Hundred Years War
would require a thick separate volume.[34] At Mauron in 1352,
a devastating ambush – which the chronicler le Bel termed "a
brilliant trap" – killed eighty-nine members of the French royal
Order of the Star.[35] Geoffroi de Charny tried to buy his way
through a gate at Calais so that the surprise of a night attack
might gain the city for the French king, its rightful lord in his
eyes.[36] Near the traditional end of the Middle Ages, Sir Thomas
Malory apparently adopted the tactic of ambush (as well as house-
breaking and extortion) in his own vigorous knightly career and
wrote several instances of ambush almost casually into his great
book on Arthurian chivalry.[37] Scholars have in the past worried
over his behavior (especially the charges of sexual assault), questioning whether an immoral man could write a moral book, but it
is possible without lapsing into mindless relativism to think all such
terms need to be contextualized in their own age and within
a nonromantic view of chivalry. Judging them by our own standards (or those of some nineteenth-century revival) will not take
us back into the medieval world we seek to understand. Flexibility
in concepts and an undoubted desire to win seem better explana-
tions for all such military ruses than any moral weakness or violations to be charged against them on the basis of a supposed
absolute and universally agreed code constructed of self-denying
rules. In short, this chapter urges a somber assessment of chivalric
warfare, agreeing with the concise view of Craig Taylor that
"medieval knights and men-at-arms were not gentlemen amateurs
playing at war."[38]

---

[33] *Deeds of Arms and of Chivalry*, 97.
[34] See the helpful analysis in Taylor, *Chivalry and the Ideals of Knighthood*, 231–275.
[35] Discussed in Taylor, *Chivalry and the Ideals of Knighthood*, 217; he cites Jean le Bel.
[36] Discussed with sources cited in Kaeuper and Kennedy, *Book of Chivalry*, 10–11.
[37] Vinaver, ed., *Malory: Works*; see Vinaver's Introduction, v, for Malory himself,
and 17, 24, 150, 301, 828 for references to ambush.
[38] Taylor, *Chivalry and the Ideals of Knighthood*, 104.

KNIGHT VERSUS KNIGHT AND A LAW OF ARMS

Violations of standards actually derived from romantic visions do not, of course, imply that chivalric warfare was formless, fought between groups of warriors without any guidelines or by men who foamed at the mouth. Only agreed ideas about the myriad issues of combat would prevent an intolerable, utterly Hobbesian environment; the interest of men-at-arms required agreement on basic guidelines for a dangerous, yet profitable occupation. Honorable reputations depended on compliance; pragmatic military practice relied on it. Experience would quickly have taught that one could lose the fight on some dark day even if glorious triumph crowned other times beneath cloudless skies. When the crucial city of Calais finally surrenders to Edward III after an exhausting siege, the exasperated king wanted the defenders and citizens to place themselves utterly at his mercy, accepting his decree of captivity and ransom or being summarily put to death. With classic pragmatism, the renowned Sir Walter Mauny advised King Edward:

It wouldn't bode well if you were to send us to one of your strongholds! By holy Mary, we wouldn't be so willing to go if you condemn these people to death as you say, for we'd suffer the same fate in a similar position, even though we were doing our duty.[39]

Mauny said what all knew: Each side would ape the measures taken by the other; some conventions clearly were needed.

Often these guidelines were driven by a mixture of prudence with a keen desire for financial gain. Capturing and ransoming prisoners offered a lucrative as well as a prudent practice for warriors who in long careers could expect to be both captors and prisoners. A captor who treated his prisoner badly, as Sidney Painter pointed out many years ago, could expect the same treatment when he fell into his opponent's hands.[40] Yet no scholars would deny that killing of prisoners continued in some circumstances and some regions. John Gillingham, Matthew Strickland, and Craig Taylor have noted significant instances of the killing of prisoners in the British Isles and in France.[41] Taylor laconically writes that "mercy was less common on

---

[39] Bryant, *True Chronicles of Jean le Bel*, 201.   [40] *French Chivalry*, 34, 44.
[41] John Gillingham, "Killing and Mutilating Political Enemies in the British Isles from the Late Twelfth to the Early Fourteenth Century: A Comparative Study," in *Britain and Ireland, 900–1300: Insular Responses to Medieval European Change*, ed. Brendan Smith (New York: Cambridge University Press, 1999), 130–134;

the battlefields of the later middle ages than chivalric legend might suppose."[42] Perhaps, he suggests, its slight actual presence explains why mercy is so emphasized by chivalric commentators.[43] Matthew Strickland has argued that men defeated and captured in fighting between the English and Celtic opponents were in danger.[44] Warren Brown cites the chronicler Froissart's claim that German captors treated their prisoners harshly to extract greater ransoms and stood, in effect, outside the zone of the chivalrous.[45] Enrique II of Castile promised to kill Don Martin Lopez de Cordoba, the Master of Calatrava and the defender of Carmona, when some royal troops were killed after they had been isolated and captured in the besieged town. Though previously Enrique had wanted to bring Lopez into his own service as a great knight, he now wanted the man dead, a goal that he achieved in brutal fashion.[46] Florentine Guelfs captured in the fortress of Capraia in 1248 by the Ghibellines under Emperor Frederick II were taken to Apulia and subsequently killed.[47] The chronicler Villani, who tells of this incident, also relates that a Florentine knight and noble, Messer Cece de' Bondelmonti, was captured in the castle Castiglione (in the territory of Lucca) in 1263; he was held honorably by Messer Farinata degli Uberti, a famous

Strickland, "Treason, Feud and the Growth of State Violence: Edward I and the 'War of the Earl of Carrick,' 1306–7," in *War, Government and Aristocracy in the British Isles, c.1150–1500: Essays in Honour of Michael Prestwich*, eds. Chris Given-Wilson, Ann J. Kettle, and Len Scales (Rochester: Boydell & Brewer, 2008), 112; Craig Taylor, *Chivalry and the Ideals of Knighthood*, provides a broad survey, 177–208.

[42] This acute phrase appeared in unpublished work of Craig Taylor. Dr. Taylor graciously assured me that he still endorses this statement.

[43] Taylor, *Chivalry and the Ideals of Knighthood*, 215. The literary emphasis on mercy, combined with vengeance, is stressed in Kaeuper, "Revenge and Mercy in Chivalric Thought," in *Peace and Protection in Medieval Europe*, eds. T. B. Lambert and D. Rollason (Toronto, 2009).

[44] Strickland, "The Vanquished Body: Some Conclusions and Comparisons," in *El Cuerpo Derrotado: Cómo trataban Muselmanes y Cristianos a los enemigos vencidos*, eds. Maribel Fierro and Francisco Garcia Fitz (Madrid: Consejo Superior de Investigaciones Cientificas, 2008), 531–573.

[45] Warren C. Brown, *Violence in Medieval Europe* (New York: Longman, 2011), 265, citing Froissart.

[46] *Chronicas de los reyes de castilla*, 3 vols., ed. Cayetan Rosell (Madrid: M. Rivadeneyra, 1975–1978), II, 20–21.

[47] Giovanni Villani, *Nuova Cronica*, ed. G. Porta (Parma: Letteratura italiana Einaudi, 1991), 259 (bk. 7.35).

Florentine knight and noble, but Farinata's brother, Messer Piero Asino degli Uberti, killed him in cold blood by striking him in the head.[48] Had he not been clad in elaborate armor, leading his captors to think he could provide a sizable ransom, the young Francis of Assisi (at that time eager for a knightly career) might well have been killed when captured in hill-town warfare between Assisi and Perugia in early thirteenth-century Italy.[49] Of course the clear disdain commonly felt by aristocrats for those below them enters any general calculation on treatment of prisoners. Men unable to pay ransoms and not protected by the law of arms might reasonably fear capture. Their danger calls to mind Gillingham's concise observation that "chivalry was essentially an aristocratic business."[50]

The multiplicity of needed guidelines was obvious. Given its importance, none could doubt the need for clear rules on distribution of loot, in what amounts, and under what circumstances. Ideas about how wars should properly begin and end were no less needed, as were settled understandings about pauses arranged by truce. Messengers under safe-conducts could carry out their missions only by common agreement that they not be harmed. Thus some actions, and especially breaking sworn word, were recognized as utterly disreputable, though late medieval writers complained that even this behavior occurred.[51]

---

[48] Villani, 317 (bk. 7.85). Cf. Villani, 378 (bk. 8.31): when the Sienese and the Florentine Ghibelline exiles were defeated in battle at the Colle di Valdelsa in 1269, the commander of the Sienese army, Messer Provenzano Salvani, was taken prisoner and then killed. Few prisoners were taken at the battle of Montaperti, the victors putting them all to death; ibid., 378–379. Though less thoroughly, Villani, 628 (bk. 9.72): when the White Guelf and Ghibelline exiles of Florence failed in their attempt to retake the city of Florence from the Black Guelfs in 1304, certain of the prisoners were killed: ibid., 628 (bk. 9.72). See ibid., 715 (bk. 10.43) for a case involving a fighting bishop killed in Rome. And see *The Chronicle of Salimbene de Adam*, eds. and trans. Joseph L. Baird, Giuseppe Baglivi, and John Robert Kane (Binghamton, NY: Medieval & Renaissance Texts & Studies, 1986), 188: Emperor Frederick II kills knightly prisoners from Parma. This chronicle notes torture and killings of noble prisoners, and later claims some were burned alive and says of the perpetrator, "I do not believe there has been a more evil man from the beginning of the world up to our own days." Ibid., 335, 369.

[49] Adrian House, Francis of Assisi (London: Chatto and Windus, 2000), 43–44, citing early biographers of Francis.

[50] Gillingham, *The English in the Twelfth Century: Imperialism, National Identity and Political Values* (Woodbridge, Suffolk: Boydell, 2000), 226.

[51] Taylor, *Chivalry and the Ideals of Knighthood*, 265–269.

These norms began to take form early. For the eleventh and twelfth centuries, as Matthew Strickland has argued, such guidelines remained rather informal; it is preferable to think in terms of custom (*mos*) rather than formally enacted law (*lex*). He notes that such pragmatic understandings among warriors (who sometimes violated them), though not a product of formal enactment by any authority, were widely discussed, debated, and practiced by fighting men. Narrative sources from these centuries allow us to detect working knightly conceptions on practices of war, for they praise some actions as exemplary (or at least recognize them as acceptable), while condemning others as violations. The Marshal, who warmly advised the tactic of deception to Henry II, nonetheless fervently hated the Lusignan family after one of them put a lance into the back of the unarmored Earl Patrick as he was just mounting his riding horse.[52] Even if, predictably, virtues shine upon the brows of those speaking and lapses besmirch their enemies, discussion of this sort retains significance.

That it has become common for historians to speak of a formal law of arms by the later Middle Ages is a tribute to the classic study Maurice Keen devoted to this topic. He sees the origin of a law of arms in the legal thought and judicial actions of the fourteenth and fifteenth centuries, especially on issues of profits of war.[53] Royal courts became involved in these issues. In France, for example, some captains suffered the death penalty because they had made war in the realm without possessing the required status that would legitimize their actions. The famous *routier* Merigot Marches claimed he had done all that a soldier "can and ought to do in a just war" and was thus not guilty of treason, robbery, murder, and arson, as charged by the justices. His claim was not accepted and he was beheaded.[54] If his case was complicated by issues of feudal ties, notions of just war, and the legitimacy of his link with the English crown, other ambitious fighters were condemned because they "completely lacked the title of *seigneur*."[55]

At a more abstract level, scholastic philosophers and canon lawyers wrestled with the difficult ideas of what warfare was just, and what

---

[52] *History of William Marshal*, lines 1645–1651.
[53] Keen, *The Laws of War in the Late Middle Ages* (London: Routledge, 1965), 63–81.
[54] Ibid., 96–100.
[55] Cases cited and sources provided in Keen, *Laws of War*, 100n1.

violence was even holy. Christine de Pizan, in a work warriors were more likely to have read or heard, drew upon these intellectual discussions in the later fourteenth century, and shows how a long tradition of philosophical norms might reach a wide audience of arms bearers. She is sure that despite all wrongs committed by wrongful people, war itself is just and is divinely approved.[56] If we can imagine warrior heads nodding in full approval, we might well picture more puzzlement registering as they discover her insistence that no seigneurial warfare can be launched without sovereign permission or her assertion that vengeance belongs to God alone.[57] Perhaps the men-at-arms waved a dismissive hand or even anticipated a line spoken to a cleric in *Monty Python and the Holy Grail*: "Skip a bit, brother."

Likely, the major deterrent to transgressive behavior was not royal legal action or intellectual disapproval, but ill fame, spread through-out the elite world. Knights in romance shout at someone about to sin against standards that he will be shame in all courts. It remains useful to remember, as Craig Taylor concisely states, that "There were no real institutional mechanisms to enforce military discipline in the middle ages."[58]

Such caution is commendable. The regulations cannot be thought carved in stone and set prominently beside each castle gate; they were not universally accepted and practiced, any more than prescriptive reform ideas in chivalric literature can be imagined as simple descrip-tions of quotidian behavior. Craig Taylor wisely suggests that the most basic rules about ransom of prisoners remained flexible and negotiable in the later Middle Ages and that deceptively clear works of Christine de Pizan and Honoré Bonet cannot be read as "straight-forward expositions of the law of arms."[59] Just as no single code of chivalry could be issued as a parchment pamphlet to newly dubbed knights, the laws of war remained to a surprising degree open for debate. In his treatise posing questions regarding joust, tournament,

---

[56] Pizan, *The Book of Deeds of Arms and of Chivalry*, 11–18. Her source was Honoré Bonet, who makes these views quite clear. See Coopland, ed., trans., Honoré Bonet, *The Tree of Battles of Honoré Bonet* (Cambridge, MA: Harvard University Press, 1949).

[57] Pizan, *Book of Deeds of Arms and of Chivalry*, 14–17.

[58] Craig Taylor has agreed to my quoting from his unpublished work.

[59] Comments from unpublished work by Craig Taylor, which he assures me repre-sent his views.

and war (*Demandes pour la joute, les tournois et la guerre*) written for the French royal chivalric order in the mid-fourteenth century, Geoffroi de Charny clearly reveals this somewhat open-ended quality of these "laws." On many points they seem still in the process of formation or even of definition of terms. Sadly, no answers to Charny's long list of questions are supplied in his treatise; the honored members of the Order of the Star were to debate the issues and respond to the twenty questions regarding joust, twenty-one on tournament, and a hefty ninety-three on war.[60] At times Charny poses questions in a concise and straightforward sentence or two before asking, "How will this be judged by the law of arms?" Often he provides mini-narratives that open even wider vistas on uncertainties in chivalric practice. Question 42 in the long section on war, for example, pictures part of a garrison riding out on a raid and asks whether the entire garrison should share in the booty won. Some of these little narrative scenes could generate plot lines for scenes in a *chanson de geste* or a romance, for they open debate on such topics as when men can leave a losing field of battle without shame and exactly how prisoners are to be taken, treated, and put to ransom. A handful of questions pose truly basic issues on the qualities of a warrior. Question 90 asks whether wisdom or prowess (*sen ou prouesce*) is to be preferred, a query accompanied by a phantom echo of the oliphant sounding in the distance.[61] A number of other questions explore proper terminology for classifying specific forms of combats and combatants. Charny wants the Order of the Star to ensure that all these matters of military chivalry be rendered clear and tidy; sorting out such unsettled issues advanced the martial enterprise and the honor that formed the very core of his existence and shaped thought in the body of men on whom he concentrated exclusively.[62]

---

[60] Michael Taylor, "A Critical Edition of Geoffroy de Charny's *Livre Charny* and the *Demandes pour la joute, les tournois et la guerre*" (PhD dissertation, University of North Carolina, Chapel Hill, 1977); for English translations, see Steven Muhlberger, *Jousts and Tournaments* (Union City, CA: Chivalry Bookshelf, 2002), and *Charny's Men-at-Arms* (Wheaton, IL: Freelance Press, 2014).

[61] Not only is this set of virtues a theme of the *Song of Roland*, but it is addressed by Ramon Llull, who states, "Chivalry and valour cannot be joined together unless there is wisdom and common sense, otherwise, folly and ignorance would be joined with the Order of Chivalry..." Llull, *Book of the Order of Chivalry*, trans. Fallows, 49.

[62] Comments by Matthew Strickland, War and Chivalry, 33–34; Nicholas Wright, *Knights and Peasants*, 43; and general discussion in David Whetham, *Just Wars and*

Some modern views suggest much more order and intellectual clarity, going so far as to argue that war was actually an enactment of legal process, as some medieval scholastic thinkers and canon lawyers wanted to imagine it. Such a view may be valid in the limited sense that warriors (like other members of the medieval elite) often had legal categories in mind and used them to justify their activities and status. Certainly good wartime propaganda could be enriched by claims that legal norms had been violated by an enemy.[63] However, caution might be useful in assessing the causative force of formal legal and philosophical ideas penned by intellectuals: to the extent that these concepts reinforced contemporary "laws" of war, their significance will be clear; Charny insists, for example, that good warfare requires that a formal defiance be given to an opponent before fighting begins, and, as David Whetham argues, the context for justifying any ruse or deception always mattered.

Scholastic and legal treatises may well have valorized warrior behavior more than they formed or restrained it, and modern scholarly prudence calls to mind T. F. T. Plucknett's characterization of the attitude of "most of the great litigants" of the time of Edward I concerning law in general: like this renowned royal knight, famous as a lawgiver, they considered law "as a mass of technicalities which might be ingeniously combined to secure . . . ends."[64] As we will see more thoroughly in the following chapter, elite warriors always carefully selected and adapted certain religious ideals in circulation to justify their military profession; they had long selectively adapted ideas from epic and romance literature that offered differing perspectives on issues of violence and even (more indirectly) on war. Of course they cherished the praise and valorization of their work written in grand treatises such as that of Ramon Llull or Christine de Pizan. Yet even authors who prescribed idealized behavior feared that the knights would not follow their ideals closely; inconvenient points of view could be modified in a highly selective fashion or quietly ignored altogether. Lull, in the *Book of Contemplation*, a work seldom read by modern scholars, unsparingly denounced knights as "the Devil's ministers" and rhetorically asked, "Who is there in the

---

Moral Victories: Surprise, Deception and the Normative Framework of European War in the Later Middle Ages (Leiden: Brill, 2009), 185–193.

[63] David Whetham shows that such charges were brought against Edward III in the campaign leading to the capture of Calais: *Just Wars*, 235–244.

[64] Plucknett, *Legislation of Edward I* (Oxford University Press, 1949), 1.

world who does as much harm as knights?"[65] He knew that his gilded
portrait of the warriors in the *Book of the Order of Chivalry* was often
more prescriptive than simply descriptive. Writing his book was an
act of whistling past the graveyard. More than a century later,
Christine de Pizan shared his worries, fearing that men-at-arms
committed acts that would "send them to hell forever." Of her
solemn warning, she admits that "many make light of this, for there
are plenty who care not a whit what the quarrel is, so long as they
have good wages and may commit robbery." Gathering force, she
continues,

And along with this, all, or most of them, forget that those who pass in the
exercise of arms the limits of proper warfare, whatever the quarrel, just or not,
as limited by law, condemn themselves to perdition.[66]

It is a remarkably frank view, quite different from that of the soldiers
to whom Shakespeare gives voice, as they sit around a fire in *Henry
V* (Act 4, Scene 1); their claim is that moral safety is secured for their
combat by the justness of their king's cause. Christine asserts that
terrible actions in war have eternal consequences for warriors, regardless of formal theological or legal justifications for the fighting.
Scholars would give much to possess a survey on attitudes to war
and its practices at the time, with standard Likert scales, boxes all
ticked, rating actions in warfare and likely consequences worldly or
otherwise.

Pragmatic concerns – including the winning of honor, of course –
seem a more likely foundation for operative guidelines in warfare
than inherent noble goodness among elite fighters or their motivation
from charity, justice, or abstract legitimacy as purveyed by scholastics,
legists, and other intellectuals. At base, customs governing conduct of
knights and men-at-arms, as Craig Taylor notes, "must reflect
a mounting awareness of the advantages to be gained through some
level of cooperation."[67] Toleration of chaos on campaign and battlefield would be as unlikely as a romantic vision of knights regularly and
willingly hobbling their chances of success or even of survival by

[65] Quoted in J. Hillgarth, *The Spanish Kingdoms* (Oxford, 1976), 60.
[66] This passage and the preceding quotations appear in her *Book of Deeds of Arms and of Chivalry*, trans. Summer Willard and ed. Charity Cannon Willard, 153.
[67] A statement from unpublished work, which Dr. Taylor has permitted me to quote. Even this level of cooperation could break down in the brutality of civil wars, as he notes.

adopting self-denying standards of campaign and combat, or by regular consultation of the most elevated ideals of scholastic or legal books.[68]

Writing prescriptively, Ramon Llull identified knights as protectors and denounced any who brought destruction to town or countryside as untrue to their calling:

> If destroying towns and castles, burning cities, laying waste trees and crops, killing livestock and robbing the highways was the office of and Order of the knights . . . the reason why Chivalry is constituted would be the same thing as its disorder and its contrary.[69]

Against this glowing ideal a candid description from the early days of the Hundred Years War can be set. Late in the summer of 1340 the army of Edward III was besieging Tournai, a town loyal to the French crown. A relieving army under Philip VI was maneuvering in the region to break the siege, but the river Marque, seemingly impassable, separated the two forces.

> Some of Edward's allies were anxious for action, as the chronicler Jean le Bel records. One evening, he reports, some Hainaulters and men of Brabant and Hesbaye, realizing that the French army was so near, conferred and agreed to go next day and reconnoiter their position, and if they saw an opportunity they'd venture an attack. They did as planned: next morning they rode up close to the enemy, but they didn't cross the river and couldn't see any French troops they could engage. Not wanting to return without leaving their mark, they set fire to two poor dwellings that remained unburnt and then rode back to their quarters.[70]

---

[68] Recognizing such a likelihood in no way diminishes the case that elite warriors had ideas and ideals; it suggests that they selected values carefully and drew more heavily on some sources than others. They seem more deeply engaged with the debates in epic and romance literature, for example, from treatises such as that of Ramon Llull, and the lay theology purveyed by sermon exempla (crusade and non-crusade) and encouragements for confession.

[69] Noel Fallows, Llull, *The Book of the Order of Chivalry*, 51. Llull later attempts to link chivalry with peace: "If justice and peace were opposites, Chivalry, which belongs with justice, would be the opposite of peace, and if it is so then those who are the enemies of peace and who love war and conflict are knights, and those who pacify the people and avoid conflict are unjust and are against Chivalry." Ibid., 55. One wonders how an audience of knights would receive the claim that they were proponents of peace and hostile to the idea of conflict.

[70] Bryant, *True Chronicles of Jean le Bel*, 90.

This fleck of an incident afloat in the swift current of a massive campaign early in the Hundred Years War raises one of the most basic issues we can discuss about warfare in the age of chivalry: how did warfare as conducted or at least led by knights affect commoners? Whatever conventions smoothed the jagged edges of interactions among warriors, we have to ask about the impact of their warfare on all others living in their world. Perhaps few nonclerical adult males were strictly noncombatants, since nearly all seem to have possessed at least rudimentary weapons and all might be summoned in an emergency to a rendezvous at a country crossroads or to rush to their positions atop the walls of an endangered town. And even the clerics were far from immune to these levies of men or, indeed, from an inclination to join the warriors.[71] The case against immunity for commoners was their support of the regime under attack, by their taxes if by no means more active. Their property and their bodies were demonstrably vulnerable to hostile forces (and at times to their supposed defenders) who looted and destroyed with remarkable frequency.[72] Indeed, Matthew Stickland asserts:

---

[71] Lawrence G. Duggan, *Armsbearing and the Clergy in the History and Canon Law of Western Christianity* (Rochester: Boydell & Brewer, 2013), provides many cases in point, as does Craig Nakashian, "'A New Kind of Monster... Part-Monk, Part-Knight': The Paradox of Clerical Militarism in the Middle Ages: The English and French Evidence" (PhD dissertation, University of Rochester, 2010); helpful evidence and interpretation appear in Christopher Guyol, "Benedictine Sermons and Coercive Violence in Late Medieval England," in *Prowess, Piety, and Public Order in Medieval Society: Studies in Honor of Richard W. Kaeuper*, eds. Daniel Franke and Craig Nakashian (Leiden: Brill, forthcoming), and in "'Let Them Realize What God Can Do': Chivalry in the St Albans Chronicle," in *Fourteenth Century England IX: Governance in the Fourteenth and Fifteenth Centuries*, eds. J. S. Boswell and Gwilym Dodd. For levies of the English clerics, see Bruce McNab, "Obligations of the Church in English Society: Military Arrays of the Clergy, 1369–1418," in *Order and Innovation in the Middle Ages: Essays in Honor of Joseph R. Strayer*, eds. William C. Jordan, Bruce McNab, and Teofilo F. Ruiz (Princeton: Princeton University Press, 1976), 293–315. For the *arriere ban* see Philippe Contamine, *War in the Middle Ages* (Oxford: Blackwell, 1984), 155–157.

[72] A survey of civilians and war in general is provided in Mark Grimsley and Clifford Rogers, eds., *Civilians in the Path of War* (Lincoln: University of Nebraska Press, 2002). Rogers offers an essay on the devastation of English *chevauchée* in the Hundred Years War. He closely investigates the campaigns of Edward III in Scotland and France in War Cruel and Sharp: English Strategy under Edward III, 1327–1360 (Woodbridge, Suffolk: Boydell & Brewer, 2000).

The habitual and ubiquitous looting of churches themselves in time of war forms one of the most striking features of medieval warfare and directly challenges any assumptions that the Christian element in chivalry acted as an effective restraint on the conduct of the warriors.[73]

All these subknightly or nonknightly males followed peacetime occupations on most days; and as noncombatants they were joined by the vast body of women and children and the aged and infirm. An inquiry into the social scope covered by martial customs is thus crucial; we must ask if chivalric norms for war were concerned with the population in general. If we know they obviously sought to protect populations within their own kingdom or lordship, was it their intent to limit death and damage among populations in the territories they invaded? How, in fact, did they treat this great mass of villagers and townspeople who were not, or not yet, securely placed under their dominion?[74]

A few qualifications are necessary. One technical issue will not be considered: the debate over whether medieval commanders and their armies ardently sought battle or prudently avoided it. Specialists in campaign and combat own that debate, which can be left in their care. Most scholars will also slip past the steel-toothed trap of moral judgment as they picture the flames licking at the vulnerable homes of two poor families and will focus on analysis rather than judgment, fearing it too facile, too readily disregarding of context. Not knowing how they would have behaved as members of that party of knights, harboring their mental set within iron helms, they can retain analytical if not emotional balance.

One point yields certainty: the minuscule incident in the Tournai campaign may be chillingly informative; but it is unusual only in the microscopic detail of knights "leaving their mark" by torching two humble houses that had somehow escaped arson on a larger scale. The evidence is not distortingly unique, not some species of outlier to a mass of contradictory documentation showing knightly concern for their inferiors decade by decade. Indeed, we have good reason to recognize that medieval warfare involved almost mind–numbingly constant ravaging, looting, destruction, and arson, frequently accompanied by rape. As we will see, classic medieval accounts and clear

---

[73] Strickland, *War and Chivalry*, 81.
[74] Bryant, trans., *Perceforest*, 145, addresses the need to protect a home population in return for revenues received.

modern analysis show these practices plainly. Either before and after, or in place of, or as a spur urging on great battles, the common medieval military technique conducted day by day was ravaging an enemy's land.

The concept of total war did not originate with William Tecumseh Sherman in the state of Georgia. As Matthew Strickland notes of eleventh- and twelfth-century war, "it was not until the advent of aerial bombing that a 'civilian' population could experience suffering greater in scale and degree than that inflicted by such systematic, regionalized harrying."[75] In some cases, such as the endemic fighting along the Anglo–Scottish border, organized state involvement may have been greater than we have previously suspected, as Alistair MacDonald has argued.[76] In the case of France during the Hundred Years War, Nicholas Wright finds war "as much a state of affairs, a condition of chronic instability, as the story of an Anglo-French power struggle."[77] As the Hundred Years War progressed, weakened central authority lost the ability to provide pay or assert control over its troops, and, given the multiplicity and local nature of many armed groups, the fighting in France reminds him of wars "in the so-called 'Third World' of today."[78] Even near the traditional end of the Middle Ages as kings and princes sought to forge more disciplined fighting forces, their objective remained military efficiency rather than humane treatment of civilian populations.

Of course there were prudent limits and specific attempts at better control. Anne Curry has carefully studied the military ordinances of Henry V and has detailed the ordinances for competing forces, English and Franco-Scottish, in a campaign of 1385, where each army consisted of multiple units (and on the Scottish side even multiple nationalities) that could require careful attempts at command and control.[79] Sadly, the chronicle evidence shows how

---

[75] Strickland, *War and Chivalry*, 273.
[76] Alastair J. MacDonald, *Border Bloodshed: Scotland, England and France at War, 1369–1403* (Edinburgh: Birlinn, 2009), 178.
[77] Nicholas Wright, *Knights and Peasants*, 5.   [78] Ibid., 3.
[79] Anne Curry, "The Military Ordinances of Henry V: Texts and Contexts," in *War, Government and Aristocracy in the British Isles, c. 1150–1500: Essays in Honour of Michael Prestwich*, eds. C. Given-Wilson, A. Kettle, and L. Scales (Woodbridge, Suffolk: Boydell, 2008), 214–249; "Disciplinary Ordinances for English and Franco-Scottish Armies in 1385: An International Code?" *Journal of Medieval History* 37 (2011), 269–294.

devastating this campaign proved to be to church property along the Scottish border and in Edinburgh. Though these ordinances mention but do not emphasize civilians, they do formally order protection of the sacred pyx (containing the host) within churches and the clerics who performed the sacrament.[80] Armies could be instructed to avoid harming not only civilians in home territories, but those in the lands of allies, actual or potential. Christine de Pizan wanly warned that arms bearers must not commit wrongful acts such as "pillaging friendly lands and various other sorts of grievances that men-at-arms carry out frequently."[81] In the campaigns of Henry V in Normandy, as Anne Curry has shown, the local population in general was expressly to be spared, for they were soon, it was hoped, to become loyal subjects of the invader who claimed to be their lawful king.

Yet the driving impulse remains clear: only when military policy or statecraft so required was any real effort made to protect subordinate social levels, that is, when usual military conduct would hinder a conquest or occupation by strengthening the will to resist. We have already seen, by contrast, that these medieval conventions, like the laws of arms, were basically made by and for the *gens d'armes* and operated within the group, among fighters whose interactions over technical points about honors and profits of war took place in tense and violent circumstances.

The massively disruptive power of this warfare cannot be doubted. When Don Pero Niño entered the fray with a naval raid on the Bordeaux region, he attacked both sides of the Gironde; on the side opposite the city he "ordered all the houses and all the corn (of which there was much in this part) to be fired, and whosoever they found there to be killed and plundered; so that in a few hours more than a hundred and fifty houses were in flames. The captain would have

---

[80] See Rory Cox, "A Law of War? English Protection and Destruction of Ecclesiastical Property during the Fourteenth Century," *English Historical Review* 128 (2013), 1381–1417. Cox cites Scottish, English, and French chronicles. It would be interesting to know if the few clauses in the ordinances pertaining to merchants produced any effect. In France about a decade later, the *Chronicle of St. Denis* records the worries over ravaging caused by the passage of a body of troops (who had been organized by Enguerand de Coucy for repressing a rising) who were now going to the aid of the duke of Orleans as they passed through the Dauphiné: *Chronique du Religieux de Saint Denys* (Paris: Grapelet, 1839), 12 vols., I, 395–398.

[81] *Book of Deeds of Arms and of Chivalry*, 152.

Figure 6 Fire was the great agency of devastation in medieval warfare, often practiced
and likely to get out of control.

liked to remain some days in the Gironde to wreak more harm on
the English lands. . ."[82] In his chronicle, Geoffrey le Baker refers tellingly to "the destructive sword," yet the blazing torch was its constant
ally and seems likely to have inflicted more widespread damage on
society and the economy (Figure 6). Medieval *gens d'armes* not only
fought and looted; they burned villages and towns, ruined monasteries
and churches, broke bridges, sank or burned shipping, and destroyed
stores of harvested crops or even those standing in the fields by torching
or trampling them; sometimes they destroyed vineyards by hacking
vines at their roots. Urban growth and the founding of countless
smaller centers had been a major sign and source of economic takeoff
in the Middle Ages. It is remarkable to note how relentlessly campaigning was directed at settlements of all sizes, from towns ringed by
protective stone walls and towers to smaller settlements waiting vul-
nerably behind only a ditch and wooden palisade. Even stout cities

[82] Evans, *Unconquered Knight*, 106; Carriazo, *El victorial*, 105–106.

could be stormed or starved into submission, of course, but the smaller places had little chance. Carquefou, inadequately defended by ditch and stockade, was easily taken, with the result that the whole town was looted, half of it was burned, and all the people were put to the sword, which was "a grievous pity," as Jean le Bel intones.[83] The eminent legist Honoré Bonet announced the taking of spoil as policy and granted that humble and innocent people might be hurt in war; yet God was the Lord of Hosts who had fought the first war in heaven and gave warfare to mankind; it could be abused, but could not be wrong in essence. Suffering in war might be a form of earthly penance allowed by divine will.[84] Determined readers of chronicle accounts of warfare in the age of chivalry might substitute "usually" for the word "sometimes" in Bonet's statement.

Reporting on the invasion of Normandy in 1346, Jean le Bel notes with some enthusiasm that he could never name all the places taken and devastated; the list would never end. Yet to provide a suitable sense of the accomplishment, he asserts that from Paris to Saint-Vaast-la-Hougue in the Cotentin, "along a front at least a day's ride wide, that whole rich land was laid waste."[85] Page by page he narrates the utter devastation of countryside so rich in potential loot that he almost stumbles in finding words of description. Normandy was found to be

a thriving country indeed, abounding in all things; its granaries were full of corn, its houses full of riches, its people possessed of carts and horses and wagons and sheep and ewes and pigs and calves and cows and oxen; and [the invaders] seized the lot and took it back to the king's army.[86]

As the attacking force, fanning out to right and left under the direction of marshals in a broadly destructive and relentlessly moving front, they found a population unprepared; they had hidden nothing as a precaution. Le Bel continues,

It's no wonder they were in a state of shock, they'd never experienced war or ever seen a man-at-arms, and now they were seeing people slaughtered without mercy, houses set ablaze and pillaged, and the land laid waste and burnt.[87]

The pattern was repeated elsewhere. A force of English and Gascon troops setting out from English Gascony in 1345 to reestablishing

---

[83] Bryant, *True Chronicles of Jean le Bel*, 116. For most towns devastated, no such lament is given by the chronicler.

[84] Bonet, *Tree of Battles*, ed. Coopland, 81, 125, 153–154, 158.

[85] Bryant, *True Chronicles of Jean le Bel*, 174.   [86] Ibid., 171.   [87] Ibid.

their control of Villefranche seized "cattle, sheep, pigs, wine, corn and flour and whatever other provisions they found."[88] In fact, le Bel's entire chronicle is generously sprinkled with terms such as looted, laid waste, devastated, ravaged, burnt, pillaged, and utterly destroyed. In a summary statement, another chronicler of the early Hundred Years War, Geoffrey le Baker, says that Edward III "spent a long time firing the towns, putting the French to flight, and burning their cornfields or trampling them under his horses' feet."[89]

These techniques, of course, were scarcely limited to English invasions of Valois France. Throughout the fourteenth century (and well beyond), the Scots and English harried lands on either side of their porous border.[90] Ravaging tactics were likewise common in the warfare that wracked German imperial lands over centuries. In 1179, Philip, archbishop of Cologne – to cite only one case in point – avenged wrongs done to him by Henry the Lion, duke of Saxony and Bavaria, by ravaging ducal lands, burning many fortified places and towns, and destroying churches and monasteries.[91] Flemish allies brought to England by those rebelling against Henry II at about the same time were described by a contemporary chronicle in similar terms,

Some speed into the farms to wreak havoc, some take sheep from their folds, and some set fire to farmsteads. What more can I tell you? Never will a tale of greater loss be told.

These words recall the description of imagined regional warfare in France at the same period. In the monumental *chanson Raoul de Cambrai*, the eponymous antihero launches deliberately destructive warfare to avenge perceived wrongs; his troops "cross the boundary of Vermandois; they seize the herds and take the herdsmen prisoners; they burn the crops and set fire to the farms."[92] Such actions significantly contravene his mother's prudent and specific advice and set off hundreds of pages of reciprocal mayhem between contending parties.

In fact, the vast body of imaginative literature purveys frankly realistic representations alongside portrayals of heroes in its representations of warfare. First-time readers may remember only the

[88] Ibid., 161.   [89] *Chronicle of Geoffrey le Baker*, 62.

[90] Alastair J. MacDonald, *Border Bloodshed: Scotland, England and France at War, 1369–1403* (Edinburgh: Birlinn, 2009).

[91] *MGH, Script. Rerum Germ. Annales S. Petri Erphesfurstenses Maiores*, 63.

[92] Sarah Kay, ed., trans., *Raoul de Cambrai*, laisse 59.

individual fights graphically portrayed in exaggerated language. The numbers of combatants existed only in wishful dreams; similarly imagined sword strokes sever entire armored bodies and sometimes cleave the warhorse as well; great knights fight all day despite wounds that gush blood. Such details must have satisfied audiences, providing specifics often disappointingly absent from chroniclers. Yet authors of these works know the reality of war as a relentlessly and broadly destructive process in society; and they almost casually employ a language of ravaging and harrying the land and its people that at times could replace sentences in chronicles or biographies. In the Merlin continuation from the *Lancelot-Grail* cycle, King Mark is said to have

fire set to the villages and slaughtered so many of the men there that few of them were left alive. After they had killed the people, burned the villages, and taken plunder, they left and went on their way, happy with the great booty they had taken.[93]

In the *History of Merlin*, Arthur's enemies "took plunder, burned towns, and laid waste the countryside everywhere they went, and they killed many people."[94] Invading Saxons had "spread out through the countryside to plunder; and these had so laid waste the land in four days' time that you would not have found a cottage or a house where a man could shelter himself or his horse, nor could you have found enough to eat to feed anyone one meal."[95] Late in the *Lancelot* volume upon that hero's arrival at Corbenic, he finds King Pelles and his people much beset, and he is hailed by the king as a deliverer:

For so long now we've wished to see you and have you among us! Thank God you've come at last. Mark me well: we're in great need of you, for our land has been so long destroyed and laid waste and the poor people have lost their meager holdings, that it's only right, if it please Our Lord, that their losses be redeemed and their possessions restored, which they've done without for so long.[96]

Such statements could be joined by hundreds of others detailing the making of war by brutal ravaging in the great *Lancelot-Grail* cycle of early thirteenth-century romances.[97]

---

[93] *Lancelot-Grail, Post-Vulgate Quest for the Holy Grail*, 240.
[94] *Lancelot-Grail, Story of Merlin*, 279.   [95] Ibid., 276.
[96] *Lancelot-Grail*, vol. 3, *Lancelot*, 163.
[97] My thanks to Terenc ("Willi") Clark, who conducted exacting word searches through the entire *Lancelot-Grail* cycle of romances. Of course clear statements of ravaging appear in other romances: e.g., Bryant, trans., *Perceforest*, 116, where an

In Arthurian literature as in life, a good leader is expected to prevent such destruction in his own land, but to enact it in the lands of his enemies. Great heroes are needed, and in their absence destruction sweeps the land; even after the catastrophic Arthurian battle on the Salisbury Plain dooms the kingdom of Logres "and many others with it," the crisis is registered in the death of great men because afterward "their lands lay waste and barren and without worthy lords, for they had all been painfully and brutally killed."[98]

In short, if individual combats are romanticized in this literature, war is viewed with brutal clarity. Yet its terrifying presence appears inevitable, for war seems almost a natural force, coming upon the land as a terrifying storm (as in repeated scenes in Chrétien de Troyes's *Yvain, the Knight with the Lion*) or in many other works as a terrifying giant or fire-breathing dragon. These natural or imagined embodiments of war speak frankly to its destructive capacities, even if great fighters are often pictured as victims rather than perpetrators.[99] The haunting image of the wasteland as territory completely blighted by war lingers in memory after reading much of chivalric literature. This is how warfare could be imaginatively reproduced in literature as well as reported in chronicles. Great acts of individual prowess were tirelessly attributed to heroes in these works, but the writers of romance and their audiences were well aware of the destructive implications of contemporary military practices.

Even idealist intellectual treatises show little interest in the need or possibility of shielding the subwarrior ranks of society from war. The destruction, again, seems inevitable. We have already seen that Christine de Pizan felt a need to sermonize men-at-arms against looting within the territory of their own side and that her warning trails off vaguely about other sorts of wrongdoing.[100] Theoretical discussions were more likely to provide backing for knightly action, perhaps in hopes of encouraging best practice. Some wars were just. And as Christine de Pizan assured contemporary arms bearers (again, drawing on the views of the cleric and legist Honoré Bonet), God sometimes even allows wars that are against all right; the men-at-arms

---

entire land is laid waste and the people driven out. Crops and fruit-bearing trees have been destroyed and cattle stolen.

[98] *Lancelot-Grail, The Death of Arthur,* 151.

[99] E.g., the adventures of Yvain with Malduit the Giant, *Lancelot-Grail*, vol. 3, 171–177.

[100] *Book of Deeds of Arms and of Chivalry,* 152.

may then be acting, in effect, as the divine scourge, punishing the people in general for their sins. Of course she idealistically admonishes the fighters to inquire carefully and learn if their cause is just, earnestly seeking advice from competent jurists or lawyers before launching or joining any war. All defensive wars, she adds, are known to be just, but, as we have already noted, she warns of hellfire for wrongdoers, possibly with her fingers crossed in the hope that such warnings will take effect.[101] Attempts to argue for immunity of noncombatants, Craig Taylor aptly notes, were equivalent to "pushing a boulder up a mountainside."[102]

Voices closest to the men-at-arms or indeed those issuing from within their own ranks, as we have seen, overwhelmingly focused on the glorious exercise of prowess to secure honor and loot; any restraint basically concerned how to treat each other and how best to distribute material gains without quarreling among themselves. If we were to ask members of the royal Order of the Star to debate not these martial technicalities that Charny emphasized, but the morality of damage inflicted on townspeople and villagers, robbing homes or destroying fields, flocks, and vineyards, we might be met with puzzled looks: these were not issues for chivalric debate. The more thoughtful knights might quickly rally and assert that looting, devastation, and killing of commoners were licit in good warfare. Some astute warriors surely would refer, with broad assent expressed among the others, that their hard work was a part of the divine plan, adding that it was not only approved by legal authorities, but was blessed by the holy fathers with their Latin learning conveying the will of God. They were fighting for their rights and justice; collateral costs to villagers and townspeople were simply incurred and inevitable.

Only occasionally can lesser voices from the medieval social scale be heard over the blare of trumpets and the clank of armor. One such voice (which often catches echoes of voices otherwise unheard) comes from Jean de Venette. This clerical chronicler castigates the failure of French nobles to provide defense and deplores the heedless devastation wrought by armed men of all stripes. Writing of conditions after the disastrous French defeat at Poitiers in 1356, he laments:

From that time on all went ill with the kingdom and the state was undone. Thieves and robbers were everywhere in the land. The nobles despised and

---

[101] See *Book of Deeds of Arms and of Chivalry*, 152–153, for this entire discussion.
[102] I quote from unpublished writing, with the permission of Dr. Taylor.

hated all others and took no thought for the mutual usefulness and profit of lord and men. They subjected and despoiled the peasants and the men of the villages. In no wise did they defend their country from its enemies. Rather did they trample it underfoot, robbing and pillaging the peasants' goods.[103]

Pointedly he retells the classic fable of the dog that abandoned his role as guard and joined the wolf in devouring the sheep. The story was commonly told, he says, and "seemed to have come true."[104] Diana Tyson has patiently explored occasional French verse written on either side of the Channel between the twelfth and fifteenth centuries and produced some other witnesses voicing outraged shouts and sorrowful murmurs. Yet such witnesses are rare, and in general the silence is deafening.

Nicholas Wright's important study adds actions taken to voices faintly heard. He emphasizes "a France studded with tens of thousands of castles, fortified churches, fortified farm houses, walled towns, and villages, whose often tiny and impoverished garrisons fought for local power with each other and with the local people."[105] French villagers hoping to survive the Hundred Years War found it necessary to rely on fortified churches, or to find safe havens in obscure caves, underground shelters, and woods. If they sometimes took offensive action, they were justly fearful of any military force, whatever cause was proclaimed by the banners carried; even those troops formally charged with local protection could prove rapacious and destructive. At some times, and especially within innumerable border zones created by the confusion of the great Anglo-French war, garrisons poorly paid or not paid at all simply lived off the countryside, eliminating the weakened central government as middleman; under the guise of taxation or simply by force, they extracted what modern gangs would term "protection money" from the surrounding countryside. In fact, garrisons formally charged to protect the local populace, as Craig Taylor suggests, represented the greatest threat to civilian populations in late medieval France.[106] Only a thin and porous line separated these *gens d'armes* from freebooters or brigands; "free companies" of fighters (bequeathing us the term "free lance") without abiding loyalty to either side left bloody and charred footprints over the realm of France and at one point even

---

[103] Chronicle of John de Venette, trans. Jean Birdsall (New York: Columbia University Press, 1953), 113.
[104] Ibid.   [105] *Knights and Peasants*, 3.
[106] Taylor, *Chivalry and the Ideals of Knighthood*, 14–16, 23–25, 118–121, 217–221.

took protection money (generously sprinkled with spiritual blessings) from the pope in Avignon.[107]

Was the common practice of siege not a special case showing more careful treatment of noncombatants? It might be tempting to argue that the sieges so frequent in medieval warfare present an exception to laws of war with a narrow social focus. Certainly, any siege concerned significant populations of nonwarriors; elaborate conventions for initiating, conducting, and concluding such operations might be thought a great benefit to civilian populations. Yet a strong counter case would argue that customs governing sieges, like other laws of war, simply regulated combat in the interests of the combatants and that the framework for any siege might depend on specific negotiations or even on strong emotions operating under the stress of specific campaigns. No generalizations can safely be based on a single case or even a small sample. A town or fortress, of course, often possessed a citadel as well as town walls and could count elite warriors among its defenders. Their obligations as warriors and the besieger's claims had to be recognized and reconciled, though as we have seen in the surrender of Calais to Edward III, defenders might find their lives balanced on a sword edge, even in surrender. Wealthy citizens would be lucky if they could buy safety; many lost all; some were carted off for ransom. Honorable surrender was often arranged for a garrison not reinforced by its overlord within a certain period of time. Besiegers could licitly threaten dire consequences if a town or castle held out beyond these limits, making swift surrender much more attractive to those under threat. Yet matters did not always work out neatly, and any resistance might bring dreadful massacres that spread bloody blotches on the pages of chronicles, though as a rule they left the conquerors' honor unblemished. The precise methods employed by the victorious in war are seldom closely scrutinized. Reading straight through the *True Chronicles of Jean le Bel* or *the Chronicle of Geoffrey le Baker* will disturb any view of the universal sway of clear and careful guidelines unvaryingly followed when an army approached a castle or fortified urban center.

Thus it would be difficult to construe benefits to civilians as the guiding motives of chivalric siege customs. Asking what motivated

---

[107] Useful comments in Taylor, *Chivalry and the Ideals of Knighthood*, 128–129; Jean le Bel says that "the Pope also gave them pardon for all their misdeeds and absolution and remission from Purgatory." *The True Chronicles of Jean le Bel*, 261.

besiegers to grant terms, Matthew Strickland supplies an uncompromising answer: "It was tactical and strategic concerns that were paramount."[108] Noncombatant refugees within a castle might be forced outside their own walls in order to conserve supplies within; those expelled might be generously treated and given safe passage. Froissart claimed that Edward III allowed exiles from Calais early in that long siege;[109] but this is denied by other sources claiming noncombatants died of starvation between the lines, as did many dwelling in Rouen when that city was besieged by Henry V.[110] Those expelled from the great Chateau Gaillard in 1202–1204 were barred by besiegers and left to die of starvation and exposure between lines of contending warriors.[111] Hard military goals always remained uppermost. Even the chivalric chronicler Froissart is sometimes moved to describe populations of a sacked city as martyrs. Craig Taylor detects ambiguity and moral qualms more generally in Froissart, whose chronicles usually seem to overflow with praise for bold knightly action.[112]

Knightly responsibility for treatment of civilians

Romantic impulses, defending idealistic images of knighthood to the last ditch, may insist that surely knights wanted to limit damage to lesser beings; only the common soldiery rather than the elite warriors did whatever moderns lament. Lesser men, increasingly recruited into armies by the later Middle Ages, simply remained beyond restraint. Such a case is abstractly unlikely and demonstrably false in detail. Far from showing a keen sense of obligation arising from a common human bond or a common Christian bond with townspeople and villagers, knights and men-at-arms seem to have regarded them almost as another species. Nicholas Wright succinctly notes, "The concerns of peasants were not only irrelevant to this matter of chivalry but the very antithesis of it: base, ignoble, unrefined, clodhopping."[113] And as Mervyn James has plainly observed, aristocrats

---

[108] Strickland, *War and Chivalry*, 209.
[109] Bryant, *The True Chronicles of Jean le Bel*, 184.
[110] Taylor, *Chivalry and the Ideals of Knighthood*, 211; 500 civilians starved between the lines during the winter.
[111] Discussed in Strickland, *War and Chivalry*, 212–213.
[112] Taylor, *Chivalry and the Ideals of Knighthood*, 39.
[113] Wright, *Knights and Peasants*, 15.

tended to consider themselves to be morally autonomous.[114] The medieval chronicler Jean de Venette's words echo in our ears: aristocrats hated and despised peasants. And this comment on moral autonomy resounds when we recall the assertive motto of the four-teenth-century Breton lord Olivier de Clisson, engraved on his seal: "Because it pleases me (*parce qu'il me plest*)."[115]

An idealistic case might argue that, at the least, the knights were by nature or training inclined to show their *noblesse oblige* by treating noncombatants well. Did they not play the role ideally expected of socially elite officers of later ages who claimed them as models? It is true that medieval aristocrats were formed by a rigorous youthful discipline; they deeply cherished their elaborate manners and saw in formal courtesy difference setting them utterly apart from those beneath them. Yet if we can grant that their manners provided social markers,[116] in war such courtliness could make little difference in the treatment of noncombatants and no transformation of the impact of campaigns on ordinary people. Elite behavioral forms represented a social, not an ethical system; they did not – and were not intended to – enact abstract morality or generate kindness; they certainly provided no significant check on violence against medieval com-moners or their possessions. Courtesy functioned best between peo-ple of broadly similar status and profession – that is, within the ranks of elite warriors. In this world, as in many worlds, honor in particular usually advanced a social rather than a moral outlook. Of course a lord might prudently protect his own tenants from invaders, but once into another lord's territory his forces burned or looted towns or villages in actions that smeared no blot on the cherished shield of honor. In fact, honor could act as a spur to such action; once he had committed himself to a militant course, a lord's honor required its successful completion to avoid dread dishonor, concern for honor thus spreading more violence than it checked. Philippe Contamine

---

[114] Mervyn E. James, *Society, Politics and Culture: Studies in Early Modern England* (New York: Cambridge University Press, 1988), 375. *English Politics and the Concept of Honour: 1485–1642*, vol. 3 of Past and Present Supplements (Cambridge: Past and Present Society, 1978).

[115] John Bell Henneman, *Olivier de Clisson and Political Society in France under Charles V and Charles VI* (Philadelphia: University of Pennsylvania Press, 1996), 209.

[116] M. Keen, "Chivalry and Courtly Love," in *Nobles, Knights, and Men-at-Arms in the Middle Ages* (London: Hambledon Press, 1996), 21–42.

cites a telling early fifteenth-century case in which a quarrel over a basket of apples – or at least over rights of jurisdiction over the act of picking or collecting them – led to warfare between the town of Metz and the duke of Lorraine.[117]

Chroniclers sometimes proudly place great lords or kings and their officials in the directive role of campaign violence. Jean le Bel reports that Edward III wished to pass by Beauvais in his single-minded desire to set siege to the port city of Calais. Yet

> his marshals passed so close to Beauvais that they couldn't resist going to attack the barriers and the suburbs on three sides of the city, and they burned, pillaged and destroyed two fine abbeys outside the city walls, along with several nearby villages and the three suburbs right up to the city's walls, and gates; they took an unimaginable amount of loot. Then they set off and went in separate directions, pillaging, burning and ravaging the countryside.[118]

Of course when enemies acted in this fashion they would be condemned. Geoffrey le Baker asserts that King David of Scotland, sitting in captivity in London (after the battle of Neville's Cross in 1346) could not be ransomed as a knight:

> For one who had no right to the kingdom of England had not been captured as one fighting for a just cause, but as a ferocious brigand who laid waste with fire and the sword everything that he touched.[119]

He would, Geoffrey said, have to make reparations to Edward III "for all that he had destroyed" in England who might then grant him "the grace of ransom." A few paragraphs later, Geoffrey swiftly asserts that Edward III was legally conducting war in France, had been elected as vicar of the German emperor, and could carry on his campaigns "until he should peacefully gain as his own the royal crown of France, which was owed to him by hereditary right." He does not explain how this process was to be accomplished "peacefully," but he illustrates that the difference between ferocious brigand and legitimate actor depended on the validity of a claim of inheritance.[120] With no qualms whatsoever he attributes the devastation wrought in France to the king leading the invasions: As we have seen, he plainly says that Edward III "spent a long time firing the towns, putting the

---

[117] Discussed, with sources cited, in Philippe Contamine, *War in the Middle Ages*, 285. Legal action and counteraction having been taken, none could claim the warfare was illicit.

[118] Bryant, *The True Chronicles of Jean le Bel*, 175.

[119] *Chronicle of Geoffrey le Baker*, 84.   [120] Ibid., 85.

French to flight, and burning their cornfields or trampling them under his horses' feet."[121] Romantics cannot awkwardly claim both that the king was simply enforcing his right and that massive destruction was merely the lamentable behavior of the subknightly soldiery.

Usually without concerning themselves with theories of legitimacy, admirers of the great routinely and approvingly noted their leadership in campaigns featuring destruction. In his *Life of the Black Prince*, Chandos Herald, writing of the sweeping mid-fourteenth-century raid conducted by the prince, records that the French king wanted to force the invading English into battle between the Seine and the Somme:

But the English to disport themselves put everything to fire and flame. There they made many a widowed lady and many a poor child orphan. They rode day and night until they came to the water of the Somme.[122]

The Black Prince described his progress in his great raid of 1355 in similar terms:

"We took our road through the land of Toulouse where were many goodly towns and strongholds burnt and destroyed, for the land was very rich and plenteous: and there was not a day but towns, castles, and strongholds were taken."[123]

During the great raid of 1359–1360, Sir Thomas Gray recorded that English forces sometimes ate poor rations as they were crossing regions previously ravaged by their countrymen who had carried on the war "outstandingly."[124] Later in this long war, Sir John Fastolf plainly advocated a scorched-earth policy by English forces,

brennyng and distruynge alle the lande as thei pas, both hous, corne, veignes and all treis thaty beren fruyte for manys sustenance, and all bestaile that may not be droven, to be distroiede.[125]

---

[121] Ibid., 62.

[122] Chandos Herald, *La vie du Prince Noir*, ed. Diana B. Tyson (Tübingen: M. Niemeyer, 1975).

[123] Quoted in H. J. Hewitt, *The Black Prince's Expedition* (Manchester: Manchester University Press, 1958), 72–73.

[124] Cited and discussed in A. King, "War and Peace: A Knight's Tale; The Ethics of War in Sir Thomas Gray's *Scalacronica*," in *War, Government and Aristocracy in the British Isles*, eds. Chris Given-Wilson, Ann Kettle, and Len Scales (Boydel Press, 2008), 155.

[125] Christopher Allmand, "The War and the Non-Combatant," in *The Hundred Years War*, ed. K. Fowler (London, 1971), 180, cited and discussed in Wright, *Knights and Peasants*, 32.

Scenes from imaginative literature once again support other evidence. The directive role of elite fighters is never doubted. Often its devastating vigor is praised as righteous violence, as in the remarkable vengeance exacted by Tristan in an Italian romance:

Now the tale tells that as soon as Tristan became a knight he avenged his father very nobly, for he killed all eight of the knights who had been present at the king's death; and he still did not deem himself satisfied with this vengeance. So he rode to the city from which these knights came, which was called Bresia, and he killed all the men and women there, and destroyed the city and its walls down to the foundations. All this Tristan did to avenge King Meliadus his father, and no greater revenge was ever taken by any knight, than the one Tristan took for his father's death.[126]

Sometimes, as in the action of Yvain in Chrétien's romance, a violent right is simply assumed in a great knight, though its consequences are like a devastating storm. Significantly, the moral dangers and societal consequences of elite violence are carefully drawn, indirectly emphasizing a tendency in need of reform. Some of the most powerfully symbolic chivalric literature imagines great knightly figures inflicting vast destruction to a land and its people. Heroes are dramatically linked with great violence, vengeance, and war. In a war pitting one faithful Christian king against another (a recent convert from paganism) in *The History of the Holy Grail*, early in the *Lancelot-Grail* cycle, King Lambor, "a good knight who loved God," then keeper of the Holy Grail, fights his neighbor, King Varlan.[127] Fleeing to the seashore in utter defeat, Varlan comes upon a wondrous and holy ship. Despite a stern warning (in golden Chaldean letters) against anyone entering it who is sullied or who lacks faith, Varlan climbs aboard and finds a beautiful bed on which lie a gold crown and a sword with remarkable powers. Though further clear statements inscribed on sword and scabbard warn him (this time in blood-red letters) and hint that the sword is reserved for use only by the Christ-like knight Galahad, Varlan draws the sword for his own great need. Meeting the onrushing Lambor, he swings the sword, completely splitting that king (and his horse) with a single stroke. God is not pleased. Yet Varlan, wonderfully exultant with the cutting power of

---

[126] *Italian Literature, vol. II: Tristano Riccardiano*, ed. and trans. F. Regina Psaki (D. S. Brewer, 2006), 18–19.

[127] This war and its consequences and the history of the marvelous sword are discussed in *Lancelot-Grail: The History of the Holy Grail*, 157–160; *The Quest for the Holy Grail*, 64–67.

the weapon, returns for the rich scabbard. As soon as he places the sword in the scabbard, he falls dead on the spot. And his death is not the only consequence, for as the story is continued in *The Quest for the Holy Grail*:

[T]here resulted from it such a great pestilence and persecution in both king-doms that the earth no longer produced when cultivated. From that time on, no wheat or other grain grew there, no tree gave fruit, and very few fish were found in the sea. For this reason, the two kingdoms were called the Waste Land; they had been laid waste by this unfortunate blow.[128]

Such rich symbolism takes many twists and turns; yet it seems significant that misuse of a sacred sword in war against a king of whom the *Quest* says that "he had the lord within him" results not only in the offender's death, but in the blighting of the land. If God sometimes allows warriors to play his scourge for widespread sin among the people, here divine wrath overflows over two kingdoms because of a great knight's great sin.

In the yet more famous case of a Dolorous Stroke, Balain, a knight renowned even more than Varlan for remarkable prowess, caps a career of serial disasters by entering the Grail chamber and there seizing (against clearly spoken divine warnings) the Lance of Longinus (the instrument completing Christ's redeeming passion on the cross in medieval accounts). When King Peleham, the Grail-keeper, rushes toward him and is about to smite him with a great pole, Balain, who has previously killed Peleham's brother in an act of revenge, now protects himself against the wrathful king by using the Lance of Redemption to maim the Grail-keeper. Once again diving wrath overflows, in this case spreading like a wave of destruction from an atomic bomb through three kingdoms. The king is rendered impotent; the kingdoms are likewise barren. So toxic is Ground Zero, the devastated Grail Castle, that a priest wearing Mass vest-ments like an antiradiation suit must accompany Merlin in guiding Balain (who has survived the blast) out of the ruins. As he flees, Balain finds utter devastation all around:

As he rode thus through the land, he found trees down and grain destroyed and all things laid waste, as if lightning had struck in each place, and unquestionably it had struck in many places, though not everywhere. He found half the people in the villages dead, both bourgeois and knights, and he found laborers dead in the fields. What can I tell you? He found the kingdom of Listinois so totally

---

[128] *Lancelot-Grail, Quest for the Holy Grail,* 65.

destroyed that it was later called by everyone the Kingdom of Waste Land and the Kingdom of Strange Land, because everywhere the land had become so strange and wasted.[129]

Balain's career ends when he and his brother, not recognizing the armor worn in a fight, inflict fatal wounds on each other. If this final installment of symbolism is powerful, in the Dolorous Stroke he had played his greatest symbolic role, provoking the wrath of God by laying bloodstained hands on the instrument of human redemption and using it to maim the keeper of the Holy Grail. His action led to devastation that exceeded the most ambitious achievements of the warfare that clerics knew only too well in their own thoroughly real world.

Clear recognition of the responsibilities of leaders for the course taken by war is sometimes presented even more directly. The great knight Galehaut eagerly questions a wise man, seeking to learn the day of his own death, in order to be prepared for judgment. As he explains his concern:

"Master," said Galehaut, "in the name of everything I owe you, that is why I am asking you when my body will die: because I want to do whatever I can to avoid the death of my soul! I want to watch out for the death of the body in order to avoid the death which is truly frightening, the death of the soul. And be assured that, whatever torment my body may undergo, my soul, please God, will accept it gladly. I would strive more to behave the right way, and more urgently, than if I were just to live out a usual life. It would help me, since I have committed many wrongs in my life, destroying cities, killing people, dispossessing and banishing people..."[130]

The moral fears caused by "a usual life" are noteworthy, and they are later repeated in the Middle English "Awntyrs off Arthur" where Gawain pointedly asks:

What will happen to us...who strive to fight, / and so trample down folk in many kings' lands, / And ride over realms without any right / To win worship in war through prowess of hands?[131]

---

[129] *Lancelot-Grail, The Merlin Continuation,* 211–214, narrates the events and provides the words quoted.

[130] *Lancelot-Grail,* vol. 2, *Lancelot,* 254.

[131] Thomas Hahn, ed., *Sir Gawain: Eleven Romances and Tales* (Kalamazoo, MI: TEAMS, 1995), lines 261–264. "How shal we fare," quod the freke, "that fonden to fight, / And thus defoulen the folke on fele kinges londes, / And riches over reymes withouten eny right, / Wynnen worship in werre thorgh wightnesse of hondes?"

At the very least, clerical authors are working to instill a keen sense of what they see as the responsibility of great knights and lords for the devastating effects of war. That some of their fellow clerics lavishly praised leadership in wars that they approved simply provides another dimension of the evidence. The interplay of violence and religion (the subject of Chapter 9) form an endlessly complicated and intensely fascinating topic. It seems likely that many elite men-at-arms were troubled by just such moral qualms and, at least in sleepless nights, worried about the work they had wrought.[132] Blaming lesser men does not seem to have eliminated their doubts and fears.

It does not matter, finally, whether knights remained firmly in their saddles while others carried blazing torches toward wooden dwellings or fields of waving grain; elite fighters led and directed these campaigns, and these were the strategies they counted on. It seems highly unlikely that they tried valiantly to eliminate methods that proved so effective and came with such relatively low risk to their own force. "Raiders, under high-ranking leaders," as Strickland concisely notes, "seem to have had clear objectives ... [and] it is hard to see how army leaders could not but be involved should acts of atrocity occur."[133] As Clifford Rogers has observed, "it was not chivalric qualms that made devastation and destruction primarily the work of common soldiers rather than men-at-arms. Rather, it was the need to reserve the best-mounted fighters for the crucial task of covering and protecting those engaged in the labor of havoc."[134] The chance to take part in just such havoc, legitimately and for good pay, was one of the attractions leading men to join an expeditionary force, though they were not obligated by high rank or tenure.

The last, thin hope for sustaining a romantic view of this warfare rests with the treatment of clerics and women. All medieval reformers, of course, prescriptively asserted that good knights showed proper restraint and respect in dealing with these particular groups. The case for sensitive care for clerics and churches sporadically gets

---

[132] An argument of R. W. Kaeuper, *Holy Warriors*.

[133] Strickland, *War and Chivalry*, 325–326.

[134] Rogers, *Soldiers' Lives through History: The Middle Ages* (Portsmouth: Greenwood, 2007), 90. Craig Taylor has commented that "it would be wrong to lay the blame for all the brutality of war on the soldiers who carried out the pillaging, burning and raping, and ignore the culpability of the knights and noblemen who gave the instructions." Dr. Taylor informs me that this unpublished statement represents his current views.

a boost in surviving evidence; kings are sometimes shown to order
one or more churches exempt when fires were lit. They had likely
heard repeated prescriptive messages such as that in the epic the
Crowning of Louis, which pointedly informed all who heard it that
the hero William of Orange, when he easily captured the town of
Saint-Giles, "acted in a way pleasing to Jesus when he spared the
church there from being laid waste."[135] Sometimes we are told
that great knights feel regretful when churches are burned and clerics
killed. In an unusual case, Henry I, says the Norman chronicler
Orderic Vitalis, formally asked the bishop of Evreux to agree to the
burning of the town as a means of defeating enemies troubling the
king; he recognized that "the innocent will suffer great harm" and
that churches would be lost, but promised generous rebuilding
of what was destroyed. This argument finally swayed the bishop,
who consulted with "practical men," and the entire town and
several churches were, indeed, destroyed. Henry publicly promised
restoration.[136] In a brutal campaign against the count of Champagne,
Louis VII burned Vitry in 1143, the conflagration engulfing the
church in which as many as 1,500 townspeople who had sought
refuge perished.[137]

Cases could be multiplied from the Hundred Years War, but only
an example or two must stand for many. As Edward III left the abbey
of Saint Lucien near Beauvais where he had spent a night, "the next
thing he knew the abbey was all ablaze; he was deeply upset by this."
Louis of Spain (Luis de la Cerda), campaigning in Brittany, took the
city of Guémené by storm, and looted and destroyed it.[138] The entire
population was put to the sword, and five churches were burned and
desecrated, "at which Louis was enraged and had fourteen hanged for
the deed." Louis was no soft campaigner, and the action is striking.
Yet it is also uncommon; and the chronicler finishes his paragraph by
adding, "A mass of booty was taken there, for it was a prosperous city
of abundant riches."[139]

[135] Laisse 50.
[136] Chibnall, ed., trans., *Ecclesiastical History of Orderic Vitalis*, vol. 6, 228–229.
[137] *Recueil des historiend des Gaules et de las France*, 24 vols. (Paris, 1738–1904), vol.
    xiii, 272.
[138] Luis de la Cerda was the son of Alfonso de la Cerda, who was once a contender
    for the crown of Castile.
[139] Bryant, *The True Chronicles of Jean le Bel*, 137–138.

Any general case claiming usual or widespread care shown to church personnel and property falls apart quickly, as a detailed study by Rory Cox has shown.[140] Matthew Strickland has likewise provided convincing evidence for what he terms the "habitual and ubiquitous looting of churches in time of war."[141] He notes that

> violation of sanctuary, the spoliation and burning of churches, and the immolation of refugees were not deeds restricted to a minority of tyrant lords, but commonplace, fully indulged in even by kings and the greatest magnates. If mercenaries were sometimes to blame, the stripping of churches was widely practiced by both lay and ecclesiastical magnates and was sanctioned by commanders of the highest rank.[142]

These facts of warfare had not disappeared by the later Middle Ages, as any reading through almost any chronicle dealing with the Hundred Years War will demonstrate.

The treatment of women by elite warriors brings more difficult questions into focus.[143] In some instances, chronicles portray leading knights whom they admire trying to prevent abuse in a captured town. When the force under Edward III captured Caen, Jean le Bel reports English knights going through the town trying to prevent massacre and save women; murder and rape were taking place. "Truly, anyone who was in a position to protect them and failed to do so," he believes, "was not a good Christian."[144] Sir Thomas Holland is specifically named. The same chronicler reports that the Earl of Derby tried to prevent rape when Poitiers was sacked and looted and its churches desecrated: "the worthy Earl of Derby [much admired by the chronicler] was enraged but had been unable to prevent it."[145] The difficulty of evaluating evidence appears in the puzzlement of the adept translator of this chronicle, Nigel Bryant: the passage describing the sacking of Poitiers actually reads "one can well imagine it." He renders this as the action "was unimaginable," but notes that perhaps, in light of similar incidents, le Bel was growing inured.[146]

---

[140] See the convincing article by Rory Cox, "A Law of War? English Protection and Destruction of Ecclesiastical Property during the Fourteenth Century," *English Historical Review* 128 (2013), 1381–1417.

[141] Strickland, *War and Chivalry*, 81.   [142] Ibid., 91.

[143] R. W. Kaeuper, "Chivalry and the 'Civilizing Process,'" in *Violence in Medieval Society*, ed. Kaeuper (Woodbridge, Suffolk: Boydell, 2000), 21–38.

[144] Bryant, *The True Chronicles of Jean le Bel*, 173.   [145] Ibid., 188.

[146] Ibid., 188 and footnote 3 on that page.

Social rank mattered: ladies and maidens must, in theory, never be sexually forced, though girls and women of lower status were often considered fair game. Both sexual violence and outright killing are at issue, and on such topics absolute certainly about the behavior of arms bearers remains extremely difficult to achieve. If chronicles provide instances of the taking of towns in which women were protected, they also often report widespread killing, including women and children among the victims, with or without adverse comment. Even kings might ill-treat women from the opposing side. Edward I infamously imprisoned two ladies, Isabel (Countess of Buchan) and Mary Bruce (Robert's younger sister) in what his biographer, Michael Prestwich, plainly terms "inhuman conditions, caged at Berwick and Roxburgh."[147] Significantly, Prestwich adds that "Edward's own subjects apparently did not condemn him for it, and it would be quite wrong to assume that honour was not a virtue which Edward valued." Even nuns could not consider themselves safe. At Origny-Saint Bénoite, as Jean le Bel reports, "a Benedictine convent was ruined and set ablaze, and many of the nuns were raped by the English, which was a grievous shame."[148] Geoffrey le Baker, in the midst of a seemingly endless string of assaults, lootings, and burnings in the invasion of Normandy in 1346, casually mentions that among the prisoners taken for ransom, "the abbess of Caen was sent to England."[149] Since her life was spared amidst much killing and rape in the town, some sense of protection emerges; but capturing and holding a lady in religious orders for ransom scarcely registers as an action that would have been credited to Lancelot. Modern historians regard some incidents reported in le Baker's chronicle as fabricated. Although usually devoted to the cause of Edward III, Jean le Bel extensively tells of that king's rape of the Countess of Salisbury,[150] a tale completely discounted by the king's modern biographer, Mark Ormrod.[151]

Tabulating cases from chronicles in columns of varying degrees of reliability could fill all waking hours and not finally prove

---

[147] Prestwich, Edward I (Berkeley: University of California Press, 1998), 109. Prestwich adds that "Edward's own subjects apparently did not condemn him for it, and it would be quite wrong to assume that honour was not a virtue which Edward valued."

[148] Bryant, *The True Chronicles of Jean le Bel*, 80.

[149] *Chronicles of Geoffrey le Baker*, 70.

[150] Bryant, *The True Chronicles of Jean le Bel*, 154–156.

[151] Mark Ormrod, Edward III (New Haven: Yale University Press, 2011), 135–137.

convincing. We might at least add evidence of other sorts. Significantly, the topic of rape concerned writers of both civil and canon law, especially from the twelfth century, indicating some level of social concern over a perceived problem needing attention.[152] Of course, the problem need not be thought limited to wartime or to elite warriors, but it would not stretch credibility to reflect that warfare has always been a solvent on social constraints.

And we might likewise recall that imagined cases of rape appear throughout all works of literature written at this time and definitely refer to elite fighters. Many cases in literature seem designed to spark discussion on male–female relations in general, with sexual violence as an extreme case. A male point of view dominates in works of literature, though exceptions can be cited. The focus falls, that is, on male honor and on viewing women as prizes won through prowess, often gained in the mock war of tournament. Little concern appears for the women themselves; they are usually pictured as accepting the chivalric framework in which they fit as distinctly subordinate parts, though again exceptions exist. That chivalric literature so constantly urged knights to protect ladies (if not all women) must, of course, to some degree reflect the reformist view, rather than accepted practice.

The only certainty may be that we cannot assume that seemingly imperishable images of stalwart knights unfailingly protecting vulnerable females provides an accurate picture of conduct in war. Exactly how much sexual violence accompanied the manifold injuries of warfare is likely beyond unqualified determination, but the rose-tinted image of knights and ladies – let alone knights and women in general – is a figment of our imaginative wish for the Middle Ages of our dreams.

CONCLUSION

Far from a colorful if tough game played by the fair-minded, war conducted by knights or under their leadership seems, like war at other times, the veritable dissolution of civil society under the impact

---

[152] Medieval views are discussed in James A. Brundage, *Law, Sex, and Christian Society in Medieval Europe* (Chicago: University of Chicago Press, 2009); Kathryn Gravdal, *Ravishing Maidens: Writing Rape in Medieval French Literature and Law* (Philadelphia: University of Pennsylvania Press, 2011); Albrecht Classen, *Sexual Violence and Rape in the Middle Ages: A Critical Discourse in Premodern German and European Literature* (Boston: Walter de Gruyter, 2011).

of military campaign, with consequences felt throughout all social ranks. The clear social limitations on forbearance in working codes of chivalry and even ghostly echoes of voices from the subchivalric point to significant differences from broad modern attempts to secure less brutal warfare such as the Geneva Accords; for the chivalric norms did little to regulate the actions of combatants upon noncombatants. Townspeople, villagers, or country folk seem to have been edged into deep shadows on the periphery of the warriors' field of vision and were scarcely central even to the theoreticians who wrote treatises on warfare. Noncombatants mattered only in the manner game is important to hunters; they represented sources of varying degrees of available wealth (to be acquired by invaders and denied to defenders) rather than fit subjects for serious ethical discussion.

The laws of war were never intended to impose serious limitations on the practitioners of war as they dealt with all those of lower social ranks or nonmilitary status. Customs or laws of war could not transform campaign and combat into a noble enterprise of altruistic protection of the weak. Arguably, the arms bearers were sometimes troubled by the disparity between what they ought to do as good Christians and what they must do as victorious fighters.[153] The tension was significant, but seems almost never crippling. Chivalric warfare could scarcely be kind or gentle where the great mass of lesser people was concerned.

In the tumult of war, the ideals of chivalry proved more important to the men-at-arms than to anyone else; these working codes affected the actors much more than those acted upon. Granted, an end to outright slaughter of defeated enemies and ceaseless slave raiding – as claimed by Matthew Strickland and John Gillingham – stands as a genuine and important early change. For centuries after that early alteration in warfare, any claim that chivalric ideals and practices essentially civilized medieval warfare for society as a whole – transforming it into a species the romantics desired – can scarcely be maintained. Basic conventions of war, it is true, prevented chaos among *gens d'armes*, though at times with only a narrow margin of success (as during phases of the Hundred Years War in France); but for most people in most regions affected by the warfare of knights and men-at-arms, the trying experience could not have differed greatly from that endured by nonwarriors across most of historic time.

---

[153] Discussed in Chapter 9 and in R. W. Kaeuper, *Holy Warriors*, passim.

To the broad assumption (often made by beginning students) that the chivalrous warriors were protective of local populations, the obvious rejoinder must be to ask what populations were at issue and against whom protection had to be provided. Historians can find no evidence of knights fighting fearful dragons, ogres, or evil sorcerers. The outside threat to townspeople, villagers, monks, clerics, and merchants, including the majority of the population composed of women and children, came from warriors on campaign. Knights were encouraged to fight infidels, but crusade (whatever attitude that form of warfare inspires in modern people) was not a full-time occupation for the vast majority of knights. As they fought each other, they found convenient and even licit targets in those unarmed people on whose support and economic productivity their enemies depended. As Matthew Strickland observed, a lord, one of whose most essential functions was the provision of protection for his own men, became in war an instrument of destruction to those of any opponent without tarnishing his knightly reputation. Had this attitude not been preponderant, it is hard to see how warriors such as William Rufus or William Marshal, still less commanders of a later age such as Edward III, the Black Prince, or Henry V, who made extensive use of the *chevauchée*, could have enjoyed the glittering chivalric reputations bestowed on them by their contemporaries.[154]

---

[154] Strickland, *War and Chivalry*, 287.

7

TOURNAMENT

A revival of jousting has become a feature of the medieval or Renaissance fairs that now dot the summer landscape of the United States, drawing large crowds especially to watch colorful combats between fully armored knights while enjoying a roast turkey leg and quaffing mead. Usually the jousting is sadly false and scripted to ensure victory by the obvious hero, but the sheer physicality of armored men atop snorting, stamping horses remains impressive enough; and on one occasion it elicited from my watching granddaughter (at age 4) a series of questions pertinent to this chapter: "Why are they doing this? Are they having a quarrel? Are they going to do it again?" Her conclusion revealed genuine concern: "Perhaps we should talk to them." This chapter at least talks about them, or rather their authentic medieval predecessors, drawing on the careful work of numerous scholars such as David Crouch, Juliet Barker, and Richard Barber.[1]

We must grant, however, that they would have been surprised by these queries, for over centuries tourneying seemed natural and self-justifying to them. Early in the massive fourteenth-century romance *Perceforest*, Alexander the Great, improbably portrayed as the founder of an English kingdom, descends on an exploratory quest into the sea

---

[1] Crouch, *Tournament* (London: Hambledon, 2005), Barber and Barker, *Tournaments, Jousts, Chivalry and Pageants in the Middle Ages* (Woodbridge, Suffolk: Boydell, 1989), and Barker, *Tournament in England, 1100–1400* (Woodbridge, Suffolk: Boydell, 1986).

within a large glass barrel towed behind a ship.[2] His great discovery is
swordfish that "tourney and battle with one another so fiercely that it
was a wonder to behold, exchanging mighty blows." Alexander sees
they are well equipped for such extreme sport, "having a head shaped
like a helmet with a shield behind and a sword clutched by the
pommel before." As a natural phenomenon, this martial play can be
read from the created universe and usefully implemented in human
society; knighthood can engage in it enthusiastically as a defining
chivalric activity. The result is that "the noble king was inspired to
establish a similar sport between his knights so that in times of peace
and rest they could practice fighting without killing and in times of
war be the readier to inflict damage on their enemies and defend
themselves if attacked."

This sport, the text continues, could be called "the school of
prowess." There must be careful rules to exclude treachery; blunted
weaponry only should be used; and no one must hit a man from
behind when he has lost his helmet. But the lure of profitable ransoming of defeated knights and capture of their valuable horses is held out,
in addition to the prospect of winning "honour, praise, and the esteem
from ladies and maidens." Thus, "by their prowess poor knights can
profit." All goes swimmingly in the imagined first tournament that
follows, though enthusiasm nearly gets out of hand: "the tournament
became so violent that Betis and Alexander had to call a halt."[3]

The remainder of this romance is stuffed with glowing accounts of
scores of later tournaments (Figure 7); yet at one point when the
practice is being introduced in a new region, the onlooking ladies
witnessing their first tournament echo the penetrating questions
with which this chapter began; for "the ladies and maidens who
had husbands or sweethearts taking part lost all sense of fun: it
didn't look at all like sport but warfare!"[4] Such passages are priceless,
even if they represent a voice all but lost in the blare of trumpets and
the clash of arms on the field. A generation earlier, Ramon Llull in his
widely read *Book of the Order of Chivalry* had enthusiastically endorsed
various forms of martial sport as essential to chivalry:

---

[2] The following quotations in this paragraph all come from Nigel J. Bryant, ed,
trans., *Perceforest: The Prehistory of King Arthur's Britain* (Rochester: Boydell &
Brewer, 2011), 40. More fighting fish with chivalric instincts appear in remarkable
scenes later in the romance, and one character describes tournament as "a perfeact
exercise for all who aspire to honour and renown in arms," 458.

[3] Ibid., 41.   [4] Ibid., 479.

Figure 7 Early tournament was close to warfare; mêlée (in a more restricted space) kept alive something of that vigorous general combat. This image shows such combat within Italian urban space.

Riding a horse, participating in behourds, tilting lances against the quintain, going about armed, taking part in tournaments, holding Round Tables, fencing, hunting deer, bears, wild boar, lions and other things similar to these are the office of a knight, for by all these things knights are trained for feats of arms and for upholding the Order of Chivalry. Hence, to scorn the training and the usage of that which better prepares the knight to practice his office is to scorn the Order of Chivalry.[5]

The popularity of the sport among elite males can scarcely be exaggerated; in fact it might be termed their obsession. For half a millennium extreme martial sport to a remarkable degree captured the imagination of the European lay elite; indeed, it constituted a seemingly necessary element in courtly life and a necessary staple in courtly literature. As centerpieces of chivalric social life, tournaments were the exigent celebratory events expected for marking a coronation, a knighting, a wedding, the beginning of a war, the ending of a war, or about any other occasion. Were tournaments somehow suddenly to be removed from romance literature, the vast corpus of such works would collapse into the cavernous gaps created. Elite society had spawned an elite sport, spectacular, highly colorful, undoubtedly dangerous (though usually without becoming

---

[5] Noel Fallows, trans., Llull, *The Book of the Order of Chivalry* (Woodstock, Suffolk: Boydell, 2013), 47. These forms of martial activity will be discussed in this chapter. Ramon Llull, in his prologue to this treatise, specifies that the wise hermit who instructs the knight had upheld the honor of chivalry "in wars and in tournaments, in assaults and in battles" before adopting the vocation of hermit. Ibid., 35.

lethal), and with more than a hint of sexuality both in the violent encounters and, more obviously, in the other encounters that all moralists were certain followed the closing wine-drenched party. Little wonder that tournament would take center stage and last for centuries.

Though the subject has sparked historical debate, it seems tournament was, as claimed by the author of the *Perceforest*, a good training ground for war, through the exercise of horsemanship and cooperative action. Granted, the assaults of besieged places, so common a part of medieval warfare, could not use cavalry directly; despite their vigor and determination, knights on horseback could not ride up ramparts. But even during siege operations, mounted warriors were necessary to drive off relieving forces and to protect the garnering of supplies from the surrounding countryside.[6] Tournament offered a chance to present oneself as a member of the lay elite (especially significant as chivalry and tournament became increasingly restricted to those who could claim noble rank in the later Middle Ages), to demonstrate prowess before the ideal audience of fellow warriors, or to catch the eye of a patron or a lovely and highly placed lady. And success on the field could be splendidly profitable.[7]

EVOLVING FORMS

Though we casually lump together all forms of the sport as tournament, it adopted varying forms throughout its long life span. As David Crouch has argued, tournament likely came into being in the first half of the eleventh century, emerging from a cluster of northwestern European counties (Flanders, Brabant, Picardy, and Hainault), and it was originally an outlet through which youthful testosterone-driven warriors could demonstrate prowess.[8] Dominique Barthélemy stresses the close relationship between early tournament and the warfare of the period, seeing the border between them almost porous.[9] In short,

---

[6] Bernard S. Bachrach, "Medieval Siege Warfare: A Reconnaissance," *Journal of Military History* 58, no. 1 (1994), 119–133. Bernard S. Bachrach, "Caballus et Caballarius in Medieval Warfare," in *The Study of Chivalry: Resources and Approaches* (Kalamazoo, MI: Medieval Institute Publications, 1988).

[7] Motives discussed in Keen, *Chivalry*, 87–91.   [8] Crouch, *Tournament*, 2–12.

[9] "Les chroniques de la mutation chevaleresque en France," *Comptes rendus de l'Academie des Inscriptions et Belles-Lettres* (2007), 1643–1665.

tournament took shape in a cockpit of contentious political entities and allowed martial competition to continue even when a temporary absence of open warfare occurred, although the line separating early tournament and war tended to blur or even vanish.[10]

As Richard Barber and Juliet Baker have emphasized, early romance literature provided a great agency for its spread. Works by the great master Chrétien de Troyes in the late twelfth century were especially important, and it seems no accident that his patrons included Henry, count of Champagne, and Philip, count of Flanders, both avid patrons of the tournament. This network of patronage spread significantly to include Count Henry's wife, a daughter of Eleanor of Aquitaine, and his brothers-in-law, Henry the Young King (who relied on William Marshal), and Henry's younger brothers Geoffrey of Brittany (trampled to death in a tournament, according to one chronicler) and the knightly king Richard Lion-Heart.[11] Unsurprisingly, the tournament quickly spread into German and Italian lands by roughly the mid-twelfth century, and its terminology appeared in Spain and Portugal perhaps a century later.[12]

We must picture all these vigorous lads initially in chain armor, rather than the substantial plate armor provided for man and mount that still defiantly shines in display cases within our museums.[13] More important, we must recognize that the competitive action took a variety of forms, although in casual usage we lump all such combat together under the single rubric of tournament. For early tournaments we must airbrush from the common image purveyed by Hollywood of a closely limited field with lanes laid out for individual combat in front of reviewing stands packed with spectators. Though we likely picture two opposed knights thundering toward each other with extended lances as spectators gasped, in fact, early tournament featured groups of mounted warriors acting in teams and riding over

[10] Crouch, *Tournament*, 1–16.
[11] Barber and Barker, *Tournaments*, 20. On the death of Geoffrey: *Chronica magistri Rogeri de Hovedene*, vol. 2, 309. "Gaufridus comes Britanniae, filius Henrici regis Angliae, in conflictu militari pedibus equinis contritus, Parisius obiit; et in ecclesia cathedral ujusdem civitatis sepultus est." (Geoffrey, count of Britanny, son of King Henry of England, was crushed under the horses' hooves in knightly conflict; he died in Paris and was buried in the cathedral of that city). His death is also mentioned by Rigord: *Œuvres de Rigord et de Guillaume le Breton, historiens de Philippe-Auguste: Chroniques de Rigord et de Guillaume le Breton*, vol. I, 68.
[12] Chronology established by regional sections in Barber and Barker, *Tournaments*.
[13] A good sense is given by the many illustrations in Barber and Barker, *Tournaments*.

a widespread swath of countryside, seeking, avoiding, and fighting their opponents. This was termed the *mêlée*, an apt name that suggests a violent mixing of warriors.

This early form of tournament is famously that of William Marshal's youth, with spectacular clashes and hell-for-leather chases over fields and sometimes through village streets.[14] Marshal's unsurpassed skill as a fighter put him ever close to his powerful patron, the Young King (son of Henry II), who delighted in this dangerous sport and wanted the Marshal always near him in combat. Tournament was the Marshal's high road to success and appears (especially in the admiring and perhaps slightly envious biography written by Sidney Painter) to have been a rollicking time of martial adventure and comradeship. Indeed, for young, ambitious, elite males, the cycle of tournaments may have seemed a real-life portal into the imagined pastel pages of life portrayed in romance. We will see that others in their world would have viewed it quite differently.

If *mêlée* quickly became the standard tournament, jousting between individuals may have provided the original, spontaneous form of sport; and it undoubtedly continued as a prelude to the massed fighting of tournament. Such contests between individual challengers also preceded many an actual set-piece battles in war where such challenges, loudly made in the presence of opposing ranks of warriors, would surely be accepted. Yet individual encounters only became the central aspect of the sport about two decades into the thirteenth century. One of its flourishing homes was the Burgundian court of the later fourteenth and the fifteenth century.[15] Formal individual combat to mark important occasions lasted longer than the traditional span of the Middle Ages, and it is obviously reenacted in this style of combat in Renaissance fairs today (ostensibly to honor some finely costumed lady solemnly seated in a pavilion on the field as Queen Elizabeth I).

[14] Crouch, *Tournament*, 51.
[15] Numerous forms of extreme chivalric sport in the court of Philip the Good (duke of Burgundy, 1419–1467) are described by Richard Vaughan, *Philip the Good: The Apogee of Burgundy* (London: Longman, 1970; new ed. Woodbridge, Suffolk: Boydell, 2002), 145–149, 182–183, 300–301. The display and expense are fully apparent. The way had been paved in the later fourteenth century by Philip the Bold (duke of Burgundy, 1383–1404). See Vaughan, *Philip the Bold: the Formation of the Burgundian State* (London: Longman, 1962; new ed. Woodbridge, Suffolk, 2002), 196.

Tournament not only lasted for centuries, it spread socially and geographically, and seems to have known many relatives in a variety of violent games. A classic regional variation appeared in the Iberian peninsula where Spanish chivalry adopted from Moorish custom the *juegos de cañas* (cane games), in which participants threw canes or reeds at one another. By the late fourteenth century this sport had become formalized. As Barbara Fuchs writes, "[T]hough the game was recognized as Moorish, it was embraced as an appropriate pursuit for Spanish nobles – a particularly Iberian version of the joust... [P]erhaps most important, the *cañas* were not only an exceptional performance; in their simpler form, they were instead a habitual practice or discipline, involving specific skills and the mastery of a particular style of horsemanship."[16]

Of course the subchivalric or prechivalric wanted some of the action that characterized an elite group. Some urban dwellers with money and social ambition inevitably aped knightly sport. In Italian communal society, practitioners of tournament present a complicated pattern (as is usually true of matters chivalric south of the Alps). Some individuals and families who considered themselves strenuous knights (and were so recognized by others) lived the knightly life intensely in all its combative and more pacific forms; they were warriors and trained for war. Other individuals and families centered their lives on commerce and banking, but might imitate chivalric form, including chivalric sport. Many considered such forms prestigious, though the chivalric elite did not simply coincide with the ruling elite.[17] Urban knightly sport could indeed be vigorous. A Venetian ordinance of 1288 required those participating in chivalric games to tie bells to their harnesses so that citizens would not be suddenly run down by enthusiastic jousters on large horses in narrow and twisting town streets.[18]

---

[16] *Exotic Nation: Maurophilia and the Construction of Early Modern Spain* (Philadelphia: University of Pennsylvania Press, 2009), 90.

[17] Peter W. Sposato, "Reforming the Chivalric Elite in Thirteenth Century Florence: The Evidence of Brunetto Latini's *Il Tesoretto*," *Viator: Medieval and Renaissance Studies* 46.1 (Spring 2015), pages unknown; idem, "Chivalry and Honor-Violence in Late Medieval Florence," in *Prowess, Piety, and Public Order in Medieval Society: Studies in Honor of Richard W. Kaeuper*, eds. Daniel Franke and Craig Nakashian (Brill, forthcoming); idem, "'That the Practice of Arms Is the Most Excellent': Chivalry, Honor, and Violence in Late Medieval Florence" (PhD dissertation, University of Rochester, 2014).

[18] Barber and Barker, *Tournaments*, 164.

In both town and countryside, in fact, a variety of tough fighting games and contests took form and showed regional and local variants. Genuine tournaments were fought within town walls.[19] But young males, both urban and rural, loved riding with lance in hand at the quintain (a target mannequin). They and their elders also engaged in a variety of spontaneous martial sports often termed "bohorts." These combative games were not limited to urban youth; even the great beyond urban walls sometimes participated.[20] If the exact nature of some forms of sport remains elusive, efforts by governing bodies to control them and an evident fear of death resulting from them suggest that they were decidedly vigorous.[21] Regulations at Bologna in 1259 and at Trevisa in 1313 stipulated that participants in these rough sports must not use their spears against any onlookers who were on foot.[22] Men-at-arms loved competing with their weaponry in any available fashion, but occasionally participating in actions known by a common name likely did not make elite warriors feel any bond with their social inferiors. In its most significant forms, tournament belonged to the elite who appear to have mocked commoners hardy enough or foolish enough to attempt imitation.[23] Formal tourneying was essentially a knightly activity that marked participants as superior beings.

These elite warriors came by the middle of the thirteenth century to favor a fashionable form of chivalric sporting event termed a "Round Table." Such festivities displayed changing tastes well: jousting replaced the mass fighting of teams, and the action was enhanced with rich and costly pageantry and drama drawn from knightly appreciation of Arthurian literature. The fourteenth-century romance *Perceforest* lovingly imagines the outfit of a tourneyer:

Estonné's handsome tunic and his horse's matching caparison, all of fine blue samite embroidered with silver clover leaves and lozenges of gold, at each

---

[19] Paoloa Ventrone, "Feste, apparati, spettacoli," in *Comuni e Signorie*, ed. F. Cardini (Florence: Casa Editrice Le Monnier, 2000), 393–412; Duccio Balestracci, *La festa in armi: Giostre, tornei e giochi del Medioevo* (Rome: Laterza, 2003).

[20] Crouch, *Tournament*, 79.   [21] Ibid., 113–114.

[22] Barber and Barker, *Tournaments*, 164.

[23] Perhaps no Middle English poem escapes controversy, but the *Tournament of Tottenham* seems to lampoon rustics fighting with farm implements while mounted on nags. The incredibly scatological thirteenth-century *Chanson d'Augier* similarly mocks French peasants who ape their betters. This *chanson* was set to music and could be sung, no doubt late of an evening.

point of which was a red rose spraying a pollen of golden bells: you wouldn't believe how splendid it was to see the sunlight dazzling from the gold and the blue, or how sweet to hear the bells' melodious ringing wherever the horse would go.[24]

Costume for jousters became even more colorful, elaborate, and even fantastic as participants paraded or competed as characters from romance or even from Christian history; an element of play or parody could be found, as when Edward III and a team once jousted dressed as the pope and cardinals.[25] Pero Niño's biographer reports that King Juan II of Castile, the Infante Enrique (Juan's son), and the King of Navarre (Juan's brother) all met at Valladolid to hold

many jousts and tourneys, and *juegos de cañas*, in which they all took great pleasure. The Infante Don Enrique held the first festival, most noble; the King of Navarre the second. And the King of Castile, the third, much greater and more noble than any of the others. . . The King of Castile had with him twelve knights, well arrayed, in the name of the twelve apostles. . . Pero Niño was one of the twelve knights who did deeds in memory of the twelve apostles, and had the name of St. Paul; and he smashed more lances, and made more encounters, than any other. And if there was something he intended to do that day, he did it, though he was at that time around fifty years old, and had days that he did not want to participate in the sport.[26]

The impact of romance literature upon such late medieval tourneying appears in another Spanish martial enterprise, the *passo honroso* of Suero de Quiñones, in 1434. Suero had, as Noel Fallows writes,

vowed to wear a large iron ring around his neck every Thursday, a gesture that was intended to represent a topos of the medieval sentimental romance, namely, that he was symbolically imprisoned by love. The only way he could be freed from captivity was by breaking 300 lances with fellow team-members against all comers.[27]

---

[24] Bryant, trans., *Perceforest*, 137. An equally elaborate costume is described at ibid., 141. The poet elaborately describes an ideal setting for tournament at ibid., 245–261, with an equally elaborate dubbing scene at 247. The setting resembles the structure built by Edward III within Windsor Castle. Interestingly, the king is urged not to engage in the tournament as it might "turn ugly." Ibid., 254.

[25] Richard Barber, "Why Did Edward III Hold the Round Table? The Literary Background," in *Edward III's Round Table at Windsor: The House of the Round Table and the Windsor Festival of 1344*, eds. Julian Munby, Richard Barber, and Richard Brown (Rochester: Boydell & Brewer, 2008), 92.

[26] Carriazo, *El victorial*, 328–329. Translation by Samuel Claussen. This portion of the biography is not included in Evans, *Unconquered Knight*.

[27] Noel Fallows, *Jousting in Medieval and Renaissance Iberia* (Woodbridge: Boydell, 2010), 14. He adds, "And let it be said that these jousts, in which seasoned jousters

Spectacle would eventually – well beyond the medieval period – edge even jousting off the field, though the physical combat lingered into the Early Modern world as a gilded anachronism. Stylized tilts could still be dangerous; a French king (Henry II) died in 1559 when a splintered segment of a lance slid through his visor; but those who thought "breaking a lance" proved and enhanced their manhood retained confidence in plate armor and sometimes used jointed lances that would shatter spectacularly; and, as a further safeguard, they rode great horses that could not dangerously collide across the wall built along the axis of the joust.[28] Well before this time, spectators lined the field, women were included in their numbers, and soon stands for viewing the action and pageantry had been built. At least in fervid literary imagination, wealthy and desired women offered themselves as prizes to be won by triumphant knights.

TOURNAMENT, SOCIETY, AND AUTHORITY

Color and pageantry were important, but, as is true when analyzing all chivalric topics, we must keep distortive romanticism at bay and be fully aware not only of what tournament meant to knights, but what impact it had on society more generally. Knightly personal enjoyment was unbounded, but chivalric pleasures can scarcely form the sole criterion for scholarly investigation. What tournament meant for villagers, merchants, and monks is significant, as are the attitudes and actions of those busily building more powerful institutions of governance and systems of law, both lay and ecclesiastical.

The sheer scope of tournament takes on significance in understanding societal impact. In its northern French homeland, as David Crouch has suggested, a site announced for tournament would actually extend over the countryside between two settled places, one of them usually a town of medium size (utilized as a base by one

---

risked life and limb in the lists at the same time that they were acting out an amorous emprise invented by Suero de Quiñones, took place long before the exercise of jousting had 'degenerated into a ceremonial breaking of fragile lances.'" Ibid.

[28] The tiltyard at the Tudor palace of Hampton Court still preserves the feature of a low wall to separate jousters and their mounts. Cf. Alan Young, *Tudor and Jacobean Tournaments* (Dobbs Ferry: Sheridan House, 1986), 110, and *The Great Tournament Roll of Westminster: A Collotype Reproduction of the Manuscript*, 2 vols., ed. Sydney Anglo (Oxford: Clarendon Press, 1968), 42 (with a description of jousting under Henry VIII).

tournament team). Dominique Barthélemy has strongly argued that the initial link with warfare of the period may have been quite close, with little more than prearrangement dividing one from the other.[29] The area utilized in early tournament could be surprisingly large; one famous designated field on the borders of Flanders spread across nearly 2,000 acres.[30] What separated the action from war, as we may recall from Dominique Barthélemy's argument, was merely the prearrangement of the tournament. Within the varied expanse of this area, thousands of men and horses would maneuver and fight, take prisoners, and seek refuge. In other parts of Europe, the site might lie close to a major town and take place over fields, plains, or meadows outside the city walls. Although tournaments on a single day may have been the early norm, by the thirteenth century the fighting often lasted for several days.[31]

Action often began on the evening preceding the formally announced opening of the tournament. Knights who could not wait for the morrow might call their evening action "vespers" as a nod to (or parody of) the last ecclesiastical service of the day.[32] Yet a genuine religious service opened the next day, for at least by the thirteenth century the knights prudently and piously heard Mass before combat that would be dangerous and might even prove fatal.[33] Teams were soon arranged, and the action commenced. If sport, it was highly serious combat: tourneyers used real weaponry, the very tools of war, as they thrust and hacked at each other, at least in the twelfth century. In the thirteenth century blunted weapons became more common, especially in the potentially lethal jousting; in the free-for-all general fighting of tournament, sword edges may have been blunted, but the practice is obscure.[34] Arthurian literature written in the twelfth century makes little or no distinction between weaponry or tactics utilized in war and those used in tournament. Was this a conservative view, reproducing old practice, or possibly – or

---

[29] "Les chroniques de la mutation chevaleresque en France," *Comptes redus de l'Academie des Inscriptions et Belles-Lettres* (2007); and "L'Eglise et les premiers tournois aux XIᵉ et XIIᵉ siècles," in *Chevalerie et christianisme aux XIIᵉ et XIIIᵉ siècles*, ed. Martin Aurell (Rennes, 2011), 139–149.

[30] Crouch, *Tournament*, 51.   [31] Ibid., 57.

[32] Ibid., 67–68. The idea of parodic language is my own suggestion and does not appear here. Vespers are mentioned in Wolfram von Eschenbach's *Parzival*, trans. Helen M. Mustard and Charles E. Passage (New York: Vintage, 1961), 49, 54.

[33] Crouch, *Tournament*, 71.   [34] Ibid., 79.

additionally – a form of flattery to please participants and patrons, suggesting the vigor and disregard of danger among the knighthood?

No more than in war was rough practice or even ruse foreign to tournament. The tactics of the count of Flanders were famous; he tended to hold back his team, pretending merely to observe the opening jousting or to allow some of his men to participate in it. Having announced that his force would not engage generally, he might suddenly rush them into combat at the moment a team was seen to be weary and dispersed. William Marshal's authorized biographer, far from condemning such practice, termed it wise and proper; the Young King's team adopted the very strategy, after suffering its use against them.[35] Footmen might march with their lord to tournaments, but their legitimate use to police the action sometimes shaded into vigorous participation in it. Darker hints sometimes were whispered about knightly participants themselves; rumors spread that some took bribes or betrayed their fellows who might bring good ransoms to the briber and a share of profits to a betrayer. The problem would inevitably arise, for the goal, of course, was to win valuable prisoners and their costly horses and gear, not to kill opponents. Whatever transpired on the field, a convivial dinner ideally closed the festivities, but all moralists warned against a tendency for the evening to end with *après tournois* sex; some clerics claimed bitterly that tournaments were breeding grounds of every mortal sin.[36]

Much that characterized tournament (especially in its early days) could never be loved by those who were building early forms of centralized authority, whether they were royal administrators, great lords, concerned clerics, or town councils. Yet the staying power of the sport is indisputable in the historical record. Over time, kings and great lay lords came to terms with tournament and even embraced it with enthusiasm (and perhaps a crafty sense of policy); churchmen slowly made their uneasy quotidian peace with it, recognizing with resignation that what could not be radically reformed, and certainly not altogether expunged, had to be accepted, though that acceptance came with frequent muttering and head shaking. They never loved this unruly child of chivalric culture, and at the level of abstract ideas

---

[35] Ibid., 85–86.
[36] These warnings could even appear in books of moral tales, such as that from the first half of the fourteenth century in British Library Arundel 506 f 43.

never ceased to condemn it.[37] Why nascent governing institutions, lay and ecclesiastical, struggled with tournament in its early days and how they came to deal with it in an acceptable way pose interesting questions.

Clearly the violence of tournament produced a social impact well beyond the combat of elite participants themselves. Tournament began life as a disruptive and even destructive force within a society endeavoring to build frameworks for an ordered life from resources always in short supply and ever under threat. Without claiming that policies of early state builders or ecclesiastical bureaucrats always worked for peace and communal harmony – a claim that the plain historical record disproves – it remains important to contextualize tournament and to unblinkingly analyze its consequences. The issues include threats to public order not only on the field of competition but also en route to that site, and also a framework of ideas that could contend with religious principles and ecclesiastical authority and with emerging systems of secular law. We must also note that some aspects troubling to critics did change over time. In significant ways, the tournament matured by the later thirteenth century and became a more controlled sport rather than a simulacrum of war. The change retains significance even if the causation of governing institutions would be hard to prove.

Yet early tournaments, as we have seen, might closely resemble warfare of the period as the combatants ranged over considerable swaths of territory, with groups maneuvering, clashing directly at opponents, setting ambushes, and chasing fleeing foes. Any awareness of danger and damage to ordinary travelers on roads or villagers working in fields or vineyards is conspicuously missing from accounts of the action such as the biography of William Marshal. The noted clerical writer Jacques de Vitry, by contrast, charged that the warriors cursed peasants who got in their way, trampled their vineyards, and cut down the farmers' hedges and brush to make room for their tents.[38] Destructiveness was not openly acknowledged by tourneyers and their admirers, but it could not have been unknown to them. By common convention, certain seasons were kept free of tournaments: Lent was avoided out of piety, and the traditional times for

---

[37] The attitude in Thomas of Cantimpré, *Bonum Universale de Apibus*, and John Bromyard, *Summa Praedicantium*, for example.

[38] Discussed in Crouch, *Tournament*, 55.

early crop growth and for later harvesting of its bounty were avoided.
Prudence seems a more likely cause than abstract altruism: Crouch
declares that "even noble landowners did not want hundreds of
knights trampling down their hay and crops and bothering their
workers."[39] That spring grass and autumn harvest had to be protected
from chivalric sport provides a telling fact.

Dangers of combat must have been obvious to participants, though
no clear sense of the scale of resulting mortality appears.[40] Who better
could appreciate the perils of weaponry or a fall to the ground among
thundering horses' hooves? Though the agreed goal was vigorous
sport and profitable captures, deep personal enmity and political or
financial advantage might, as already noted, darken a scene so easily
pictured in pure scarlet and gold. And it can come as no surprise
that scores could be settled – even assassinations attempted – under
cover of vigorous action on the tourney field.[41] Of course extreme
sport could likewise generate resentment. Gutierre Díaz de Gamez
reported that from vigorous encounters in a tournament held by
Spanish royalty "there were engendered many animosities and
hatred."[42] Michael Prestwich cites a good case of a tournament
canceled in 1265 because of fears of trouble between the sons of
Simon de Montfort and supporters of the earl of Gloucester.[43]

[39] Ibid., 33.
[40] Perhaps several score of references to deaths in tournament appear in Barber and
Barker, *Tournaments*. Crouch discusses the issue in *Tournament*, 98–101. Matthew
Paris in his *Chronica Majora*, vol. iii, 404, writes of an English tournament at Blyth
(1237): "Quod odium fere in lamentabili judicium propuperat, in torneamento
commisso apud Blie … et commissum est non hastiludium, *sed hostile bellum*
[emphasis supplied]." Ludwig, son of Ludwig II, duke of Bavaria, was killed in
1290 when a lance pierced his throat in a tournament at Nurnberg: *Bayerische
Chroniken des XIV Jahrhunderts*, ed. Georg Leidinger (Hannover, 1918), 43. Horst
Fuhrman, *Einladung ins Mittelalter*, lists numbers of knights known to have been
killed in certain regions of Germany for certain years, and Joachim Bumke, *Courtly
Culture: Literature and Society in the High Middle Ages*, trans. Thomas Dunlap
(Berkeley: University of California Press, 1991), 249–250, mentions a number of
noble deaths in German tourneys as well. But all such evidence obviously cannot
be taken as an indication of representative number or frequency of deaths in
tournament.
[41] Barber and Barker cite cases, *Tournaments*, 146, 148.
[42] Carriazo, *El victorial*, 328–329. Translation by Samuel Claussen.
[43] Prestwich, *Edward I*, 48. Prestwich describes tournaments in the mid-1260s as
"violent contests, barely distinguishable from battle," ibid., 60.

As Maurice Keen warns, "tournaments offered an easy cover for the pursuit of established rivalries, and in the fury of confrontation self-restraint was easily lost sight of."[44] Experiencing such ferocity on the part of knights led by Baldwin V, count of Hainault, at a tournament in 1168, the count of Flanders brought a strong force of footmen into the action.[45] Baldwin himself characteristically had such a force on hand for protection during the confused fighting of the mêlée.[46] Ferocity seems to have abated by the end of the thirteenth century, as Keen notes, but the competitive spirit could still turn to wrath, and the settling of political scores could still be feared.[47] The "little war of Chalon," which took place on the return journey from crusade of Edward I in 1274, pitted a body of English knights against all comers in what Michael Prestwich has characterized as "from the outset barely distinguishable from a full-scale battle" involving infantry assaults as well as cavalry action on the part of the Burgundians.[48] Arthurian literature shows elite awareness that tournament could turn deadly serious; even in the world of Camelot, personal ambition and corrosive family feuds could seep to the surface and find an outlet in martial sport.[49] Perceforest, in the romance bearing his name, calls out to his lads, "My lords, you've done enough! It's best to leave the game while it is in good spirit! It was begun so, and so I'd have it end."[50]

A wider set of difficulties would be apparent, in fact, even before the opening of any particular tournament. As David Crouch has argued, bands of armed men traveled to the site of a tourney in high spirits (some fueled, no doubt, by ample wine no less than innate male vigor); their behavior may have presented more of a danger to public order than the formal combat to come.[51] Raucous high spirits could disintegrate into theft, oppression, and violence. Any band of armed men traversing the countryside could represent a problem in the eyes of local people; even friendly forces in wartime might be

---

[44] Keen, *Chivalry*, 86. Malcolm Vale notes this problem in *War and Chivalry*, 63–68.
[45] Crouch, *Tournament*, 28.   [46] Barber and Barker, *Tournaments*, 23.
[47] Keen, *Chivalry*, 86–87.   [48] Prestwich, *Edward I*, 84–85.
[49] E.g., *Lancelot-Grail*, I, *Story of Merlin*, 336. To take only one example from Malory, in his description of a disguised Lancelot winning the Grand Tournament, King Arthur becomes "wrothe oute of mesure that he and hys knyghtes might nat prevayle that day." Vinaver, *Malory: Works*, 647.
[50] Bryant, *Perceforest*, 142.   [51] Crouch, *Tournament*, 42.

perceived as a threat.[52] If the tourneyers were no worse, they may have been little better. Even William Marshal robbed a runaway priest of a hefty moneybag he counted on to support himself and the young lady eloping with him. The Marshal claimed the justification that this money would be lent at usury; his companions (with whom he shared the loot) revealingly expressed surprise that he had not taken the horses and baggage of the pair as well.[53] In general the behavior of tourneyers generated enough clerical outrage that taking clergymen's evidence would require patience and an organized queue. In written sources we possess, they complain that they have been taunted and humiliated, if not actually robbed.[54] Of course we can no longer hear the laments or outraged shouts of cheated inn-keepers or robbed villagers, but indirect evidence of a most informative sort comes from royal legislation. Richard Lion-Heart, no innate foe of chivalric sport, ordained that en route to a tournament,

no knight, earl, baron, or any other tourneyer may take unlawfully without permission any food or supplies from anyone else: he ought to buy everything he needs in the market place. He should not confiscate anything from anyone on the road on his own behalf or on behalf of any of his men. He ought not to permit anyone within his power to be harassed unjustly either by himself or his men... The earls and barons of England, and all who want to go to tournaments, must swear that they are within the jurisdiction of the king and his chief justiciar, and will maintain the king's peace with all their ability, untroubled and whole, going to and from tournament, particularly in the king's forests and markets.[55]

---

[52] In a striking case, a petition to the English crown complained about foreign troops committing depredations while passing to a port on the Channel; they were, in fact, foreign only in being English troops from another county. See against "foreign troops" who turn out to be soldiery from another county marching to a port on the Channel, from which they would be shipped to the war in France: *Rotuli Parliamentorum*, iii, 80.

[53] *History of William Marshal*, lines 6854–6864.

[54] Jocelin de Brakelonde, "Chronica," in *Memorials of St. Edmund's Abbey*, vol. II, ed. Thomas Arnold (London: Eyre and Spottiswoode, 1890), 260. A number of knights are given the right to hold a tournament at Thetford by Richard after his return in 1194. Although Abbot Samson prohibited them from holding the tournament, twenty-four noble youths (*juvenes filii nobilium*) arrived at Thetford fully armed (*plenis armis*) to harass the abbot, causing a disturbance in the town as they drank, danced, shouted, and caroused. Eventually Abbot Samson excommunicated them.

[55] Quoted in Crouch, *Tournament*, 44.

The "ought to," "should not," "ought not," and "must" fall like a drumbeat, leaving the reader to wonder how many tourneyers obediently marched to this restrictive royalist tune.

Early increases in royal power, especially noteworthy in England but operative on both sides of the Channel, led kings to attempt to regulate tournament as a potential danger to a basic level of public order that they claimed as their right and duty to maintain. Their most formal utterances (upon taking the crown or when issuing general rulings) focus on securing "the king's peace." Although royal prohibitions had formally blocked tournaments in England since the time of Henry II, the first surviving legislation comes from his son Richard I, from which a bit was just quoted. The ordinance licensed tournaments only by royal grant (fees adding welcomed funds to the king's coffers). Five permitted sites were stipulated (in Wiltshire, Warwickshire, Suffolk or Lincolnshire, Northamptonshire, and Nottinghamshire); the regulations stipulated a sliding scale of fees for those knights who wished to participate, an earl being charged 20 marks, a baron 10, a landed knight 4, and a landless knight 2. Unless a knight swore to pay his fees, he would be arrested and his lands possibly confiscated.[56] Scores of tournament prohibitions issued from the royal chancery across the thirteenth century and into the fourteenth century, reaching a peak in the reign of Edward I, who ordered sheriffs to deliver the message rather than send out the friars often favored by his father, Henry III.

At the most pragmatic level, royal administrators would have remembered antiroyalist baronial gatherings against King John and King Henry III that met behind the opaque screen of tournaments. What is more, a king such as Edward I could announce with public outrage that trouble in the realm flouted his lordship.[57] As Maurice Keen has stated, "The reduction of bloodshed and restraint upon the rancours which were so easily engendered in the heat of affray were clearly among the principal objects of the rules of tournaments which were drawn up by the English kings Richard I and Edward I."[58] Keen is referring to the 1292 *Statuta Armorum* by which Edward sought to limit the dangers represented by armed supporters who attended tournaments in significant numbers and were inclined to join in the fray on behalf of their lord. Exactly how a single sheriff (even with some escort of his own) convinced large bodies of armed men eager

---

[56] *Foedera*, ed. Thomas Rymer (1816), vol. I, pt. I, 65.   [57] Ibid.
[58] Keen, *Chivalry*, 86.

for a show of prowess to desist and return home is unclear; whether he could even recognize or fully record who was present so that their names (or family crests) could be reported to the central administration is uncertain. By the time of Edward III, the king's serjeants-at-arms were sometimes empowered to supervise sheriffs and to arrest offenders; some tourneyers felt enough concern to obtain royal licenses for their sport, and a few who did not are known to have been imprisoned.[59] The general efficacy and enforcement remain interpretive problems. The hands of the royal official holding up his wand of office and declaring a halt to a tournament may have trembled; he was, after all, requiring vigorous men ready for action to practice *conflictus interruptus*.

Yet even a king as certain of his role and rightful mastery as Edward I also breathed the atmosphere of chivalry and recognized its benefits for martial culture in a reign replete with warfare. As Keen sharply observed, tension had long characterized English royal attitudes toward tournament, which kings could accept so long as they could be in control. Could they only pose as patrons, "all they had to be concerned about was that the magnificence of their own tournaments should outshine that of any gathering that a subject of theirs might bring together."[60] Edward I richly appreciated tournament when he was the sponsor; famously, he held a Round Table at Nefynin in 1284 to celebrate his conquest of Wales, and another at Falkirk in 1302, when progress in Scotland seemed assured. At Whitsuntide in 1306 he knighted the future Edward II, along with several hundred other young men, in a festive ceremony at Westminster that would not seem out of place in a romance.[61]

Perhaps even more clearly, by the reign of his grandson, Edward III, the crown came to see the need to escape a conundrum threatening its very well-being. It was trying to maintain a needed and desired relationship with lay elite warriors, who formed a key element of

---

[59] Sources in R. W. Kaeuper, *War, Justice and Public Order*, 205n64.

[60] Keen, *Chivalry*, 87.

[61] Prestwich grants that the king shows some surprisingly romantic streaks, but warns against thinking Edward I was an Arthurian: *Edward I*, 120–121. For an argument that Edward I utilized the pageantry of his Feast of the Swans to harness the younger generation of English aristocracy to his campaign against Robert the Bruce, replete with vows of vengeance, see Andy King, "Treason, Feud and the Growth of State Violence," in *War, Government and Aristocracy in the British Isles, c. 1150–1500*, 105–106.

Figure 8   Individual combat eventually dominated tournament and filled many pages
of romance literature, where it appears to settle most pressing issues.

armed force, while prohibiting or closely regulating the extreme
sport beloved by this elite. Even the short-lived regime of Queen
Isabella and her lover Mortimer (acting before Edward III took
personal control in 1330) seemed determined to tread the authoritative path of the young king's grandfather. The tournament prohibition of 1329 was issued "as the king, who is going to parts beyond sea,
wishes his peace to be firmly observed in his absence, and he considers
that his peace may easily be broken by assemblies of men-at-arms
during his absence."[62] Coming into his own, and with the fearful
memory of his father deposed and murdered, Edward III soon found
a solution. Rather than prohibit, he decided to permit and to lead.
More precisely, Edward decided that as royal patron he played
a role that allied him with elite subjects and permitted him to
prohibit only on those occasions when specific royal interests
demanded it. Famously, he founded the Order of the Garter in the

---

[62]   *Calendar of Close Rolls 1327–30*, 544–545.

mid-1340s – originally as tourneying groups at the peak of society. And he broadly identified himself with the mythical King Arthur.[63]

This royal turn benefited from the changing nature of tournament itself. The rise of individual jousting (Figure 8) and the more restricted scope of the action made the royal romance with tourneying more likely. Extreme chivalric sport was distancing itself from its early resemblance to warfare or any challenge to royal sovereignty; that entry into tournaments was increasingly tied to noble status likewise made it more attractive to the crown seeking the full cooperation of great lords in lucrative and honored military enterprises across the Channel.

Royal power vis-à-vis tournament developed on a different timetable within France, but by the second half of the thirteenth century French kings, too, sought some regulation and prohibition of tournament.[64] As is true in many aspects of medieval French kingship, Louis IX took a founder's role, combining strictures against tournament, judicial duel, and private war within the royal domain.[65] This combination of targeted practices is obviously of interest, even if the exact chronology and scope of royal action across the vast French realm remain cloudy.[66] Since Louis's son Philip III loved to tourney and rewarded followers of similar tastes, no continuity of policy developed at once; tournaments would be temporarily prohibited and then allowed; one pause was occasioned by Philip's son suffering brain damage when his helmet was beaten down about his head by repeated blows while he was participating in the sport. Philip IV, the Fair, ever concerned about royal sovereignty, prohibited more consistently, though with shifting justifications: sometimes the priority of the king's war over sport was asserted; sometimes the view of Holy Church was evoked; once a tournament under royal sponsorship to celebrate the knighting of his son was specified; in December 1311

[63] Mark Ormrod, *Edward III* (New Haven: Yale University Press, 2011), 300–308. Ormrod holds that even though originally finding its basis in tourneying groups it became restricted to a more exclusive membership.

[64] This discussion is based on evidence cited and analysis in R. W. Kaeuper, *War, Justice and Public Order*, 208–211, and *Chivalry and Violence*, 98–102, which provides references to primary sources.

[65] William Chester Jordan, *Louis IX and the Challenge of Crusade* (Princeton, 1979), 204, comments on these policies and the difficulties of establishing intent and applicability within the realm of France.

[66] Discussed by William Chester Jordan, *Louis IX and the Challenge of Crusade* (Princeton: Princeton University Press, 1979).

the prohibition stated an intent to secure the peace of his kingdom, and its violation was linked to the offense of *port d'armes*, the carrying of offensive arms within the realm. The policy continued under his successor, Philip V, but the series of prohibitions then stopped. Crown emphasis may have shifted to measures against *port d'armes* and private warfare as greater threats to peace. As the earlier practice of warriors riding roughshod over the countryside was reduced to jousts within a restricted area, tournament may have been perceived as a lesser danger. All such issues paled, of course, once the single great issue became repeated invasions from across the Channel.

Had these measures won any more success within the vast expanse of the French kingdom than those proposed in the more compact and relatively more governed realm of England? French prohibitions and regulations (*ordonnonces* and *mandements*) rail against continued actions in violation of previous legislation that make new enactments necessary; surviving legal records show no signs of widespread or truly effective prosecution of violators. On both sides of the Channel, the impulse for royal regulation is clear, but the result seems to have fallen far short of announced goals. Though generalization is difficult, in other regions of the continent, governing agencies seemingly invested less effort strictly to prohibit or contain tournament and came more swiftly to the strategy of adopting a leading role in the phenomenon. In the stoutly royalist legislation of Frederick II for the kingdom of Sicily in 1231 tournament is not mentioned, but the carrying of various sorts of arms by people of various specified groups is attempted.[67]

Were ecclesiastical efforts at prohibition or restraint of tournament any more effective? Avid tourneyers must have thought that ecclesiastical disapproval and condemnation hovered over the fields of their sport like dark clouds blocking welcomed sunlight. Clerics saw matters differently. Maurice Keen states,

[T]he real bedrock basis of the church's condemnation of [tournaments] . . . and the original mainspring of the papal prohibitions, was the encouragement that they gave to the turbulent spirit of secular knighthood, in which the ecclesiastical authority had long seen a direct threat to the good ordering of Christendom, and which led to homicide, destruction, and disorder.[68]

[67] James Powell, *The Liber Augustalis or Constitutions of Melfi*, legislates about the carrying of arms; see 15–16, 18.

[68] Keen, *Chivalry*, 96.

Such condemnations had, of course, served to buttress the regulation attempted by kings, great lords, and town councils. Clerical hands had long been uplifted in blessing for efforts toward an ordered society, which they knew to be necessary to maintain their religious mission. Even though these hands could never be cleansed from all stain of war and violence, the clerics shared motives with lay rulers; their own disapproval had roots beyond the search for peace and order secured by the lay authority they always blessed and sometimes exercised. They worried about sin. As early as 1130 a church council at Clermont prohibited violent chivalric sport. The fathers were not certain of the proper terminology for the phenomena they disapproved; with evident distaste they hurled several phrases at their target, calling them "detestable markets or fairs at which knights are accustomed to meet to show off their strength and their boldness . . . at which the deaths of men and dangers to the soul often occur."[69] But they provided a theoretically potent enforcement clause: no knight killed in the sport could be buried in sacred ground. For half a century succeeding church councils would repeat this prohibition and threat, the last in the series emerging from the Third Lateran Council of 1179 (at which the more accurate noun *torneamenta* replaced the earlier, approximate language). Concern for homicide and pride, both deadly sins, animated this line of thought, but resourceful and prolific critics such as Bishop Jacques de Vitry soon claimed that all seven deadly sins flourished at tournaments. That claim rolled across succeeding centuries: senseless killings and even pride in prowess were obvious wrongs, but so were wrath, envy, and lust (as ladies or less respected women attended), and even sloth could be detected (for depression and inaction might follow defeat in combat).[70] The determination required in clerical critics comes into focus as we realize that they were denouncing a sport in its springtime growth, the very age in which William Marshal rode close by the Young King, sword at the ready to protect his great patron.

---

[69] Quoted in Barber and Barker, *Tournaments*, 17; the authors speculate that the odd terminology may reflect the markets that sold food, drink, clothing, and armor to the participants.

[70] Discussed in Keen, *Chivalry*, 95. For primary texts, see Crane, ed., *Exempla of Jacques de Vitry* (Folklore Society, 1890), 62–64, 193. Cf. H. von E. Scott and C. C. Swinton, eds., trans., *Dialogue of Miracles [by] Caesarius of Heisterbach* (London: Routledge, 1922), 2 vols., II, 303–304, and British Library Arundel 506 f 73.

Brows beneath tonsures must have furrowed as the sport continued unabated. Heedless of the conciliar legislation, local clerics were officiating at the burial in sacred ground of participants killed in tournaments. Understandably, these accommodating clerics showed more concern about local society – often the family that had appointed them and continued to supply essential patronage – than distant popes and formal conciliar prohibitions. Yet formal clerical critiques continued. If in time the councils ceased to reissue the prohibition of 1130, tireless efforts turned to other approaches. Many efforts originated with a concerned individual cleric and so were local and sporadic, but a realistic view granted that if knightly vigor could not be stanched, its outlet might be transformed by renewed emphasis on a means already at hand.

Crusade as the better cause might provide an outlet that could draw the warriors away from sin toward virtuous fighting that would contribute mightily to their salvation. Let them stop smiting each other out of pride, greed, and wrath, and fight the good fight that was thought to please God. The saintly Louis IX of France in his regulation of 1260 gave royal support to this clerical line of thought, encouraging knighthood to prove its martial worth on crusade.[71] To their bold, flanking assault on tournament, clerics added endless guerrilla attacks carried out in sermons and collections of the exempla that animated them. These lively (and sometimes ghoulish) stories constantly lauded crusaders, showing them as recipients of divine love and forgiveness, while picturing vile tourneyers being punished in the flames of perdition.

A thirteenth-century sermon exemplum penned by Thomas of Cantimpré, as told to him, he says, by the widow of a prominent German knight, provides a good example, much appreciated and retold for centuries. The distraught widow saw her late husband in her dreams, surrounded by flames, with demons performing a devilish parody of an arming ceremony that would prepare him for the lists; they attached red-hot pieces of armor to his body with long spikes and – skipping the actual fighting – led him directly to his accustomed post-tourney bed for recreational sex – the bed now transformed into a flaming iron frame, where his waiting sexual companion was a horrid toad. The widow told her confessor she

[71] Jordan, *Louis IX*, 204n124.

could not free herself from the images.[72] Tourneyers reached by the story, it was hoped, would have a similar reaction.

Crusaders, in contrast, died piously in the Holy Land, the exemplum sometimes adding that golden crosses were found on their hearts, even bearing (as the story was retold) a Latin tag expressing their love for God; while alive they had fought manfully, had fervently prayed at the Holy Sepulchure, and had emerged to find that their divinely guided stallions had trotted off to reserve the best inn within the city for them by steadily blocking the doorway to other potential lodgers.[73]

In one final blast of prohibitional authority, Pope Clement V in 1312 issued sweeping instructions to European leaders on their duty to recapture the Holy Land and to ban all violent chivalric sport as well, naming tournaments, jousts, and Round Tables. A storm of reactive protest swept back against his injunctions; the French royal publicist Pierre du Bois (who, it is interesting to note, also wrote in favor of a major new crusade) produced a significant formal rebuttal of the papal case for prohibition. This counter case claimed with some merit that clerical prohibitions only damaged church authority, as their open defiance showed; moreover, excommunicated knights would not go on crusade, he argued, or if they did they would provoke divine wrath, not the blessings of victory. Twisting the rhetorical blade he had already thrust home, du Bois asserted that a wiser policy would be to restrict the right to tourney to crusaders alone. The view, if not the specific case, of Philip IV and Pierre du Bois won the day not long after, for in 1316, only eleven days after his accession, the new Avignon pope, John XXII, arguably under intense French pressure from Philip V, lifted the ban on tournament. He "looked the facts in the face" in the concise phrase of Maurice Keen. He had learned, the bull states, that some men refused to take up knighthood if they could not engage in chivalric sport; the crusade was actually being impeded by the prohibition. The turning point is striking, for critics with the rhetorical clout of Saint Bernard had claimed nearly two centuries before that tournament represented heedless killing and stood as the antithesis of crusade. Throughout the remainder of the traditional Middle Ages, tournament and

---

[72] Georgius Colvenerius, ed., *Thomas Cantimpratanus, Bonum universale de apibus* (Douai, 1597), II, li, 3, 366–368.

[73] See, e.g., British Library Royal 7DI, f 90; Arundel 52, f 113b.

crusade stood as accepted pillars of chivalric culture, even though
determined opponents, such as John Bromyard, continued to rage
against knightly sport in works that remained a rich source for
sermons and treatises.[74] The famous treatise of René d'Anjou
(c. 1460) recommended to tourneyers that they lodge in religious
houses; the cloisters could provide such wonderful spaces for displaying the colorful armor during festivities anticipating the action soon
to commence on the field.[75]

Few components of chivalry better display the confidence and
assertive independence of the elite warriors than the persistence and
triumph of tournament. Its determined practitioners rode through
the hellfires threatened by ecclesiastics and brought the nascent
regulatory power of early states to accept their right to practice
extreme sport embodying so much of their ethos. In the long run,
church prohibitions faded into background grumbling; kings and the
greatest territorial lords learned they must lead what they could not –
and often at base did not intend to – utterly prohibit, worry though
they might about threats to public order and to emerging sovereignty.
So remarkable a triumph would, of course, never have transpired had
tournament not transformed itself significantly in the process, moving
slowly from the simulacrum of war to a more limited space and
a more controlled spectacle, while retaining a high-voltage practice
of limited violence wired into its core. The evolutionary process was
remarkable and also highly informative; few phenomena could better
display the strains and tensions in the practice of chivalry within an
emerging society forming along religious, governmental, and legal
dimensions.

[74] John Bromyard, *Summa Praedicantium* (Venice, 1586), with topics arranged alpha-
betically to aid those preparing sermons.
[75] See René d'Anjou, *Traité de la Forme et Devis d'un Tournoi* (Paris: Verve, 1946). For
a fifteenth-century treatise by a Dutch scholastic, Hencricus de Leuwis (c.
1401–1470), or Dionysius Cartusianus, see *Opuscula insigniora* (Cologne, 1559);
but this treatise denounces tournament in terms of greed, avarice, and violence.

Part IV

CHIVALRY, GOVERNING INSTITUTIONS, AND IDEALS

—————— • ——————

Thinking about knights and kings will likely bring to mind vivid scenes in stories and especially films about King Arthur and his knights of the Round Table. It is easy to picture them feasting together (inconveniently wearing full plate armor) in joyous harmony, their rich goblets lifted to toast a common sense of purpose and destiny. Thinking about chivalry and the clerical hierarchy may conjure fewer vivid scenes; it requires us to recall that governing powers rested in great ecclesiastics no less than kings whose very knightliness more readily fills the eyes and mind. Yet the popular mental picture that surfaces will likely remain rosy-hued, perhaps featuring a bishop, solemn beneath his mitre, with gloved and ringed hand uplifted in blessing while knights bow heads in obedience and reverence. Both imagined scenes are not foreign to medieval life: kings, knights, and great clerics (joined by ranks of monks and parish priests) had good reason to cooperate; all knew that their thoughts operated within a common religious worldview encompassing a special role for kings and clerics as well as knights.

Yet reality was not always so simple and amicable, especially when actual and effective governing power was at issue. If harmonious scenes are readily imagined, tensions and difficulties can swiftly be spotted. A good witness can be summoned in the person of crusty old Girart, duke of Burgundy, as imagined in the great twelfth-century epic poem *Chanson d'Aspremont*. An utterly unreconstructed conservative, scornful of all advancing institutions of governance, he sings out an assertion of full independence from any governing authority.

Though, in company with other epics, this *chanson* is set in an imagined Carolingian world, the poem wrestles with issues of the time of its composition. As the duke lectures Archbishop Turpin, who has been sent to secure his assistance in Charlemagne's campaign against Muslim invaders:

> Now if my memory is clear,
> There are three thrones chosen and set apart:
> One is called Constantinople,
> Rome is another, and this city makes three –
> The fourth is Toulouse which is part of my heritage.
> Across my own realm I have my own priests;
> Never for baptism or any Christian service
> Do we need the pope's authority.
> I'll make a pope myself, should I so please!
> In all my possessions whatsoever
> I hold not the value of one shelled egg
> From any earthly man, but from the Lord God alone.
> Your king will never be loved by me
> Unless he is kneeling down at my feet![1]

Girart had, in fact, planned to attack Charlemagne's lands while the great emperor was fighting the invading foe, a scheme that was quashed only by the duke's plainspoken wife, who had shamed him into turning from war as usual ("killing people or causing hurt . . . [and] committing crimes") to an engagement in what all contemporaries considered a more holy form of warfare.

This imagined duke is scarcely presented as an unambiguously admirable character in the epic, and his degree of independence from all external clerical and lay authority is likely pushed deliberately off the end of the scale. Yet some subterranean approval for his hardy contrariness seeps to the surface, and the goal in the *chanson* may well have been (as so often in such texts) to generate debate on a basic issue. The duke's speech and his wild behavior (in wrath he attempts to stab Archbishop Turpin with an impressive knife) raise significant questions about attitudes toward the power and authority of governing agencies in a world of proudly independent warriors of various social ranks. Just how much cooperation would they offer, and how much intrusion would they tolerate from those building governing institutions and formulating guiding ideas?

[1] Lines 5012–5017, my translation slightly modifying that of Michael A. Newth, *The Song of Aspremont* (New York: Garland, 1999).

It is worthy of note that chivalry grew up alongside major institutions of governance in "church" and "state" that were busily extending their reach. What R. W. Southern, in an overview of medieval church history in social context, termed its "age of growth" (c. 1050–1300) coincides with our classic phase of chivalric development.[2] This chronology also coincides with the opening era of what J. R. Strayer termed "the medieval origins of the modern state."[3] Reactions between and among all these high medieval siblings were compounded of cooperation and competitive tension. This complexity can be ignored only by indulging in a romantic conception of chivalry as ideal restraint exercised within perfect hierarchical loyalty on the part of knights who were unfailingly guided by the most elevated and abstract Christian principles – a view completely at odds with the evidence that we will explore. If complexities and conflicts in church–state relations have stimulated scholarship for generations, exploring how the proud and independent-minded men of chivalry related to both of these growing agencies of governance has received less attention. Understanding this subject sets the goal for the chapters in this part. Cooperation and conflict between kings and knights are explored in Chapter 8; the emergence of a religious ideology of chivalry is examined in Chapter 9.

Kings and knights shared much common ground. Kings stood at the apex of the lay aristocracy and – the cause of much controversy – together they had long dominated the clerical hierarchy within their realms, with heavy hands on clerical appointments and church property. Over time, kings came to consider themselves as members of the knighthood and personally led armored hosts into battle. Their unsurpassed patronage bonded followers, great and lesser, to them in intense loyalty (though it had to be renewed regularly). Yet if kings were keenly aware of their obligations to defend the realm in armor, they also swore coronation oaths about keeping the peace within the realm, defending the church, and providing justice. They had no standing armies. Pay could recruit mercenaries, but a key part of the force required came from the ranks of knights rooted in the countryside, some of whom might, in fact, constitute the problem. Kings were definitely not – despite the image beloved in film and, indeed,

---

[2] R. W. Southern, *Western Society and the Church* (New York: Penguin Books, 1990).

[3] J. R. Strayer, *On the Medieval Origins of the Modern State* (Princeton, 1970, repr. 2005).

in many literary works – simply leaders of a war band writ large. They collected taxes; they made and enforced laws and had a genuine role in legal cases, either through direct jurisdiction (as was so widely the case in England) or through appellate jurisdiction (as was more common on the continent); they thought they should at least regulate tournaments. Perspectives could clash, for if kings considered themselves knights, the warriors considered themselves at least kinglets within their own territorial spheres. That is, they could never forget their rights in regional or local use of armed force and adjudication. Boundaries of authority on all such issues could be ragged and contested. The outrage occasionally felt by constrained lords was made in unforgettable if inelegant terms by a knight who was hauled into a French royal court in 1327 to answer for his misdeeds. This was not the first judicial effort to restrain him, and he was clearly informed that the entire royal administrative and legal hierarchy demanded his submission. His plain reply – no doubt scribbled hastily and in disbelief on parchment by the clerk – declared that he would not give for the king, his local representative, or their subordinates so much as "one large turd."[4] The scene and the speech could come from a *chanson de geste* featuring rebel barons. Of course one constituent branch of *chansons de geste* in general featured barons in revolt.

Issues of authority and directive scope were even more complex in the case of the church than in that of the state. In one sense, the church functioned almost as a state, as the great scholar F. W. Maitland long ago noted in lapidary fashion:

The medieval church was a state. Convenience may forbid us to call it a state very often, but we ought to do so from time to time, for we can frame no acceptable definition of a state which would not comprehend the church. What has it not that a state should have? It has laws, lawgivers, law courts, lawyers. It uses physical force to compel men to obey its laws. It keeps prisons. In the thirteenth century, though with squeamish phrases, it pronounces sentence of death.[5]

We might even amplify these elegant assertions that Maitland characteristically drew from legal categories. The scope of ecclesiastical governance was in important respects different from and much vaster

<hr/>

[4] *Actes du parlement de Paris*, 1st ser., 1254–1328 (Paris, 1920), 7916: "Ego non darem de te, de cleric tuo, de Rege tuo et comite, unum magnum stercus." The comment earned a mention in Elizabeth Crozet-Pavan, *La derision au Moyen Age* (Paris: Sorbonne, 2003), 253.
[5] F. W. Maitland, *Roman Canon Law*, 100.

than that of royal administrations. The clerics maintained the essential sacramental system and facilitated pious actions of believers in the world in order to produce the human society desired by divine will.

Despite a remarkable elaboration of administrative and legal structures, limitations in seeking sound religious practice based on true belief had to be recognized; deep or detailed belief seems sometimes only formally demanded, and perhaps compliance represented the most that could be required.[6] Moreover, elite churchmen were enmeshed in the web of warrior relations and ideas; bishops and abbots usually came from the same families that produced knights. The clerics, possessing vast tracts of land, were closely tied into the business of war and quotidian judicial judgments. They supplied military service to the crown and judged accused criminals; they paid their taxes, usually employed in warfare, and helped the crown collect such sums from the realm at large. We cannot imagine them as pacifists in theory or distant and uninvolved critics at a distance from worldly action. They, too, went on crusade, and sometimes even on home turf donned armor and took up weapons, despite all efforts by idealistic reformers to distance them from weapons as well as women; the scriptures they read and all their devotional literature were replete with military imagery, however much it may have been spiritualized in intent or interpretation. If they knew that the knights could be troublesome allies, they had to be fully aware that elite arms bearers ideally were esteemed patrons and protectors of church property and personnel.

Yet clerics were undertaking immense tasks. Royal administrations faced less daunting tasks – they by and large regulated behavior rather than a framework of belief, dealt with this world rather than the next, worked primarily through legal measures and courts (when not relying on brute force), and prescribed sanctions of loss of property or even loss of life or limb. Though the church famously handed over sinners it deemed obdurate to be taken to the dread stake and fire by "the secular arm," it moved beyond even the goals of the

---

[6] See Andre Vauchez, *The Laity in the Middle Ages*, trans. Daniel Bornstein (Notre Dame, IN: University of Notre Dame Press, 1993). The rudimentary instructions given Perceval by his mother in various works of literature are interesting in this regard. In many *chansons de geste* a Muslim hero sees Christianity triumphant on a battlefield and after baptism is instantly a Christian hero. Some miracle stories stress the need for true piety that will spur charitable acts, but the emphasis falls on external signs in most of this genre.

state by claiming spiritual governance with results stretching into eternity. Reaching across all emerging political units, the church sought to direct Christendom, declaring and requiring orthodox beliefs and pious practices that took souls to heaven or hell from every kingdom of Europe. Its broadest and most powerful sanctions had to work in a spiritual and otherworldly dimension and might be enforced not in the public space of law courts so much as in the searching and private process by which a sinner felt contrition, made confession, and performed penance. Just as it did not haul great bankers into court on usury charges, it could not force knights at all levels into church courts to answer for violation of just war principles, nor could it deny them the sacraments or burial in sacred ground for participation in proscribed tournaments. Remediation guided by clerics had to work through appeals to conscience, through treatises written, sermons preached, and confessions heard.

If their task was immense, ecclesiastics who had been stirred by ideas of reform since the Gregorian revolution, beginning in the second half of the eleventh century, proclaimed clerical leadership within Christian society. Reformers sought clerical independence from the strong, controlling grip that the warrior elite had exercised over church offices, high and low – just the sort of dominance old Duke Girart proudly proclaims as his undoubted right. The struggle for the independence of the church famously sparked the intense quarreling now termed the "investiture controversy," which has rightly become a staple for study by scholars. Yet as the fireworks from that struggle – so fraught with political conflicts – began slowly to dissipate, the ardent desire for broad reform in society continued. By the late twelfth and early thirteenth century this effort had gained renewed energy and emphasis from reformers in Laon and especially in Paris, closely studied by John Baldwin.[7] Proper use of military force was one of the important topics debated. The effort to shape knighthood in general, though less openly spectacular than the quarrel over appointment to clerical offices, played an essential role in shaping medieval society within which chivalry stood tall as one of its most essential pillars.

---

[7] John Baldwin, *Masters, Princes and Merchants* (Princeton University Press, 1970).

8

KINGS AND KNIGHTS

——————— • ———————

CHIVALRY AND THE EMERGING STATE

During the age of chivalry, kings and great lords (and urban communal governing bodies) were busily extending their reach (Figure 9). They expanded administrative structures, increased the flow of legislation, bolstered law enforcement, and increased financial exaction within societies producing new forms and deposits of wealth. The kingdom of Sicily, where Richard Lion-Heart may have seen a draft of the *Chanson d'Aspremont* (quoted in the introduction to this part) while on crusade, provides a good case in point, as more famously did Richard's own territories on the continent and his kingdom of England with its central royal court, the great administrative gyroscope of the exchequer, itinerant justices on circuit throughout the realm, and emerging methods of taxation that produced appreciable results.[1] The French kingdom under his fellow crusader and bitter rival Philip II (Augustus) provides another case in

---

[1] For Sicily, see Hiroshi Takayama, *The Administration of the Norman Kingdom of Sicily* (Lieden: Brill, 1992); Evelyn Mary Jamison, *The Norman Administration of Apulia and Capua: More Especially under Roger II and William I, 1127–1166* (Dulles, VA: David Brown Book Company, 1987). For England, see Ralph V. Turner and Richard Heiser, *The Reign of Richard Lionheart: Ruler of the Angevin Empire, 1189–1199* (New York: Routledge, 2013); John Gillingham, *Richard I* (New Haven: Yale University Press, 2002). For France, see John W. Baldwin, *The Government of Philip Augustus: Foundations of French Royal Power in the Middle Ages* (Berkeley: University of California Press, 1986). A good entry into the vast body of

Figure 9 Chivalric ideals and practices had to accommodate increasing royal power. The scepter of Charles V (1364–1380), topped with a gilded image of Charlemagne as enthroned emperor, vividly embodies royal aspirations to power and authority.

point with its territorial acquisitions and its administrative advances in justice and finance.[2] Such processes on either side of the Channel generated what Joseph Strayer termed "the medieval origins of the

scholarship on Angevin governance is provided in Robert Bartlett, *England under the Norman and Angevin Kings* (Oxford University Press, 2000).

[2] John W. Baldwin, *The Government of Philip Augustus* (Berkeley: University of California Press, 1991).

modern state."[3] And they can be found south of the Pyrenees as well, if on a slightly later chronology. Thirteenth-century Castile witnessed a move toward centralization of political power, especially under Alfonso X (r. 1252–1284). Evidence includes not only the great law book, the *Siete Partidas*, but also the beginning of the appointment of *corregidores* – royal officials appointed at the local level to oversee the meting out of justice, some control over the use of armed force, and general oversight of administration.[4] If conditions were more mixed and complex east of the Rhine and north of the Alps, regional governing powers still developed within growing towns and lay and ecclesiastical lordships.[5] It is at least interesting to note that Wolfram von Eschenbach in his *Parzifal* pictured King Arthur prohibiting his knights from undertaking any joust without his permission.[6]

---

[3] J. R. Strayer, *On the Medieval Origins of the Modern State* (Princeton, 1970).

[4] See Agustín Bermúdez Aznar, *El Corregidor en Castilla durante la Baja Edad Media (1348–1474)* (Murcia: Universidad de Murcia, 1970). Although the reign of Fernando (Ferdinand) IV and the early reign of Alfonso XI were marked by relative royal weakness, the famously powerful queen mother María de Molina actively worked to check the power of the high nobility by cultivating a political alliance with the interests of the lower nobility and the urban elites. These latter groups had, in 1315, formed an *hermandad* precisely to counter the predations of the upper nobility, and María de Molina shared the governing of the realm with the *hermandad* in order to protect the crown's judicial and administrative prerogatives. Later in his reign, Alfonso attempted to expand the crown's authority, checking urban autonomy and striving to reduce internal strife. He was only partially successful. See Teofilo F. Ruiz, *Spain's Centuries of Crisis: 1300–1474* (Malden, MA: Blackwell, 2011), 51–63. The Trastámara monarchy of the late fourteenth and then the late fifteenth centuries really began establishing itself as a more complete sovereign power. See Emilio Mitre Fernández, *La extensión del regimen de corregidores en el reinado de Enrique III de Castilla* (Valladolid: Gráf. Andrés Martín, S.A., 1969).

[5] The broad pattern in Europe and in the German empire is concisely discussed by Eva Havercamp, *Medieval Germany, 1056–1273*, 2nd ed. (Oxford University Press, 1992), 21–29. Benjamin Arnold, *German Knighthood, 1050–1300* (Oxford University Press, 1985), 2, considers a "centralised empire . . . not a practical possibility." See his *Princes and Territories in Medieval Germany* (Cambridge University Press, 1991) and his *Medieval Germany, 500–1300: A Political Interpretation* (University of Toronto Press, 1997). Cf. the essays presented by Björn Weiller and Simon MacLean, *Representations of Power in Medieval Germany, 800–1500* (Turnhout: Brepols, 2006); Len Scales, *The Shaping of German Identity: Authority and Crisis, 1245–1440* (Cambridge University Press, 2012); and Björn Weiler, *Kingship, Rebellion and Political Culture: England and Germany, c.1215–c.1250* (Basingstoke: Palgrave Macmillan, 2007).

[6] Mustard and Passage, *Parzifal*, 152. As Arthur reminds Sagremors later, he has sworn to the king to hold his "folly in check" (158).

In short, early working notions of sovereignty – especially evident in the Anglo-Norman and Capetian efforts – did not have to await formal declaration of theory by the French jurist and political philosopher Jean Bodin in the late sixteenth century. Kings on either side of the Channel were exercising genuine power and showing a revealing touchiness about setting the exact borders of their realms and clarifying and extending the exercise of their authority; within these boundaries they worked toward regulation of violence (at least the violence not of their own choosing), including private or seigneurial war and unauthorized tournament; they extracted money from subjects for what they claimed was the common defense; in England the king exercised original jurisdiction over a wide and expanding set of crimes and disputes; in France the crown proclaimed its willingness to act as the guarantor of justice through a process of appeal, receiving complaints about injustice from lesser jurisdictions.[7] On a somewhat later chronology, the process can be seen in Scandinavia.[8] Drawing on Carolingian traditions, German emperors were issuing peace legislation from the early twelfth century, and these efforts were extended by Frederick Barbarossa in the second half of that century.[9] The legislation of Frederick II for the kingdom

[7] William Chester Jordan, *Louis IX and the Challenge of Crusade* (Princeton, 1879); Joseph R. Strayer, *The Reign of Philip the Fair* (Princeton, 1980). This theme is also discussed in Richard W. Kaeuper, *War, Justice and Public Order* (Oxford, 1988).

[8] *The Chronicle of Duke Erik*, trans. Erik Carlquist and Peter C. Hogg (Lund: Norse Academic Press, 2012). For a detailed overview of Swedish, Danish, and Norwegian medieval state development, see *The Norwegian Domination and the Norse World, c.1100–c.1400* (Trondheim: Tapir Academic Press, 2010), and Sverre Bagge, *Cross and Scepter: The Rise of the Scandinavian Kingdoms from the Vikings to the Reformation* (Princeton: Princeton University Press, 2014), 50–169. A. Winroth emphasizes that the key shift in Scandinavian medieval state formation began "when rulers began to collect taxes and other fees from their own people rather than stealing someone else's wealth": *The Conversion of Scandinavia* (New Haven: Yale University Press, 2012), 167.

[9] See Hanna Vollrath, "Ideal and Reality in Twelfth-Century Germany," in *England and Germany in the High Middle Ages*, ed. Alfred Haverkamp and Hanna Vollrath (New York: Oxford University Press, 1996), 93–104. Karl Leyser's interpretation holds that Barbarossa, in utilizing regularized judicial and administrative procedures, in part derived from Carolingians' modes of governance, "did not try to institutionalize this authority," unlike his French, Angevin, and Iberian counterparts. Karl Leyser, "Frederick Barbarossa: Court and Country," in *Communication and Power in Medieval Europe: The Gregorian Revolution and Beyond*, ed. Timothy Reuter (London: Hambledon Press, 1994), 143–156.

of Sicily in 1231, with significant concerns for peace and public order, is well known.[10] Specialists in various regions of Europe could supply case studies; this chapter will draw particularly on the rich documentary deposits of the kingdoms of England and France.

The study of knighthood in relationship with governance by kings offers a slightly less harrowing challenge than analyzing chivalry and the church (to be considered in the following chapter), since the goals sought by royal administrations (aided by the mass of available evidence) are relatively more straightforward on the secular side. Medieval kingship, as it developed, claimed clear goals: leadership in defensive and aggressive war; preeminence in making and enforcing – or at least supervising by way of appeals – the body of law to regulate interactions among subjects and between subjects and the crown. At home kings came to assert a role against violence perceived as a threat to public order, whatever the complications created by their own violent measures. They always claimed the right to some of the wealth of those within the realm and meticulously collected and recorded its acquisition, largely for the purposes of war. The emphasis of royal action fell on measures encouraging a broadly safe, more or less peaceable, prosperous, and ideally just realm. Of course the results of royal administrative action could be viewed differently, although purely political and constitutional history lies beyond the present inquiry. Significant power backed royal claims: rebels were warned about consequences to their property or even their bodies and lives. For the crown, the catch, of course, was the lack of a standing army or even an effective police force; an active military force depended on sufficient loyalty among great and lesser lords or at least a sufficient yield of taxation to hire men to fight.

Working toward these ambitious goals did not wreck a sense of solidarity between kings and their knights. We have seen that kings came to consider themselves members of the knighthood and relied on their elite warriors on campaign, in battle, and for essential roles of governance both at the center and in localities, no less than on diplomatic missions beyond borders. In an unusually clear case, key elements of governance in the English countryside depended in no small measure on the unpaid service of "knights of the shire" who

[10] See James Powell, *The Liber Augustalis*, for a study and English translation of this legislation.

served on a variety of juries and commissions and attended meetings of parliament.

As so often, William Marshal represents the exemplar we seek for some chivalric virtue. His loyalty is a quality often extolled in his biography. This work, commissioned by his son, carefully hides contrary evidence, showing how much importance was attributed to the virtue of loyalty. Of course the Marshal could claim to be loyal in the original sense of faithfulness to word and obligation; but he was likewise loyal to the Plantagenet monarchy in the persons of five kings of quite different personality and character (Henry II, the Young King, Richard, John, Henry III), and of course to that unforgettable queen, Eleanor of Aquitaine. The wisdom and reward of such loyalty were proved by his spectacular rise from sturdy tournament companion to earl and finally to regent of England. Striking parallels (and some important differences) flash back and forth like summer lightning between the historical William and Lancelot do Lac imagined in romance literature. The historical and imagined men each had serious faults, but if William's lapses in loyalty – such as serving King John while prudently sending a son to the side of French invaders – are airbrushed out of his narrative, Lancelot's treasonous adultery was manifest and becomes a fulcrum on which dramatic action turns in romance.[11] Yet in each career a close, ideal bond joins king and knight through loyal, personal martial service by a great knight, whatever the complications.

Others of our set of model knights stand as witnesses to these bonds of service and loyalty, even if they, too, show relationships somewhat corroded by intense upward ambition or fractured by the sheer downward pressures of power. Don Pero Niño unfailingly fought with his characteristic vigor at the direction of Castilian royalty. The near breach came with an affair of the heart; for he married in secret a woman for whom the infante had planned a union politically advantageous for the crown. Yet his basic loyalty to the crown is unquestioned, and we can perhaps sense behind him the great story of El Cid, who for a time joined the Muslim forces in frustration with a king who treated him badly, but was fundamentally loyal.[12]

[11] Richard W. Kaeuper, "William Marshal, Lancelot, and the Issue of Chivalric Identity," *Essays in Medieval Studies* 23 (2006), ed. Anita Riedinger, 1–19.

[12] R. Menendez Pidal, ed., *Cantar de Mio Cid*, 3 vols., 4th ed. (Madrid: Espasa-Calpe, S.A., 1964).

Geoffroi de Charny provides fewer complications. He died protect-ing his king on the battlefield of Poitiers, though exactly how much royal intervention in his own rights outside of royal campaign and battle he would have accepted might be questioned.[13] Malory iden-tified with his hero Lancelot, "the best of sinful men," despite the infamous and treasonous love affair (which led finally to war) forever associated with him. Yet as he narrates the "Day of Destiny" that brings the collapse of the civilization centered on the Round Table, Malory speaks in famous words directly to his own generation, wracked by the terrors of civil war. Malory counseled complete loyalty to the monarchy, specifically on the grounds that it is the sustainer of chivalry:

Lo ye all Englysshemen, se ye nat what a myschyff here was? For he that was the moste kynge and nobelyst knight of the worlde, and moste loved the felyshyp of noble knyghtes, and by hym they all were upholdyn, and yet might nat thes Englyshemen holde them contente with hym. Lo thus was the olde custom and usayges of thys londe, and men say that we of thys londe have nat yet loste that custom. Alas! Thys ys a greate defaughte of us Englysshemen, for there may no thyngeus please no terme.

No doubt as he slowly won the crown of the Scottish kingdom, Robert Bruce, exhausted by endless fighting against both the English and dissident Scots, would have warmly seconded Malory's senti-ment. He embodies, of course, the combination of strenuous knight and powerful monarch, illustrating in his own person the compat-ibility of kingship and chivalry.[14]

Yet almost surreptitiously tensions have surfaced even in our quick survey of model knightly cooperation with royalty. Such tensions must also register in our analysis of *chanson de geste* and romance, the imaginative literature that features knightly life and values. Positive images abundantly appear: this literature often imagines kings and knights joyfully conjoined in battles against common enemies and in tournaments, hunts, and sumptuous banquets that spiced their social

[13] Contrasting his language about kingship with that of, say, Louis de la Tremoille, a great Burgundian lord of the late fifteenth and early sixteenth century, might show this point with special clarity. I intend to devote a study, already in progress, to a comparison of these two great knights and their link with crown service.

[14] G. W. S. Barrow, *Robert Bruce and the Community of the Realm of Scotland* (Edinburgh: Edinburgh University Press, 2005). Jean Flori, *Richard Coeur de Lion: Le roi-chevalier* (Paris, 1990), translated as *Richard the Lionheart: King and Knight*, by Jean Birrell (Westport, CT, 2006).

lives. Knights gathered at a chivalric court seem almost a glorified *comitatus*, a traditional war band now decorated with samite and enlivened with silky amours. Yet even in this imagined paradise serpents of discontent slither.

If we instantly recall the most infamously destructive adulterous love affair in Camelot, we must first note that *chansons de geste* portray political tensions earlier and even more openly. For much of this vast body of literature viscerally struggles with the impact of newly energized royal power. In fact, medieval French tradition, not modern scholarly analysis, sorted epics into three great cycles of poetry. In each cycle the relationship of warriors to kingship is at issue; in fact, the knightly obedience to any agency of governance, lay or ecclesiastical, can be critically examined. The cycle of the king advocates loyal support for monarchy (while recognizing the strength of opposition); the cycle of William of Orange (sometimes termed that of Garin de Monglane, his ancestor) praises William's service to his king, but recognizes a distinct failure of royal gratitude in response for this support; the cycle of the rebel barons celebrates heroic resistance of warriors to royal authority. Throughout these texts, issues of clerical directive authority also come under scrutiny and critique. The major determinant, however, remains the stance taken by the warriors toward royal authority.

The crucial concept of loyalty (as briefly noted in the case of the Marshal) is under new construction, shifting from a sense of personal reliability and faithfulness to word and obligation in general, and toward a greater emphasis on lordship and in particular the support owed the lord king. In a work such as the famous *Song of Roland* from the cycle of the king, we can read a highly positive evaluation of late eleventh-century kingship as superior even to the sacred taking of personal vengeance for injured honor.[15] These contemporary (and

---

[15] Gerard J. Brault, *Song of Roland: An Analytical Edition, vol. 1. Introduction and Commentary* (University Park: Pennsylvania State University Press, 1978; Paul R. Hyams, "Henry II and Ganelon," *Syracuse Scholar* 4 (1983), 23–35; Larissa Tracy, *Torture and Brutality in Medieval Literature: Negotiations of National Identity* (Rochester: Boydell & Brewer, 2011), 70–107, in particular 75–96; Emanuel J. Mickel, *Ganelon, Treason, and the "Chanson de Roland"* (University Park: Pennsylvania State University Press, 1989); Stephen D. White, "The Ambiguity of Treason in Anglo-Norman-French Law, c. 1150–c. 1250," in *Law and the Illicit in Medieval Europe*, eds. Ruth Mazo Karras, Joel Kaye, E. Ann Matte (Philadelphia: University of Pennsylvania Press, 2010), 89–102.

contested) values are set, of course, in the Carolingian period, centuries before the composition of the epic, and the great Charlemagne is the featured ruler, but issues of interest in the late eleventh and twelfth centuries are at stake. If heroic warrior capacity is still lauded to the skies in all epics, loyalty to the king/emperor trumps even heroic vigor in defense of honor, and treason against the king by Ganelon (whose warrior qualities are undoubted) is savagely punished in the end. Loyalty to Charlemagne was easy to praise, but in an epic from the cycle that bears his name William of Orange is shown loyally serving a king whose weakness and wrongheadedness lead to unfair distribution of land. The hero resolutely rejects calls from his subordinates that they should abandon King Louis to his fate (literally to the devil) and get on with their own lordly concerns. We can, that is, hear the voice of resistance as well as the corrective view intoned.

The rebellious end of the spectrum, in the cycle of barons in revolt, has already appeared in lines quoted from the *Chanson d'Aspremont* in which the imagined old duke lashes out against claims made by any overlord. Yet the classic text in this vein may be *Raoul de Cambrai*. This *chanson* offers voices and commentary that debate obligations of lordship and vassalage working under extreme pressure. The characters denounce an unjust king as an impediment to the real business of sorting out loyalty and lordship, and gaining estates. At the close of its first component – the text was composed in stages – lords who have been occupied with remarkably vigorous and seemingly endless feuding come suddenly to the realization that King Louis is the problem; in effect striking the heels of their hands to helmeted foreheads in a moment of sudden clarity of vision, they attack the king, and burn Paris for good measure.[16] The depth of chivalric assumption of rights to practice violence may seem surprising. As a *chievtain de guerre* a knight was entitled to fight no less than to sit in judgment over disputes of lesser mortals, and to hang thieves publicly on a cherished lordly gallows. The incentive of social markers reinforced any urges for personal direct action. What have kings to do with this? All chivalric literature tirelessly shows

---

[16] Sarah Kay, ed., trans. *Raoul de Cambrai.* Throughout the Middle Ages, Raoul provided the model for villainy as a church burner and nun slayer; yet his sheer martial vigor and unstinting actions command a subterranean admiration from the poet and presumably from the audience. See the discussion in R. W. Kaeuper, *Chivalry and Violence,* 244–252.

heroes settling issues by violence and taking vengeance to restore honor, celebrating noisily afterward.

This strong division of views on kingship surfaces anew in the remarkable series of animal fables written in northwestern Europe in the late twelfth century. They center on Reynard the Fox, simultaneously a wily animal and a great baron in the Lion King's court. These popular stories were written by numerous authors who often focus on hopes for good governance and functioning legal systems, which are usually disappointed. These stories, in fact, present a general societal unease straddling the gap between ardent desire for more royal action (especially that taken in interests of internal peace) and dark fears that such action will only feed into the problems and be turned to the interests of the powerful. These witty and satirical stories, with animal characters instantly morphing into humans and back again with ease, were avidly read or heard in their own time (and still repay attention by modern readers). Their mudslinging hits all targets: the king's law courts are necessary, but fail miserably, for justice disappears, and ambush and brawl take its place; oaths quickly made are just as quickly broken; even crusading and the great Saint Bernard are splattered in the free-for-all. Great lords (who sometimes appear in fur as wolves or bears) are no better than the Lion King, who tries to restrain their self-seeking and crude violence, but finds he needs their force for his own purposes. The world is nature red in tooth and claw, with only faint hopes of redress through governing institutions. If these texts circulated widely and obviously moved beyond a knightly audience, they complement the epic complexity of view on effective kingship.[17]

Some of these issues surface in romance literature, though the urgency seems to climb only occasionally and only to a temperature short of the boiling point. In the *Lancelot* (a component romance in the great Vulgate Cycle), the admired knight Bertelay is disinherited by a panel of powerful kings and knights for actions that offended King Leodigan: he killed a knight without seeking royal judgment. Overruling his defense that he had maintained personal loyalty to his king, the verdict states that "he took it upon himself to judge the

---

[17] These texts and themes are cited and discussed in R. W. Kaeuper, "The King and the Fox: Tales of Reynard the Fox and French Kingship in the Twelfth Century," in *Expectations of the Law in Medieval Europe*, ed. A. Musson (Boydell & Brewer, 2001).

knight he killed, and at night, but justice was not his to mete out."[18] Superior royal jurisdiction over knightly violence is vindicated here; but only a few such clear cases appear in romance. The fact of centralizing government is generally and broadly accepted in romance, even if its specific operations may be questioned. Kingship and knighthood have prerogatives mutually accepted, whatever adjustments are still debated. The details of quotidian governance must have seemed deadly dull to most poets, who did not even want to find words to rhyme with such technical terms as exchequer or writ. Recording tax receipts on parchment rolls must not have seemed a heroic enterprise to such writers or their audiences. Great courts of kings and counts functioned as the nerve centers of glorious chivalric life; feasts and festivals – and tournaments above all – brightened even overcast climes; and from these courts featured knights are imagined to sally forth on the individual knightly quests in which a maturing chivalry could be tested and its values debated and constructed. Successively featured knights could roam the forest as central characters on the stage of imagination before returning to a court where some great lord or king provided a base for chivalry; there the heroic knight could ideally be rewarded for his high performance. Tensions could flow beneath the surface, as in Chrétien's *Yvain*, where the hero acts independently of the court and even confronts it when he has won a lady and her land.[19]

How the relationship between kingship and chivalry was portrayed in literature varied over time and depended upon place; it could obviously readily reflect basic political circumstances. English kingship provides a good case in point. It likely continued a closer link with Anglo-Saxon foundations than France did with its Carolingian past; and in England sheer capacity had been added to royal power and knightly cooperation by the Norman Conquest during a crucial era of chivalric history. That no existential debate over kingship informed a massive production of epic literature in England – in contrast to the lands of *chanson de geste* just across the Channel – can be understood. Kingship in England was an incontrovertible reality.[20] The searing tensions that appeared in the French epic tradition, with

---

[18] *Lancelot-Grail Cycle*, III, *Lancelot*, trans. Rosenberg, 263.
[19] Golden, trans., *Yvain, the Knight with the Lion*, 20–23, 63–69. Yvain even waits for Arthur to come to his tent, rather than presenting himself to the king in the royal pavilion.
[20] An argument advanced in R. W. Kaeuper, *War, Justice and Public Order*, 153–156.

one entire branch of literary work opposed to kingship, does not appear. And in romance writing in general, kingship is accepted as the capstone of the chivalric arch. Kings appear as leading knights and as leaders of the knighthood.

KNIGHTHOOD AND AN ORDERED REALM

Yet the relationship between kingship and chivalry would always be complex and, despite imaginative reconciliation in most romance writing, tensions long continued. Evidence from the precocious English royal administration with its well-preserved archives is particularly telling. That long-range goals of kingship and knighthood continued to move at times on differing trajectories appears with clarity in a series of orders regarding the bearing of arms within the realm sent out by the fourteenth-century crown to local administrators; both the disruption of tournaments and the unhindered meeting of courts of law were at issue. On June 18, 1320, Edward II ordered all his sheriffs to forbid

any earl, baron, knight or other from tourneying, etc. or making assemblies in breach of the peace [and to arrest violators]. The king has ordered his justices who hold pleas before him to proceed against and punish the persons so attached [i.e., arrested] according to the sheriffs' certificate.[21]

Under the same date an order went out to the justices assigned to take assizes, juries, and certificates in all the counties of England. They were to cause proclamation to be made at each of their sessions prohibiting anyone

from presuming to come armed before them, or from inflicting damage or hindrance upon the parties, jurors, or others there or coming to the place of their sessions or returning thence under penalty of forfeiting all that they may forfeit ... as the king is given to understand that many persons come armed before his justices and so threaten the king's ministers, the parties suing, jurors, and others. . .

To prevent any armed interference with sessions of these courts, sheriffs are to arrest the malefactors.[22]

On July 12, 1330, the young Edward III issued to all his sheriffs another tournament prohibition (against "tourneying, jousting, seeking adventures, etc., or doing any feat of arms without the king's special licence"). But in this case, royal fears of misdirected knightly

---

[21] *Calendar of Close Rolls, 1218–1322*, 243.   [22] Ibid., 232.

violence are complicated by the king's need for armed men. Sheriffs
are to arrest those who act thus, in violation of another royal order
(sent out that same day), which is identified as the king's proclamation
"for knights and men to arm themselves."[23] This proclamation,
which was also sent to all sheriffs (and was entered on the parchment
record just above the tournament prohibition), ordered

> all knights and others able to bear arms [to] prepare themselves with horses and
> arms as speedily as possible, ... so that they shall be ready to come to the king
> or those whom he shall appoint with all their power summoned, to set out
> against certain contrariants and rebels who lately withdrew secretly from the
> realm, and who have assembled a multitude of armed men ... and prepared
> ships of war ... and who propose entering the realm to aggrieve the king and
> his people.[24]

On July 14, 1348, these themes regarding the licit use of knightly
force and weaponry fuse in a single directive sent to all sheriffs

> to cause proclamation to be made that no one shall tourney, joust, or seek
> adventures or do other deeds of arms upon pain of imprisonment and the
> forfeiture of his horses, arms, and all other things, but that everyone of that
> bailiwick shall provide himself with arms befitting his estate and prepare
> himself for the defence of the realm against the malice of the king's adversaries
> of France as the truce between the king and those adversaries has recently
> expired and the king wishes to provide for the defense of the realm.[25]

Violators are threatened with imprisonment and forfeiture of horse and
arms.

This series of administrative orders embodies a fundamental problem faced by medieval monarchy: the crown necessarily relied to
a significant degree on the armed force of the same men who –
though they might generally be relied on – sometimes forced sleepless
nights on royal officials worried about illegal gatherings of armed men
and their temptations to use such power for their own ends. Expected
to be armed to the teeth and ready to fight the king's enemies at home
(meaning some portion of the elite arms bearers gone astray) or
abroad, the chivalrous must likewise be sternly ordered not to employ
their beloved weaponry in unauthorized martial sport, in political
movements, or in private score-settling; ideally, swords were to be
unsheathed and banners unfurled only when and where and against
whom the king gave permission and direction. No standing army

---

[23] *Calendar of Close Rolls 1330–1333*, 147.   [24] Ibid.
[25] *Calendar of Close Rolls 1346–1349*, 549.

existed to answer a crown call; no police force awaited royal directions; local elites and their armed force had to respond when the
royal trumpet sounded. The difficulty became acute if these men
were at any juncture, in fact, the problem – that is if they were
considering rebellion, were unhappy about the likely results of
a crucial lawsuit in a royal court, or simply thought a neighbor
had to be taught a hard lesson through satisfyingly direct action in
defense of sacred honor.

Challenges to such directive supervision of peace and justice seriously offended the crown; they openly exposed its failure to carry
out basic duties, and offended a sense of unique royal capacity.
At some threshold level that varied with king, kingdom, and the
chronology of state formation, any volume of complaint about countryside or urban violence outraged the crown's sense of right and
duty. The preambles to several English statutes issued under Edward
I decry continuing and unacceptable violence; when law-and-order
commissions known as trailbastons began to be sent out from 1305,
the issuing documents fulminated against the

> numerous evildoers and disturbers of our peace who wander about the
> countryside committing murders, outrages, burnings, and other great offenses
> night and day, to the great peril both of local inhabitants and travelers.[26]

The commissions for later trailbaston justices continued to decry
horrible felonies and trespasses committed and criminal confederacies
formed "*in lesionem pacis nostre et terorem populi nostril* (to the dimin-
ishment of our peace and the fear of our people)."[27] The relevant
point is not that these commissions were aimed at arms bearers
specifically or solely, for the charge was general in scope, nor can it
be that royal administrations were agencies working for greater peace
in the world generally, for they surely spent much of their time raising
taxation and leading armies in war. What the crown increasingly
insisted on was its superior directive power, which translated into
a distinct sensitivity to disorder and disregard for royal judicial
authority at home. This sensitivity was stated most baldly in English
sources in an internal government memorandum from 1305 that
characterizes efforts "to suppress the disorders, tumults, and outrages
of the past, which were like the start of war and which flouted the

---

[26] National Archives, London, C66/125, C66/126.
[27] National Archives, London, C66/153.

lordship of the king."[28] By then English litigants already knew that the key to opening a case in a royal court was to charge that an enemy had come "*vi et armis et contra pacem domini regis* (by force and arms and against the lord king's peace)."[29]

Yet in record evidence, as in literature, if the king's courts were sought by litigants, including the socially elite, they were also sometimes feared and resented. As the royal enactments on arms bearing have shown, knightly force might become a real and present danger to the orderly operation of law courts. Any scholarly investigation through legal records and petitions to the crown will document overawed court sessions, attacks on sitting justices, and suborned jurors acting as fear or greed dictated. At Louth in Lincolnshire in 1352 Sir Robert Darcy

made various hostile assaults on [one of the justices] in hall where they were sitting for judgment and with drawn sword before all the people would have killed him, whom he took violently by the throat, if he had not been prevented by others and would likewise have killed other serjeants and ministers of the king if not prevented.[30]

Sir John Deyvill of Egmanton had greater success. Angered by an adjournment in a land case important to one of his relatives, he brought knights and squires to break up a meeting of the county court for Lincolnshire in 1301.[31] Sir Roger Swynerton and his relatives surrounded a court hall in Stafford, forcibly closed the doors, and issued threats, stopping legal action being transacted against them.[32] Other vigorous knights saw no need to let matters come into a law court at all, as was charged in a petition by John of Massingham. His petition (with perhaps unintended irony) states that "Sir Thomas Ingaldesthorp, knight, who is keeper and maintainer of the peace in Norfolk and Suffolk" broke into John's mother's house where John thought he was secure "in the peace of God and in the peace of our lord the king" and brutally assaulted him and his mother, who was calling for help, before

---

[28] National Archives, London, *King's Remembrancer Memoranda Roll* 79, Trinity Recorda, m. 41d; pr.: CCR 1302–1307, 454–455. Discussed in G. O. Sayles, *Select Cases*, vol. iv, p. lvi.

[29] R. W. Kaeuper, *War, Justice and Public Order: England and France in the Later Middle Ages* (Oxford: Clarendon Press, 1988), 158.

[30] *Calendar of Patent Rolls 1354–1358*, 166.

[31] National Archives, London, SC1/49/122.

[32] John G. Bellamy, *Crime and Public Order in England in the Later Middle Ages*, 19; G. Wrottesley, ed., *Staffordshire Historical Collections*, vol. 10, 54.

imprisoning John until he provided the knight with a sealed bond for twenty pounds; the issue was property held by John but sought by Sir Thomas.[33] Jurors could be bought, of course, or might less subtly be warned not to think of indicting a knight and his men.[34] One juror who could not act against conscience claimed he was imprisoned in chains for indicting one of his betters.[35] The knight Henry of Lincoln, who had actually been indicted in a criminal case, caught one bold juror outside the safety of the city of Lincoln; after he had stolen the juror's horse and harshly beaten the man, Sir Henry announced that he would let him live in order to tell the others: were he to catch them in open countryside they would die, or (he added, on reflection) each would at least lose a limb.[36] The most concise statement may come from a commons petition stating that "many rich/powerful men (Riche gentz) are like kings in their home territories."[37]

If we cannot determine the truth of charges more than seven centuries old, we can at least note endorsements of local violent self-help in such romances as "The Tale of Gamelyn" in which a wronged hero, the son of a knight, overawes a court and assertively declares himself the agent of justice for that day; he acts the part vigorously, proceeding to hang all the corrupt personnel of the court gathered to condemn him. Echoing the distant hope of the Reynard stories, the romance pictures the king as warmly endorsing these actions against his own unworthy judicial agents and gratefully relying on the stout hero for high administrative duties in the future.[38] On this basis no knight could object to royal judicial action.

Using force or violence to achieve goals had in theory (and sometimes in practice) long violated the king's peace in England. It could bring retributive royal legal action. Though it is often said that Henry I prohibited "private war" in his realm, that term has fallen from

---

[33] National Archives SC8/158/7851,7852. *Calendar of Patent Rolls 1313–1317*, 43.

[34] For an example of jurors being bought, see National Archives, London, SC 8/143/7135: *"par lour grant dounes procurent un faux enqueste,"* the victim claims. For a case of jurors warned off indicting a knight and his followers, see SC8/39/1921.

[35] National Archives, London, C81/231/9595.

[36] National Archives, London, SC8/130/6498.

[37] National Archives, London, SC8/80/3956.

[38] Stephen Knight, trans., "The Tale of Gamelyn," in *Medieval Outlaws: Twelve Tales in Modern English Translation*, ed. Thomas H. Ohlgren (West Lafayette: Parlor Press, 2005), 264–289; Richard W. Kaeuper, "An Historian's Reading of the Tale of Gamelyn," *Medium Aevum* 52 (1983), 51–62.

scholarly favor. Justifiable medieval war did not neatly exist in two categories of public and private, but ran the gamut from quarrels between individuals or families to campaigns between sovereigns. Whatever we call the royal effort, it could not eliminate local and regional quarreling and combat, for fairly regular civil war and rebellion provided opportunities to achieve objectives through martial vigor by taking one side or the other, or by switching sides as circumstances demanded.

The complexities that could link king and knight, licit and illicit violence, and standard legal proceedings appear in extreme form in the case of Lord John Fitzwalter, who, with his followers, from 1342 "began spreading terror and destruction throughout the county of Essex."[39] If such actions were blatantly illegal, by indenture with the Black Prince he served in the siege of Calais, and as so many others, received a pardon for any offenses as a part of his reward for good military service; licit violence excused illicit violence. But he then continued his vigorous and criminal militancy at home, while also appealing to royal law when it suited his interests in protecting his own property.[40] Fitzwalter was finally arrested and tried on collected charges that fill five long parchment membranes, front and back, in the record of King's Bench from 1352. More than once his actions are said to have "drawn royal power to himself by nullifying the laws of the present lord king (*attraendo sibi regale potestatem in adnullacionem legis domini Regis nunc regalis*)."[41] He had besieged the town of Colchester, setting ambushes that brought trade to a standstill (until the townsmen bought off the siege). He had thwarted royal justices, would not pay taxes, and for long could never be arrested, for he threatened to break the arms and legs of any who dared try and to leave the crippled man to die. Upon conviction in Westminster in

---

[39] E. C. Furber, *Essex Sessions of the Peace, 1351, 1377–1379* (Colchester, 1953) 61. The following discussion is based on Furber's work and acknowledges "Compromises with Late Thirteenth and Early Fourteenth Century Public Order," the unpublished senior project written by Samuel Boyer at the University of Rochester in 2007. The relevant Kings Bench records are National Archives, London, KB27/366, with six additional membranes inserted between mm 30 and 31 devoted to the Fitzwalter case.

[40] As argued in an unpublished paper by Samuel Boyer, "Compromises in Late Thirteenth- and Fourteenth-Century Law and Public Order" (University of Rochester, senior project) drawing on the printed Calendars.

[41] Quoted by Furber in *Essex Sessions of the Peace* from the National Archives, London, KB 27/66.

1352 he received a comprehensive pardon for an almost numbing list of crimes (including offenses against royal judicial and administrative personnel); the price for pardon was a fine large enough that its payment occupied his attention for the final decade of his life. Many of Fitzwalter's followers likewise obtained pardons based on past or promised war service. As usual, licit violence wiped the record clean of illicit violence, illustrating once again the paradox of royal power reliant on elite arms bearers.

The Fitzwalter case is obviously extreme, but it is not unique. The Statute of Northampton of 1328 had included prohibitions of riding armed and intimidating justices.[42] Legislation seldom is enacted to combat nonexistent problems. An attack on a royal court sitting in Liverpool in February 1345, for example, was made (perhaps by as many as 180 men) with banners displayed "as if in war" and resulted in the deaths of 27 men; once again the malefactors were pardoned on condition of military service with the king's army in France.[43] Contemporary troubles the crown experienced with the Molyns family or with Thomas de Lisle could quickly add to the evidence.[44] The problems could not easily be averted for the remainder of the Middle Ages.

If English evidence has proved especially rich and plentiful, across all of Europe tensions between crown and knights and men-at-arms could blossom over the same basic issues; for the lay elite practiced what amounted to warfare within the political unit of any realm, principality, or city; they enthusiastically engaged in raid, feud, and pitched battle; and (as in England) they proved willing to use force to overawe law courts when their interests were closely involved. As already noted briefly,[45] the legislation of Frederick II for southern Italy and Sicily outlawed violence that would have been licit in much

---

[42] *Statute of the Realms*, vol. I, 257–258.

[43] *Calendar of Patent Rolls 1343–1345*, 495; *Victoria County History of Lancashire*, vol. 2, 204; Tupling, *South Lancashire*, lix; *Calendar of Close Rolls, 1346–1348*, 48–50. This case is discussed in the MA thesis of Stephen Ehrstein, "Gentry Behavior in Fourteenth-Century Lancashire" (University of Rochester, 1996).

[44] Natalie Fryde, "A Medieval Robber Baron: Sir John Molyns of Stoke Poges, Buckinghamshire," in *Medieval Legal Records* (London, 1978); John Aberth, "Crime and Justice under Edward III: The Case of Thomas de Lisle," *English Historical Review* 107 (1992), 283–301.

[45] In Chapter 4 on the second chivalric phase.

of continental Europe. It uncompromisingly ordered the death penalty for inciting war within the kingdom:

A count, baron, knight, or anyone else who publicly incites war in the kingdom should be punished by death after all his goods have been confiscated. Moreover, he who makes attacks or counterattacks should be condemned by the proscription of half of all his goods.[46]

Declaring the intent to prevent as well as punish wrongdoing, the emperor declares,

[W]e order that none of the *fideles* of our kingdom should dare to carry sharpened and prohibited weapons: small knives with points, swords, lances, breast-plates, shields or coats of mail, iron maces, or any others which have been made more to cause injury than for some beneficial purpose.[47]

The stern language sags, however, as knights and their sons and townsmen are formally exempted; but this leniency applies only when they are traveling outside of their locality and wish to carry swords. If they are received as guests, they are to put away weaponry, as they are also required to do upon return home.[48] And for the future, carrying prohibited arms brings specified fines for count, baron, or simple knight.[49] And any mortal wound inflicted with prohibited weapons is to cost the one who acts the hand with which he acted.[50] Specific imperial protection covered certain individuals, and their murderers would be killed – ordinary men by hanging, knights or their superiors by the more honorable beheading sword stroke.[51] Precise rules and penalties were provided for blows upon a knight of greater status, by one knight against his fellow of equal status, or by a lesser or a rustic against any knight.[52] Precisely how all these rules about knights and violence worked out in practice may remain a bit murky; but the desire to control action and the assumption of having the right to declare such control remain significant. This royal impulse appears clearly in an edict against "Whoever receives new knighthood or seizes it at any time against the happiness, peace, and integrity of our kingdom." Unless he is descended "from the stock of a military family," such a disruptive upstart will "lose completely the name and profession of knight."[53]

---

[46] James M. Powell, *The Liber Augustalis*, 15. [47] Ibid.

[48] Ibid. Curials and their servants staying at court with the emperor or traveling on his business were granted permission to carry all of these weapons. Castellans could send armed men to the service of the court (18).

[49] Ibid., 14–16. [50] Ibid., 17. [51] Ibid. [52] Ibid., 129–130. [53] Ibid., 141.

Kings of France found it harder to attempt so global a set of measures as their English rivals and imperial Sicilian contemporaries enacted. They were working within a much larger realm composed of more compact and independent lordships; but efforts aimed at restraint appear from the late twelfth century and come to a new level from the second half of the thirteenth century. Louis VII (joining to his effort several great lords, lay and ecclesiastical) declared a 10-year truce among quarreling parties in France beginning in 1155, a measure that seems to be both admired and satirized by some of the imaginative and widely enjoyed tales of Reynard the Fox.[54] A more sustained effort came under Louis IX, who around the mid-thirteenth century prohibited private warfare (along with reliance on the judicial duel). William Chester Jordan considers the action against judicial combat more effective, and notes the uncertainty of the general applicability of the decree against private war. That such restrictions on lordly privileges were distasteful to aristocratic sensibilities appears in the poetry of Rutebeuf.[55] Similarly, this king's unsparing action against Enguerrand IV de Coucy, heavily fined for summarily hanging several lads caught poaching on his land, generated aristocratic displeasure, not in the least mollified by the king's assertion that he would enforce justice even against nobles.[56]

Louis's imperious grandson Philip IV issued a series of ordinances that sometimes prohibited all nonroyal warfare during a time when he was conducting royal warfare and sometimes even prohibited all nonroyal warfare altogether. One of these ordinances justified itself as a measure "for the common benefit and necessity of the realm," another "for the prosperous state of our realm."[57] Another ordinance even evoked the need to avert danger to the commonwealth (*res*

---

[54] Themes are analyzed and several editions of the texts are presented in Richard W. Kaeuper, "The King and the Fox: Reaction to the Role of Kingship in Tales of Reynard the Fox," in *Expectations of the Law*, ed., Anthony Musson (Boydell Press, 2001), 9–21.

[55] William Chester Jordan, *Louis IX and the Challenge of Crusade* (Princeton: Princeton University Press, 1979), 204.

[56] Discussed, with sources provided, in Jordan, *Louis IX and the Challenge of Crusade*, 208–209.

[57] *Les Olim ou Registres des arrêts rendu par la cour du roi*, ed. Arthur Beugnot, 3 vols. (Paris, 1839–1848), 2:409; *Ordonnances des rois de France*, 22 vols. (Paris, 1723–1849) 1:390. These ordinances are cited and discussed in Justine Firnhaber-Baker, "From God's Peace to the King's Order: Late Medieval Limitations on Non-Royal Warfare," *Essays in Medieval Studies* 23 (2006), 19–30.

publica).[58] Moreover, the royal acts claim the prohibition of nonroyal warfare as a right and duty divinely ordained, for the king has been deputized by God (*divinis deputati*). Such actions, the ordinance of 1304 asserts, "befit the royal dignity," which justly carries out vengeance that should be forbidden to subjects; it is a "corruption" for them to carry out what is a king's function.[59] The language recalls the sentence in the imagined trial of the knight Bertelay in romance nearly a century earlier.[60]

By the early fourteenth century the French crown had issued royal safeguards to particular individuals or religious houses, imposed truces on quarreling parties, and bequeathed *panonceaux* (insignias bearing the royal coat of arms) to favored individuals who might affix them to their homes, gallows (signs of possessing high jurisdiction), or ships in witness of royal protection.[61] The step was not always effective and seems to have generated heated resentment, for these *panonceaux* were sometimes ripped down, hacked with axes, and shot with crossbow bolts, provoking crown efforts to prosecute violators of the royal insignia. Nearly 400 such cases are recorded in French royal records between 1328 and 1350. In a 1341 assault, Etienne d'Anglure attacked Jean de Vlandwes in his house (he claimed), inflicted a head wound with a lance, and nearly choked the man with his own hood; gasping for breath, Jean pointed to the royal *panonceau* affixed atop his house in witness of the king's protection; but the imperious Etienne responded "that he shat upon that."[62]

Whatever the fate of French royal power during the first half of the fourteenth century, these prohibitions continued and, as Justine

---

[58] *Ordonnances*, 1:492–493, cited in Firnhaber-Baker, art. cit.

[59] *Ordonnances*, 1:390, 492–493, cited in Firnhaber-Baker, art. cit.

[60] Rupert T. Pickens, trans., *The Story of Merlin, Lancelot-Grail Cycle*, vol. 2, ed. Norris J. Lacy (Cambridge: D.S. Brewer, 2010), 336–337. R. W. Kaeuper, *War, Justice and Public Order*, 241–242. Struggles over higher jurisdiction form a major theme in Firnhaber-Baker's examination of the war between Sicard de Lescure and the city of Albi, which raged throughout the 1360s: "Guerram publice et palam faciendo: Local War and Royal Authority in Late Medieval Southern France" (PhD dissertation, Harvard University, 2007), 28–97, esp. 60–62.

[61] The discussion that follows draws on F. L. Cheyette, "The Royal Safeguard in Medieval France," in *Studia Gratiana XV Post Scripta* (1972), 631–652; R. W. Kaeuper, *War, Justice and Public Order*, especially for roughly the first half of the fourteenth century; Justine Firnhaber-Baker, *Violence and the State in Languedoc, 1250–1400* (Cambridge University Press, 2014), especially for the southern part of the kingdom.

[62] *Actes du parlement de Paris*, 2nd ser. 3676.

Firnhaber-Baker argues, took on increasing theoretical confidence, speaking in the reign of John the Good in more abstract terms of the damage done to the king's lordship and sovereignty by such nonroyal warfare. If, by this time the Anglo-French struggle had brought many *routiers* into the countryside, there is good reason to think they were joined by nobles pursuing their own agendas through the opportunities that warlike violence offered.[63]

The very competence of royal jurisdiction could be denied by the most ardently independent among the elite arms bearers. The French crown did not have the impressive original jurisdiction exercised by their English cousins whose courts in theory judged all major crimes (felonies and trespasses) and became the desired locus for settling property disputes. In fact, the fragmented nature of judicial rights in France, divided among hundreds of elite possessors, became an additional source of conflict often vigorously pursued by armed men.[64]

Claiming rights to violence was claiming noble status. As kings and their advisors demonstrated increasing willingness to hear cases on appeal and acted in the interest of royally supervised general peace within the realm, conflicts could only be expected, especially during the most vigorous periods of royal effort beginning with Louis IX and continuing under Philip IV and the early Valois monarchs Philip VI and John II. Such royal efforts could readily seem intrusive to those possessed of traditional rights of jurisdiction. Such *seigneurs* also claimed a right to take violent steps to defend their rights; they often intimidated or physically dissuaded those within their jurisdiction who appealed a legal case to the crown in Paris. When directly accused and convicted of blocking appeals, their response could generate unforgettable scenes. In 1327 the lord of St-Sanflieu, who had refused to pay amends he owed the crown for offenses committed, was outraged to find royal officials collecting the sums from his lands. He angrily appeared in the court of the royal *bailli* of Senlis, first to accuse royal agents of robbery, then to claim that he had already paid all, and finally to announce loudly to all present that he

---

[63] Justine Firnhaber-Baker, "Local War and Royal Authority," 24–25.

[64] For what follows, see the discussion in R. W. Kaeuper, *War, Justice and Public Order*, 163–174; Justine Firnhaber-Baker, "Seigneurial War and Royal Power in Later Medieval Southern France," *Past & Present* 208 (2010), 37–76; and Firnhaber-Baker, *Violence and the State in Languedoc, 1350–1400* (Cambridge University Press, 2014), passim.

would not give for any of the royal officials or for the king so much as "one large turd."[65]

The stakes could be even higher, as royal action against Jourdain de l'Isle Jourdain, lord of Casaubon, demonstrated in 1323. Capping a career of violence and disregard of legal charges, he hanged two men who were under royal safeguard and were appealing their case to the king. Summoned to Paris, he appeared, but "with a great company and in haughty pride." His confidence was misplaced; condemned to death for brigandage, murder, arson, and killing of women and children – and denied the justification of having committed these acts in licit war – he was dragged to the gallows and hanged. At the end he confessed that he deserved to die, yet apparently in puzzlement kept insisting "that it was in war."[66] Such statements and actions, of course, show the rougher edge of the terse but challenging motto we have already noted a fourteenth-century Breton lord, Olivier de Clisson, placed on his official seal: "Because it pleases me."[67]

CONCLUSION

The defining age of classic chivalry coincided with the early formative age of the state in Western Europe. The result could only be a shifting and complicated relationship between kingship and knighthood, bringing both cooperation and conflict. Perhaps to many modern observers the responsibility of the state for securing and maintaining internal peace and for carrying out external war is simply taken for granted, thus losing sight of the centuries-long process that transformed these once novel principles into common assumptions. Governing power did not – indeed could not, and did not want to – contest the key chivalric goal of prowess winning honor. Kings not only led knights; they became knights without ever forgetting that they were exercising genuine powers that could seem as divinely given as prowess securing honor seemed to elite warriors who likewise claimed to know the divine plan. For their part, knights and

---

[65] *Actes du parlement de Paris*, 7916.

[66] Monique Langlois and Yvonne Lanhers, *Confessions et jugements de criminels au parlement de Paris (1319–1350)* (Paris: S.E.V.P.E.N., 1971), 37–39.

[67] John Bell Henneman, *Olivier de Clisson and Political Society in France under Charles V and Charles VI* (Philadelphia: University of Pennsylvania Press, 1996), 209.

men-at-arms loyally served kings without losing pride in their status as mini-kings and much-needed elite fighters.

Chansons de geste conducted a vigorous debate over the very role of kingship as it dealt with knighthood, special attention being devoted to just rewards of great fighters who should receive broad estates and good marriages. That these rewards were not always forthcoming helped to create one entire branch of epic writing that celebrated barons in revolt. Characteristically, England, with its early and strong tradition of functioning governance, did not generate such a body of literature.

Throughout Europe, tension and debate over newly effective governance did not completely disappear in romance writing, but the tendency was strongly to minimize the differences in goals of kings and knights and to imagine them in a world centered on idealized warrior bands, the rest of the world fading into the background. The countryside of romance seems thinly populated (or at least to harbor tillers of the soil who seldom need mention), and even towns function as settings and resources more than active centers with agendas of their own. Above all, there is almost no evidence of emerging structures of governance. Plentiful loot and largesse supplied the warriors joyfully following their warrior king on campaign. No scruffy administrative ranks bearing rolls of closely written parchment records intervene; no tax collection was necessary; injustice was rectified by the quest of a stout knight who volunteers to help when the wronged elite maiden or wounded knight suddenly appeared in court seeking help. Instructively, romance turns a blind eye on the law, justice, and finance shaping its world, to dream of an Arthurian world with the king and his stalwart men seated at a plentiful table waiting for the next wonder that will evoke chivalric prowess and honor.

We can usefully recall (from earlier chapters on phases of chivalric chronology) that as the interactive process analyzed in this chapter began there was only the material from which both the early state and chivalry could fully be constructed. As our chronological span closes, chivalry has undoubtedly emerged to dominate the social, cultural, and military world for generations; but the early state is well on its way to broad and decisive triumph. Chivalric honor has lost none of its social luster and still shines with special radiance when reflected on armor; but kings and other governors control dispensation of its glories and prizes, controlling them like a laicized treasury of merit.

Prowess likewise still elicits ringing cheers and awed murmurs; but its best employment is increasingly seen in the service of the king and kingdom. The elite claim to generous personal or familial autonomy, so long unarguably established as personal right – "Because it pleases me" – is coming to be replaced by hopeful phrases about the res publica, the commonwealth, and the common good, which elite warriors are to serve. The process cannot be hurried in analysis, for visceral impulses no less than a sense of rights possessed urged direct action to secure dominance; violence as a right possessed could only with difficulty be relegated to royal agents, possibly figures of unimpressive social origins with ink-stained hands.

With some care, we must also note that this absorption of chivalry into the mechanisms of the state did not inaugurate a reign of peace. Each governing agency always had its own program to hand, seemingly always requiring violence for its achievement. The issue was never chivalric violence versus the nonviolence of authoritative governors. If tensions persisted, it was because behind all these transformative actions the issue of licit violence loomed. Who was to carry out licit violence? Who was to decide what violence was actually licit? Such questions in medieval society could be answered only within a religious framework. Exploring this framework for chivalry is the goal of the chapter to follow.

9

CHIVALRY IN DIALOGUE WITH RELIGIOUS IDEALS

Two extreme views stand out in sharp contrast when knighthood and piety are placed within the same analytical frame. The cynical view merely dismisses the importance of piety to the arms bearers, whose entire thought went in other directions; the flagrantly romantic view asserts that the link between knighthood and religion not only was close, but took the ideal form desired by clerics. These distortions represent twin nightmares of any scholar hoping for close analysis and genuine understanding of a complicated and fascinating relationship that was undoubtedly essential to medieval civilization.

Those expressing the first, cynical view (with a shrug of the shoulders and upraised hands) assert that of course a gaping chasm separated religious ideals from actual knightly conceptions and behavior. The gap can surely come as no surprise, for these were hard men of war operating in a tough environment, and they were worldly men thinking of dominance, wealth, and courtly pleasures, not of spiritual values, not even of divine retribution for sin. Enthusiastic violence and a relaxed view of sexuality could scarcely be eliminated from their lives. Abstract religious ideals in general, this view might conclude, seldom change behavior in any historical period, at least not when their enactment would prove inconvenient to those socially dominant. Never in the least troubled by abstract thought, the medieval arms bearers simply and impatiently brushed aside homilies and warnings from carping clerics and tiresome intellectual reformers and got on with it. Religious or reforming ideals could only have touched them in the most superficial manner, and religion could only

Figure 10 Practitioners of chivalry wanted and needed religious valorization. Their undoubted piety became independent only when status or military profession was challenged. Clerics, whatever their moral qualms, accepted elite armed force. This image shows a mounted warrior boldly carved on a capital in an eleventh-century Tuscan church.

mean unwelcome constraints on behavior as usual (Figures 10 and 11).

To the contrary, this chapter will argue that the knights needed and knew they needed religious ideals. In significant ways, the knights were fully cooperative with clerics and were traditionally religious, often enacting the pious and obedient role ascribed to them as sons of Holy Mother Church in the pages of medieval (and much modern) writing. From childhood knights would have learned the omnipresence of sin and its dire consequences and regularly experienced the directive and mediatory role of the clergy, with some representative

Figure 11   Recognizing moral dangers, this image (from mid-thirteenth-century
Sainte Chapelle, Paris) pictures Holofernes' army (invaders of ancient Jewish lands) as
contemporary knights.

likely residing in the family household. Learning and practicing the
hard profession of arms would quickly convince them that knightly
lives were especially fraught with moral as well as physical perils,
some of which must have seemed virtually unavoidable. They knew
that the scales of judgment had finally to be balanced.

We can, for example, see our model knights enact pious roles and
may almost hear them talking in the pages of their own books
(Charny, Malory, and, indirectly, the Marshal) or through their
biographers (the Bruce and Pero Niño). William Marshal gratefully
accepted clerically announced remission of his sins as recompense for
his defense of the boy king Henry III and his troubled realm of
England; he died beneath a Templar robe likely obtained many
years earlier and with unqualified praise from leading clerics present
at the bedside echoing in his ears.[1] Geoffroi de Charny's piety, of

---

[1] Discussed by all of Marshal's modern biographers: Painter, *William Marshal*,
   275–289; Crouch, *William Marshal*, 185–195; Duby, *William Marshal*, 1–11.

a distinctly martial tenor, nearly spills out of lines of his *Livre de chevalerie*; divine gifts endow warriors, who must accept them with gratitude and exercise them with utmost effort as a pious act.[2] Robert Bruce, in company with the others, finds divine will behind his arduous triumph; his army, Barbour specifies, heard Mass before the decisive battle at Bannockburn.[3] Pero Niño's biographer assures readers that his hero was thoroughly taught the Catholic faith while young and accepted the imperative for its armed defense; he records a crucial moment when Pero Niño argues his sailors out of disabling superstitious fear.[4] Worldly failures on the part of the clergy seem not to have troubled him: chasing some pirates in the Mediterranean, he even accepts that he cannot attack, for he learns that they are the Lord Pope's pirates.[5] William Marshal is reported to have been a crusader, and Charny certainly was. Robert Bruce's heart was literally in the crusade: having been removed from his body, the heart was taken to Spain and hurled at the non-Christian foe in a bold charge.[6] Pero Niño fought Muslims in his early Mediterranean campaigns and later battled the Muslim kingdom of Granada on behalf of a Christian kingdom of Castile.[7]

Most of our model knights combined piety and military vigor with donations to religious foundations. The Marshal left gifts to religious houses in England and Ireland and became a Knight Templar on his deathbed.[8] Charny founded a church at Lirey and is a likely candidate for ownership of what we now call the Shroud of Turin; he certainly carried into his last battle the Oriflamme, the sacred banner of French kingship kept reverently in the abbey of

---

[2] Kaeuper and Kennedy, *Book of Chivalry*, passim.

[3] Barbour, *The Bruce*, passim. For the Mass before battle, see *Barbour's Bruce*, bk. 11, lines 381–390: "On Sonday than in the mornyng / Weile sone after the sone rising / Thai hard thar mes commounaly / And mony thaim schraiff full devotly / That thocht to dey in that melle / Or than to mak thar contre fre. / To God for thar richt prayit thai, / Thar dynit nane of thaim that day / Bot for the vigil off Sanct Jhane / Thai fastyt water and breid ilkan."

[4] Evans, *Unconquered Knight*, 155: the hero convinces his sailors to abandon superstitious fears.

[5] Ibid., 59–64: Pero Niño ceases pursuit of corsairs near Marseilles when he learns they are under the protection of the pope.

[6] *Barbour's Bruce*, bk. 20, lines 309–365.

[7] Evans, *Unconquered Knight*, 192–202; Carriazo, *El victorial*, 290–299.

[8] Crouch, *William Marshal*, 130.

Saint Denis.[9] Robert Bruce included gifts to ecclesiastical establishments in his testament.[10] Malory's book is enriched by almost
reflexive piety, even if it would be hard to claim that his life was
always guided by it.

Of course tension with some religious principles was unavoidable
in the hard knightly profession, exercised in a deeply pious environment. Though they gradually took their proper place at the pinnacle
of lay society and saw themselves as unfailingly orthodox, the knights'
path was pitted with spiritual sinkholes: courtly life was far from
ascetic, far even from monogamous; their beloved sport of tournament was long condemned not only as wasteful of men and mounts,
or as morally dangerous combat, but as a site for sexual license. War in
all its forms and dimensions was undoubtedly perilous both to body
and soul and could be massively disruptive to an ordered Christian
society rather than providing its protection. The daunting contingent
of pride, greed, envy, lust, and wrath assuredly fought for the Devil
and stalked all paths taken by *gens d'armes*. Could they be sure a major
gift or a late monastic retirement would settle the mounting bill for
all sins? Did going on crusade wipe the slate clean, even if sinning
stubbornly continued while upon crusade as upon return home?
Steady as a drumbeat came warnings about spiritual consequences
from unexpected death that could prevent a final, cleansing
confession.[11]

They inhabited a world shaped and utterly suffused by judgmental
religion as the ultimate valorizing force. The afterlife looming just
beyond inevitable death was constantly portrayed for them in sermons, in books of moral tales, and in graphically sculpted tympana
beneath which they regularly walked on entering a church; and inside
the church vivid wall paintings continued to deliver the message
about sin, retribution, and salvation. Fitting their lives and work
into a religious frame was a necessity, not some frilly option.
Regularly aided by clerical critics and allies, men-at-arms could and
did think creatively and critically about their profession in religious

[9] R. W. Kaeuper, *Holy Warriors*, 42–51.
[10] *Barbour's Bruce*, bk. 20, lines 164–169: "His testament than has he maid / Befor
bath lordis and prelatis, / And to religioun of ser statis / For hele of his saule gaf
he / Silver in gret quantite. / He ordanyt for his saule weill."
[11] General discussion of these themes appears in R. W. Kaeuper, *Holy Warriors*; the
evidence of exempla can be of particular usefulness for illustrating the warnings
given to arms bearers.

terms. Not only were iron helms never impervious to ideals in circulation, but the brains beneath these helms animated men who actually thought about basic issues. As the thirteenth-century Florentine Brunetto Latini observed, a good warrior had an active brain: "to tell the truth, armor is of little value outside when there is no sense inside."[12]

William Marshal provides a classic example; he is pictured on his deathbed by his biographer reflecting over an early lifetime on the tournament field and over the competing demands of lordly generosity and pious charity. Coming finally to resolution, he declares that gains from tournament do not imperil his soul and that robes may be distributed to members of his household as usual, with garments left over going to charity. In the process he complains that "the clerks shave us too closely," but with pious assurance puts his soul into the hands of God, confident that his life energy has gone into worthy efforts.[13] The warriors could pose hard questions and debate ideas about chivalry and morality. Such debates constantly appear in the treatises they wrote and in the literature they read, patronized, and sometimes composed. Dialogue was internal to knighthood no less than a multilayered discussion linking them to the religious world in which they lived.

We will see that the vast body of writing for, about, and by knights – chronicles, vernacular manuals, epics and romances, treatises, and biographies – registers both their sense of moral peril in their knightly life and work and a valorization and glorification of the high calling to which God has summoned them. Understandably for an elite and essential group in society, acknowledgment of the moral gap that could open between knighthood and religious principles may often be suppressed; on sunny days when all was going their way, men-at-arms must have felt their status and profession dampened the distant fires of hell. But worry existed and left its traces. Even the esteemed Templar knights evidently worried enough about combining the profession of warrior with that of monk to elicit a famous treatise from Saint Bernard. Don Pero Niño's fellow warrior and admiring biographer Gutierre Díaz de Gamez wrote with feeling about the moral uncertainty even his ever-resolute hero felt over

---

[12] Brunetto Latini, *The Book of the Treasure (Li Livres dou Tresor)*, trans. Paul Barrette and Spurgeon Baldwin (New York and London: Garland, 1993), 235.

[13] *History of William Marshal*, lines 18480–18481.

devastating the homes of fellow Christians during a raid on the island of Jersey in the early fifteenth century.[14] In chivalric literature the need for assurance is never far from the surface. Lancelot's great friend and ardent admirer Galehaut in the early thirteenth-century romance *Lancelot* prudently seeks advance notice of his own death "since I have committed many wrongs in my life, destroying cities, killing people, dispossessing and banishing people."[15] Gawain in the later Middle English *Awntyrs off Arthur* pointedly asks:

"What will happen to us . . . who strive to fight, / and so trample down folk in many kings' lands, / And ride over realms without any right / To win worship in war through prowess of hands?"[16]

More commonly, chivalric literature gives us the voice of reassurance, or at least ideas of reform to reinforce such assurance that knights needed. Both worry and reassurance speak to the importance of piety. Valorization for the importance of religion within chivalry appears throughout the body of chivalric literature produced throughout Europe over several centuries.

Recognizing the importance of religion in the lives of knights does not justify the other extreme view on chivalry and piety. This approach takes as a given that knights were indeed religious; but it extends and simplifies such characterization to make elite arms bearers in essence uncomplicated and unquestionably obedient sons of Holy Mother Church. They become imagined standard medieval Christians who were all pressed from a single mold operated by clerics. They could not create or possess any religious thoughts of their own. These warriors humbly accept all critiques and dutifully follow only ideas helpfully provided by those wearing tonsures. Such ecclesiastical guides seem, at heart, pacifists, except when preaching crusade or other violence considered necessary for causes blessed by ecclesiastical doctrine, authority, or interest. The clerical guides in this view seem also to display unanimity of thought on all matters

---

[14] Evans, *Unconquered Knight*, 174–175; Carriazo, *El victorial*, 270–272. The incident has the ring of truth, for no such scruples had troubled Pero Niño earlier and the direct appeal to compassion and a common religion on the part of the locals, noted at length, seems to have sown doubts. Rather than creating a plaster-cast bust of commendable piety, the biographer records tension and unease breaking through the heroic mold.

[15] *Lancelot-Grail*, 2, 234; for the original French, see Micha, ed., *Lancelot*, vol. 1, 61.

[16] Translating the Middle English lines in Thomas Hahn, ed., *Sir Gawain: Eleven Romances and Tales, Awntyrs off Arthur*, lines 261–264.

relating to chivalry. To inquire closely about knightly piety becomes unnecessary, for it was simply the common medieval piety, the concepts and practices of all Christians in the Middle Ages. With lives piously regulated at home, the knights all seem to ride off to their characteristic warfare of crusade humming "Onward, Christian Soldiers," while thumbing well-worn pages of the uniform and restraining codebook for chivalry prepared for them, with the original Latin in which it was composed translated into their respective vernaculars.

This interpretation forms a part of the general view through rose-tinted lenses of romanticism that has already fallen (or rather has been repeatedly pushed) off the table in this book. Yet romantic views persist, seemingly possessing more lives than a cat, and so must be done to death one more time. How the warriors could throughout the age of chivalry (often with the cooperation and blessing of clerics in their region) enthusiastically kill fellow-Christian enemies, loot and burn churches, or devastate the nonknightly or subknightly populations is insufficiently confronted by romantics. That the very category "cleric" covered a wide range of opinion, some of it extremely close to the practice and thought of knights whom they served, is likewise ignored.

In more realistic lines of sight, the many issues that crowd the canvas show hues of storm clouds, not merely sunny pastels. Clerics, far from forming a solid phalanx of thought, worked throughout the spectrum of ideas on chivalry (as they had done on the vexed issue of lay investiture). That clerical mandates and advice were not automatically followed appears as soon as we recall some well-known evidence of knightly independence and resistance. The continuing popularity of tournament, denounced by clerics, and dubbing to knighthood, which never came under clerical control, show that elite warriors could disregard or resist specific clerical claims to a directive role in society. Knights would have their beloved extreme sport with all its morally questionable trimmings, despite strong disapproval from clerical pen and pulpit; and they retained control over the making of new knights.

Like the cynical extreme, the romantic view blocks progress toward understanding of the complex and crucial dialogue between chivalry and religion. Romantics and cynics share one set of distortive views: both assume that knights could fashion no structure of religious ideals in their own interest; both conceive of religious conceptions primarily as restraints on any independent chivalric thought or action, though the romantics imagine such restraint worked whereas the cynics scoff. The more the knights were independent, in both views, the less they could have been religious.

Were either of the extreme views valid, this chapter would be utterly unnecessary, religion being either effectively absent or unremarkably standard-issue piety. In fact, the relationship between knighthood and religion involved subtle complications that are as informative as they are fascinating. Elite arms bearers were as unlikely simply to ignore religious precepts as they were unlikely passively to absorb and enact each dictate or searing criticism from the most censorious clerics or the most idealistic intellectuals. Dialogue would never have occurred had the most judgmental abstract views prevailed. Certainly analysis cannot be based on an assumption of clerical pacifism versus knightly militarism, for the clerics readily accepted violence in what they recognized as licit causes, and the knights, as we will see, necessarily and readily incorporated religious ideals in their operative thought.

Rejecting reductive cynicism and myopic romanticism, we need a new approach. It cannot simply occupy middle ground between extreme views in prudent hopes of lessening scholarly controversy; an entirely different analysis is required. Contending against both views, the counterargument of this chapter holds that knights and men-at-arms managed, in alliance with clerics close to them, and with confidence in their own piety and orthodoxy, to craft a religious framework suited to their particular requirements. Without disregarding the broad framework for Christian life offered to all believers, they found a set of ideas that valorized and blessed their particularly hard work as warriors, even as this framework offered guides for its ideal practice that they could accept. Queried about their piety, they might have loudly insisted on their orthodoxy, noting that they piously and prudently took every available path to redemption, in the process honoring the essential mediation of clerics (at least of those not culpably serving their enemies or uncompromisingly denouncing knighthood). Over generations, knights followed common pious practices such as attending Mass, providing donations to religious houses, giving traditional alms, going on pilgrimage, and collecting and venerating relics. As good Christian warriors, they proudly enforced and defended right religion with their swords both at home (where they dealt summarily with heretics) and abroad, on crusade (where they vigorously killed "God's enemies"). Many could rightly claim that they, or some honored ancestor, had founded the local church; all expected burial near the altar containing sacred relics. If they possessed the resources, they maintained a confessor in their household. They claimed the special patronage of saints in the heavenly court and of the queen of that court, the Blessed Virgin Mary, who came to their aid in repeated miracle stories they must have cherished.[17]

Granted, signs of anticlericalism surface regularly among the knighthood. Debates between a cleric and a knight became a subgenre, and unsubtle barbs against clerics peppered epic and romance writing.[18] But these outbursts hardly constitute the issue to be explained; rivalry and sniping at the clerics are simply what we might expect from proud laymen who were aristocrats or from men hurrying along their way to that status. The timeless parallel with family quarrels comes quickly to mind. Indeed, the participants were often close relatives, intensifying both cooperation and conflict. Piety and anticlericalism easily coexisted. The piety remained an active force, and it was substantial. Orthodoxy was never in doubt in knightly self-conception.

Rather than anticlericalism, the feature of their piety that needs emphasis and close examination is their degree of independence concerning specific issues. This independence was never global, for, as we have seen, they accepted the mediatory function of the clergy on most issues. But that independence focused intensely on maintenance of their status and valorization of their profession as warriors. Whenever these fundamentals came under critical discussion, the temperature of emotional reaction could rise sharply. Knighthood, in effect, drew a line in the sand; they were acutely aware that the Lord of Hosts could not intend His clerical servants to cross that line by interfering with honored warrior status or the labors that secured it. On their side of the line, knights knew that their position and function were part of the divine plan. As French knights angrily reminded clerics in a confrontation at the French royal court around mid-thirteenth century, "the kingdom was

---

[17] Many examples are discussed in R. W. Kaeuper, *Holy Warriors*, passim.

[18] E.g., the sharp thrusts in the debates between William of Orange and the abbot of the monastery he joins (with remarkable results) in the second redaction of *William in the Monastery*; see Wilhelm Cloetta, ed., *Moniage Guillaume: Les deux redactions en vers du Moniage Guillaume* (Paris: Firmin-Didot, 1906).

neither acquired by written law nor by the arrogance of clerks, but by the sweat of war."[19]

Shouting matches, however much they show depth of feeling, were never the mechanism by which the chivalric religious framework was created. Most of the work went forward quietly and often out of sight, proceeding through collaboration between arms bearers and clerics close to them who understood their needs and warmly appreciated their role as fighters no less than patrons, much needed in a world beset by many dangers. The men-at-arms had no doubts that they needed religion within a society all of whose most basic principles claimed religious referents. They had to sustain campaign and battle, with all the moral murkiness doing so entailed. It might be exceedingly difficult for them to count on the "good end," the anticipated death in a state of grace, with confession made and blessings received, that all medieval Christians thought the most secure gateway to paradise. Geoffroi de Charny spoke for many a man-at-arms in asserting that a knight must be the best Christian of all because of his hazardous life; he knew that in their dangerous vocation death was always just a sword stroke or arrow flight away, and he admonished warriors to think regularly of their souls (an otherworldly parallel to their lively concern for honor in this world).[20] Perhaps showing confidence teetering on the sword edge of fear, he insisted that knights should and could indeed achieve salvation within their profession.[21] Wolfram von Eschenbach's Parzifal declares plainly that "knighthood with shield and spear can win renown in this life and Paradise for the soul as well."[22]

The specifically chivalric piety that Charny shows so clearly had gradually come into being. Knights and men-at-arms obviously drew upon fundamental ideals of medieval Christianity, but the sets of working concepts that we are seeking were no simple replication of abstract theological or legal pronouncements somehow imposed on unwilling knighthood by stern clerics or subtle intellectuals. Working chivalric religious conceptions, that is, were not limited to the justifications and restrictions of violence, war, and sexuality elaborated in

---

[19] H. R. Luard, ed., *Matthew Paris: Chronica Majora* (Rolls Series LVII, London, 1872–1884), 7 vols., IV, 593.

[20] Kaeuper and Kennedy, *Book of Chivalry*, 122–123, for example.

[21] Ibid., 164–167; for general discussion of Charny's religion, see Kaeuper, *Holy Warriors*, 42–51.

[22] *Parzifal*, stanza 472.

learned treatises. Unsurprisingly, knightly views enthusiastically adapted praise and justifications in what they heard and read, but they deftly circumvented restrictions on actions or motives theoretically imposed in these learned treatises. It would be convenient for modern scholars to read only John of Salisbury, Etienne de Fougeres, Ramon Llull, or Christine de Pizan and think they have comprehended what chivalry meant to knighthood as an operative force in the medieval world. But such a shortcut actually leads into a cul-de-sac. As always, the hard effort of trying to determine actual chivalric notions among historical knights remains. These working conceptions – the common currency of talk at table in a hall or discussions around a campfire on campaign – must be extracted from a more comprehensive and diverse body of sources ranging from classics of abstract thought (which show ideals and problems if not behavior) to chronicles, vernacular treatises (such as Charny's), and biographies or autobiographies of practicing knights, along with the vast corpus of imaginative chivalric literature.

The knights and their allies gradually put together a cluster of ideas that fitted elite warriors into a world steeped in religious values, most of which they admired and respected. No single document or decade can be expected to reveal the birth of such fundamental constructs, but crucial elements appeared during the transition into what we have termed the classic or second phase of chivalry. Initial hostility to the military profession on the part of significant clerical reformers changed to endorsement, as significantly real as it was ever qualified. The thoughts and actions of Pope Gregory VII (1073–1085) show the shift,[23] as does the generously encouraging preaching of the first crusade and all its successors, the founding and defense of the Knights Templar,[24] and the expansion of the idea of a society of orders

---

[23] Gregory VII, the great reforming pope, at first thoroughly condemned the military life; yet he later attempted to transform knighthood into a "militia sancti Petri," a military force that might produce right order in the world when guided by Saint Peter's vicar. Only a few years after his death, the first crusade was launched, with its valorization of participating knights.

[24] Saint Bernard of Clairvaux, who wielded a pen as sharp as a sword, savaged knighthood in general over its inherent sinfulness, but his famous tract "In Praise of the New Knighthood" eased troubled minds among even the select minority of early Knights Templar, uncertain that they could combine the knightly and monastic professions. Bernard likewise enthusiastically endorsed the second crusade in his mesmerizing preaching. See the discussion in Jean Leclerc, "Un document sur le debuts des Templiers," *Receuil d'études sur*

(*ordines*) to include rising *milites*.[25] Among the knights themselves, ubiquitous tournaments served as flowing fountains of chivalric conceptions and conduct. By mid-twelfth century the crucial agency of *chanson de geste* was actively at work, soon to be followed by romance writing. The seemingly ceaseless flow of these works of literature as much as any other force created, debated, and disseminated chivalric ideals. By the twelfth century, in other words, the religious ideology of chivalry was taking on recognizable form. Its development continued throughout following centuries, culminating in the later Middle Ages.

We cannot thus expect any single work to put it all neatly together. One work may emphasize and link two or more ideals; in another work, one line of thought from this first set may be bonded with new concepts, and so the process likely proceeded, the framework taking shape in broadly shared views over time. If this process generated a variety of particular expressions, the result, as argued before (in the chapters of Part I), was a core of chivalric beliefs broadly held, with a shifting outer perimeter of valorizing and directive notions shaped by local circumstances. All these valorizations were at least to a significant degree the creation of warriors themselves, and none were hostile to their needs. In this sense chivalry was their creation, not an imposition grudgingly and only partially accepted by men who did not want it. Working conceptions represent their code, however much they relied on friendly clerical cooperation; it was designed to meet the requirements of their order of society.

Given the challenge of extracting views held by arms bearers most of whom were in initial chivalric phases illiterate, scholars will lament that they cannot sit among them as plentiful wine and talk flowed – especially at that unique time of night (and level of helpful inebriation) when life's large questions can be discussed. Lacking a capacity for time travel, we must, especially for the earliest chivalric centuries, derive views of the warriors from their actions or from careful reading of the mediating voice of clerical authors who often speak about them and sometimes speak ostensibly for them. These writers reveal much as they praise or condemn knightly

---

Saint Bernard (Rome: Apud Curiam Generalem Sacri Ordinis Cesterciansis, 1966), 2: 87–99, and Malcolm Barber and Keith Bate, *The Templars* (Manchester University Press, 2002), 54–59.

[25] Classic discussions in Jean Flori, *L'essor de chevalerie*.

behavior, or speak in their name by writing their formal documents.[26]

Through the centuries we can observe action at a distance, even when we cannot directly see or hear our subjects at close hand. In time, unmediated voices come to us from literate and highly thoughtful arms bearers. All evidence we can muster suggests a process in which knighthood absorbed basic religious formulations that underwent selection (there were some quiet, specific exclusions) and much creative adaptation. Only thus could the knights have achieved needed support for their rising status in society and requisite blessings upon their hard professional labor at arms. Their piety fused with significantly confident independence in its application to crucial aspects of their lives.

CONTEXT: CRUSADE AND WARFARE IN GENERAL

Two basic features of the cultural context in which chivalry matured can help to explain the emergence of a basic religious framework of knighthood. These features – the enterprise of crusade and an intense focus on meritorious ascetic practice – intertwined in chivalric thought and practice, but each will be emphasized in turn. Each phenomenon, in fact, takes on double importance for this investigation: not only do crusade and asceticism represent fertile conceptual seed beds, but each also shows how men-at-arms interpreted and enacted them through selective borrowing and characteristically creative chivalric adaptation.

Many aspects of crusade have been intensively studied and will seem well known. Famously, throughout the age of chivalry many knights took the cross and set off to fight on the frontiers of Spanish kingdoms, in the Holy Land, in the later expeditions in the Levant or Baltic, as well as on campaigns within established regions of Europe (notably against Cathars and their allies in what would become southern additions to the kingdom of France). Admirable scholarship over generations has examined these expeditions and explored the flood tide of crusade propaganda, which generated crucial justifications for specific dimensions of knighthood.[27] The importance of

---

[26] As argued in R. W. Kaeuper, *Holy Warriors*, 23–32.
[27] The discussion begins with Carl Erdman, *The Origin of the Idea of Crusade*, trans. Marshall W. Baldwin and Walter Goffart (Princeton University Press, 1977). For

these great waves of men and ideas can scarcely be overestimated, even if the detailed arguments over precisely what campaigns constituted crusade must be left to specialists. What is needed for present analysis is a distinctly new orientation on the bonding of chivalry with crusade emphasizing actual warrior behavior and the independence inseparable from piety.

Crusade always represented an especially honored and pious component of a knightly career, even its culmination. That many knights went on crusade demonstrates active piety in response to a clerical call, with repeated surges of crusading undoubtedly shaping emergent chivalry. Geoffroi de Charny, we can recall, praised crusading as "righteous, holy, certain and sure."[28] Sermons advanced the message repeatedly, and the miracle stories that enlivened them – or those heard or read in castle halls and chambers as well as churches – assured knights of divine gratitude for their work against the "enemies of God." In these stories at least the fictional crusader may piously decide not to return to his homeland and to worldly action stained with sin, but rather to die wearing the cross as an act of self-cleansing atonement. Crusading in this view was thus not only elevated above ordinary knightly action; it also served to wipe from knightly slates the smudged record of a sinful life. Clerics worked to instruct knights that this form of fighting is purer, it is especially blessed by God, and it offers an active form of atonement, in addition to the usual warrior pleasures. Not only was its goal approved, since the warriors fought a thoroughly demonized foe, but crusade also required more effort: long and dangerous voyages, absence from home and family,

more recent studies with a variety of points of view, see Jonathan Riley-Smith, *The First Crusade and the Idea of Crusading* (Philadelphia: University of Pennsylvania Press, 1991; 2nd rev. ed., Continuum, 2009); Christopher Tyerman, *God's War: A New History of the Crusades* (Cambridge, MA: Belknap Press of Harvard University Press, 2006); Susanna A. Throop, *Crusading as an Act of Vengeance 1095–1216* (Aldershot: Ashgate, 2011); Jean Flori, "Ideology and Motivation in the First Crusade," in *Palgrave Advances in the Crusades*, ed. Helen J. Nicholson (Basingstoke: Palgrave Macmillan, 2005), 15–36. For an important collection of republished articles, see *The Crusades*, ed. Andrew Jotischky, 4 vols. (Routledge Critical Concepts in Historical Studies; Routledge, 2008); see especially vol. I for ideology. For the Iberian crusade, see *Reconquest and Crusade in Medieval Spain* (Philadelphia: University of Pennsylvania Press, 2003). Overviews of crusades scholarship appear in Christopher Tyerman, *The Debate on the Crusades, 1099–2010* (Manchester: Manchester University Press, 2011), and Norman Housley, *Contesting the Crusades* (Malden, MA: Blackwell, 2006).

[28] Kaeuper and Kennedy, *Book of Chivalry*, 164–165.

desperate combat. It thus merited more divine blessing than ordinary fighting at home. Sermon exempla and religious tales regularly made the point. One crusader in a thirteenth-century book of religious tales is said to have a crossbow bolt lodged in his head after combat, but refuses the offer of friends to arrange for its removal; he wants the bolt in place on Judgment Day to demonstrate his meritorious fighting beyond cavil.[29] Another crusader is said in a fourteenth-century book to prolong his departure to the Holy Land so that the meritorious suffering of leaving for this warfare will increase his spiritual benefit.[30]

Yet we cannot simply project prescriptive clerical stories as if they portrayed actual and representative knightly behavior on crusade. Strong elements of chivalric independence appear in both the thought and the behavior of the historical body of men who took the cross – and we must remember that they represent an unknown percentage of all European knighthood over centuries. Though they revered the enterprise of crusade, their actions while wearing the cross differed very little from conduct of their military careers at home. They were not suddenly transformed into ideal models of piety and probity by donning crusader garb. And most knights who survived the experience chose to return to that quotidian life in Europe with its accustomed pleasures of tournament, border raid, or war against fellow Christians; they likewise returned to a courtly world with an undisguised focus on the pleasures of sexuality.

Even while wearing the cross, knights are often said to honor the chivalry and nobility of non-Christian foes;[31] within their own world of crusading knighthood, the warriors likewise show concern over prickly issues of worldly honor and advantage that could trump any simplistic and theoretical predominance of crusading merit over the usual warrior mentality and action. Intense royal rivalry sent Philip Augustus back to France, crusading success unachieved, to gain advantage over his fellow crusader Richard Lion-Heart, who con-tinued fighting in the Holy Land. Famously, Richard was captured

---

[29] British Library Additional MS 2799b, f 11.
[30] British Library Additional MS 1846, f 125b.
[31] The tendency is especially clear in Wolfram von Eschenbach's *Willehalm*, but examples there and in other works are so numerous they defy citation. Of course an opposite and even more common stance is to view the non-Christians as monstrous, as is classically the case in the *Song of Roland*. This attribution of "otherness" to the Saracens highlights the minority view of chivalric inclusiveness everywhere it can be found.

on his way home, despite the special protection that in theory guarded crusaders. The Sire de Joinville threatened to leave the first crusade of the saintly Louis IX unless that king choreographed a formal rite of satisfaction when one of Joinville's men was merely shoved while entering the royal tent in Egypt.[32] Joinville, moreover, refused to join his king's second crusade, asserting that his higher duty was to remain at home and protect his men from rapacious royal administrators.[33] The dismay of that most lordly pope, Innocent III, at the diversion of the fourth crusade into attacks on the Christian city of Zara and the great Christian metropolis of Constantinople is well known. That crusades could veer far from the course intended by clerical direction cannot be doubted; but such recognition makes the point, and what the majority of crusaders actually did cannot be forgotten in analysis, for it speaks powerfully to the complex relationship between chivalric prowess and the touchy concern over honor intermixed with undoubted religious piety. Knights answered the clerical call and donned the cross, but doing so did not entail their simple and obedient following of clerical hopes and directives in detail, nor did it effect their suppression of all warrior values in exchange for spiritual benefits. We cannot understand what crusade meant to the arms bearers by reading only prescriptive clerical texts. If clerics gave crusaders blessings and preached ideal goals and standards for their service, how the message was received and utilized is also crucially important. In effect, knights accepted the blessing far more readily than any directive or restrictive elements that came as their yokefellow.

Though a distinctly minority view, some authors even doubted that the killing of non-Christian foes could be fitted within the spiritual demands of their Christian belief. Such a view famously appears in the *Willehalm* of Wolfram von Eschenbach, which is a faux or proto-crusading epic written in the twelfth century, but featuring cross-wearing Christian warriors of the Carolingian period fighting Saracens. The message is delivered by the spouse of the eponymous hero Willehalm (who is named Guiburc here, but may in other poems be called Guibour, Guitburgi, or Guibourg); this fascinating lady has been converted from Islam to Christianity. She

---

[32] M. R. B. Shaw, ed., trans., *Joinville and Villehardouin: Chronicles of the Crusades* (Baltimore: Penguin, 1963), 293.

[33] Ibid., 346.

sends off her husband's warriors with the admonition that "you should act so that your salvation will be assured. Pay heed to the advice of a foolish woman: spare the creatures of God's Hand."[34] The case she makes emphasizes tolerance, the following of the divine example of mercy, and a broad understanding; after all, the earliest humans could not have been other than unbaptized "pagans."[35] Near the end of this text Wolfram returns to the theme and speaks out directly to his audience, posing a provocative question:

Is it a sin to slaughter like cattle those who have never received baptism? I say it is a great sin, for they are all the creatures of God's Hand and He maintains them, with their seventy-two languages.[36]

A companion quickly tries by injunction and argument to brighten Willehalm's dark mood, "scolding him and diverting him." Willehalm is told not "to act like a woman" over losses and is reminded that from battlefield success "what we gain is sweet." The sinfulness of killing the unbaptized is not touched unless there is an oblique reference to this troubling issue in the rhetorical question put to Willehalm, "Who ever yielded us land or its treasure without bloodshed and sword's point?"[37] The clinching case is an injunction to "remember that God has honoured you here and increased your fame."[38]

It is likewise worth noting that the stories warriors enjoyed in *chansons de geste* pictured remarkable – perhaps fantastic – spiritual benefits earned by this fighting; these benefits extended far beyond what any canon lawyer or text would grant. To encourage a reluctant

---

[34] Gibbs and Johnson, *Willehalm*, 155–158.

[35] Ibid. Gibbs and Johnson suggest that Wolfram is taking issue with the current theological view that salvation was denied to the unbaptized. Guiburc's attitudes have been the subject of much scholarly controversy. See Martin H. Jones and Timothy McFarland, eds., *Wolfram's Willehalm: Fifteen Essays* (Woodbridge: Boydell & Brewer, 2002); the essay by Martin Jones is of particular interest and relevance. Cf. Stephanie Hathaway, *Saracens and Conversion: Chivalric Ideals in Aliscans and Wolfram's Willehalm* (Oxford: Peter Lang, 2012), 117–176. The respectful burial of even Saracen dead at the end of the poem is noteworthy, as is Willehalm's commendation of the Saracen king Matriblieiz to God, "for your heart has never abandoned virtue." Gibbs and Johnson, *Willehalm*, 225.

[36] Gibbs and Johnson, *Willehalm*, 218.

[37] All of these quotations appear at Gibbs and Johnson, *Willehalm*, 221.

[38] Ibid., 222. Willehalm is not convinced and continues to mourn the loss of his friends, but acknowledges that he must act as if he were happy, as the duty of a good leader.

William of Orange to fight the threatening pagan champion Corsolt in *The Crowning of Louis*, the imagined pope proffers a relic of Saint Peter, prince of the apostles, for William to kiss, and he promises much else:

> Look, here is St Peter, the guardian of souls; if you undertake this feat of arms today on his account, my lord, then you may eat meat every single day for the rest of your life and take as many wives as you have a mind to. You will never commit any sin however wicked (so long as you avoid any act of treason) that will not be discounted, all the days of your life, and you shall have your lodging in paradise, the place Our Lord keeps for His best friends; St Gabriel himself will show you the way.[39]

Multiple wives permitted and treason prohibited as the only sin reserved for dire judgment reveal the lay rather than ecclesiastical wellsprings of this imagined offer. Here is a cleric who appreciates knighthood and the rewards knights deserve! Overwhelmed, William can only accept the combat and mutter thanks: "Ah! God help us! . . . never was there a more generous-hearted cleric!"[40]

In their zeal for the cause, those preaching sermons and creating dramatic sermon exempla often moved beyond the careful limits and prescriptions of canon law with as much enthusiasm as the epics. These enthusiasts promised outright forgiveness and paradise to warriors bearing the cross on their tunics.[41] The significant language of suffering, merit, and martyrdom floated like a halo above fighters popularly recognized as crusaders, whether they were campaigning in the Holy Land or elsewhere. Sometimes such men-at-arms were acting in response to a clerical call, and sometimes on their own initiative, though with clerical blessing. In the German *Priest Konrad's Song of Roland* the great emperor Karl (Charlemagne) is said to have "won the kingdom of heaven" and his men were

---

[39] *The Crowning of Louis*, trans. David Hoggan, in Glanville Price, ed., *William of Orange: Four Old French Epics* (Herts: Letchworth, 1975), laisse 18.

[40] Ibid.

[41] Christoph T. Maier, *Crusade Propaganda and Ideology: Model Sermons for the Preaching of the Cross* (Cambridge University Press, 2000), provides numerous examples. The Norman chronicler Ralph of Caen reported that the great knight Tancred, active in southern Italy and Sicily, was convinced that the crusade preaching of Pope Urban had offered crusaders forgiveness for all sin: *RHC* III Occ., 605–606, discussed in Marcus Bull, *Knightly Piety and the Lay Response to the First Crusade* (Oxford, 1993), 3–4. In *The Song of Aspremont* the fighters anticipate full pardon without confession: Brandin, ed., *Chanson d'Aspremont*, laisse 236, line 4309: "sans boce regehir."

"willing to risk their lives for the welfare of their souls" and even "to die in God's service and win heaven through suffering."[42]

Such offerings fondly imagine the overflowing cup that God's ministers should ideally extend to God's good fighters. Blessings of this character and specificity could scarcely emerge from clerical orthodoxy, and certainly not from the programs of vigorous reformers trying to produce a directive clerical caste and right order in the world. Rather, they represent justification of the warrior life in terms the warriors could appreciate. Valorization descends upon the fighters from a heavenly realm where they are understood and to which they will be carried in glory after suffering a heroic death.

Authors of *chansons de geste* portray clerics as full participants in the meritorious asceticism of righteous armed combat. These are clerics as they must have appeared in chivalric dreams, and sometimes in real life.[43] Remarkably knightly in thought and action, these churchmen fight and suffer alongside the cherished warriors.[44] Repeatedly and in multiple epic poems, Archbishop Turpin, the very model of a medieval clerk in warrior fantasy (joined by an occasional pope or abbot), hews many an enemy as a knight, in clear sign of the basic worth of such combat. Of course his hallowed hands not only grip weapons, but also bless, absolve, and consecrate his fellow warriors, fulsomely assuring them that their hard labors open the lofty doors of paradise.

Audiences of epic could hear grand knightly clerics articulate – as well as see them enact – radically chivalric views.[45] Early in the *Song of Aspremont* Archbishop Turpin pointedly gives a clear message to the pope:

---

[42] J. W. Thomas, trans., *Priest Konrad's Song of Roland* (Columbia, SC: Camden House, 1994), 17; a martyr's death brings ascent to heaven, ibid., 19; and "the soul ... will never suffer the torments of hell if one zealously serves the Lord," ibid., 35. Turning prescriptive, the poet intones later, "Even though they were upright youths who were ready to suffer for the good of their souls, they were careful to prepare for death through confession." Ibid., 51. The usefulness of confession is stressed again at ibid., 94.

[43] Craig Nakashian, "A New Kind of Monster ... Part-Monk, Part-Knight: The Paradox of Clerical Militarism in the Middle Ages" (PhD dissertation, University of Rochester, NY, 2009).

[44] As Craig Nakashian has convincingly shown, at least some paler versions of these imagined, outsized militaristic clerical figures stride boldly about in fully historical records; moreover, they are generally praised – or at least are condemned solely for worldliness rather than militarism: "A New Kind of Monster."

[45] Craig Nakashian, "A New Kind of Monster."

Father, don't take amiss these words of mine;
It is our duty to cherish all brave knights;
For when we clerics sit down to eat at night,
Or in God's service sing matins at first light,
These men are fighting for our lands with their lives;
So Abbot Fromer here and you and I
Should empty all our coffers for their supplies;
Each one of us should give so much alike
They'll honor us and serve us all the time.

The theme would have brought sage nods from a warrior audience. And as the tale inevitably turned to the good archbishop's knightly feats, it might have brought them to their feet with loud cheering. Such epic literature provided the lineaments of a militant moral world, making sense of fighting and dying in armor.

If a separate volume would be required fully to demonstrate the religious valorization of combat in romance, the flavor at least can be seen in the *Alliterative Morte Arthure*. During the Arthurian council that advocates war against the Romans, Duke Cador sings out, "Now we shall have war, thanks be to Christ!"[46] And late in this great text Gawain finds that he and his men are surrounded by the forces of Mordred (demonized as Saracens, though the fight is on English soil). Resolutely Gawain shouts,

We'll work like loyal men for the court of Christ,
And yonder Saracens, I swear on my troth,
We'll sup with our Savior in ceremony, in heaven,
In the presence of the King of Kings and Prince of all others,
With prophets and patriarchs and the noble apostles,
Before His gracious face, who formed us all!
Now on to yonder japes' sons: he who yields
While quick and still in health, unkilled by their hands,
May he never more be saved or succored in Christ,
But Satan sink his soul deep down in hell![47]

King Arthur soon collects the precious blood flowing from Gawain's lifeless body in his clean, gilded helmet, converting it into a chivalric reliquary, almost a chalice; he declares to his men that when death comes to them they will reach the gates of heaven before their bodies have gone

---

[46] Line 257 in Larry D. Benson, *King Arthur's Death, the Middle English Stanzaic and Alliterative Morte Arthure* (Exeter: University of Exeter Press, 1986): "Worshipped be Crist!"

[47] John Gardner, trans., *The Alliterative Morte Arthure* (Carbondale, IL: Southern Illinois University Press, 1973), 100.

half cold. With such views reverberating in the cultural atmosphere, it is no surprise to find Galahad presented as the knightly image of Christ in *The Quest for the Holy Grail* or to witness Christ jousting against the devil for human salvation in Langland's *Piers Plowman*.

Such literary expressions coincide with techniques adopted in chronicles. These traditionally historical sources, of course, tend fully to promote the rightness of the combat they narrate. One technique, as we have just noted, involved visualizing Saracens among the enemy. In the very real world, opponents were frequently declared to be "worse than Saracens," suggesting that fighting them was justifiable or even spiritually meritorious.[48] Of course, merit may simply be asserted, without recourse to Saracens. The French chronicler Rigord lavished praise on the young King Philip Augustus when he campaigned in 1179 against local "tyrants" troubling churches and clerics in Berry and Burgundy. Philip, he says, is a "knight of Christ" who has "waged his first war consecrated to God."[49] We can recall that William Marshal claimed to lead the Army of God against French invaders in England during the minority of Henry III, whatever the current views on the righteousness of one side or the other coming from the papal curia. Though no one would confuse him with an intellectual, the Marshal, as we have seen, famously spoke his definite and independent ideas about religion and the knightly life – even about the proscribed mock warfare of tournament – near the end of his own life, with judgment and the fate of his soul in the next life looming.[50] Northern French knights could boast they attacked Cathars in the south with explicit papal blessing; yet those who resisted them argued that God blessed their own cause.[51]

Throughout more than a century of Anglo-French warfare during the later Middle Ages, as for several centuries before, shields and banners on both sides were boldly and brightly emblazoned with images of the saints and especially of the Blessed Virgin Mary, leading irreverent postmedieval writers, including Henry Adams, to observe drily that she fought on both sides in most medieval conflicts.[52]

---

[48] Discussion and sources provided in R. W. Kaeuper, *Holy Warriors*, 104–105, 110–113.

[49] H. Francois Delaborde, ed., *Oeuvres de Rigord* (Paris: Renouard, 1882).

[50] *History of William Marshal*, lines 18468–18482.

[51] R. W. Kaeuper, *Holy Warriors*, 106–107.

[52] E.g., Henry Adams declared in his *Mont-Saint-Michel and Chartres* that "the greatest French warriors insisted on her leading them into battle, and in the actual mêlée

Sacred power could even be imagined endorsing the tourney ground. A famous miracle story features the Blessed Virgin jousting for a knight who had become lost in devotion to her in a wayside chapel while en route to chivalric competition.[53] Needless to say, she won the prize for her knight while ignoring clerical strictures on chivalric sport.

Revealing war cries in the great Anglo-French conflict seemed to pit God and Saint George on the English side against God and Saint Denis backing the French. Like a magnet near iron filings, much knightly violence attracted religious blessing, though some fervent idealists and all those targeted by knightly violence would press opposing views. As each lord or king claimed or assumed that God's blessing descended upon his work, medieval or modern canonists might again justly claim distinctions between this particular blessing and a broad canonical definition of crusade. What the warriors wanted, however, was simpler: they needed and thought they merited divine approval and believed their good fighting placed hefty weights upon the looming scales of eternal judgment. The historical record shows that from our second and classic phase of chivalry, the men-at-arms experienced little difficulty in securing sufficient clerical assurance of divine favor, whatever the careful caveats of university scholars, joined, by the later Middle Ages, by great legists.[54]

Of basic importance, all this evidence suggests that the very fact of religiously blessed warfare helped to spread a cloak of righteousness over knightly fighting in general. This result may have been far from clerical intent, but the reality must register in analysis. Religious justification could be expanded broadly in knightly conception; it could bleed into valorization for the usual warfare at home. Did not all knights fight solely in good causes? This religious justification, heartily desired by knights, was broadly claimed by their own statements and was supported by the voices and pens of clerics close to their interests. The knights were all considered members of an *ordo* of fighter; they knew their military role was necessary and that it had been ordained by God. His clerical agents, never pacifists, sanctified any warfare – in the Holy Land or within Europe – that they saw as

---

when men were killing each other, on every battle-field in Europe, for at least five hundred years, Mary was present, leading both sides."

[53] E.g., British Library Additional MS 33956, f 75b, column 2.

[54] Even the faux war of tournament outlived fiery blasts of clerical condemnation, as discussed in Chapter 7.

aligned with divine will as interpreted by clerical authority. Some of these clerics inevitably stood closer to local knightly lords and patrons than to more distant theologians, canon lawyers, pontiffs, or university scholars.

In fact, as a contextual force in chivalric life and thought, blessings on crusade-like fighting seem to have been regularly extended beyond strict definitions of crusade. That the idea of crusade-like spiritual merit spread to cover all good fighting is clear in *chansons de geste*. As the warriors fight wrongful enemies, whether pagans or fellow Christians, these epics famously portray their deprivations and horrific bodily suffering in pitiless anatomical detail. None could doubt that the fighters pierced by enemy spears, riddled with darts, and holding intestines within slashed bodies were suffering.[55] No more could they doubt the rectitude of the cause for which the warriors fought and suffered. That this vast body of epic literature is usually set in an imagined Carolingian age several centuries earlier than their composition in no way reduces their value to our analysis; for these epic poems anachronistically show warriors gaining heavenly blessings from crusade-like combat before there were crusades, and their authors may be utterly untroubled if both sides in combat are Christian. The poets claim moral high ground no less enthusiastically than the warriors they portray sought advantageous battlefield terrain.

Significantly, heroic fighting in the interests of king, kin, or lord garnered no less merit than fighting "the enemies of God." Coyly, the author of the *Song of Aspremont* explains that his imagined fighters (as usual, pictured in a setting that predated the crusades by centuries) placed red crosses on their tunics in order to distinguish friend from foe in the confusion of battle.[56] In *The Crowning of Louis* when William of Orange moves from combat against the invading pagans, led by their champion Corsolt, to defense of King Louis in France against misguided Christians, no change of tone occurs, and no loss of merit is noted; in fact, as William provides this good martial service to legitimate kingship, he is said

---

[55] In Wolfram's *Willehalm*, for example, Vivianz's entrails spill out over his saddle: Gibbs and Johnson, *Willehalm*, 28. The young hero rips a banner off the lance and binds his entrails so that he can enter the combat once again.

[56] See laisses 213, 236, 244, and 288 in the *chanson*. See also Gibbs and Johnson, *Willehalm*, 165, for another scene of warriors before crusade wearing and carrying crosses.

to have "suffered great penance (*grant peneance suffrit*)" through his fighting against the rebels.[57]

Similarly, in Wolfram's *Willehalm*, if on a more limited scale, the epic fight against Saracens is interrupted by a quarrel with a magistrate over payment of demanded tolls in order to pass through the town of Orleans, which the poet terms a sinful plan. When Willehalm prefers fighting to paying, the urban militia is summoned by the town bell. Willehalm's drawn sword beheads the offending official. The widow's complaint to Arnalt, count of Narbonne, brings only that lord's contempt: no knight should be confused with a merchant who pays tolls; had Willehalm killed all his urban opponents, Arnalt would have remained dry-eyed. Yet fearing an unworthy man is using a royal battle cry ("Montjoie!"), he gathers knights and men-at-arms, citing the king's interests and the honor due to the queen, his sister. In the pursuit, Willehalm unhorses Arnalt, but calm returns when this man turns out to be Willehalm's brother. Yet messages about knightly right have been delivered in the midst of a quasi-crusading text, and Willehalm has justifiably charged even (misguided) fellow Christians using his wanted battle cry.[58] More concisely, even the Grail knights in this poet's *Parzival* are said to fight as a form of penance: "Always when they ride out as they often do, it is to seek adventure. They do so for their sins."[59]

Emphatically, the sense of rightful combat with religious blessing did not remain restricted to the subset of knights who went on campaigns that would fit all modern scholarly categorization as crusades. In fact, religious praise and spiritual blessings usually descended on most knightly combat – at least from clerics within their realm or territory. Bernard of Clairvaux might uncompromisingly separate the faithful in Templar costume or heroes of the second crusade he had

---

[57] Ernest Langlois, ed., *La Couronnement de Louis* (Paris, 1924–1925), lines 2089–2090; Hoggan, trans., *The Crowning of Louis*, in Glanville Price, ed., *William of Orange*, 42. For numerous other examples, see Kaeuper, *Holy Warriors*, 104–115.

[58] Gibbs and Johnson, *Willehalm*, 68–71. The dead magistrate and his irate widow fade; Willehalm and Arnalt discuss their *lignage*. He and his men are soon given hospitality by monks who do not know him. The top orders in society seem here to be emphasized shortly after merchants have not appeared in a good light. Ibid., 73. Soon after this, however, a merchant born of a noble family is hospitable to Willehalm when the royal court is unwelcoming. Ibid., 75.

[59] Mustard and Passage, *Parzifal*, 251. Fighting by these knights to win pardon for sins is repeated at ibid., 263.

promoted so effectively from the wretched sinners who formed the ranks of ordinary knighthood, fighting in their ordinary quarrels, but even his great energy and the sharp scalpel of his sarcasm could not prevent appropriation of blessings for a wide range of combat in practice. If the goats thought they were faithful sheep, they were encouraged in their confidence by local clerics who preached to them, confessed them, blessed them, and finally buried them amidst resounding chant and clouds of incense.[60] In the minds of most knights, the merits of sanctified warfare and the glow of holiness could not be limited to the minority of fighting men recognized by high and distant clerics.

Idealists, both medieval and modern, prefer strictly defined and clerically initiated crusading warfare to be considered as the true function of knighthood, an alternative to destructive combat among coreligionists. Yet elite medieval arms bearers were less insistent on rigid borders between crusade and other licit warfare; they warmly endorsed crusade without condemning what could be viewed as noncrusading warfare, or even fused the two in their thinking. A species of crusading mentality (however false in the view of canonists, medieval or modern) spread throughout idealized descriptions of warfare in general in chivalric texts as in chivalric life.

Fulsome praise and blessings that theoretically should have been reserved for crusade went to causes writers endorsed. This is true of all our sources, literary, chronicle, treatise, biography – all show an expansion of blessing to all fighting by warriors they approved. Almost all such fighting could be imagined as at least crusade-like. William Marshal's claim to be leading the Army of God against French invaders in early thirteenth-century England comes quickly to mind.[61] More than a century later Geoffrey le Baker could only term the King of France the "crowned one" as he assumed divine blessing on Edward III and the Black Prince, who were gaining control of swaths of that realm.

The tradition of religious blessing of valiant fighters had a long pedigree. Before an English army fought invading Scots in 1138 at the Battle of the Standard, they had been assured in a sermon that they were doing God's work, and they were accompanied by a wagon

---

[60] As David Bachrach has shown in detail in *Religion and the Conduct of War*, the practice was as old as the Carolingian era and immediately post-Carolingian era.
[61] J. C. Holt, *Magna Carta* (Cambridge University Press, 1965), 263, 364.

bearing a tall standard displaying a consecrated host and sacred banners.[62] Well before that, as David Bachrach has shown, armies in tenth- and eleventh-century German lands, as elsewhere, when setting off on campaign included platoons of priests to bless their work, after fellow clerics at home had laid a foundation of intercessory prayer.[63]

Elite warriors were claiming divine blessing on all their good fighting, and were certain that all their fighting was good. From the twelfth century they were specifically, in effect, grasping the blessed mantle of legitimacy offered to crusaders and stretching that shimmering fabric over all elite arms bearers engaged in hard and meritorious labor at arms. If these knights were fully convinced that they engaged in no unjustified warfare, it was an opinion often seconded by at least some prominent clerics within their region. Granted, to take the cross and fight "unbelievers" was undoubtedly a capstone to a knightly career, but it required no vast stretch of mind to consider all fighting in good causes as spiritually meritorious.

If Charny shows a highly positive attitude to crusading,[64] we must remember also his insistence that men-at-arms could save themselves within their profession.[65] And he repeatedly shows the hard lives and hard fighting of men-at-arms as pleasing to God, an enactment of divine endowments, and a form of penitential practice. Moreover, Charny enacted in dramatic ritual a veritable religion of battle. The goal was the triumph of the king of France and the defense of the kingdom of France. With minimal mental effort we can visualize the imposing ceremony by which the Oriflamme, the royal sacred banner, was entrusted to Messire Geoffroi before the campaign that led to his death on the disastrous field of Poitiers. The ceremony classically blended religious and chivalric ideals. In the holy setting of the church of Saint Denis, within the aura spread by chests of powerful relics, within the scent of swirling clouds of incense, and with the sound of chanting and powerfully pious language, this renowned knight swore to bear the banner with honor into war; after being kissed by the king of France, he had the sacred cloth draped around

---

[62] John R. E. Bliese, "Aelred of Rievaulx's Rhetoric and Morale at the Battle of the Standard, 1138," *Albion* 20 (1988), 543–556.

[63] David Bachrach, *Religion and the Conduct of War*, passim.

[64] Kaeuper and Kennedy, *Book of Chivalry*, 164–165; he terms crusade a "righteous, holy, certain and sure" form of combat.

[65] Ibid.

his shoulders for the recessional down the aisle of the church, surrounded by great knights and eminent churchmen.[66]

CONTEXT: CULTURAL OBSESSION WITH ASCETICISM

Evidence on crusading and other combat has repeatedly taken us into
a realm of thought featuring meritorious asceticism, but to calibrate
its force within maturing chivalry requires a closer and more specific
examination of this remarkable phenomenon. Though asceticism
will seem utterly foreign to modern conceptions, it was basic within
the medieval world. As a contextual element in chivalry, asceticism
has received much less attention than crusade. Yet it played an
essential and powerful role in the emergence of the chivalric religious
assurance we are trying to understand.

Clearly, asceticism could readily mesh with chivalry, given the
emphasis placed by arms bearers on physical exertion and heroic
endurance. But to sense the significant power of asceticism, we
must see it within medieval society as a whole. The presence of
asceticism within medieval piety is generally recognized, but we
might plainly declare it foundational, for the individual or group
showing the most avid ascetic beliefs and practices merited the most
respect from God and society. This admiration was evident as surging
waves of monastic reform periodically flowed through the medieval
world and elevated those religious orders claiming a purer and more
austere life. Showing greater ascetic rigor assured them of enthusiastic
support among the laity as well as the formally religious; endowment
flowed on this tide to these new practitioners of a hard life of pious
self-denial. Immured anchorites provoked admiration and provided
advice even to the great. Busy flagellants, alone or in groups, left
bloody footprints as they periodically crossed the historical stage,
striving to elicit divine mercy. Painting and sculpture show an unrelenting focus on anatomical details of martyrdom suffered by the
saints, no less than punishment endured by sinners in the afterlife;
by later generations, images of the crucified Christ become almost
unbearable in their intense portrayal of meritorious physical suffering.
Clearly, in this view, God required such penance for sin and was
mollified by physical suffering in atonement. Human salvation had, of

---

[66] Kaeuper and Kennedy, *Book of Chivalry*, 15–17. Many a knighting ceremony, if on
a less grand scale, reproduced the symbolism valorizing combat.

course, depended on the meritorious suffering and atoning death of the Son of God on Calvary and on its regular mimetic repetition in the singing of the Mass.

This emphasis on meritorious suffering in medieval *mentalité* has not traditionally been linked with chivalry in scholarly analysis. Yet the link has already been apparent in the evidence, and appreciation of its significance can be intensified under closer analysis. In what might be termed a chivalric sermon on the eve of knighting a number of young men, Perceforest, in the romance bearing his name, plainly intones, "You cannot win without suffering; if you wish to win, you must learn to suffer."[67] Opening his *Willehalm*, Wolfram von Eschenbach intones the principle clearly, addressing God, whose hand steered Willehalm:

Thy mercy knew how to guide him to works of such a kind that with manly courage at his disposal and by means of Thy Grace, he was capable of making amends. Thy Help often saved him from peril. He risked a twofold death, of the soul and of the body too.[68]

Concisely in his *Parzifal*, Wolfram declares that knighthood "has a knotted whip of sorrows for a tail."[69]

As an active model knight, Geoffroi de Charny provides the ideal exemplar. Charny clearly found physical suffering inherent in the vigorous practice of knighthood to be spiritually meritorious. His denunciations of pampering the mere body through sloth, rich diet, plentiful sleep, or even stylish clothing would do credit to an

---

[67] Bryant, trans., *Perceforest*, 268.

[68] Wolfram virtually canonizes Willehalm, assuring every knight that he may call upon the hero and "be assured that he will never be denied it, but that Guillaume [his French name in Wolfram's source] will declare that same distress before God." Willehalm is a "noble intercessor" who "knows every sorrow which can befall a knight" and is said, in elaborate language, to know the martial technicalities of a lifetime in arms. Wolfram's invocation to him, calling out to him "as a saint" follows. Even love is termed one of the griefs suffered. Ibid., 18–19. He later describes his heroes as "purchasing a place in heaven," but soon adds that the rewards were twofold: the love of ladies on earth and the joys of heaven upon death. Ibid., 24. The rewards are specified often, perhaps most explicitly when (ibid., 185) Wolfram specifies that "the Christians suffered misery and gained the twofold reward. Noble ladies bestowed reward on those who came back alive, but those who died there went into those Hands which are able to grant payment above all other payment." The young Vivianz, dying in combat with non-Christians, takes on a similar role: "every knight can call upon God in the name of [his] martyrdom when he finds himself in distress!" Ibid., 38.

[69] Mustard and Passage, *Parzifal*, 97.

uncompromising monastic reformer. He is sure that as Lord of Hosts, God has ordained a knighthood in which "practice is hard, stressful and perilous to endure." But Charny knows that such suffering is essentially beneficial because it is the price to be paid for the glorious enterprise of prowess securing honor in this life and it provides a welcomed aid to salvation awaiting the good knights in the next. Men-at-arms accomplish all this

through suffering great hardship, making strenuous efforts, and enduring fearful physical perils and the loss of friends whose deaths they have witnessed in many great battles in which they have taken part; these experiences have often filled their hearts with great distress and strong emotions.

The constant effort must be physical and the suffering must be willingly endured, for, as he preaches to French knighthood,

If you want to continue to achieve great deeds, exert yourself, take up arms, fight as you should, go everywhere across both land and sea and through many different countries, without fearing any peril and without sparing your wretched body, which you should hold to be of little account, caring only for your soul and for living an honourable life.

Men-at-arms who perform their great deeds of prowess "to win God's grace (*pour avoir la grace de Dieu*)" and "for the salvation of their soul (*pour l'ame sauver*)," he is certain, "will be set in paradise to all eternity and their persons will be forever honored (*sont mises en paradis et sanz fin les corps touzjours mais honorez et rameneuz en touz biens*)." Piety pours forth in his prolix prose and his orthodoxy is undoubted, but he also indulges in some revealing jabs at the monks who emphasized merit won through constraints on their food and sleep, the hard hours spent on their knees in religious observances, and sexual abstinence. Charny proudly asserts that knighthood is the most rigorous order of all. As for the suffering of the religious,

this is all nothing in comparison with the suffering to be endured in the order of knighthood. For whoever might want to consider the hardships, pains, discomforts, fears, perils, broken bones and wounds which the good knights who uphold the order of knighthood as they should endure and have to suffer frequently, there is no religious order in which as much is suffered as has to be endured by these good knights who go in search of deeds of arms in the right way.[70]

---

[70] Kaeuper and Kennedy, *Book of Chivalry*, 174–175.

Suffering as a man-at-arms is not only spiritually meritorious; it is important enough to form the basis for spiritual competition among the orders constituting Christian society.[71]

Charny's views in no way represent some idiosyncratic or outlying strain of thought among knights. Henry, earl of Lancaster, his English contemporary (and knightly opponent in Anglo-French warfare) voiced similar thoughts and can usefully add another dimension to knightly ascetic piety. In his fervid devotional treatise, *Livre de seyntz medecines*, he wrote:

I pray you, Lord, for the love in which you took on human form, pardon my sins and watch over me, dearest Lord, that henceforth I be able to resemble you in some ways, if wretched food for worms such as I can resemble so noble a king as the king of heaven, earth, sea, and all that is in them. And if, dearest Lord, I have in this life any persecution for you touching body, possessions, or companions, or of any other sort, I pray, dearest Lord, that I may endure willingly for love of you, and since you, Lord, so willingly suffered such pains for me on earth, I pray, Lord, that I may resemble you insofar as I can find in my hard heart to suffer willingly for you such afflictions, labors, pains, as you choose and not merely to win a prize [*guerdon*] nor to offset my sins, but purely for love of you as you, Lord have done for love of me.[72]

Earl Henry wants to suffer in imitation of Christ's sacrificial suffering. In this intensely pious utterance he even claims a motive of pure mimetic love rather than advance of his personal redemption, though one can scarcely doubt that his hopes for heaven have been amplified by the endurance of suffering that he tirelessly mentions throughout his treatise.

Chivalric literature in general sings the same tune. Wolfram's hero Willehalm knows he is suffering the future pains of purgatory as he sees his faithful men killed in battle against pagans and thinks longingly of his wife even on the battlefield.[73] In the pages of epic and romance, troops of pale hermits (many of them former knights now

---

[71] A classic debate about chivalric and clerical orders appears in the second redaction of the *Moniage Guillaume*, written around 1180; it includes a claim that a good knight can save himself in his own order. See Wilhelm Cloetta, ed., *Moniage Guillaume: Les deux redactions en vers du Moniage Guillaume* (Paris: Firmin-Didot, 1906). I hope to work with specialists in Old French literature on a new edition and English translation of this second redaction of "William in the Monastery."

[72] Henry of Lancaster, *Livre de seyntz medecines*, ed. E. J. Arnould (Oxford University Press, 1944), my translation.

[73] Gibbs and Johnson, *Willehalm*, 39. Vivianz thinks any showing of cowardice will damage his soul. Ibid., 47.

living in puritanical austerity in the woods) aid and guide knights; over a little barley soup they may interpret dreams, give counsel on moral issues, even (after the thin soup) provide penitential discipline – all made possible and valid by their lives of abstention and simplicity. Some of these ascetic heroes lived and carried out at least some such work in the very real world.[74]

Of yet more basic importance, the blood-red thread of knightly asceticism that can be traced throughout the vast fabric of imaginative chivalric literature presents knightly suffering as a licit form of penance. The very occupation that brings the knights into spiritual danger provides them with a physical mechanism for spiritual atonement. Out of the vast body of evidence in both epic and romance only a handful of examples must suffice to illustrate the suffering of men-at-arms on campaign and in battle serving as a form of enacted penance.[75] Warriors in the *Song of Roland* are told by Archbishop Turpin that he assigns them only one penance for their sins, "to strike (*ferir*)"; and Duke Girart is told in *The Song of Aspremont* that he should do penance with his sword for the terrible sins he has committed as a warrior.[76] In the latter epic a knight named Godfroi speaks the theme concisely when he is asked to carry a relic of the true cross into battle; though an honor, it will inhibit his capacity to fight fully, so he responds, "Why should I not strike mighty blows for Jesus / and pay to God the debt of all believers?"[77] Of warriors on the ghastly battle-field of the Archamp in the *Song of William*, the poet says, "St Stephen and the other martyrs were no better than all of those who died for God in the Archamp."[78] The *History of the Holy Grail* (the opening

---

[74] Discussed in R. W. Kaeuper, *Holy Warriors*, passim, and Angus Kennedy, "The Hermit's Role in French Arthurian Romance," *Romania* 95 (1974).

[75] This theme is extensively developed in R. W. Kaeuper, *Holy Warriors*.

[76] In the *Song of Roland* Turpin's assignment of penance comes at the end of laisse 89, which also refers to the warriors as martyrs. For the injunction to Girart, see Newth, trans., *The Song of Aspremont*, lines 1447–1450. In the German *Song of Roland* the penance is said to be all the heathens the knights can kill. Thompson, trans., *Priest Konrad's Song of Roland*, 55.

[77] Newth, trans., *Song of Aspremont*, Louis Brandin, ed., *Chanson d'Aspremont* (Paris, 1970), lines 3969–3971: "Je n'irai par ma foi. / Armes ai bones et ceval a mon qoi; / Jo nel la'rai que grans cols n'i employ / Et rendrai Deu tot ce que je li doi; / M'armes et mon cors quitement li otroi/."

[78] Ibid., laisse 44. The quotation appears at lines 545–548: "Car saint Estephne ne les alters martirs / ne furent mieldres que serrunt tut icil / Qui en Larchamp serrunt pur Deu ocis!"

romance in the *Lancelot-Grail* cycle) declares that "the good . . . will undertake to suffer the difficult burden of earthly exploits of chivalry in order to learn about the marvels of the Holy Grail and the lance."[79] Arthur, in the *Alliterative Morte Arthure*, assures his men that following death in righteous battle their souls will reach the gates of heaven before their bodies are half cold. A veritable religion of combat infuses all these works, based on a knightly asceticism of meritorious suffering. Recognizing this bond of the redemptively sacred with the physicality of chivalry is essential.

Of course there were limits; clerics, however willing to valorize good combat, always wanted to assert the superiority of their *ordo*. Guibert of Nogent, among others, happily and proudly tells stories of such conversions.[80] Caesar of Heisterbach's treatise allows us to visualize one spectacular instance in which a renowned German warrior rode fully armed upon his great warhorse up to the high altar of a monastic church, there to leave the world and enter the cloister.[81] The funeral of Bertrand du Guesclin brought no fewer than eight warhorses into an abbey church.[82] Even if seldom described so visually, many such conversions took place. They could not come soon enough from a clerical perspective, and the miracle stories they wrote repeatedly warned that counting on such last-minute measures incurred eternal risk; violating such a commitment was even more risky.[83] Pious impulses stood behind all such foundations, donations, and conversions; they suggest how thin and bereft a picture is purveyed by a purely negative conception of religion on the part of warriors.

THEOLOGICAL CONSTRUCTS AS CHIVALRIC BUTTRESSES

Though clerics may sometimes have been of two minds, elements of chivalric religious valorization fit together like pieces of a puzzle.

---

[79] *Lancelot-Grail*, vol. 1, 51.
[80] John F. Benton, ed., *Self and Society in Medieval France: The Memoirs of Abbot Guibert of Nogent* (University of Toronto Press, 1985).
[81] Caesar of Heisterbach, *Dialogue on Miracles*, trans. H. von F. Scott and C. C. Swindon (London: Routledge, 1929), I: 45–46. The knight is Waleran, joining a Cistercian house.
[82] Information cited in Malcolm Vale, *War and Chivalry*, 92.
[83] E.g., the story "How William Mauvoisin Became a Monk," told by the Benedictine monks of Notre Dame of Coulombs: *Recueil des historiens des Gaules et de la France*, 14: 245–246.

We can appreciate the constructive strength of these bonds by examining three particular yet fundamental lines of thought under discussion in the era when classic chivalry emerged. In each case, ideas swirling around a theological view still in the process of formation were creatively adapted and forged into valorizing links between chivalry and religion. Whatever the precedents, they appear clearly in the central, classic phase of the emergence of chivalry and continued their development into the later Middle Ages. Though complete uniformity of clerical opinion on major issues is sometimes imagined, it is seldom encountered. On some weighty issues, religious doctrine was only coming to clear formulation. This very diversity of clerical views opened windows of opportunity for knights and their clerical allies; they could choose a position or, more commonly as we will see, could draw strength from both sides of the issue. Such flexibility was crucially important to them, for it allowed their characteristic selective borrowing and adaptation to protect chivalric status and vigorous professional labor. The process will be examined through three basic religious concepts: soteriology (the explanation of how Christ brought salvation to humankind), the role of human labor in the divine plan for the world, and the sacramental system based on confession and penance.

Soteriology

Among many theological concepts under construction in the central Middle Ages, even so fundamental an issue as the precise manner in which Christ ensured human salvation remained at issue.[84] Either of two theological views could be emphasized. From one perspective, Christ could be conceived as a warrior who had come to Earth to conquer Satan and rescue humanity from his foul dominion that would condemn them to an eternity in hellfire. Parzival is told by the hermit bringing about his repentance, "Since He was once a man, and true, and fought against all that was false, you should make your peace with Him."[85] In some of the many variants as a master strategist, he even wears armor made of human flesh to trick the Devil into the fatal misstep of jousting with God's son. Continuing the chivalric tone, the church may be pictured as his lady, loyally awaiting his

---

[84] Discussed in detail in R. W. Kaeuper, *Holy Warriors*, 116–131.
[85] Mustard and Passage, *Parzival*, 249.

return in triumph after a merely mortal and temporary demise in combat. Such imagery would obviously appeal to knighthood, which could identify with a heroic warrior image of Christ and identify as well with his victory over an evil enemy force.

Yet, in another perspective (classically formulated by Anselm of Bec at the turn of the twelfth century), Christ appears rather as the "suffering servant" who gave his life for mankind, not through martial combat, but in willing sacrifice, personally paying the vast human debt for sin and reconciling fallen humanity with divine love. With only a slightly greater stretch, knighthood linked its mission with this theological theme as well. Figures in *chansons de geste* readily cry out that Christ has died for his men and so they, too, must give their lives for their men in righteous fighting. Duke Girart, here the voice of orthodoxy, states the principle concisely in the *Song of Aspremont*. Reflecting on the death of so many good fighters, he addresses Christ, concluding that "here is the only homily to be drawn; / You died for us and we should die for your sake."[86] Wolfram von Eschenbach elaborates the theme in a speech given to the great knight Bertram of Berbester:

It was never right for a noble man to turn from fame... Now, heroes, remember that you have endured suffering to gain much fame in France. If you forsake the Marquis [Willehalm or William of Orange] now, when he is in such dire straits, this will not match the intention of the lady of any one of you. I know, too, that He will hate you for this who on the Day of Judgement will come forward bearing in His mouth the sword... If only we may behold the five wounds [of Christ] which are still open! He shed his blood for us... His flesh and blood gained blessing for us, He who came riding with no thought of flight... He accepted death for our sake.[87]

The poet gives Willehalm an even clearer statement on knightly atonement late in the text bearing his name. As he grieves over the loss of his men in battle, the great hero calls upon God as the Highest (Altissimus):

O God, if You have pity, may all the angels in Your company recognize my loss! Let this be my purgatory, since my bodily joy is dead for ever more. Altissimus, since the heathens have given me such pain, keep me from losing

---

[86] Brandin, *Chanson d'Aspremont*, lines 476–477; my translation, slightly modifying that of Newth, *Song of Aspremont*.

[87] Gibbs and Johnson, *Willehalm*, 154. Shortly after this speech comes the much more famous view of Willehalm's wife Giburc (ibid., 155–159). Her views have been discussed earlier.

You on Judgment Day and from the eternal lament that You do not turn aside! May Your mercy send me such consolation that my soul shall be freed from its bonds![88]

In the Old French *Song of William*, Vivien at first invokes the aid of the Blessed Virgin to escape death on the battlefield; but quickly repenting such weakness, he blames himself for "thinking that I could save myself from death, when the Lord God Himself didn't do it, suffering death for us on the Holy Cross to redeem us from our mortal enemies. Respite from death, Lord, I may not pray for, since You would not spare Yourself from it."[89] Earthly warriors fight and triumph in imitation of the warrior Christ, but they also suffer in imitation of the willing servant who sacrificed himself. In the German *Rolandslied* or *Song of Roland* Archbishop Turpin instructs crusading knights that they are martyrs "following their Creator, Whose death had set them an example," adding that "His holy humility led him to redeem men and women by allowing Himself to be nailed to the cross."[90] Such imaginative linking of the knight with Christ speaks with special clarity to the fusion of chivalry with fundamental religious ideals. The complex and symbolic romance *Perlesvaus* clearly endorses the formula:

There are no knightly deeds so fine as those done for the advancement of the Law of God, and we should toil for Him more than anyone, for just as He exposed His body to pain and suffering and destruction for us, so must every man risk his body for Him.[91]

This theme appears in chronicle as well as epic and romance. Geoffrey of Monmouth's *History of the Kings of Britain* gives a speech to Bishop Dubricius addressed to King Arthur and his court:

---

[88] Gibbs and Johnson, *Willehalm*, 220.
[89] Francois Suard, *Chanson de Guillaume* (Paris: Bordas, 1991), lines 818–824.
[90] Thompson, trans., *Priest Konrad's Song of Roland*, 73. Yet when Roland, speaking to his sword, Durendal (a gift from heaven), lists the conquests he has achieved with it, the list includes Christian lands won for the emperor, and not merely crusading enterprises. See ibid., 84. In short, what the poet considers virtuous fighting spreads beyond holy war, or perhaps engulfs all fighting by the hero in that sanctified category.
[91] Nigel Bryant, trans., *High Book of the Grail: Perlesvaus* (Ipswich: Brewer, 1978), 238; William Nitze and T. A. Jenkins, ed., *Le Haut Livre du Graal: Perlesvaus* (Chicago, 1932, 368): "il n'est nul si bele chevalerie come cele est que l'on fait por la loi Deu essaucier, e por lui se doit l'on miex pener que por toz les autres; autresi com il mist son cors en paine e en travaill e en exill por nos, si doit chascuns le sien metre por lui."

The Sacred text teaches that Christ laid down his soul at His enemy's feet for our sake: lay down your soul for Christ's limbs, which are being torn by the insanely motivated tyranny of the Saxon people... To the just man death brings glory, to the sinner eternal punishment... He who has fought the good fight will be given a crown in recompense... Reverence is owed to martyrs along with Christ, Himself a martyr, to Whom be glory, power and honour for all time.[92]

Joinville, in his firsthand narrative of the first crusade of Louis IX of France, admiringly writes, "as our Lord died for the love He bore His people, even so King Louis put his own life in danger . . . for the very same reason."[93]

In short, a chivalric ideal could draw on both theological streams explaining soteriology. Through their hard feats of arms, the elite warriors triumphed over evil as Christ had done; and like him they willingly enacted the role of suffering servants, enduring much travail and even sacrificing their lives. Christ's suffering and victory, combined in his Passion, became a model for knightly endurance and victory.

Labor

Though we may not associate knights, swords, and lances with labor,[94] chivalric sources tirelessly speak of the hard work performed by knights. Since it had been assigned to them by divine will, the nature of knightly labor was crucial to their self-conception. They would draw on current discussions about human labor in general, which were likewise under intense theological scrutiny as chivalry matured. Again, as with soteriology, two main lines of thought contended. From one stern viewpoint, labor had been imposed on humans as punishment for sin and possessed no inherent redeeming quality. Manual labor posed particular issues for knighthood, as it bore a distinct social stigma. With smooth hands free from telltale calluses, clerics, the other

---

[92] Neil Wright, *The Historia Regum Britanniae of Geoffrey of Monmouth*, 5 vols. (Cambridge, 1984–1991), V, 182–185 (facing page, Latin text and English translation).

[93] Shaw, trans., *Joinville*, 167; Natalis deWailly, ed., *Histoire de Saint Louis* (Paris: Renouard, 1868), 7: "aussi comme Diex morut pour l'amour qu'il avoit en son peuple, mist-il son cors en avanture par plusieurs fois pour l'amour qu'il avoit à son peuple."

[94] Discussed in more detail in R. W. Kaeuper, *Holy Warriors*, 131–167.

major elite order, elevated the host in the climax of the Mass; with the same hands they dipped pens into inkwells and wrote sacred words on costly parchment. Could the knights whose hands gripped weapons claim immunity from the social stigma of truly physical hands-on work? Could their hard labors, in which they took such pride, be characterized as punishment for sin?

In another view of labor under discussion, human work could be patterned on the work God did in glorious creation of the world; he had, what is more, assigned the honorable labor of tending the garden to Adam and Eve even before sin darkened creation. Labor thus had, in this view, genuine value. The world was, in fact, organized into many socio-professional orders, each with a characteristic labor given it by God. Each group had to accept its assignment. The list of such *ordines* varied with the writer and gradually grew longer, with groups multiplying well beyond the traditional three – the clerics, warriors, and common laborers. Those who pray, those who fight, and those who work were cogs in the great machine of the divine plan, and all had to do their part. Doing so was not punishment, but acceptance of order, even a movement toward salvation while carrying out their assignments, whatever their particular form.

Again, all the lines of thought – if carefully modulated – could be appealing to knighthood, for they could consider the labor assigned them to be both penitential in its difficulties, hardships, and dangers and redemptive in that their performance of it defined them as one of the elite orders within the divine plan. Ordinary laborers simply endured hard work, achieving some merit by humbly enduring. Suffering was generally considered spiritually meritorious. But the great majority of people were socially stained by the soil they tilled, the cloth they dyed, or the leather they worked. It was far different for the knighthood, for if rough campaigning and hand-to-hand fighting featured truly physical toil, even manual labor, its practice elevated them socially and secured their dominance while increasing their wealth and glory. Their hardened fists grasped sword and lance, and with them they did the labor God had assigned them, using the bodies he had endowed with great physical capacities. William Marshal's biographer outlined several of these themes, observing,

> What is armed combat? Is it the same
> as working with a sieve or winnow,
> with an axe or mallet?
> Not at all, it is much nobler work,

for he who undertakes these tasks is able to take a rest
when he has worked for a while.
What, then is chivalry?
Such a difficult, tough,
and very costly thing to learn
that no coward ventures to take it on.[95]

The exceptional labor of knighthood links its nobility with its difficulties; there is no respite, and the physical demands and dangers deter
all cowards. Pointedly, Charny notes that clerics are approached by
those who want to honor them and learn from them, but the knights
are confronted by those who wish to dismember or kill them and rob
them of everything, including honor.[96]

In the process of their labors, of course, the arms bearers maintained elite status and sustained it with the booty that licitly came to
good fighters. And through suffering, hard campaigning, wounds,
fears, or even death, they repaid some part of the debt owed to God
for sin. Reducing that debt in this world was wise policy; suffering the
torments of sinners in the next world would be a vastly more grim
prospect. As Henry of Lancaster observed in a combination of piety
and frankness, the atonement of knighthood meant a tough life, but
ultimately represented a good deal (*un bon marchandise*).[97]

Confession and penance

Perhaps the sacramental system of confession and penance[98] best
shows the knightly degree of independence no less than its selectivity
and adaptation of important theological ideas. Characteristically, the
knights both incorporated what they found most helpful from current
theological discussion and adapted it to fit chivalric needs or norms.
Within the traditional physicality of the general medieval system of
atonement, the warriors found conceptions that they could readily
understand and imaginatively infuse into their pious practice; for an
old tradition from the early medieval church often specified that
penance take the form of a dramatic act of great physicality, publicly
performed. In the process, these sinners had sometimes been set apart
as a distinct group. The meritorious suffering of knights as divinely

[95] *History of William Marshal*, lines 16853–16863.
[96] Kaeuper and Kennedy, *Book of Chivalry*, 180–183.
[97] *Livre de Seyntz Medecines*, 97.
[98] Discussed in detail in R. W. Kaeuper, *Holy Warriors*, 167–194.

endowed fighters in righteous causes fit into this tradition of heroic
atonement as easily as a hand slipped into a mailed glove. At least they
could understand difficult and dangerous pilgrimages or the rigors of
fasting as feats of penance, close cousins perhaps to their own prized
feats of arms; sexual abstinence would scarcely be so acceptable, and
beating with rods might not appeal (though it served Henry II after
Becket's murder).

There was a tradition of arranging penance for warriors following
significant military service. From the late Carolingian period, sins
committed during major military campaigns were often confessed
and penance assigned by formal arrangements involving the armed
force as a whole; the participating warriors, in effect, were cleansed by
a program supervised by leading clerics. Battlefield killing seems to
have been the focus, though a scale of penances for other wartime sins
could be provided in an effort to make the punishment fit the crime.
A late example of just such a set of penances was overseen in
1067–1070 by Norman bishops after their Duke William and his
men had conquered England. But this is a late example and the
phenomenon seems to have waned by the end of the eleventh
century; this concept of practice does not appear in the great canon
law book of Gratian, c. 1140.

A renewed lay theology based on confession and penance occupied the thoughts of reformers first gathered in the cathedral community of Laon and then in Paris, where Peter the Chanter stood at
the center of the effort. This group, closely and classically studied by
John Baldwin, worked vigorously at a range of basic issues in lay life,
including the practice of warfare and its inseparable links with tournament and even the dangers posed by money.[99] These clerics
wanted to provide guidance for lay life as it had to be lived amidst
the hubbub of temptations in daily life, including the clink of coins
and the shouts of battle. Elite arms bearers, that is, were included no
less than other lay folk as reformers picked up a broadly reforming
thread from the Gregorian reform of a century earlier; producing
right order in the world required the infusion of Christian principles
into society.

One high point of their work appeared in the legislation by the
Fourth Lateran Council of 1215, in which article 21 significantly

[99] John W. Baldwin, *Masters, Princes and Merchants* (Princeton University Press,
1970), passim, esp. 205–228.

mandated annual confession and penance for all adult Christians. Preaching tours were organized and handy manuals were produced for parish priests who were expected to serve in the forefront of the effort. Though knighthood was only one segment of the population affected, it represented the lay elite possessed of much power and influence and a vocation that was undoubtedly necessary but confronted with seemingly endless moral and social dangers. A renewed emphasis on a sacramental system with regular inspection of conscience, confession of sins to a priest, and penance assigned, might, it was hoped, prove highly effective as pastoral care and amelioration of social problems. Recognition of personal wrongdoing and acceptance of divine grace through the mediation of the church would ideally bring all of society closer to the model intended in the divine plan.

Elite arms bearers managed to combine old and new features of the sacramental system based on confession and penance. If they accepted newer views of repeated penitential acts, they could view them through a lens unique to their *ordo*: as we have seen, men-at-arms could claim that in an adult lifetime of professional campaign and combat they repeatedly performed penitential acts. The professional labor God expected of them was a form of physical and heroic penance, repeatedly endured, that earned spiritual merit to offset punishment for sin. On campaign they slept rough, ate badly, had to travel dangerously by land and especially on the uncertain sea, and finally fought hard, risking and enduring grievous wounds or even sudden death. Exactly how such penance enacted through professional labor would fit within the ecclesiastical system was unclear.

Indeed, how readily proud and independent knighthood would accept the full implications of the system of confession and penance remained unclear. The knights were instructed that they, in common with all other Christians throughout Europe, must, at a minimum, annually examine their conduct and feel and express contrition for all sins committed. As for all sinners, weeping was encouraged. The men-at-arms were required to confess their wrongs humbly to their parish priest, who would declare God's forgiveness to them and assign appropriate (and usually nonheroic) penance that they were faithfully to perform. The manuals composed to aid priests/confessors sometimes suggested helpful questions to be posed to the various ranks of society. The list of issues raised could include pillage, extortion, oppression of their tenants, attacks on churchmen, burning of churches, participating in tournaments, encouraging warfare, and killing in battle.[100] Such specific inquiries and the general process raise the obvious question of how proud and socially dominant warriors would receive such mandates as central elements of the economy of salvation.

In seeking answers, we are brought back to the romantic and cynical extremes outlined earlier. Again avoiding extremes, a case can be made that simple and humble acceptance is as unlikely as utter rejection. Characteristically, the knights may have accommodated the new system on terms that they could accept. To understand knightly caution, we must picture the likely scene as confession was made and penance assigned. No confessional boxes existed in the Middle Ages to provide privacy. The penitent sinner – the knight, no less than the cobbler who repaired his boots – was expected to kneel before the seated confessor and then whisper his grievous sins into the priest's ear. Only the broad hood circling the priest's head provided a degree of privacy, and the parish church was the likely space for this humbling ritual. Little imagination is needed to picture a queue of waiting sinners straining to hear whether their lord mentioned that night with the shepherdess that was the talk of the village or the terrible incident in his last raid when the wind shifted so that many dwellings were consumed in flames. Was the local church thus cleared of ordinary sinners so that the lord and his family might mutter their sins in privacy? Our evidence is sadly sparse, but this option seems at least likely. For members of the knightly elite who could afford it, keeping a household chaplain would be an attractive option; he not only could perform routine religious and educational services, but would be willing to hear private confession in the chapel built into the castle structure or standing adjacent to the manorial hall. Wearing his lord's livery, might he not seem all the more suitable an agent of the process for neutralizing sin and assigning penance at an elevated social level? Such a man might be more sensitive to chivalric pride and less likely to spread what he had heard, theoretically spoken to him in confidence.

---

[100] See the *Liber Poenitentialis* of Robert of Flamborough, ed. J. Frances Firth (Toronto: Pontifical Institute, 1971), 134, 185, 226–227; *Summa Poetentia* of Ramond de Peñaforte (1224–1226), quoted in Peter Biller's introduction to Biller and Minnis, *Handling Sin*, 17; and, from mid-fourteenth century, *Memoriales Presbitorum* in Michael Haren, *Sin and Society in Fourteenth-Century England*, 119–124.

The romantic assumption will hold that such measures were unnecessary, since knights must have acted the role of obedient parishioners; but the evidence of a series of exempla reinforces the contrary case. Regularly and with urgency clerics pressed upon knighthood the need for confession to a priest and acceptance of penance assigned. It is hard not to draw from this telling, if indirect, evidence that the knights were seen as reluctant and troublesome participants in this sacramental system. Evidently they required convincing. The very scale and persistence of this effort calibrate the knightly reluctance. Exempla intended for use in sermons and books of moral tales pointedly praise the spiritual efficacy of the sacrament and give dire warnings of the consequences of disregarding it. Knights are reminded that death can strike them down at any moment and that they must be prepared to face a great accounting. Stretching a point revealingly, some clerical stories even assure knights that one who has confessed will do better in his next tournament. Dead knights return in visions to urge their living comrades to practice confession and perform the penance set by a priest.[101] Clerics evidently knew it would be a challenge to gain full knightly cooperation; handbooks prepared for confessors even suggest a bargaining process by which the confessor can identify a penance that the reluctant knight will accept and actually perform. In miracle stories these techniques are said to work, bringing decidedly reluctant knights into the process.[102]

In sum, it seems likely that chivalric ideas accommodated to the new lay theology by making good fighting a form of penance that was repeated through a hard life, but that the chivalrous only slowly and somewhat reluctantly could be brought routinely to confess to a priest as their social inferiors were doing more commonly. The remarkable blend of piety and independence that we see here characterized the overall dialogue between chivalry and religion and helps us to understand how chivalry can be interpreted as one of the significant exemplars of lay piety within medieval Christendom.

---

[101] Discussed, with many examples provided, in Kaeuper, *Holy Warriors*, 129–164. A classic case of a moral tale featuring confession appears in *Le Chevalier au Barisel: conte pieuse du XIIIe siècle*, ed. Félix Lecoy (Paris: Champion, 1955).

[102] Numerous examples are discussed and cited in R. W. Kaeuper, *Holy Warriors*, 167–194.

CONCLUSION: CHIVALRY AS A SPECIES OF LAY PIETY

As admirable scholarship has emphasized, multiple forms of lay piety lived within the overarching framework of medieval Christianity.[103] A part of the vitality of medieval religion, it can be argued, came from various social and professional groups crafting elements of the common religion into particular configurations to meet their specific needs. Other scholarship objects, asserting that multiple forms of medieval piety are a myth; clerical direction secured essential uniformity of thought and practice throughout medieval society. Yet specific forms of piety seem manifestly at work within specific elements of the lay population; with considerable fervor, these groups often formed around professions and sought religious valorization and guidance. These impulses gave special religious dimensions to an expanding set of guilds and lay confraternities. Piety flourished among Waldensians, Beghards and Beguines, and Brethren of the Common Life.[104] Many individual mystics played prominent roles. Sometimes this religious enthusiasm steered within orthodox limits; sometimes it generated clashes with orthodoxy, as is well known.[105] A variety of conceptions were declared heresies, such as the Poor Men of Lyon. But views considered orthodox also sprouted like mushrooms in soil enriched by religious, cultural, and socioeconomic changes, especially from the twelfth century. Humiliati and the original followers of Francis of Assisi carefully guarded their

---

[103] Recent studies on lay piety in general, with a focus on the later Middle Ages, include Mark D. Johnston, *Evangelical Rhetoric of Ramon Llull: Lay Learning and Piety in the Christian West around 1300* (Oxford University Press, 1996); Ulrica Hascher-Burger, *Between Lay Piety and Academic Theology* (Leiden: Brill, 2011); Ronald K. Rittgers, *The Reformation of Suffering: Pastoral Theology and Lay Piety in Late Medieval and Early Modern Germany* (Oxford University Press, 2012); Derek Rivard, *Blessing the World: Ritual and Lay Piety in Medieval Religion* (Washington, DC: Catholic University of America Press, 2009).

[104] Tanya Stabler, *Beguines of Medieval Paris* (Philadelphia: University of Pennsylvania Press, 2014); Dayton Phelps, *Beguines of Medieval Strassbourg* (Stanford University Press, 1995); John H. Van Engen, *Sisters and Brothers of the Common Life: the Devotio Moderna and the World of the Later Middle Ages* (Philadelphia: University of Pennsylvania Press, 2008); Robert E. Lerner, *The Heresy of the Free Spirit in the Later Middle Ages* (Berkeley: University of California Press, 1972).

[105] R. I. Moore, *The Formation of a Persecuting Society: Authority and Deviance in Western Europe, 950–1250* (Malden, MA: Blackwell, 2007); Peter A. Dykema and Heiko Oberman, eds., *Anti-Clericalism in Late Medieval and Early Modern Europe* (Leiden: Brill, 1993).

relationship with clerical authority, to be joined by lay groups clustered around orders of friars and even around their houses.

Despite all its particular differences from such groups, the knighthood can reasonably be situated within that broad tradition of lay piety that sought a variety of religious experience to meet certain needs without any desire openly to contest the religious authority of the clerical hierarchy. Of course much in knightly piety mirrored the common currency of medieval religious life and thought, as we have seen. Yet the knights constituted the most socially elevated manifestations of pious lay groups requiring particular religious expression and valorization. The work God had given them was especially demanding and dangerous. They defended Christendom and proudly enforced true religion with their swords. Despite unsurprising bursts of anticlericalism, their piety was substantial and took shape in close cooperation with clerical allies. As we have seen, they drew intensely upon values and ideals that were deeply religious but not closely restraining of their characteristic work. As *bellatores* within the divine plan, elite arms bearers were certain they needed and should have special consideration, even in spiritual terms. Their crucial degree of independence was buttressed by a conviction that God (and the Blessed Virgin, surrounded by the entire heavenly court) stood behind their profession with appropriate favor and gracious understanding. This support sustained confidence as they happily absorbed – or creatively reconstructed – basic moral guidelines offered by clerics for their hard profession. In effect, they incorporated all praise lavished on them, but listened to critiques through a dense filter of confident professionalism that they considered a secure part of their piety. Even at first glance we can recognize their disregard of some elements of clerical criticism or templates for reform (e.g., denunciations of tournament) and their acceptance of others (e.g., the spiritual merits of ascetic practice). Their working ideals achieved the requisite result.

All elite arms bearers came to be quite certain, as their status rose, that they were essentially different from the mass of peasants, prospering merchants, or even the hosts of monks and secular clergy; they could not simply hold the exact views or find full satisfaction in the religious practices that suited craftsmen in the growing towns or the masses walking behind oxen in muddy fields. They were socially elite professional fighters and both characterizations made a crucial difference. However much certain beliefs and religious rites touched all medieval Christians, some particular beliefs and practices of arms bearers would have to be accommodated. Within an overarching framework, specific forms of lay piety had to address these unique dimensions of their lives. Theirs was a highly particular variant of lay piety, formed by a remarkable combination of religious ideals, willingly absorbed, with lines of thought specific to warriors that were energized and enabled by their generous degree of independence; the fusion of these elements formed the crucial religious dimension of chivalry.

If a theology of ascetic atonement has not been routinely featured in the study of medieval chivalry, it helps us to understand chivalry as a species of lay piety. However hardheaded and pragmatic the arms bearers may have been, they found this religious valorization eminently practical. Living within an intensely religious society with richly complex ideas about sanctity and asceticism, violence and war, they needed to be as sure that God awarded success or failure in the present life as they knew a fearsome balancing of accounts came in an afterlife just beyond the grave. Of course the specific framework of their piety buttressed their status and blessed their profession of fighting (whatever cautions theoretically applied); and it spoke reassurance in the most potent terms and concepts of the age. If finding some flexible bond to link religion and licit violence constitutes a challenge common to all ages, the solution in the age of chivalry came through warrior adaption, appropriation, and even re-creation of specifically medieval religious elements, shaped to meet warrior needs.

Religious justification for the order of fighters became significant features of medieval society. Pacific efforts of some leading clerics and earnest goals of revered saints could scarcely limit and obviously could not prevent ceaseless warfare in which elite knights claimed to be following Christ in meritorious suffering no less than glorious triumph. That Christ could be transformed into a warrior suggests how powerfully major religious ideals then under construction could be co-opted for the military elite. Perhaps from a modern perspective this transformation seems to turn basic spiritual principles such as forgiveness and humility upside down. Any castigation makes little sense when directed from a safe distance of modernity; but scholarly recognition of ideals, practices, and their consequences in that long-gone world remains a necessity. Religious elements of chivalric ideology could have worked as well as they did and for as long as they did only by resting upon sturdy paradoxes that could fit abstract religious principles into a world full of threats and dangers. If hard campaigning and fighting constituted penitential labor for the knights, widespread devastation and costly battle could scarcely be uniformly denounced as sinful. Knightly manual labor did not degrade its practitioners, but, while enacting penance, it assured their envied status and enabled the amassing of the loot that sustained it. Claims for the subknightly humble and downtrodden could be deftly brushed aside by elite warriors who proudly combined worldly social dominance with claims to heavenly honor well earned.

Part V

THE WORLD OF CHIVALRIC EMOTIONS

Modern cinematic audiences must feel they understand knightly emotions. The righteous wrath of knights fills screens with a swirl of bodies, blades, and blood. In fact, "getting medieval" on someone has come, in common parlance, to suggest unrestrained violence fueled by equally unrestrained emotions. Yet from another angle and with little sense of contradiction, the imagined chivalrous show deliciously amorous sensitivity; with hearts thumping in ample chests, they speak soft, poetic lines about intense feelings of love, or perhaps even sing them with lute accompaniment, to demure ladies on balconies. Although usually strong, silent types, when standing tall amidst a courtly audience the knights express finely felt pride in birth and accomplishment, or project outrage at any imputed dishonor, employing elaborate speech, with dramatic gestures to match.

Such popular views can claim at least some historical merit, catching a panoply of intense emotions that infused chivalric thought and actions. Distinct traces of such feelings and consequent actions appear throughout a wide range of sources, from narratives within chronicles to vividly dramatic scenes in imaginative literature. All this evidence presents displays of intense emotions that accompanied important occasions and conveyed or enhanced their meanings.

Yet popular books and films assume that our medieval forebears were in essential ways and at all times and social levels just like us. Is this not how they appear in popular media? Their costumes may be more dashing and colorful, their speech charmingly quaint, but their emotions appear simply cut along lines of an eternal pattern. From such an ahistorical viewpoint, any questions about medieval emotions simply self-destruct. Why should emotions among the chivalric elite require any special focus when we can look within ourselves and understand all?

In fact, medieval evidence contradicts this common line of thought. Even if some broad affective human traits appear in every era, the relative importance of particular emotions and their embodiment in social roles and relationships have surely varied. A modern emotional template cannot be force fit upon medieval society in general or on the knights in particular. Contrary to the modern commitment to casualness and informality (coupled with at least theoretical egalitarianism), medieval emotions proudly operated in formal and heroic mode and in the service of social, political, and religious hierarchy. Speech best conveyed meaning and secured assent when delivered in the high style; actions that were formally dignified and dramatically presented best secured results. In the modern world, social media may seem to enact social life on a limitless virtual stage, each player providing, in theory, his or her own script. Medieval social life necessarily took place face-to-face on a local or regional stage, with a distinct hierarchy of actors, and with every word and gesture, every sword stroke watched closely and critically. These players knew how key emotions worked as they practiced or submitted to power relationships that were sometimes balanced on a knife edge.

We can step at once into that medieval emotional world by noting that the knightly self-image included remarkably nonmodern, frequent, and copious bouts of weeping, along with fainting spells. Clearly vigorous and dominant warriors saw refined behavior in such actions. Though these displays might seem "feminized" behavior in other ages, they are pictured in the age of chivalry as consequences of refined, elite male emotional makeup. Before dismissing such images out of hand as picturesque nonsense, we might recall scenes related by the mid-fourteenth-century chronicler Jean le Bel. In one, his patron, Jean of Hainault, "began to weep fervent tears of pity" when he learned of the exile of Queen Isabella and her young son, Edward III.[1] Similarly, any arms bearers, he tells us, wept for pity when Edward III initially threatened to hang leading burgers of

---

[1] Nigel Bryant, ed., trans., *The True Chronicles of Jean le Bel*, 68.

a surrendered Calais.[2] Vivid scenes might also be recalled from the biography of William Marshal, written more than a century earlier. As the Young King, son of Henry II, lay dying, the poet muses that "if tears were of any avail, [he] might have better expectations of recovery" for "never had God brought into the world a knight so worthy to be mourned."[3] The account of William's own death features similar weeping. His wife and daughters had to be escorted from the chamber, but William's son and all the knights remained present, sobbing tears of sorrow.[4]

Of course great joy could produce similarly emotional scenes, as could fearful concern. Richard I, ransomed and returned from crusade, was met with tears of gladness.[5] When some of William Marshal's men in Ireland were confronted with charges of disloyalty, they "wept pitifully" and sought his forgiveness symbolized by the kiss of peace.[6] Yet the most emotional scene occurred as the Marshal shouldered responsibility for the young lad who had just become King Henry III and was faced with great dangers. Little Henry wept, the Marshal wept, and all present wept tears of compassion. William's heart is said to overflow, with tears streaming down his face.[7] Emotional equivalents of rain gauges for calibrating historical tear production are hard to come by, and smelling salts may not have been carried in each suit of armor, but the idealization of refined and powerful emotions remains significant. In the perceptive words of Dorothy Sayers,

There are fashions in sensibility as in everything else. The idea that a strong man should react to great personal and national calamities by a slight compression of the lips and by silently throwing his cigarette into the fireplace is of very recent origin.[8]

Even the greatest heroes in medieval imaginative literature not only sob, but drop senseless to the ground, as does King Arthur himself. The death of beloved companions may bring repeated episodes of fainting to the great king, especially late in his story as his band of heroes is diminished.[9] "In his sorrow he said that he had lived too long when he saw that

---

[2] Ibid., 202.   [3] *History of William Marshal*, lines 6916–6919.
[4] Ibid., lines 18261–18287. Unsurprisingly, the servants, too, are in tears, but the significant display of emotion on the part of knights retains significance.
[5] Ibid., lines 10015–10016.
[6] Ibid., lines 14005–14015. Cf. ibid., lines 14077–14083, 14124–14125.
[7] Ibid., lines 15281–15284, 15647–15652.
[8] Sayers, trans., *The Song of Roland* (Baltimore, 1966), 15.
[9] *Lancelot-Grail*, IV, *Death of King Arthur*, 148.

those whom he had nurtured had died a terrible death."[10] Even the nearly suprahuman Charlemagne faints at the appropriate moment.[11] Individually and collectively, knights are repeatedly imagined weeping out of pity for the sufferings and losses that the hard practice of their profession inevitably brings – as a prelude to easing their hearts with vengeance – or upon hearing of the insults and perils faced by elite ladies. Such behavior inscribes an exclusive social circle, elevating those within; no more than these elite warriors can we imagine peasants or urban cloth workers fainting from overpowering emotions or, while working in their fields or shops, weeping uncontrollably over issues of honor. The elite were certain that peasants especially could feel no elevated emotions at all; in one demeaning fabliau the knights who enter a beautiful meadow think of jousting, but some peasants coming by can imagine no use of a beautiful woodland clearing other than as an outdoor toilet.[12]

If most modern scholarship would dismiss views equating chivalric and modern emotions as active social forces, these scholars continue to debate exactly how to characterize the world of medieval emotions in general and those at the chivalric level in particular. One influential approach posited a rudimentary medieval emotional pattern that was swept away once the Middle Ages came to a close; only then, in this grand narrative of progress, could a recognizably modern emotional framework for life emerge. The Early Modern era of European history, it is claimed, brought the needed restraint in affective life, a feature absent in the Middle Ages, or at best only foreshadowed in the twelfth century, if not (perhaps more faintly) in the tenth century. Civilizing restraint on socially dangerous emotions had to await the agency of princely courts in the sixteenth century.[13] One scholar has aptly termed this

---

[10] Ibid., 124.   [11] See *Song of Roland*, laisse 206.

[12] The role of weeping or fainting in clerical circles stands beyond the scope of this study. An initial impression would at least suggest that clerics' weeping, when it occurred, stemmed from different causes and sought different goals, being more pastoral in nature and less a matter of social markers. See Geoffrey Koziol, *Begging Pardon and Favor: Ritual and Political Order in Early Medieval France* (Ithaca, NY: Cornell University Press, 1992); Jean-Charles Payen, *La Motif du repentir dans la littérature francaise médiévale* (Geneva: Droz, 1968). My thanks to Peter Sposato for these references.

[13] Norbert Elias, *Über den Prozess der Zivilisation* (Basel: Verlag Haus zum Falken, 1939), English translation by Edmund Jephcott, *The Civilizing Process* (New York: Urizen Books, 1978).

view of slow, linear-progressive, and postmedieval progress "the historicizing of Freudian concepts of the super-ego."[14] Somewhat childlike, medieval people were sadly unable to control their surging emotions as their Early Modern successors did.

A growing body of scholarship urges new directions. The study of medieval emotions, pioneered by Barbara Rosenwein, Stephen White, Stephen Yaeger, and others, has challenged any view that medieval people should be considered thinly disguised primitives who simply seethed with uncontrolled emotions. They have suggested, instead, that the medieval elite possessed a particular and purposeful understanding and use of the emotions.[15] This scholarship pictures medieval society richly overlaid with emotional groups, each constructing ideal patterns of affective behavior for highly pragmatic reasons.[16] Emotions did not simply erupt and flow uncontrolled, like volcanic lava rushing down a slope; rather, a set of developed and powerful emotions served the elite as proof of social status and projected entitlement and authority; they demonstrated and communicated power.[17] The pattern of emotional programs adopted by each group was far from simple; many overlapping groups existed and, inevitably, the standards of some infringed or contradicted others; their goals might be prescriptive rather than simply descriptive. As a result, any one of these groups could roughly aggregate members who sometimes mitigated or violated the standards ideally upheld.

The relevance and usefulness of such analysis for the study of chivalry are obvious, for the knighthood can, in broad terms, be considered a significant emotional community within early European

---

[14] Daniel Gorlon, *Citizens without Sovereignty* (Princeton, 1994), 89.

[15] A brief consideration of these issues also appears in R. W. Kaeuper, "Chivalry and the 'Civilizing Process,'" in *Violence in Medieval Society*, ed. Kaeuper (Woodbridge, Suffolk: Boydell, 2000).

[16] Rosenwein reviews the long historiography in "Worrying about Emotions in History," *AHR* 107 (2002), 821–845. Her work is reviewed in papers from a conference available online (http://cem.revues.org/12520) under the title "De Cluny à Auxerre, par la voie des 'émotions': Un parcours d'historienne du Moyen Age." I questioned the narrative of Norbert Elias as it relates to chivalry in "Chivalry and the Civilizing Process," in *Violence in Medieval Society*, ed. Kaeuper (Woodbridge, Suffolk: Boydell, 2000), 21–35.

[17] Stephen D. White, "The Politics of Anger," in *Anger's Past: The Social Uses of an Emotion in the Middle Ages*, ed. Barbara H. Rosenwein (Ithaca, NY: Cornell University Press, 1998), 127–152.

society, one with a recognizable and pragmatic emotional program. As is true for chivalry generally, specialist scholarship can point to regional and chronological particularities, yet to use once more the telescope rather than the microscope allows us to take in a view of considerable continuity. Elite arms bearers had good reason to claim a special relationship to powerful emotions; their enviable status, elite military function, and self-valorizing ideology entitled them to effective use and display of emotions as a language of power.

Exercising caution, we can realize that chivalrous emotions could be purposeful, performative, and, in a formal sense, fully rational, without transforming those who expressed them into perfectly cool and calculating gentlemen, utterly free from intense feelings. They decidedly do not appear as unemotional role players in the literature they read and patronized, and do not perform in this fashion in chronicles that record their actions. Rather, they fall hopelessly in love, boil or gag with rage, or nearly go out of their minds with anger and grief. In company with their own contemporaries, we must retain full awareness that the warriors could be hellishly dangerous. If we must not caricature them as emotional children with too much strength and too little restraint, we cannot ignore the terrifying reality of vengeance and warfare fueled – or at least catalyzed – by strong emotions as well as close political calculation. Rationality about ends is not incompatible with glandular zeal propelling means; genuine emotional force can be channeled toward carefully planned goals; in some cases the emotion force, we can guess, was primary. Far from acting out a pretense of emotional display, the knights are shown to emote freely, at length, and with enthusiastic force – at times to a degree we may find surprising or even disorienting. A wise old Master Elias in the *Lancelot* assures the great knight Galehaut that he knows a cure for a sick heart:

The sick heart is cured by avenging the wrong done to it, and then it is wholly changed and returned to health. Imagine that someone tomorrow mocked and insulted you; your heart would not find peace till it were freed of the shame, and that, by giving hurt for hurt. If it were well avenged, it would be rid of the filth and poison clogging it, just like a man freed of worry and anger.[18]

---

[18] *Lancelot-Grail*, 2: 250 (Samuel N. Rosenberg); for the original French, see Sommer, *Vulgate Version*, 4:20. "Ore y a autres maladies dont on prent medecines Car quant li cuers est malades dedens de duel et dire ou daucune honte qui au cors a este faite si en puet on bien venir a garison par ueniance prendre del forfait. Car

Little evidence suggests strong feelings are absent or repressed (as though the lads had been trained in some hard British public school tradition). In showing good form, their emotional energy was functional; that the results were neither infantile nor irrational does not make them unfelt or unreal. Thrusting aside images of emoting monsters or moderns before their time, we need to understand how and why men-at-arms were rationally medieval, with no loss of impulse or energy for physical action.

If such emotions, as they claimed, helped to set them apart, did the knights actually share nothing of daily emotional life with the non-knightly or subknightly in their world? We can imagine that in company with all their contemporaries they must have experienced the joys of a fine day's hunting, felt sudden flashes of pleasure or anger in family and household interactions, and savored moments of peace and friendship in quiet chambers. And in social ranks below them, even men and women who spent their days struggling simply to make a living surely used emotional displays to enhance such power and control as were on offer at their social level. Some humble urban and rural folk, for example, have been shown making good use of these emotions.[19]

qui vous feroit vilonnie li cuers ne seroit iamais a aise deuant ce que vous en series vengies. Chest de rendre honte por honte Et lors series deliures de lordure et del venin qui en vous seroit. Aussi com li homs seroit fors des pensees quant il est aquites de ses detes."

[19] Daniel Lord Smail, *The Consumption of Justice: Emotions, Publicity, and Legal Culture in Marseille, 1264–1423* (Ithaca: Cornell University Press, 2003); "Faction and Feud in Fourteenth-Century Marseille," in *Feud in Medieval and Early Modern Europe*, eds. Jeppe Büchert Netterstrøm and Bjørn Poulsen (Aarhus: Aarhus University Press, 2007), 113–132; "Enmity and the Distraint of Goods in Late Medieval Marseille," in *Emotions and Material Culture*, ed. Gerhard Jaritz, *Forschungen des Instituts für Realienkunde des Mittelalters und der Frühen Neuzeit. Diskussionen und Materialien* 7 (Vienna: Der Österreichischen Akademie der Wissenschaften, 2003), 17–30; "Hatred as a Social Institution in Late-Medieval Society," *Speculum* 76 (2001), 90–126; "Common Violence: Vengeance and Inquisition in Fourteenth-Century Marseille," *Past & Present* 151 (May 1996), 28–59. Also, Paul Freedman, "Peasant Anger in the Later Medieval Ages," in *Anger's Past: The Social Uses of an Emotion in the Middle Ages*. Of course those seeking to join chivalric ranks would have gazed upward and imitated. We can well imagine that some lesser creatures, gazing socially upward in ardent hopes of ascent, might try for a speaking part in the theater of honor featuring the language of power. In early chivalric generations, even arms bearers, as we have seen, hovered near the margins of elite status hopeful for a place on the great stage; and in later generations, lawyers and administrators could be observed queuing in the wings.

Historians can scarcely know if in clinical terms the pure distillate of emotion these common folk felt exactly replicated that of an aroused lord. Scholars can, however, note the significant assumptions of complete superiority registered in fine emotions on the part of elite arms bearers, and also their greater employment of resources to act in response to emotions. As we move up the social hierarchy, a difference in degree of emotional response mutates into a difference in kind. As a prime case in point, the elite were certain that only they truly experienced love. Of course those near the broad base of the pyramid in libidinous haste sought a suitable haystack or a dark urban nook, but this scarcely represented refined love.

Not only could the elite claim to be set apart by such refined emotions, but they could also manage to link emotional displays to action on a scale far beyond most townspeople or villagers. Significant resources of energy, time, money, and physical force made a difference when honor or status was challenged. Action by the elite resulted in vastly greater social consequences. Not only were aristocratic emotional displays more lavish, but their vengeance might escalate into veritable warfare ravaging neighborhoods or entire regions. In contrast, emotional theater as enacted by ordinary people involved no public audience considered truly significant, and unleashed minimal real power. For the vast majority in medieval society, the social niche that they could possess remained low and the vial of precious honor discouragingly small.

The chivalrous elite by their classic phase had little trouble employing emotional forms as social markers separating themselves from such smaller folk. The rising bourgeoisie may have given them many more concerns about demonstrating their sense of superiority, but we cannot forget that competition among knightly families was keen, sometimes leaving emotions raw. Frontiers of social status shifted constantly, and daily watchfulness was needed even within the charmed circle. The violence that provided remedy against any detractors of honor could rest on a foundation of publicly displayed emotions.

Analyzing the societal role and impact of these chivalric emotions constitutes the goal of the chapters in this part. Though to facilitate analysis the spotlight will fall on major individual emotions or closely interlinked sets of emotions, it will be obvious that all such affective sets form an integrated whole. Ideals about refined love between men and women and among male friends will come first and, as a vast and contentious topic, will generate the greatest challenges. The topic is venerable. Recently more attention has been paid to other emotional forces as scholars investigate the chivalrous as elite warriors no less than as idealized lovers and close friends. Since vigorous knights virtually worshipped the dangerous physical competition of a violent profession, they experienced the intense feelings generated by hand-to-hand combat. Fear will thus be considered, followed by the sharp emotional trident of anger, wrath, and the urge to take vengeance.

Though each of these emotions could amply fill a separate volume of analysis by a specialist, all must be considered in summary fashion here. Yet an overview may have its value, for taken together these emotional elements form at least a skeletal affective framework of the chivalric *ordo*. Such an overview can give us a more nuanced sense of themes we have followed throughout this book, for in looking at emotions, as so often before, an obsession with honor links knightly function, status, and ideology. As Stephen White has usefully emphasized, statements in chronicles about displays of anger and grief may not convey simple reporting from eyewitnesses, but they certainly show how a figure possessed of such status and exercising such a function should ideally behave; he is demonstrating power, achieving honor, and avoiding shame.[20] Contemporary narrative accounts – and even more clearly the imaginative literature that adds voluminously to the evidence – convey an emotional ideology, valorizing what the knights do and where they stand in society.

---

[20] White, "The Politics of Anger," in *Anger's Past: The Social Uses of an Emotion in the Middle Ages*, passim 133–140.

10

LOVE AND AMITY, MEN AND WOMEN

—————— • ——————

As one of the grand words spoken or written in medieval Latin and the various vernacular languages, love was wide-ranging in its implications and powerful in its use and impact (Figure 12). R. W. Southern argued eloquently that love between humanity and God came to a new level of understanding and emphasis in the long twelfth century,[1] and even a focus on purely human relationships involving the chivalrous reveals an impressive range of meanings. As so often, the *Song of Roland* provides perspective. A furious Ganelon, thinking he has been betrayed by his nephew Roland, responds by saying publicly and in deadly earnest that he does not love him and will take revenge, the love that is lost here conveying crucial bonds of loyalty that have been broken and bonds of kinship now severed.[2] William Marshal, dying slowly and almost operatically, calls his wife to his bedside, addresses her fondly as "ami," and kisses her for the last time, his love for her embedded in amorous, conjugal friendship.[3] Lancelot's love for Queen Guinevere, providing a central pivot around which stories of Camelot turn and finally spin out of control, readily comes to mind as a classic account of heterosexual, romantic, passionate attraction, overwhelming in its compulsion, however disastrous its

---

[1] R. W. Southern, "Medieval Humanism," in *Medieval Humanism and Other Studies* (New York: Harper & Row, 1970), 29–60, specifically 33–37.

[2] See laisses 13–21 of the *Song of Roland*. The deep affection of Roland and Oliver, of course, shows love in action within a field of warrior honor.

[3] *History of William Marshal*, lines 18371–18372.

Figure 12 Understanding refined love and participating in its forms and expressions became important social markers of chivalric status. Tirelessly depicted in romance literature, this love also became a subject for artists and craftsmen.

consequences. Richard Lion-Heart and Philip Augustus are reported, early in their careers, to have shown openly that they feel a bond that leaves modern analysts struggling to characterize it adequately and accurately.[4] Even if in all these instances love fails to conquer all, it seems to have captured an impressive range of

[4] *Roger of Hovedon, Gesta regis Henrici II*, ed. William Stubbs, Rolls Series, 49: 2, p. 7, cited and discussed in C. Stephen Jaeger, *Ennobling Love: In Search of Lost Possibilities* (Philadelphia, 1999), 11–13.

emotional territory central to chivalry, through the affective life of characters both historical and fictional.

Given the almost crushing weight of scholarship on every aspect of love in the Middle Ages, with strongly held modern interpretive positions laid out like battlefield dispositions beneath banners of accomplished scholars, attempting any necessarily contained discussion of the role of the emotions of love in chivalry may resemble tap-dancing a route through minefields thickly planted within more than one academic department. Yet an overall historical perspective with a focus on the role of love within chivalric ideology and practice allows at least some contentious issues to be left to the care of specialists.[5] Historians must often peer closely between lines of glorious prose and poetry to seek behind the textual page the pattern of ideas and behavior in dialogue with social life, searching for the role played by powerful feelings of love among the lay elite.

PRELIMINARY CAUTIONS

In launching this inquiry, several initial cautions come swiftly to mind. Analysis, in the first place, requires more than a simple rehearsing of some supposedly universal system of courtly love that comprehends all love in the age of chivalry. This virtual equation of chivalry with such courtly love, sometimes still encountered, does scant justice to the range of meanings invested in love in these centuries and is as hopelessly reductive as imagining all of medieval European society ordered into a uniform manorial system beloved by elementary school curricula. So severely limiting a formulation is obviously not the point of view adopted in this book, which holds that chivalry was vastly more than courtly love, which was, itself, much less universal and determinative than popular proposals would allow. No single unified and broadly disseminated doctrine of courtly love effectively governed elite relations between the genders; medieval love appears as possessed of many splendors and tonalities.

---

[5] The work of Andreas Capellanus provides a prime example of ideas closely analyzed and disputed in scholarship. His *De Amore* lays out the formula for love (defined as suffering and meditating on that suffering) enhancing character in its opening section: see *The Art of Courtly Love*, trans. John Jay Parry, edited and abridged by Frederick W. Locke (New York: Frederick Ungar, 1957). How much irony he embedded in his text and how he was read by medieval audiences have been disputed.

It is fascinatingly true that in romance literature that elite males heard, patronized, and even sometimes composed they sometimes pictured themselves meekly obedient to ladies they loved and admired. Lancelot, the prince of prowess, fighting well at the command of Guinevere and then switching to fighting poorly when she signals this desire, can stand for this tradition.[6] It is also true that many medieval texts blatantly advocate male superiority and assert it as a self-evident and natural truth. Ramon Llull declared that men possess "more wit and understanding" than women and was sure they are "stronger by nature" and so surpass women in honor, though he worries that men may be more vicious.[7] The massive mid-fourteenth-century romance *Perceforest* continues the theme of male superiority, but adds qualifications to prohibit rape, in line with the wish of the god of nature. The knight Belinant asserts:

Although the female should be obedient to the male, and the male should be the stronger and more imposing, the male shouldn't treat the female with disrespect or contempt but should honour her as his equal. And so the god of nature established this most noble condition: that the female should have the rule of her own body, and the male should not use force against her will. And to ensure the female's freedom, the god of nature instituted a safeguard known as consent.[8]

If slightly less one-sided, such a view sharply contrasts with any elaborate ideal of courtly love. At minimum, many writers assume that women loved along the lines males had constructed for their lives. Wolfram von Eschenbach suggested that an elite man might

direct his heart towards service in pursuit of the reward of ladies, when one learns to recognize the sound which comes from spears cracking through shields, and to know how women rejoice at this and how a beloved woman soothes the anguish of her lover.[9]

A second caution concerns limitations on the societal spread of formal ideas about love. Far from dealing with amorous feelings motivating medieval Everyman and Everywoman, interest and discussion in our sources is focused determinedly on elites; knights and

---

[6] The scene appears in Chrétien's romance, in the *Lancelot-Grail*, and in Malory's *Morte d'Arthur*. Jaeger discusses this incident in *Ennobling Love*, 136–138.

[7] Ramon Llull, *Book of the Order of Chivalry*, ch. 3.

[8] Nigel Bryant, trans., *Perceforest* (Cambridge: Brewer, 2011), 80. Belinant later prevents rape by four knights who are his relatives: ibid., 106.

[9] Gibbs and Johnson, *Willehalm*, 152. He repeats, and not for the first time, that twin rewards await the valorous knight – "heaven and the approval of noble ladies."

ladies scarcely represented men and women in general. For chivalric commentators, romantic love is a rarefied emotion and an important elite social marker. Refined love belonged to them and distinguished them from rustic villagers or scruffy townsfolk. Though such people might become infatuated and surely copulated, even domestic animals could rut. And even a medieval university student enjoying sex with a miller's daughter, though he could cherish some hopes for a toehold on the ladder to social advancement, was a figure of bawdy fun; neither sexual participant would likely be transformed by their experience (unless the young woman's irate father appeared on the spot or she became pregnant). By contrast, Lancelot, in Chrétien's romance bearing his name, finds Guinevere's comb entwined with a few golden strands of hair and is enraptured and enmeshed in refined, transformative love that will fuel his deeds of arms.[10] Such magic comes to males only from devotion to elite ladies. Peasant girls are simply used and forgotten.[11] If Malory's *Morte Darthur* unfolds as a lovers' chess game of knight, queen, and king, it is sobering to recall that the young Arthur (conceived, of course, through a deceitful and exploitive sexual union) engenders two bastard sons within two pages early in the narrative.[12]

Even within privileged society, ideals directing males toward respect and restraint remained prescriptive rather than unfailingly descriptive of behavior. Sexual violence appears even at high social levels in all accounts and stories: even elite women could become victims in literature and in life. Guinevere's father, King Leodigan,

---

[10] Chrétien de Troyes, *Lancelot: The Knight of the Cart*, trans. Burton Raffel (New Haven: Yale University Press, 1997), 46.

[11] E.g., King Pellinor in *The Post-Vulgate Cycle: Merlin Continuation* engenders a child on "a shepherdess whom the king found in a field watching her beasts." The king found her beauty so great that he "took a fancy to her, and lay by her and fathered Tor," *Lancelot-Grail*, IV, 238.

[12] Vinaver, *Malory: Works*, 26–27. Of the first woman we hear nothing more, though Malory assured readers her son became a knight of the Round Table. The second lady is King Lot's wife, and the son is Mordred. These unions are said to be consensual, but Arthur is a rapist in the *Post-Vulgate Quest for the Holy Grail* (*Lancelot-Grail*, V, 215), the victim being a pretty girl he simply came upon while hunting. She was a young woman who "still knew nothing of such matters, ... she began to cry out while he was lying with her, but it did her no good." In this case her father, to whom she reveals all, confronts the king, but can take no revenge, given the disparity of power.

in the *Story of Merlin* brutally rapes the wife of his seneschal.
Crawling into bed with her,

he told her to keep quiet; if she shouted a single word, he would kill her with
his sharp sword, or if she thrashed about in the least. The lady defended herself
with words as much as she could, but she did not dare speak out loud, so her
arguments availed her very little.[13]

If knightly conquest was usually thought of as political and territorial, it could also be achieved sexually. Kathryn Gravdal has noted
that the Old French verb for taking a city by force also has the
meaning of rape, a link that many accounts of the fall of medieval
towns and villages to an advancing military force would bear out.
Bernier's mother, in *Raoul de Cambrai*, is a nun who has been raped
and impregnated by a great lord.[14] In a mini-plot with many twists in
the *Lancelot*, a lady of status escapes the Arthurian hero Guerrehet
(who has already enjoyed sex with her and killed her abusive husband) only by joining a nunnery at which they stop for rest; she tells
him in a frank speech that only thus could she escape the shame and
degradation he has brought upon her by forcing her to journey with
him like a camp follower.[15] The historical Isabella de Fortibus,
countess of Aumale, similarly escaped a son of Simon de Montfort
who had designs on her vast estates.[16] Italian courts in Bologna and
Florence of this era, as Carol Lansing writes, assumed that a magnate
exercised his power in sexual as in other ways, and would play the
"rapacious wolf."[17] Simply to recall such salient facts provides
a vantage point far removed from simplistic notions that principles
in chivalric literature or knightly attitudes and behavior in
a straightforward manner elevated the status of all ladies, let alone
all women.

[13] *Lancelot-Grail, Story of Merlin* (Pickens trans.), 248.
[14] Sara Kay, ed., trans., *Raoul de Cambrai*, laisse 65.
[15] *Lancelot-Grail*, III, *Lancelot*, 116–127.
[16] J. R. Maddicott, *Simon de Montfort* (New York: Cambridge University Press,
1994), 325 (the details are in the *Placitorum in domo capitulari Westmonasteriensi
asservatorum abbrevatio: Temporiubs regum Ric. I., Johann., Johann., Henr. III., Edw.
I., Edw. II.*, 172. Jean le Bel, *Chronicles*, 154–156, provides a harrowing account of
the brutal rape of the Countess of Salisbury by Edward III in his chronicle, which
is otherwise unfailingly laudatory of the English king, but Mark Ormrod discounts
the charge: *Edward III*, 136.
[17] Comment in Judith Bennett and Ruth Karras, eds., *Oxford Handbook of Women
and Gender in Medieval Europe* (Oxford University Press, 2013), 123. Lansing's
discussion at 118–132 provides general background and many sources.

That elaborate ideals about love existed remains important to our analysis, even after granting that they could, unsurprisingly, be violated. Such ideals formed a structural element of historical reality taking us into that contested zone linking professed values and social enactments, evasions, and outright negation. Significant thought about love characterized the classic age of chivalry, and a cult of romantic love in particular left indelible imprints on how elite men-at-arms thought and often how they acted with regard to women and other men. Evidence is plentiful, appearing especially, as Maurice Keen emphasized, in tournament practice, in chivalric biographies, in the statutes establishing and guiding chivalric orders founded by kings and nobles, and in romance.[18]

As with chivalric ideals in general, no single, mandatory code embodied in a convenient handbook existed to settle all amatory questions. We are dealing with social conventions surrounding issues that continued to provoke the discussions and debates that demonstrate the importance of the topic; but the results do not emerge from simple molds of the sort found in textbooks.

Yet as with chivalry in general once again, some notions about love and gender relations formed a core of ideals in medieval elite discussions and enactments. Such core values held that good arms bearers should protect the honor and person of ladies and damsels, the corollary being that knights were inspired by them to achieve notable feats of arms and were rewarded with admiring love. Love inspired prowess; prowess inspired love. The chivalric ethos, in other words, combined potent amorous forces with martial zeal, just as it combined disparate qualities of warrior ferocity with religious piety.

Such principles may seem at first glance simple, but significant questions were left hanging in midair, such as what limits might constrain this love (morally or hierarchically, for example), whether the love was to be physical and to be kept private, or even whether the love must be mutual.

[18] Keen, "Courtly Love," in *Nobles, Knights, and Men-at-Arms in the Middle Ages* (London, 1996), 21–42. This evidence is fully analyzed and readily found in Keen's essay. The intent in this chapter of the present book is to add to this evidence from other sources. Malcolm Vale, *War and Chivalry: Warfare and Aristocratic Culture in England, France, and Burgundy at the End of the Middle Ages* (Athens, GA: University of Georgia Press, 1981); D'Arcy Jonathon Dacre Boulton, *The Knights of the Crown: The Monarchial Order of Knighthood in Later Medieval Europe, 1325–1520* (Rochester: Boydell & Brewer, 2000).

STARTING NEAR THE END WITH MALORY'S VIEWS

With initial cautionary thoughts in place, investigation may usefully begin near the chronological end point of chivalry by looking at developed ideas of love splendidly presented in Sir Thomas Malory's *Morte Darthur*.[19] Though written in Middle English in the late fifteenth century, it draws heavily on concepts and images created centuries earlier. Much of basic plot and characterization had begun in the late twelfth-century romances of Chrétien de Troyes, adapted and elaborated in the Old French *Lancelot-Grail* or Vulgate Cycle written in the early thirteenth century; Malory also incorporated the complexities of the Middle English *Alliterative Morte Arthure* from the late fourteenth century. This cumulative inheritance, of course, in no way eliminated Malory's own views and creativity, but it allows us to see Malory as summing up much that we rightly consider classically constitutive elements of medieval love. These ideals, and the dangers inseparable from their fallible practice in human society, offer a great tapestry of amorous chivalric emotions. With this base secured, we can then turn briefly to other works of literature and to more traditional historical sources, with special attention to the lives and views of our other model knights. The goal cannot be to "correct" Malory and his literary forebears, but to gain the dual vision possible when seeing both ideals and recorded behavior within a single framework.

Of course Malory provides classic and intense love stories, not only of Guinevere and Lancelot, but of Iseult and Tristan (who stands at the head of a queue of other male hopefuls), along with a score of others. This world seems to feature festive courts and colorful pavilions set in greenwood glades. Whenever clouds hide the sun, it may be only to darken the mood as a featured knight launches his quest into the dangers of forest and moor, endlessly seeking to prove his worth to ladies who are pictured subscribing to his standards of worth in knighthood. Lingering over these pages, we most readily associate chivalry with love that was romantic and consensual, framed and enacted among lithe, heterosexual females and males of elite status. In fact, it seems scarcely possible for Malory to say "knights" without at once adding "and ladies." Knights not only ardently hope to win the love of a lady, but their intensity of desire may leave them feeling ill, fearful of dying. "I am seke for angere and for love of fayre

---

[19] My thanks to Sebastian Bezerra, who conducted word searches through Malory's text and offered helpful observations.

Igrayne, that I may not be hool," says Arthur's father, King Uther.[20] More colorfully, Sir Bewmaynes cannot sleep, but only "wallowed and writhed" for love throughout the night, and Sir Gareth felt a love "so hoot that he wyst nat were he was."[21] Knights rescue ladies in classic fashion and fight over them tirelessly. The love of ladies relentlessly inspires their prowess, and the process also works in the other direction. Ladies are sometimes chided for not sufficiently loving valiant knights, and those few knights who do not love ladies are a cause for wonder and some disbelief, sometimes expressed with spears.[22] All these attitudes and emotions would play easily in romantic films.

Yet it takes barely a second glance to realize how much more complicated are the forms love takes in Malory and the literary tradition he embodies. Romantic love does not stand solitary and dominant. Of course the love of God is invoked (often as sworn assurance that some action will be taken). Love is assumed as natural between blood relatives and regularly is said to bond knights with their lords, unless some villainy has soured the affection. What moderns might call political allegiance is often characterized as love. As Camelot falls apart, those in Lancelot's party fiercely decide "we shall gadir togyder all that we love and that lovyth us, and what that we woll have done shall be done."[23] The declaration has an ominous ring, and in so many cases amity and satisfaction are far from the consequences love unleashes. If a knight will do anything for love, he may be manipulated, or even linked to sorcery.[24] Famously, the great love affairs involving Lancelot and the queen, Iseult and Tristan, are actually love triangles with results well known. Not only does love hurt; it wrecks.

---

[20] Vinaver, *Malory: Works*, 4.   [21] Ibid., 201, 204.

[22] Ibid., 125: Nynyve, the Lady of the Lake, intones there is "no joy of suche a proude lady that wall have no mercy on suche a valaunte knight." This knight is Sir Pelleas. Ibid., 94. Later Lancelot is rebuked for one lack in his character: he loves no lady or gentlewoman, except for rumors about the queen. And Tristram announces that "a knight may never be of proues but yf he be a lovear." *Works*, 420–421). He knocks a disagreeing Sir Dynadan off his horse and crows, "Mesemyth the lover hath well sped." Ibid.

[23] Vinaver, *Malory: Works*, 679.

[24] Ibid., 208, where Sir Ironside, called the Red Knight of the Red Lands, confesses that "all the shameful customs that I used I ded hit at the request of a lady that I loved." King Uther famously uses Merlin's sorcery to have the duke of "Tiyntigail" killed and to bed the duke's wife.

Even more significant, the expression of intense affective bonds between knights is often privileged over romantic love. This can be a form of love that involves only the warriors themselves, without the involvement of ladies at all. It is heavily based on intense admiration or worship, by which Malory means the honor won by the prowess that elevates knights. Prowess, that is, inspires a species of love not only between men and women but among elite fighting men. Sir Segwarydes tells Tristan he should hate him most of all men living, since he came between him and his wife. Yet the knightly bond predominates, he asserts, because "I woll never hate a noble knight for a lyght lady, and therefore I pray you to be my frende, and I woll be yourys unto my power."[25] At one point Sir Palomedes is told he must secure his commitment to a course of action by taking an oath "for the love thou owyste unto knyghthoode."[26] The warriors who love each other also feel love for their hard profession and are frequently shown to intensify their bonds either by witnessing marvels of combat or through testing each other in the fighting that characterized their order. Such competition may be a feature of male interaction in many times and social settings – a topic far beyond the present inquiry.

Examples of a primacy given to warrior love could easily be multiplied from Malory's text, but the heartbreaking scene that shatters the Round Table can make the point. Hearing the news that Lancelot and the queen have been caught in her private chamber, Arthur responds with three clear statements.[27] The first comment is that Lancelot, who has fought his way out through the press of knights at the door, killing many companions of the Round Table, is a wondrous knight: "'Jesu mercy' seyde the kynge, 'he ys a mervaylous knight of proues.'" Arthur's second thought is that the fellowship of the Round Table is doomed: "'And alas,' seyde the kynge, 'me sore repentith that ever sir Launcelot should be ayenste me, for now I am sure the noble felyshyp of the Rounde Table ys brokyn for ever, for wyth hym woll many a noble knight holde.'" His third thought is that Guinevere must go to the stake: "'And now hit ys fallen so,' seyde the kyneg, 'that I may not with my worship but my queen muste suffir dethe,' and was sore annoyed." The rank

[25] Vinaver, *Malory: Works*, 275.   [26] Ibid., 367.
[27] All three appear in Vinaver, *Malory: Works*, 682.

ordering of his thoughts is informative: prowess first, knightly fellowship second, the queen's judicial death last.

Clearly the importance of the phenomenon of warrior love demands recognition and deserves support from more widespread evidence, even if only a sample can be presented.[28] This search, as the scholarship of C. Stephen Jaeger would argue, should ideally begin in the Carolingian and post-Carolingian centuries (though it echoed ancient models), for that period witnessed a widespread phenomenon of "ennobling love." It touched more than the warrior elite, for it originated in monastic and clerical circles and spread to elite laymen.[29] As an intense and public form of affection between elite males, this love, he argues, elevated and educated those involved; they were showing mutual respect, forming alliance, and encouraging friendship. Jaeger insists that it was decidedly not sexual. The great change in the elite social framing of love came in the later eleventh and twelfth centuries when women gained significant entry into courtly society, a move that generated important new possibilities and new tensions. Could love elevate if it became actually or potentially sexual? Jaeger's answer is negative. This broad explanatory paradigm has stimulated admiration and provoked argument well beyond the scope of the present discussion; but for understanding chivalry it is highly useful, suggesting a long-standing tradition of powerful affective male relationships rooted in the earliest period of chivalric origins and a dramatic change that followed in the dawning of the classic age of chivalric growth.

Leaving detailed discussion to specialists, we can recognize that a wide range of our sources reveal warrior affection and eventually

---

[28] As exclusive, aristocratic practice, the adventures imagined for knights may have won the love of fictional ladies, but "it is still the adventures that fill more lines of the poem than anything else," Keen observes, soon adding that we need not think "amorous passages were considered to have the same kind of contemporary relevance as their tales of martial courage and achievement." Keen, "Courtly Love," in *Nobles, Knights, and Men-at-Arms in the Middle Ages* (London, 1996), 24, 27. Yet tournaments seem, he observes, to draw their emotional and erotic charge from current ideals about love, which also left their mark on secular orders of chivalry, which often featured amorous emblems, mottos, and regulations. More than a mere "genuflection" to ideals of love found in literature is involved. Cf. the comments of Judith Bennett on the tournament at Hem, *Oxford Handbook of Women and Gender in Medieval Europe*.

[29] Jaeger, *Ennobling Love: In Search of a Lost Sensibility* (Philadelphia: University of Pennsylvania Press, 1999).

add romantic love. In *chansons de geste* men often speak specifically of love for fellow knights after having witnessed their feats of combat and demonstrations of loyalty. It is these essential bonds between warriors that generally, though not exclusively, are termed love in these works. The spectacular epic *Raoul de Cambrai* offers a classic case in point. It can speak of the love of God (at least in the form of sworn oaths)[30] and recognizes maternal, paternal, and filial love.[31] After Raoul's death in battle, Helois, his betrothed, even gets a brief scene in which she views his body, laments her loss, and hopelessly implores her "dear friend" to kiss her.[32] Most often, however, mentions of love connect fighting men who are linked by landholding (as a material underpinning to affection). As the epic opens, the king of France is said to love Raoul, Raoul is said to love the young men sent for training in his service, and Bernier (at this time Raoul's beloved vassal), we learn, stands surety for the behavior of others in a tenurial quarrel out of love for Raoul.[33] But the love-in goes south swiftly and the intensity of emotion shows itself most clearly as the dreaded inversions of love dominate action. Utter enmity and hatred take center stage, splitting apart the love of warriors with almost nuclear explosive force. Feud leaves a bloodstained landscape. As Bernier says in rebuke to Raoul, "A false friend I have found in you. I have served you and loved you and helped to make you powerful; I am ill rewarded for my good service."[34] Though Raoul tries to retrieve Bernier's love, approaching him humbly, wearing rough clothing in a species of secular penance, "there was no love shown at the parting."[35] Statements of pure hatred soon rise on all sides like toxic bubbles breaking the surface of a swamp. Bitter fighting breaks out, and each conflict leads to others, as revenge must be taken for losses endured. Raoul, we learn, will consider himself a contemptible coward "if he fails to take revenge on those who killed one he loved."[36] After Bernier kills Raoul, Guerri the Red (Raoul's uncle) curses Bernier, since it was Raoul "who knighted you at the first and loved you dearly."[37]

Warrior love with all its complications and powerful inversions reappears in the *Histoire* of William Marshal, for in this text, too, love

[30] E.g., *Raoul de Cambrai*, laisses 72, 152, 205, 237.
[31] E.g., ibid., laisses 126, 176, 184, 208.   [32] Ibid., laisse 180.
[33] See ibid., laisses 18, 45.   [34] Ibid., laisse 84.   [35] Ibid., laisse 88.
[36] Ibid., laisse 160.   [37] Ibid., laisse 167.

generally conveys a sense of political and military linkage. After John Marshal, William's father, left his wife and married a sister of Earl Patrick, his prospects increased with his new ally, the earl, for "there was love and harmony between them."[38] As William matured into a great knight he is deeply loved by the Young King – more than any other knight – especially for aid and protection given his patron in the rough tournaments of that day.[39] This "love which bound him to his lord" made other members of his entourage jealous and would later cause trouble.[40] Yet in general the list of worthy males loving the Marshal seems to expand endlessly. While he is in the Holy Land, those who loved him for his great chivalric qualities include King Guy, the Knights Templar, and the Knights Hospitaller.[41] Meiler fitz Henry, a man the Marshal "most loved and cherished" in his Irish lands, is one "in whom he placed his greatest trust."[42] Essential elements for achieving love appear in William's deathbed comment on his son Ancel:

"Ancel is very dear to me. If he lives long enough to become a knight, and even though he has no land, provided he strives for his honour, he will find someone who will love him and honour him greatly."[43]

To many modern parents, finding someone to offer love for a son might mean an appropriate spouse; to William Marshal it means someone secured through the vigorous practice of knighthood, an aristocratic patron as the source of love; thus a politico-military career can be advanced and honor possessed. This had been the Marshal's own upward path, of course.

Yet some refinements of love involving women had undoubtedly gained cultural strength in the Marshal's lifetime and left their mark in his biography; glimmerings of romantic love just blossoming within chivalry flit through the poem. The Young King is said to have taken personified Generosity as a bride and to have loved her truly.

He did not use her as a concubine, for their marriage was a very good one: as long as he lived he loved her as a true lover and she him.[44]

---

[38] *History of William Marshal*, lines 370–377.
[39] Ibid., lines 3634–3642. William's prowess in tourneying earned love from others; see lines 6036–6040, 6179–6181, 6294–6304.
[40] Ibid., lines 5127–5129.   [41] Ibid., lines 7289–7293.
[42] Ibid., lines 13683–13684.   [43] Ibid., lines 18141–18146.
[44] Ibid., lines 3660–3668.

Famously, the poet also claims that William was accused – falsely, of course – of having an affair with his lord's wife, though he assures readers that once the lie (fabricated by men jealous of William's bond with the Young King) was exposed, love between lord and man was renewed and intensified.[45] Modern scholarly opinions on this supposed affair vary; but whether we take the view that William's behavior was blameless or was being whitewashed in the *Histoire*, or consider the entire business invented by the poet simply to make William fit fashions of the early thirteenth century, the evidence remains telling. Romantic love is slipping, if not quite striding, into chivalric life.[46]

This incident aside, much talk of love in the Marshal's *Histoire*, as in *Raoul de Cambrai*, characteristically involves males busily engaged in their military capacity or political alliances. In William's case it can come as no surprise, for he is endlessly praised as a prince of prowess and loyalty, "so worthy and loyal, so esteemed and loved, and also so feared."[47] This unbeatable combination garners praise more than once: he is "such a worthy knight, such a valiant man and proven as such, so feared and yet so loved."[48] Of course, the inversions of love are once again particularly powerful: betrayal transmutes love into hate: famously, William hated the Lusignan family for treachery. In extreme cases, as Marshal's biographer reports, the inversion of love could bring despair: Henry II, when

---

[45] Ibid., lines 5683–5687.

[46] Painter, *William Marshal*, 46–48. "As it was the age of courtly love, one can conceive of William as the 'true knight' of the young queen, but hardly as her paramour" (47). Crouch, *William Marshall*, 48–50. "In the fact of such ambiguous evidence I would put down the allegations of adultery with Queen Margaret as a strategy of the author of the *History* derived from contemporary romances and erroneous gossip, not taken seriously at the time but a welcome distraction from the more difficult accusation lèse-majesté." Duby, *William Marshal: The Flower of Chivalry*, 48–50, 52–53. Duby is more willing to entertain the affair as reality; however, he does put forward the question of to what extent were the "memory of deeds done, as it is established in the *Histoire de Guillaume le Marechal*, inflected . . . by the echo of the dreams provoked by tales the knights never tired of being told?" (53).

[47] *History of William Marshal*, lines 14513–14516.

[48] Ibid., lines 15524–15526. Other knights win similar praise: Alexander Arsic was "so brave, so valiant and handsome he was loved by all." Edward III, the chronicler Jean le Bel asserts, was so loved and feared by his men that none would disobey him. Bryant, ed., trans., *The True Chronicles of Jean le Bel*, 182.

he learned that his most loved son, John, had joined his enemies, lost the will to live.[49]

Times of testing could, of course, increase a sense of love and harmony. Joyous love is more commonly emphasized: Richard of Devizes's chronicle reports that in a crisis on Sicily while en route to the Holy Land, Richard Lion-Heart is supposed to have addressed his followers in significant terms: "I am your lord and king, I love you and am solicitous for your honor."[50] With even more emphasis, Barbour's poem on the trials and triumph of Robert Bruce speaks much of love, almost always in the sense of warrior loyalty and faithful, efficient prowess, exercised in the service of king and country. Such conceptions of love would readily dominate an account of the harrowing wars of Scottish independence from English domination; but the specifics of the language are full of interest and significance. Posing a question that would have pleased Geoffroi de Charny, Barbour asserts that in a battle the Scottish king killed more of his enemies than "alt Tydeus of Thebes" (a hero of Greek mythology), yet the latter was a more effective fighter; he asks which one should be the more loved.[51] Barbour, who loved to keep scorecards of chivalric achievement, was certain that the valiant Douglas had merited love: though personally vanquished thirteen times, he had gained victory fifty-seven times.[52] Giving credit where due, Barbour grants that Philip Mowbray, who mowed down Scots fighters in order to escape capture, was loved for his chivalry.[53] William Sinclair, Bishop of Dunkeld, is reported to call out to his fellow Scots on a battlefield that doing well they will show who loves their king that day.[54] Honor and love are often joined in the lines Barbour composes or quotes. And Malory would have approved his assertion that for their worship and bounty warriors would be lastingly loved

---

[49] *History of William Marshal*, lines 9079–9084. Cf. *Chronica Rogeri de Hoveden*, 366–367, for a description of Henry's reaction and his death shortly afterward.

[50] *Chronicles of the Crusades*, 16; Richard Devizes, *Chronicles of the Reigns of Stephen, Henry II., and Richard*, vol. iii. *Rerum Britannicarum Medii Aevi Scriptores*, ed. Richard Howlett (London: Longman & Co., 1886, 398). "Ego dominus et rex vester vos diligo, ego de decore vestro solicitor."

[51] *Barbour's Bruce*, bk. 6, lines 281–286.   [52] Ibid., bk. 8, lines 432–436.

[53] Ibid., bk. 8, lines 105–106.

[54] Ibid., bk. 16, lines 628–629. He is identified only as "Ye gud byschap" (621) and "Ye byschap yat wes rycht hardy / And mekill and stark raid forouth ay" (633–634).

and finally brought to everlasting love in heaven.[55] As this assertion suggests, the love of God and for God gets some mention, often linked to martial success.

Love involves ladies, however, only a few times in the *Bruce*, as when the king sends off to safety the ladies who had been traveling with his forces. The scene is emotional, with weeping, beseeching, and farewell kisses.[56] Barbour has already intoned that love, and here he means romantic love, has power to lighten all burdens, after praising these ladies for being partners of their husbands' pains, out of loyal love.[57] That there is little emphasis on romance can occasion little surprise, however, in a panegyric on the achievement of Scottish independence, and perhaps Barbour comes close to summarizing his view in general by declaring in straightforward terms that men who desire and achieve honor will be loved.[58]

This mixture of warrior love with romantic love takes on more equal proportions in the major treatise of Geoffroi de Charny. In fact, in his pages the high vault of honor spreads inclusively over conjoined forms of passion and prowess.[59] Charny imagines a festive court scene in which one woman glows with inner pride as her lover enters a great hall for a feast and is abundantly honored and welcomed by all for his deeds of prowess. Both types of love, the warrior and the courtly, fuse in this scene, for "in addition to the true love for one another which they share, he is in addition loved, esteemed, and honored by all."[60] To heighten his point, Charny contrasts the dismay of a second woman whose lover enters the hall unnoticed and is lost in the crowd. He is, Charny says with curled lip, a "miserable wretch who, for no good reason, is unwilling to bear arms"; he cannot be known for great deeds, though he has "no excuse except lack of will," and so his love "can be worth nothing, nor can it last for long without the ladies wanting to have no more of it . . . nor can [he] put forward any arguments to persuade . . . ladies to behave differently."[61] Charny's scorn cannot be contained:

How do such people dare to love when they do not know nor do they want to know about the worthy deeds that they should know about and ought to perform, especially those who for good reason should undertake them?[62]

---

[55] Ibid., bk. 16, lines 538–542.   [56] Ibid., bk. 3, lines 346–351.
[57] Ibid., bk. 2, lines 515–524.   [58] Ibid., bk. 6, lines 325–327.
[59] The quotations from Charny that follow all come from section 20 of Kaeuper and Kennedy, *The Book of Chivalry*.
[60] Ibid., 120–121.   [61] Ibid., 122–123.   [62] Ibid.

The link between romantic love and knightly prowess is absolutely clear to him:

Therefore men should love secretly, protect, serve, and honor all those ladies and damsels who inspire knights, men-at-arms and squires to undertake worthy deeds that bring them honor and increase their renown. And these noble ladies should, as is their duty, love and honor these worthy men-at-arms who, in order to deserve their noble love and their benevolence, expose themselves to so much physical danger as the vocation of arms requires from those who aim to reach and achieve that high honor through which they hope to deserve to win the love of their ladies.[63]

The word "secretly" in his prolix statement must not be missed. Charny wants love to be true and loyal, by which he seems to mean steady and private. His valorization of love, as he has already made clear, leaves no tolerance of male boasting of sexual conquests:

The greatest pleasure to be derived from love is not to be found in saying "I love so and so" nor in behaving in such a way that everyone will say: "That man is the lover of that lady." And there are many who say that they would not want to love Queen Guinevere if they did not declare it openly or if it were not known... And we should know for certain that the most secret love is the most lasting and the truest and that is the kind of love for which one should aim.[64]

Clearly Charny endorses love that clerics might condemn, yet he nonetheless insists repeatedly that elite warriors understand that love must be loyal to increase honor:

But make sure that the love and that loving are such that just as dearly as each of you should cherish your own honor and good standing, so should you guard the honor of your lady above all else and keep secret the love itself and all the benefit and the honorable rewards you derive from it; you should, therefore, never boast of the love nor show such outward signs of this in your behavior that would draw the attention of others.[65]

Clearly his view endorses the principle that prowess inspires love and love inspires prowess, with both closely bonded with honor.[66] But we must remember that this is true not only in a romantic sense intertwining male and female affection. Charny's famous scale of merit among elite males rises with increasingly demanding and corporally destructive deeds of prowess, for "he who does more is more

[63] Ibid. [64] Ibid., 118–119. [65] Ibid.
[66] A great knight in *Perceforest* (trans. Bryant, 243) exclaims, "God protect Love, the source of all prowess!" Another knight (ibid., 589) intones, "a knight without renown isn't worthy of being loved."

worthy."[67] As he embraces love, so, too, he deeply values its powerful inversion. Almost as a maxim, he urges, "Love and serve your
friends, hate and harm your enemies, relax with your friends, exert
yourself with all your strength against your foes."[68] Men-at-arms of
supreme worth are "more honored, loved and prized than any other
men at arms," he says plainly; and a *prudhomme* loves those he knows
have done great deeds.[69] He can insist on the love owed to great
men-at-arms and earned by them.[70] He instructs that

you should love, value, praise, and honor all those whom God by his grace has
granted several good days on the battlefield, when they win great credit and
renown for their exploits, for it is from good battles that great honors arise and
are increased, for good fighting men prove themselves in good battles.[71]

So fascinating does Charny find the overlapping circles of prowess,
romantic love, and honor that he constructs a remarkably complex
hypothetical question in his set of *Demandes*, the questions he wrote
to be debated by members of the French royal Order of the Star.
In a town situated between two warring towns, he imagines, damsels
invite their lovers from one town to party with them throughout the
night. As the satisfied men-at-arms leave the next morning, they
confront a band of their enemies coming from the opposing town,
who are about to enjoy a similar party with their lovers who (aware of
the previous night's festivities) have sensuously offered similar joys.
What Charny wants the veterans of the French royal chivalric order
to debate is which group of men will be more motivated to win
honor in the ensuing fight between groups of arms bearers, those with
the glow of satisfied love still animating them or those charged with
its expectation.[72] Had this discussion taken place and been recorded,
we might have been bequeathed a treasure trove of frank personal
reminiscences, however high the style of expression. Sadly, the
question, like all of Charny's *Demandes*, stands unanswered.

Significantly, the particular expression of love that Charny most
fears is a form of self-love that demands pampering of the body and

---

[67] Ibid., 96–97.   [68] Ibid., 138–139.
[69] Ibid., section 35, 154–157. Cf. section 43, 100–105.
[70] Ibid., sections 18, 23, 35, pp. 106–107, 128–133, 154–167.
[71] Ibid., section 7, pp. 88–91.
[72] Michael Taylor, "A Critical Edition of Geoffroy de Charny's *Livre Charny* and the
Demandes pour la joute, les tournois et la guerre" (PhD dissertation, University of
North Carolina, Chapel Hill, 1977); Maurice Keen, "Chivalry and Courtly
Love," in *Nobles, Knights and Men-at-Arms in the Middle Ages*, 34.

leads to the detriment of hard physical enterprise. Only an unswerving commitment to prowess can join warrior affection and romantic love with precious honor. He pours vitriolic scorn on concern for bodily comfort, adornment, or ease that demand soft beds and elaborate food, along with stylish, form-fitting, and highly decorative clothing, studded with gems. Such self-love smothers the desire for daring deeds that turn the interlocked gears of the multilayered machinery of love: if a worthy man loves those he knows have performed great feats of chivalry, he likewise loves ladies "who inspire men to great achievement and it is thanks to such ladies that men become good knights and men-at-arms. *Hence* all good men-at-arms are rightly bound to protect and defend the honor of all ladies."[73]

Charny was a witness to a declaration of warrior affection that remains impressive even though the term "love" was never mentioned. Jean le Bel records the potent admiration for skill at arms dramatically spoken at the celebratory banquet Edward III held after he foiled Charny's attempt to wrest Calais from English control. This king offers fulsome praise of one of his captured enemies, the French knight Eustace de Ribemont. Edward's encomium overflows with admiration for prowess and significantly links his high regard (dare we say his love?) for Eustace as a knight to the love Eustace gives to ladies and receives from them:

I've never seen any knight in all the world assail his enemies more valiantly than you, or defend himself with more skill, nor has any knight in any battle given me a sterner test in fighting man to man. I award you the prize above all others in this day's combat.[74]

To honor him, Edward removes a "gorgeous chaplet, richly adorned with pearls" from his own head, saying,

"In token of the prize I give you this chaplet, and with all my heart I pray you wear it this whole year whenever you're in the company of lords and ladies and damsels – of whom I understand you're very fond! – and give me your word that you'll tell everyone that I gave it to you and why."[75]

It is courtly speech, capped with a love token between warriors.

This incident recalls the florid declaration of an imagined knight who has seen Lancelot perform wonders in a tournament, late in the

---

[73] Kaeuper and Kennedy, *Book of Chivalry*, 94–95, emphasis supplied.
[74] Bryant, ed., trans., *The True Chronicles of Jean le Bel*, 208.   [75] Ibid.

work bearing his name in the Vulgate Cycle of Romance. Here love between warriors is given even more elaborate language:

"[I]t takes a lot more to be a worthy man than I thought it did this morning. I've learned so much today that I believe there's only one truly worthy man in the whole world. I saw the one I'm talking about prove himself so well against knights today that I don't believe any mortal man since chivalry was first established has done such marvelous deeds as he did today."[76]

He leaves no doubt about the marvelous deeds that prove a man's worth:

I could count more than a thousand fine blows, for I followed that knight every step to witness the marvelous deeds that he did; I saw him kill five knights and five men-at-arms with five blows so swift that he nearly cut horse and knights in two. As for my own experience, I can tell you he split my shield in two, cleaved my saddle and cut my horse in half at the shoulders, all with a single blow... I saw him kill five knights with one thrust of his lance... [I]f it were up to me, he'd never leave me. I'd keep him with me always, because I couldn't hold a dearer treasure.[77]

This deep affection among arms bearers occurring within a framework of honor continues unabated in the biography of Pero Niño. Amorous relations with women, in fact, now take on greater importance than in any of our previously examined texts. We encounter the hero in love, not merely speaking about love, though Gutierre Díaz de Gamez, his admiring biographer, does indeed speak at some length on the subject in the abstract. Early in the text Díaz de Gamez announces the fusion of love and prowess: "Just as Pero Niño was a man of great adventure in arms, so he was most valiant and well noted in love."[78] In these pages love often refers to politico-military bonding, yet more often and more intensely it involves ladies and feats of arms. Speeches and conversations at festive banquets bring out these ideas. At such an occasion in the home of the admiral of the king of France, "as long as the meal lasted ... anyone who wanted to could speak of arms and love and would have conversation on such,"[79] just as at a banquet in Seville the men had talked of war and love.[80] Women inspire men to achieve great feats, Díaz de Gamez asserts, as in the case of a skirmish between Castilian and Portuguese forces:

[76] Micha, ed., *Lancelot*, 4: 198–199, Kibler, trans., in *Lancelot-Grail*, 3: 161–162.
[77] Ibid.   [78] Evans, *Unconquered Knight*, 15.   [79] Ibid., 137.   [80] Ibid., 53.

[T]he fighting was very close and very dangerous, and in a very good place for those who should want to do deeds of arms for the love of their ladies, for all the ladies of Pontevedra watched from the ramparts of the city.[81]

Such discussion seems common: at the conclusion of the banquet in Seville, the host spelled out the theme:

I see here a most noble company who all purpose good deeds; I see likewise that my lord the Captain [Pero Niño] and all his gentlemen are in love. Love is a virtue which pricks on and sustains those who seek to prove themselves worthy by feats of arms. Therefore, in order that we may see who best loves his lady, and has the firmest purpose to do good deeds, let the Captain and all his gentlemen, for the greater honour of the feast, boldly make a vow, each one according to his courage and estate.[82]

Pero Niño's vigorous and wide-ranging career seems to have won for him the differing forms of love a knight might crave. Unyielding prowess and bold leadership secured for him the affection and loyalty of men who fought at his side on the Mediterranean, along the English Channel, and on the Spanish peninsula. Díaz de Gamez, who may love chivalric scorecards even more than Barbour, claimed proudly that his hero was, as the title of the biography trumpeted, unconquered. As obsessive as Charny about his themes, Díaz de Gamez introduces a discourse on love and the art of loving with another expression of the great fusion:

[J]ust as he was valiant and excelled in arms and chivalry [outshining] all the other knights of his day, so did he distinguish himself by setting his affections high; and likewise just as he brought to a fair end all the emprises of arms that he enters upon, and was never vanquished, so wherever he loved was he loved in return, and yet never incurred reproach by reason of it.[83]

After all, Díaz de Gamez reasons, it is only natural that a youth "so accomplished, who had shown so much prowess, who was so much praised by all men, to have early knowledge of love." If he was the sort of young man who would be esteemed in the households of queens and great ladies, these "fair and gentle ladies, such as are worthy of love, think to have gained honour when they know that they are loved by such men and praised of them." Charny would not have changed a word of these declarations, nor with the asserted consequence: for Díaz de Gamez says the knights

---

[81] Ibid., 35–36.   [82] Ibid., 53.
[83] Ibid., 44. The word "outshining" is missing from the Evans translation.

know that for love of [such ladies] do they become better knights and acquit themselves more magnificently, that they achieve prowess and great labours of chivalry, whether in arms or in sports, that they set forth on great adventures to do them pleasure, and go into strange realms, bearing their [heraldic] devices, seeking chance encounters and encounters in the lists [i.e., in tournaments], each praising and exalting his lady and mistress.[84]

Parting company with Charny on the score of secrecy, Díaz de Gamez says that some knights make known their love by writing songs and poems, whereas others are less public. And the women, if only they were free to choose for themselves, might find men "more gentle [i.e., noble] and of better character" than those imposed on them, "because love seeks not great riches nor great estate, but a man brave and bold, true and loyal."[85] Pero Niño's marriage with Dona Costanza made such a bond, as a "work of love."[86]

To explain his view, Gamez proposes three stages of love and, like Charny, asks his reader to picture a lady in love. For both Díaz de Gamez and Charny even to enter imaginatively into a feminine consciousness seems significant, however much we may recognize that it is actually male imagination that is guiding the process. Admiration begins the process, when the lady merely hears of the knight and begins to love him without having seen him. Predilection comes when she actually sees him and finds in him more goodness than even had been reported. She loves him, has him for her own, and "holds this knight in her power." Devotion, the final stage, brings her to such a state of love and closeness that she dies if separated from him. Striking though these stages are, Díaz de Gamez is clearly thinking more of mythical or classical ladies who appear in his books than the several real ladies in his hero's life. With self-conscious display of learning, he discusses his stages of love using a progression of mythical ladies including the Queen of the Amazons and Queen Dido of Carthage.

Though Díaz de Gamez shows off his learning in such passages, he does turn to Pero Niño's relationship with the three very real women. At least one aspect of Díaz de Gamez's schema looks valid, for Dona Costanza, first wife of Pero Niño, was a wealthy young widow of a prominent family who was able "to marry whomever she would and she had determined in her heart what manner of man she

---

[84] Ibid., 44–45. [85] Both quotations from Evans, *Unconquered Knight*, 45.
[86] Ibid., 44.

would espouse."[87] Having heard that Pero Niño was "in all things as he should be," she was guided, we learn, by reason and God to choose him, all her family and friends approving the marriage.[88] Dona Costanza died young, being only "four or five years wedded to Pero Niño."[89] Though she had given birth to a son who resembled his father and so, in time, "won the love of the King and all the Court," sadly "illness and death ended this young man's promising life at age twenty-seven."

We learn much more about Pero Niño's second love: Jeanette de Bellengues, the wife and then widow of Sir Renaud de Trie, the admiral of the king of France. This lady became the lover of Pero Niño while he was staying in France on business of the Castilian crown. The account Díaz de Gamez gives reads almost like incidents from a romance and perhaps bears literary imprint. The admiral, now old and ill, lived in retirement after a trying career as a stern knight had left him "broken by his armour." The setting certainly favored amour rather than armour – a house worthy of Paris set in the Norman countryside, surrounded by orchards along a stream, with every facility for hunting and idyllic social pastimes. The admiral's young wife, who was of course the most beautiful lady in France, had her own dwelling, separated from the main house by a drawbridge. In shady groves, books of hours were read, chaplets of flowers woven, stories told, and songs sung. "I declare to you," Díaz de Gamez sighs, "that if a man who was there could have made it last forever he would have wished for no other Paradise." Pero Niño, invited there often, naturally fell in love, as the film that will someday be made of the story will make obvious. Throughout the meals, as we have already noted, discussion turned to arms and love (*en armas e en amores*), a potent pair of topics.[90] And as soon as the meal ended and tables were cleared, dancing began, with each knight kissing his partner. There were picnics along the stream, torchlight processions through the night, with beautiful singing. As it became clear that the admiral would soon die, the lady Jeanette asked Pero Niño about his plans, suggesting he talk with her father. The hard business of war intruded, however, Pero Niño going to Paris to obtain payment owed by the French government for his raids on the English coast. And then the sport of tournament ensnared him for a time, ever victoriously (even at night

---

[87] Ibid., 46.   [88] Ibid., 45–46.   [89] Ibid., 43–44.
[90] Ibid., 137; Carriazo, *El victorial*, 553.

by torchlight), Díaz de Gamez assures readers. News of the admiral's death reached Pero Niño as he prepared to return to active warfare, at which time, his biographer asserts, the knight and Jeanette became lovers. Suddenly – almost as if borrowing a leaf from Chrétien de Troyes's *Yvain* – Díaz de Gamez tells of an urgent tournament call from great French lords to be fought "for the honour of knighthood and the love of your lady."[91] In Paris, soon thereafter, Pero Niño received a gift of a fine horse and helmet from Jeanette, whose letter urged him not to fight, though she knew he must if his honor was at stake. In fact, the French king forbade this tournament and made peace, temporarily, between the great dukes involved in dispute.

Plans for a marriage were rumored, but action was delayed by the short time the lady Jeanette had been widowed and by Pero Niño's need to return to war and to seek permission from his king to marry. The couple agreed to a two-year delay for these reasons and the narrative shifts from love to war, first along the English Channel and then in Spain when the hero was recalled to Castile by his king.[92] He still thought of Jeanette in far-off Normandy, for after severe combat with the Moors he sent that lady his hard-used sword, "like a saw, toothed in great notches, the hilt twisted by dint of striking mighty blows, and all dyed in blood."[93] The gift combined chivalric relic with love token. Being made a captain of one unit of the king's guard, he realized he could not return to France and so wrote to ask Jeanette to be released from their compact. Díaz de Gamez is sure of the rectitude of this step, "so that so great a lady should not go on trusting in his return, as she had done heretofore, according to the agreement."[94] The colorful and highly romantic second love had come to an end.

Appropriately, his third love was inspired by his unsurpassed jousting. Dona Beatriz and other ladies are pictured as discussing the fine points of the sport as they watch with interest, and Díaz de Gamez insists that on that day the new love began, she drawn by his prowess, he enamored of her approving comments (reported to him by a squire). "And just as Pero Niño used to adventure himself upon other great affairs," Díaz de Gamez rejoices, "so he adventured on this also." He tells how his hero sent word to Dona Beatriz "that she was the one lady in the world whom he would most desire to serve

---

[91] Evans, *Unconquered Knight*, 150.   [92] Ibid., 185.   [93] Ibid., 196.
[94] Ibid., 202.

for his honour."[95] So standard a link between honor and love is weakened somewhat by Dona Beatriz's reported awareness of rumors "that great ladies have lost their good name for his sake, and [she adds] 'I would not myself be numbered among them.'"[96] Pero Niño, however, contrived a public meeting while she was riding and urged her "to be well assured that his desire was to love her uprightly and loyally, to the honour of them both." It was a view, and even a set of linguistic frames, that Charny would warmly have approved, and it worked, in time, though she first countered that men's words could not be trusted and that she would take advice. Pero Niño convinced her brother to give him support and, however serious her doubts, they were put to rest.[97]

Yet the more powerful negative catalyst in the equation was not her fears but the desire of the Infante (acting as regent at the time) to wed Beatriz to his own son. With great boldness, the couple resorted to a clandestine marriage, with a select group of witnesses only. As the news inevitably leaked into court circles and a joyous Pero Niño did little to keep the marriage private, storm clouds gathered. As ever, Pero Niño's prowess rode to the rescue, though it required a devious route. Both he and Beatriz boldly responded to charges by the Infante, but in the moment of crisis (when Pero Niño had gone to the queen and her son, still a minor), he played Lancelot or William Marshal and demanded that the case be settled by combat.[98] He would prove his innocence "according to the law of knights' decrees in such a case, holding the field from one sunrise to the next" against any two opponents.[99] He would kill them, drive them off the field, or make them confess he has done no wrong in marrying Dona Beatriz; meanwhile the young king was to guarantee that Pero Niño's wife could come to him. Pressing his case through the virtue of largesse, he promised to give his challengers enough gold to provide good horses for the fight. When the Infante rejected this judicial duel and sent men to harm Pero Niño, the hero's reputation for prowess left them in inactive fear and Pero Niño crossed over into Gascony for safety. The needs of war finally broke the impasse. Fighting the Moors, the Infante needed Pero Niño's sword arm, no less than the Young King

---

[95] Ibid., 206.   [96] Ibid., 207.   [97] Ibid., 207–209.

[98] Famously, Lancelot defended the queen's innocence; William Marshal, denying the charge that he had an affair with the Young King's wife, offered proof by battle, at which point all challengers turned silent.

[99] Evans, *Unconquered Knight*, 216.

had needed William Marshal's or the imagined Arthur had needed the imagined Lancelot's. He pardoned and recalled Pero Niño. Love had conquered all, at least as warrior love allied with superb and reliable prowess.

THE INTENSITY OF WARRIOR ATTRACTION

The continuing presence and strength of warrior affective bonds, lasting throughout what is usually considered an age of purely hetero-sexual romantic love, have raised contentious questions among scholars who debate whether love between arms bearers might have represented, stemmed from, or easily led to physically erotic relationships between these arms bearers. Scholarly interest and dispute have ended a long period of scholarly silence, during which the subject could barely be broached. If we recognize that details from private lives of elite warriors have commonly disappeared within the mists of centuries long past, we must also exercise caution over any simple categorization. C. Stephen Jaeger has argued that the gender of a sexual partner during the Middle Ages did not create a defined sexual orientation.[100] The ennobling love that he analyzes as a force of male affection was ideally kept separate from physical intimacy. The very existence of homosexuality as a classification of affective and physical desire has been denied for this and other periods before fairly recent times.[101]

Even if we again leave such difficult generalizations to specialists, we must still register the power of intense male affection as a force within chivalry.[102] The public display of deep affection between Richard Lion-Heart and Philip Augustus, briefly noted at the beginning of this chapter, provides a classic case from chronicle sources. Roger of Hovedon reports that the two men "ate every day at the same table and from the same dish, and at night their beds did not

---

[100] Jaeger, *Ennobling Love*, 17.

[101] Helmut Puff comments that "the term 'gay' is rarely used by scholars of the premodern period" in "Same-Sex Possibilities," in *Oxford Handbook of Women and Gender in Medieval Europe*, eds. Bennett and Karras. My thanks to Ruth Karras and Helmut Puff for collegially providing a copy of this study in advance of publication.

[102] See Paul Dingman, "Ethics and Emotions: A Cultural History of Chivalric Friendship in Medieval/Early Modern Times," PhD dissertation, University of Rochester, 2012.

separate them. And the King of France loved [Richard] as his own soul."[103] In a famous later case, two well-known English knights, John Clanvowe and William Neville, termed themselves brothers; Clanvowe's love for Neville was characterized as "no less than for himself" and Neville died of grief after Clanvowe's death. The two knights were buried in the same tomb beneath a monument showing them sharing a stylized kiss and with their coats of arms "impaled"; that is, each bore on half of his escutcheon the family crest of the other. Such practice was common with spouses or bishops and their sees.[104]

Such affection also appears, with the greater articulation of interior emotions possible in imaginative literature, in the love between the great heroes Galehaut and Lancelot in both the *Lancelot do Lac* and the *Lancelot* within the Vulgate or *Lancelot-Grail* Cycle.[105] Galehaut sees Lancelot (who is disguised as the Black Knight), now fighting valiantly on foot after his last horse has been killed beneath him. He is performing classic wonders of prowess on the battlefield, defending King Arthur's land against invasion by the much more numerous forces of Galehaut.

Right and left he struck without respite, his sword constantly dealing blows. He split helmets, he cut shields apart, he battered hauberks upon shoulders and severed arms from knights; he performed wonders for all to see.[106]

Galehaut sees it all and the result can only be termed love at first sight. Deterring his own troops, Galehaut twice makes certain Lancelot is remounted and continues to watch his unfailing displays of prowess with utter admiration. Finally speaking with him as darkness ends combat, he promises to grant Lancelot any wish if he will stay with him that night in his pavilion. After a meal with elaborate

---

[103] Quoted and translated by C. Stephen Jaeger from *Gesta Henrici II*, in *Ennobling Love*, 12. Jaeger argues that the chronicler's words "do not convey, imply, or suggest homosexuality. In fact their intention may be to rule out suggestions of an illicit love." Ibid., 13.

[104] Helmut Puff, "Same-Sex Possibilities," in *Oxford Handbook of Women and Gender in Medieval Europe*, eds. Bennett and Karras, 382–384. He cautions, "Rather than ask whether particular relationships involved genital contact – a somewhat fruitless question – we need to recognize that eroticism could be present in many different ways." Ibid., 385.

[105] Discussed by Paul Dingman in "Ethics and Emotions."

[106] *Lancelot-Grail*, II, 134 (Carroll, trans.). Helmut Puff argues that "such displays of love between aristocrats did not reflect personal sentiment, let alone sexual predilection," but were a "politically motivated set of diplomatic niceties." "Same-Sex Possibilities," 385.

entertainments to provide pleasure, Lancelot retires to a large, richly decorated bed.[107] As soon as he sleeps, Galehaut lies beside him, as do two other knights. Galehaut remains awake, listening to Lancelot's troubled murmur in his exhausted sleep. In the morning, Galehaut is momentarily aghast when Lancelot makes his request: Galehaut must submit to King Arthur, whom he could actually count on defeating that day. Quickly recovering, Galehaut announces he will do as requested. Moving beyond simple adherence to his promise, he assures Lancelot that he would give him the world if only he could be sure of having his company.

As the news of Galehaut's decision reaches the Arthurian court, and as Galehaut himself is warmly welcomed there, conversation turns to the marvelous Black Knight (still unrecognized as Lancelot by the Arthurian circle); each major figure formally and publicly imagines how he or she would manage to secure the Black Knight's constant company. Arthur states that he would give up everything but the queen to secure this goal. Gawain states a wish to be the most beautiful maiden if only the Black Knight would love him above all others. To polite courtly laughter, Guinevere sidesteps the issue by remarking that Gawain has offered all that a lady can give. With obvious seriousness, Galehaut intones that he would turn his great honor into shame "if I could be as sure of him as I would wish him to be of me."[108] Yet the amorous atmosphere swirling through this part of the romance quickly becomes complicated by tensions Lancelot feels between what Corin Corley terms "friendship with a companion in arms and love of a man for a woman."[109] In short, Galehaut and Queen Guinevere are rivals for Lancelot's love. That the queen gains her desire is well known, but the significant outcome for present analysis lies the depth of Galehaut's disappointment; a false report of Lancelot's death reaches him with fatal force. And Lancelot, facing his own death, decides to be buried in the tomb he has created for his great knightly admirer.[110] Powerful

---

[107] For general discussion of such a phenomenon, see Jaeger, *Ennobling Love*, 128–133.

[108] *Lancelot-Grail*, II, 140.

[109] Corin Corley, trans., *Lancelot of the Lake* (with introduction by Elspeth Kennedy) (Oxford University Press, 1989), xii.

[110] *Lancelot-Grail: The Death of Arthur*, 136: the inscription on the tomb proclaims, "Here Lies the Body of Galehaut ... And with Him Rests Lancelot of the Lake ... The Best Knight Who Ever Entered the Kingdom of Logres."

though the emotions of the story remain, the tale itself did not create a continuing tradition; it soon disappeared from the Arthurian canon and we are left pondering its medieval resonance.[111]

In chronicle and literary accounts of intense male friendship of the sort just examined, what stands out, in what can only remain regions of controversy, is the important link of enacted prowess for male affection. Galehaut, followed by leading figures in the Arthurian court, fall into some species of love with the Black Knight after seeing his unexcelled personal prowess. As we have seen repeatedly in this book, such prowess is taken as a reliable litmus test revealing an entire range of chivalric qualities. It is important to recognize the multiplicity of values that these observers see as they witness sword strokes delivered boldly and in disregard of personal danger; such sword strokes are the crucial indicators of a larger cluster of characteristics that can inspire what we can only term, in the broad sense of that era, chivalrous male as well as female love.[112]

In fact, throughout imaginative literature intense knightly affection is often shown to blossom not only when one knight witnesses wonders of prowess performed by another, but after the experience of personal combat with such a hero. In Chrétien's *Erec and Enide*, Guivret the Short (a diminutive dynamo of a warrior) daily scans the horizon from his tower, hoping to see a passing knight so that he can "exhaust himself in combat, / or the other would wear himself out / and declare himself defeated." After Erec finally wins the all-day fight, the two knights kiss and embrace;

> Never from such a fierce battle
> Was there such a sweet parting,
> For, moved by love and generosity,
> Each of them cut long, broad bands
> From the tail of his shirt,
> And they bound up each other's wounds.[113]

---

[111] Paul Dingman suggests in "Ethics and Emotions" that though Galehaut as a named character does not continue in English and French literature, the theme is carried out in later romances, using other characters.

[112] R. W. Kaeuper, *Chivalry and Violence*, 138–143. A distinct physicality, which could be bloody and visceral, constituted prowess as deeds done in combat both in literature and in historical accounts of knightly combat.

[113] Carleton W. Carroll, ed., trans., *Erec and Enide/Chrétien de Troyes* (New York: Garland, 1987), lines 3629–3889.

Some scholarship holds that the tail of shirts worn by males could carry phallic significance in literature and see the close of this combat as a mutually agreed end to phallic aggression between Erec and Guivret. At least the cyclical link of love and prowess, which Robert Hanning astutely noted for heterosexual love, can be seen to have at least a shadowy presence between males as well.

The combat need not even be life-threatening, as with the indomitable Guivret and the hero Erec. In the *Milun* of Marie de France (to cite one case of many), when a father fights another knight (not knowing that it is his son), he is handily unhorsed at once, only to declare,

> I never once fell from my warhorse
> because of a blow from another knight.
> You knocked me down in a joust –
> I could love you a great deal.[114]

Those in a profession with a violent core would easily declare a species of love for its most adept practitioners, even if, as imagined by Marie, they fail to recognize their true bond. At least in this sense, medieval arms bearers stood in a long tradition of deeply felt, mutual warrior affection that has appeared in a variety of social settings.

CONCLUSION

Concepts of love were woven into the fabric of chivalric thought, but, paralleling the pattern we saw joining religion and chivalry, the pattern could be complex and even surprising. To a significant degree, elite lay males exercising crucial military and governing functions utilized amorous ideals not only out of pleasure, but as buttresses for their social status and further valorization for the demanding practice of their profession. Their success could not have been achieved, of course, without generating debate and dissent. Surely not all knights in any festive court or camp would have held congruent views on every issue, as Charny's sermonizing against sexual boasting and untrue love (delivered even in a time of crisis, requiring a positive approach to arms bearers) clearly indicates; he was certain some views held by knights needed amending. Amid the

---

[114] Robert Hanning and Joan Ferrante, eds., trans., *Lais of Marie de France* (New York, 1979), 174. Other cases are cited in Kaeuper, *Chivalry and Violence*, 215–219.

expression of a variety of points of view, clerics were certain of the sinfulness of some cherished chivalric views. Attitudes of women, when we can learn their frank views rather than the sometimes cartoonish representations of female thought projected by male imaginations, could be sharply critical. Sharp satire in several *lais* by Marie de France make the point decisively.[115] In "The Unfortunate One," a tournament held to decide which of three suitors will get the lady leaves two dead and one emasculated from a lance stroke. Equally sharp, Marie seems to slash at chivalric notions that all issues can ideally be settled by fighting.

On so vast and intricate a topic as love within chivalry, in short, only a variety of voices could be expected. The working codes of chivalry that we constantly seek seem to have been touched – at one level, and to a degree stemming from individual receptivity – by greater awareness of divine, forgiving love, which encouraged human love as well as fear in response. These working codes were likewise touched by romantic love between knights and ladies, and by truly intense warrior attachments, resembling and often expressed as love. In a highly chivalric mind like that of Geoffroi de Charny, all the pieces of the puzzle fit together perfectly, forming a stable foundation on which knighthood stood proudly and securely in place. He could not repeat the pattern enough: God granted great gifts of knightly endowments of strength so that good men could courageously enact the role these gifts enabled and thus carry out the hard, meritorious work of the elite warrior; in the process they would win not only the deep respect and affection of their peers, but the love of the ladies whose main function seems to have been to inspire them. Priestly quibbles could be brushed aside like gnats; the world should work according to the plan of the Lord of Hosts. Charny was ever the chivalric idealist no less than the cultural conservative.

In the autumn of the Middle Ages, however, Thomas Malory, drawing on the massive corpus of earlier writing, provides more active and complex roles for females; he also embodies the nostalgic idealist who must regretfully purvey doom, channeling all the dark warnings that had flowed for centuries like subterranean streams beneath the colorful valorization of a complex literature featuring love, prowess, and honor. Tragedies of triangular amorous

---

[115] Marie de France, "Le Chaitivel," in *Lais of Marie de France*, eds., trans., Hanning and Ferrante, 190–196; "Lay le Freine" in ibid., 73–92.

relationships replace simple, bright binaries; outcomes of even glorious displays of prowess – so often exercised in the quest for love – generate moldering hatreds that finally ignite the great conflagration consuming Camelot.

Both Charny and Malory were strenuous knights, full participants and significant actors in their chosen profession. The variations of views are striking and important. Yet on much they could agree; both saw the centrality of prowess seeking honor, and both knew it animated the arms bearers they so admired, as it animated each of them in thinking and writing about love, likely even in acting on their ideals.

ANGER, WRATH, FEAR, THIRST FOR VENGEANCE

——————— • ———————

TAKING THE PULSE OF KNIGHTLY EMOTIONS

What might seem, from an idealistic modern perspective, a triumvirate of the nasty emotions – anger, wrath, and a thirst for vengeance, hot emotions working in tandem with their first cousin, icy fear – actually constituted sturdy pillars upholding structural elements of chivalric ideology. In fact, this daunting trident of emotions (with fear ever hovering) addressed basic chivalric concerns about acquiring and preserving honor and status and avoiding dread shame. The chivalric life, says Wolfram von Eschenbach in his *Parzifal*, gives two rich possessions to its practitioners: one is good faith (the loyalty we have repeatedly encountered); the other gift is "a true sense of the shame which brings honor, today as of old."[1]

Any challenge on these fronts could spark these emotions into living flame. As men obsessed with status and honor, knights knew they must show enemies – and also demonstrate to their fellow arms bearers in a competitive world – that they would not submit to any perceived debasement; that they would vigorously enact appropriate responses in order to secure social position; and that they, with a little help from friends, subordinates, or right-minded superiors in the military–tenurial hierarchy, would restore their corner of the world to its rightful state. In Middle High German, to take only one relevant case in point, the noun *leit* can mean not only sorrow, but insult and

---

[1] Mustard and Passage, *Parzival*, 173.

dishonor.[2] Our sources thus focus on these emotions as correctives to intolerable challenges. And the case of fear provides the spur, showing deep worries about the possibility of loss.

That these powerful forces were abundantly active in the mental framework at the peak of elite lay society can readily be seen in the emotions and political actions of kings. Their vigorous personalities inspired or provoked a relatively rich supply of sources. Wrath, anger, and revenge functioned as expected and lauded royal traits. Their wrath easily enacted mini-dramas of power; their desire for vengeance could move armies. Contemporary medieval sources point to a *furor Teutonicus*, a rage in battle that marked German combat. With reason pushed aside, this battle fury could motivate fighters.[3] Wrath was often, of course, displayed by individuals, especially those in power. The *History of William Marshal* provides a striking scene of battlefield wrath on the part of King Stephen; when his surprise attack on Newbury castle provoked unexpectedly stout resistance, the constable of the besieged castle threatening to kill besiegers and warning the king to prepare ample biers, the royal response was wrathful:

> The King directed his anger against their side,
> and he swore by the birth of Christ:
> "I'll be sure to take my revenge on the low villains,
> they will all fall into my hands.
> Now, to arms, my valiant squires,
> my valiant men-at-arms and archers!"[4]

The *Histoire* is punctuated with displays of the famous Plantagenet rage, which could lead the poet to compare Richard I, for example, to a wild boar.[5] These kings, as J. E. A. Jolliffe showed many years

---

[2] Francis G. Gentry, "Key Concepts in the *Niebelungenlied*," in *A Companion to the Niebelungenlied*, ed. Winder McConnell (Rochester, NY: Camden House/Boydell, 1998), 68–69. As a result, Gentry says, "The only way for a member of heroic society to reclaim honor is through revenge."

[3] Len Scales, "War and German Identity in the Later Middle Ages," *Past & Present* 180 (2003), 41–82. Cf. Florin Curta, "Furor Teutonicus: A Note on Ethnic Stereotypes in Suger's *Deeds of Louis the Fat*," *Haskins Society Journal* 16 (2005), 62–76.

[4] *History of William Marshal*, lines 413–432.

[5] Ibid., line 11658. Bertran de Born compared Richard to a raging boar: "Introduction" in *The Poems of the Troubadour Bertran de Born*, ed. William D. Paden Jr., Tilde Sankovitch, Patricia H. Stäblein (Berkeley: University of California Press, 1986), 36–37. See poems 11, 14, 32.

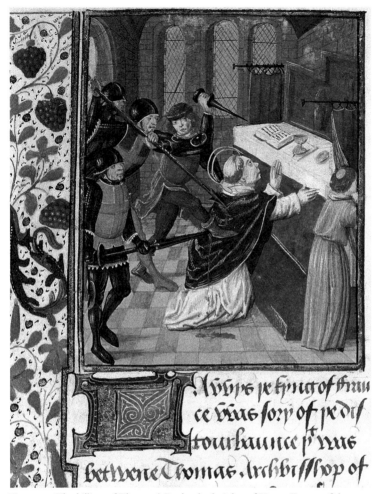

Figure 13 The killing of Thomas à Becket by knights of Henry II, one of the most noteworthy events of twelfth-century history for medieval writers and artists, shows wrath as it could overflow from, in this case, severe royal displeasure.

ago, could display their "*ira et malevolentia*" as a veritable tool of governance, leaving subjects willing to placate or pay off the crown in order to escape effects of such royal "wrath and ill will."[6] (See

[6] J. E. A. Jolliffe, *Angevin Kingship* (London: Adam and Charles Black, 1955). Clause 39 of Magna Carta makes interesting reading in this regard, as it strings together words that might restrain such wrath and ill will: "No freeman shall be

Figure 13.) At one point, unwanted advice given to the mercurial Henry II to curb his anger against his eldest son changed the king's initial courtly reception of ecclesiastical messengers into a blast of hot wrath against advisers who had put the Young King on a path of opposition to his father. Scowling, Henry swore upon his soul that "never will there be a single day that my anger will not be shown to them and their heirs, either in the morning or the evening."[7] Scenes of anger, rage, and fury multiply in this source as Henry's troubles with his sons continue and as William Marshal must deal with the yet more mercurial King John.

French royal counterparts are also said to display rage and anger over military defeats, and they almost lose their minds with rage over lost territory. After a frustrating military setback and fruitless negotiations in the conflict with his Plantagenet rival in 1181, either Philip II of France or his barons ordered the destruction of the great elm tree at Gisors, the traditional meeting place for the two sides. An account in the *History* pictures the dismantling of the symbolic tree under baronial rage, with Philip's own anger directed at the barons; the king is reported to have said that never before had such shame fallen on the crown of France and declared "in anger for all to hear" that the campaign had accomplished nothing and that he was not a woodsman![8] Whoever wielded the axes, both baronial and royal wrath are easily pictured as dramatic responses to shame. The authors of the Old French *Lancelot-Grail* cycle several times attributed to their fictional kings (Arthur, Rion, and the Grail King) the very "wrath and ill will" that served the Angevin kings so well.[9]

Recognition of the reality and dangers of royal wrath appears across the Pyrenees no less than across the Channel. His tutor warns the young Pero Niño that while serving the Castilian king he must guard against lethal royal shifts of mood, for like a lion, the king can kill in play; then, changing images, he says no wise person embarks on

captured or imprisoned or disseised or outlawed or exiled or in any way destroyed, nor will we go against him or send against him, except by lawful judgment of his peers or by the law of the land." Carl Stephenson and F. G. Marcham, *Sources of English Constitutional History* (New York: Harper & Brothers, 1937), 121.

[7] *History of William Marshal*, lines 2352–2355.

[8] See the accounts in W. L. Warren, *Henry II*, 620, and John W. Baldwin, *The Government of Philip Augustus*, 21 (where the action is attributed simply to "the French"), and *History of William Marshal*, lines 7768–7778.

[9] *Lancelot-Grail*, I, 293 (Arthur); ibid., IV, 211 (Grail King).

the sea when it is turbulent.[10] We have already observed Pero Niño heading for the border in haste when his marriage displeases the Castilian court.[11]

If we can observe many such scenes of royal wrath and their consequences, we cannot doubt that rage, threats, and acts of vengeance played well throughout elite ranks in general. The attitudes are classically encapsulated by Ganelon in the *Song of Roland*. When enraged by Roland's mocking laughter, the undoubtedly great knight Ganelon famously and publicly asserts that he will take vengeance and, when finally captured as a traitor, confidently claims that his actions were entirely justified, even though they had led to the deaths of so many heroes and the loss of the entire rear guard of Charlemagne's army. After all, his honor had been offended; wrathful vengeance was required. Even the circle of great lords standing around Charlemagne accepts this argument, so that divine judgment through trial by battle must settle the issue; only then can Ganelon be condemned to a horrid and shameful death.[12]

Intensely personal feelings about wrath, honor, and vengeance likewise move the action in the denouement of the most famous story in romance, that of Arthur, Guinevere, and Lancelot. But the pivotal figure demanding vengeance is Gawain. Early in the story, Malory has said of him through the voice of a disapproving Sir Gareth, "where he hated he wolde be avenged."[13] He was, in short, "a passing hote knight of nature."[14] This pronouncement is famously proved true. Lancelot, in rescuing the queen from being burned alive, by chance kills Gawain's brothers. Though Arthur might even then be led toward peace with Lancelot, Gawain will have none of it; the war with Lancelot grinds on and deprives Arthur of the one man who might have checked the destructive power of Mordred. Camelot tumbles into destruction, and even Gawain, albeit too late, recognizes the role his unrelenting wrath and urge for vengeance have played.[15]

[10] Joan Evans, *Unconquered Knight*, 28.   [11] See Chapter 8.
[12] See *Song of Roland*, laisses 13–23 and laisses 275–289.
[13] Vinaver, *Malory: Works*, 224.   [14] Ibid., 613.
[15] Common sentiments are heightened by contrast when Lancelot turns away from vengeance and fights only defensively against Arthurian might, leading the great French literary scholar Jean Frappier to suggest that *The Death of King Arthur* might more accurately be entitled "The Spiritual Ascent of Lancelot." See his splendid *Étude sur La Mort le Roi Artu* (Geneva, 1961), 218–258.

These scenes from the most famous *chanson* and romance form only sharp peaks rising above the seemingly endless mountain ranges of chivalric literary terrain. In no way do these famous instances of emotions at work represent uncharacteristic or outlying expressions; in fact, they can be amplified from shelves sagging beneath the weight of literary works, chronicles, and biographies packed with accounts of wrath felt and desired vengeance taken through vigorous prowess. Suffering dishonor – or even anticipation of the loss it entails – clearly ignited our tough trinity of emotions.

Great lords declare, in the *History of William Marshal*, that they will know no peace until revenge is achieved; they advise others to take "rightful revenge,"[16] and they know that to fail to take vengeance brings accusations of being lily-livered;[17] for wrath and the desire for revenge fuel prowess that secures honor. Regularly, a sense of dishonor is likewise said to generate hot wrath in the heroes of chivalric literature who show a keen desire to take vengeance that will be long remembered, at least by survivors. All know that just as honor forms the great chivalric goal, to suffer dishonor energizes the imperative desire for revenge.

This drive is apparent as cravings for revenge provide the leitmotif for many a *chanson de geste*, where it often motivates a wronged vassal to seek restoration of impugned honor. Of course securing rightful possession of productive estates can be considered a distinct matter of honor as well as revenue. The spotlight in epic usually remains centered on honor, for to be denied broad acres brings shame, as does any affront. The title character in *Raoul de Cambrai* is told by his circle of barons that he cannot be surprised if his faithful vassal Bernier is angry with him: "You have burnt his mother in her church, and, as for him, you have broken his head. God's curse on anyone who blames him if he wishes to avenge himself."[18] A universe disordered by wrong must be put right, as even divine wisdom recognizes. This epic is truly a poem of vengeance ardently sought and violently achieved; emotion and action are repeatedly proclaimed as virtuous and are exultantly described; tellingly, the action continues until, as Sarah Kay has noted, all the leading male characters having been

---

[16] *History of William Marshal*, I, lines 784–786; II, line 1481.
[17] Ibid., I, lines 784–786; II, lines 1481 and 6163. The Old French term translated as lily-livered is "*molement.*"
[18] Kay, ed., *Raoul de Cambrai*, laisse 85.

killed, the text closes.[19] If, as can be argued, the poem is an unfolding sermon against such mayhem, the need for its message still makes the sociocultural point.

Romance literature does not abandon the valorization of tough emotional responses. The portrayal of the hero Lancelot shows these interlinked emotions actively at work. It is instructive that at one point in the massive romance bearing his name Lancelot and a huge opponent named Tericam continue their combat after unhorsing each other in the standard opening joust; though "gushing with blood from lance wounds" they "felt no pain for they were so in the grip of anger and wrath that they thought of nothing except avenging the cause of their grief."[20] When, early in this romance, he is called "a disgraced son of a whore" after he has ridden in a common, decidedly uncourtly cart, Lancelot becomes sufficiently "angry and full of wrath" that he thrusts his lance through his detractor's shield, his hauberk, and his body, and drops the imprudent man lifeless to the ground.[21] Lancelot can even feel "wrath and vexation" if an opponent holds out against him longer than he expects.[22] A hero must achieve his inevitable victory swiftly; there is so much to be accomplished elsewhere. Equally telling is a description of a fight in which Lancelot has been hit atop his helm hard enough to cause him to stumble and almost fall. Stunned for a moment, the hero was "ashamed of it" and "showed his wrath" by splitting the offender's head and neck down to his shoulders.[23]. Plainly, honor requires his revenge against a knight who has for but a moment disabled him, delaying his expected victory.

The sentiment (even if it does not always spark such spectacularly successful violence) is quite common; it is scarcely limited to Lancelot. He could appreciate that in a challenging situation King Arthur goes nearly mad with wrath when an opponent in combat forces him temporarily down upon the neck of his warhorse.[24] Lancelot could likewise feel no surprise that the sword of the revered knight Bors in *The Story of Merlin* is tellingly named Wrathful (*couroucesse sespee*),[25] or that "filled with wrath," Bors enters a battle in which "he began to do wonders with his fighting."[26] This is the

---

[19] Ibid., Introduction, lv.   [20] *Lancelot-Grail*, III, I, 213.   [21] Ibid., III, 14.
[22] Ibid., III, 234.   [23] Ibid., II, 309.   [24] Ibid., I, 318.
[25] H. Oscar Sommer, ed., *Vulgate Version*, 2:235.
[26] *Lancelot-Grail*, I, 386, and note that we are repeatedly told that King Ban has a sword named Wrathful. Ibid., 246, 276, 296.

emotional frame of all great fighters in Arthurian literature, heroes
and villains alike. After his troops are routed in battle in this same
romance, the imagined King Rion becomes "as full of wrath as
anyone could be."[27] He does his utmost, engaging in fierce personal
combat with King Arthur; they charge each other, "full of wrath and
ill will, the one eager to win honor and renown and the other craving
to avenge his shame and hurt."[28] When he is castigated as a weakling
by Gaheriet in *The Story of Merlin*, Agravain becomes "filled with such
wrath that he was a wonder to behold . . . he turned red with anger
and shame."[29] If these are the emotional responses attributed to great
heroes, even minor characters show the emotional response to
diminished honor. Having witnessed the slaying of his brother by
Arpian, Danubre "took his sword and struck Arpian so wrathfully
that he made his head fly more than a lance length from his body, and
he said, 'Oh, Arpian, you've killed my brother, but you haven't
gained anything by it.'"[30]

The sheer force of the desire for vengeance – leading characters to
declare they will die if it is not satisfied[31] – can be seen in a remarkable
ideological construct that appears repeatedly in the pages of the vast
Lancelot-Grail cycle. Writers devised a compromise by which satisfying vengeance is allowed to men who are said to be "sweating with
spitefulness" or who have "burned with wrath" in battle.[32] This
ideological compromise combines satisfying vengeance with moral
imperatives. Pious injunctions about mercy are simply followed *after*
initial vengeance has been taken. In the personal combats that stud
the narrative of these works, the hero defeats his opponent, stands
towering over his enemy's prostrate body, rips off the helmet, tears
away the armor protecting the throat, and threatens instant decapita-
tion; a little encouragement to yield is provided in hard cases by
bashing the face of the defeated with the pommel of the victor's
sword. Yet the winner will then agree to spare his opponent's life if
the man openly admits defeat and asks for mercy, while lying flat on
his back, wounded, weaponless, and vulnerable. Thus the hero can
show the blessed quality of mercy (urged upon him by the most
ardently forgiving), but need grant it only after achieving the deep

---

[27] *Lancelot-Grail*, I, 293.
[28] Ibid. The reappearance of the terms "wrath" and "ill will" is notable.
[29] Ibid., I, 365.   [30] Ibid., V; *Post-Vulgate Quest for the Holy Grail*, 230.
[31] *Lancelot-Grail*, III, 66.   [32] Ibid., I, 37.

emotional satisfaction of much-loved vengeance. Striving through valorous physicality to erase a challenge or some other stain on his honor, the knight will not find the entry to heaven barred before him at the close of his life.[33]

This formula for vengeance in chivalric romance at least roughly parallels the political and emotional practice of kingship we have observed in action. If a knight defeated in single combat in a scene from romance has been forced to put himself utterly at his vanquisher's mercy, a subject who has incurred the wrath and vengeance of his royal superior finds himself at his lord's mercy; each man falls completely under the power of another and must humbly seek release, if not life itself. In each case, dominance has reasserted honor to one, and loss of agency has brought shame to the other.

Granting mercy after taking vengeance may seem minimal restraint. Some voices urged greater caution. Powerful though the impulse for vengeance was, daunting dangers obviously might result, and warnings sometimes appear in the sources. Thoughtful commentators questioned when and to what degree honorable violence might be practiced. One of the most powerfully imagined admonitions comes in advice given to King Claudas (ever in need of moral guidance) early in the *Lancelot*:

[A]n honorable man must bear his wrath and pain and harm within rather than commit some act of disloyalty or treachery that would lose him the honor of this world, toward which all prowess struggles, and the honor of the other, everlasting one, which is the great joy of Heaven.[34]

Caution about wrath is here linked to notions of honor and religious reward, a bonding whose potency we have already explored.[35] Complications become apparent if we note the words with which this passage begins:

"But whatever harm a man has suffered, whatever wrath he feels, he must safeguard his honor and fear shame on this earth, for no man, if he has eyes to see, can endure disgrace and still go on living in this world. And anyone who does not maintain his uprightness has the door to Heaven barred to him forever."

---

[33] Discussed in Richard W. Kaeuper, "Vengeance and Mercy in Chivalric *Mentalité*," in *Peace and Protection in the Middle Ages*, eds. David W. Rollason and T. B. Lambert (Toronto: Pontifical Institute of Mediaeval Studies, 2009), 168–180. For a classic case from German literature, see Mustard and Passage, *Parzival*, 115–116.

[34] *Lancelot-Grail*, II, 39.   [35] Chapter 9.

The correct course required an armored man to walk a tightrope. A just man-at-arms must act to redeem honor, but take no wrongful steps in the world that bring divine disapproval. Pharian, the fascinatingly complex character speaking these words, is tragically torn between loyalty to his morally questionable lord, Claudas, and his steady desire to do what is right, which could mean violating that very bond. The path to honor is not always obvious, and wrathful action can prove morally no less than physically destructive. At times even the heroes know it must be curbed. Having been entrapped in a magic dance by a lady, Lancelot draws his sword, only to apologize, explaining to her that he did this from anger and wrath.[36] In *The Story of Merlin*,[37] the queen counsels young Gawain that "anger has blinded many a man and has made the wise seem foolish for as long as the wrath lasts." He smiles and blesses her for her wise advice.[38] Merlin's mother, in the same romance,[39] is told by a priest, "I bid you, do not let yourself be wrathful, for the devil likes most to be where wrath is."[40] Some voices in the *History of William Marshal* warn against wrath and urge restraints upon knightly anger.[41] As we have seen, fears of anger, wrath, and revenge also dogged many a tournament, both historical and imagined.[42] Perhaps knightly wrath can properly drive a man to triumph in battle, but tournaments should, in theory, be kept free from such emotional overdrive.[43] Arthur worries over this issue for good reason: tournaments frequently turn deadly in literature as they sometimes did in life. Proud armed men powerfully thwacking each other in a simulacrum of war could easily take the short step to the real thing.[44]

Yet concerns and cautions over these emotions never formed the main line of discussion. The seemingly endless endorsement of tough emotions that we have found throughout a range of chivalric writings

---

[36] *Lancelot-Grail*, III, 165.   [37] Ibid., I, 352.

[38] As in the source cited in the previous note, sometimes wrath and anger must be forgotten and forgiven.

[39] *Lancelot-Grail*, I, 169.

[40] Her wrath later gets her into trouble (ibid., 170). This is a case of a priest speaking to a woman, of course. Whether or not the cleric would give similar advice to a practicing knight is unclear.

[41] E.g., *History of William Marshal*, I, lines 6861–6862.   [42] Chapter 7.

[43] Cf. *Lancelot-Grail*, I, 346, 385, where King Arthur will not let Round Table knights joust as they wish with foreign knights because he is afraid of wounding that will impair his forces.

[44] E.g., *Lancelot-Grail*, I, 348.

shows the majority view. It even drew on religious blessing. We have seen that a vengeful course of action is often simply assumed to receive divine blessing; and the lines from *Raoul de Cambrai* quoted earlier) show warriors confidently calling for divine curse on those blaming righteous vengeance. In the *History of William Marshal*, lay lords comfortably and confidently implore the Lord God to take vengeance on their enemies, and offer thanks to God who has given them opportunity to take personal revenge.[45] After all, God can be honored with the unforgettable title of "Supreme Avenger."[46] Were he not the divine taker of vengeance for human wrongdoing, no less than a divine source of forgiveness, the system of sin and redemption would not be possible or even necessary.[47] With the Lord of Hosts blessing their just actions, the knights could feel righteousness as well as elite social approval in their wrath and vengeance. They seem to have felt a sense of entitlement – or even of duty – to exercise revenge fueled by wrath. Evidence beyond written texts was once literally thick on the ground, for over centuries and over a wide swath of territory many a charred village and devastated field or vineyard could once have mutely testified to the reality of hot chivalric wrath that wiped out some perceived stain upon honor. Of course loot and territorial gain added balm to wounded pride. So much of the violence evident in the world we are examining was at least formally justified on the basis of righteous wrath linked to assertion or restoration of honor.

Obviously, we have no magnet or suitable solvent to separate components of pure power politics and acquisitiveness from deeply felt outrage over honor impugned. Yet such a distinction must have blurred in the minds of the militant elite as well. Rage and political calculation need not come in separate packages. When his men returned empty-handed from a raid (while on the North African

---

[45] "May the God who advances the cause of all worthy men take revenge for him on all those who have done him harm and ill" (*History of William Marshal*, I, lines 6290–6291).

[46] *Lancelot-Grail*, IV; *Post-Vulgate Quest for the Holy Grail*, 214.

[47] E.g., confession of sins works, says the *History of the Holy Grail*, "to God's honor and to the devil's shame." *Lancelot-Grail*, I, 27. Out of hundreds of possible examples, see the wrath and anger of Jesus Christ in the *Quest for the Holy Grail* (*Lancelot-Grail*, I, 130), or the famous Dolorous Stroke by which God lays waste several kingdoms in wrathful retribution for mere human hands grasping the sacred lance from Calvary.

coast), Pero Niño sternly lamented not merely the loss of loot, but the impairment that their failure had brought to his honor.[48] Moreover, it remains significant that wrath, acquisitiveness, and honor were usually blended into violence at all levels of conflict, from a personal quarrel or regional feud to the sweeping campaigns of the Hundred Years War. The ravaging that we have seen (in Chapter 6) formed so large a role in warfare could be linked to wrath as well as greed. The witness of Don Pero Niño is again helpful. Assuring a Moorish king in North Africa that he intended no further raiding against his people, Pero Niño said, literally, that he would not impose his anger on him any further, for the present (*"Je que non le entien do fazer mas henojo agora de presente"*).[49] The link between wrath aroused and prowess enacted appears so frequently and in so many sources as to defy citations; but any reader of *Barbour's Bruce* will recall how often feelings of wrath and anger are assuaged by either the Scots or the English taking bloody vengeance on the other side. As Barbour intones early in his narrative, despite the odds against the Scots, God allowed them to avenge the harms and oppressions imposed on them by the English.[50] A classic chronicle of the early phase of the Hundred Years War by Geoffrey le Baker considers widespread devastation in the realm of France to be righteous action taken against the Valois "tyrant" or "crowned one" whom he will never call king of France. For Baker, Edward III should wear that crown and can bring his wrath with fire and sword against those who deny him that honor.[51] In this case, as in so many others, actively to claim a right is to achieve honor; to experience denial of rights imposed dishonor, requiring correction with any degree of violence needed.

It is notoriously difficult to take accurate emotional temperatures at a distance of many centuries. But we need not consider elite arms bearers as simply out of control, as slaves to emotional pressures they could not guide or repress, though descriptions of such cases can be found. Granted, the righteousness of the great in both literature and life is sometimes said to be so intense that they are described as nearly

[48] Evans, *Unconquered Knight*, 81; Díaz de Gamez, Carriazo, *El victorial*, 124.
[49] Evans, *Unconquered Knight*, 76; Díaz de Gamez, Carriazo, *El victorial*, 119.
[50] *Barbour's Bruce*, bk. 1, lines 450–464; he continues with a comparison of the Scots to the Maccabees.
[51] Geoffrey le Baker, *The Chronicle of Geoffrey le Baker of Swinbrook*, 46: "In fact I prefer from now on to call him the tyrant of France, seeing that he was an enemy of the common justice and a usurper of the holy kingdom of France."

speechless, mad, or out of their minds with rage. They attack enemies and strike brutal blows spurred by rage. The long and intensely admiring description of Lancelot as a young lad shows the tenor of such descriptions, which appear abundantly in many a romance; it includes this passage:

His eyes were bright and smiling and full of delight as long as he was in a good mood, but when he was angry, they looked just like glowing coals and it seemed that drops of red blood stood out from his cheekbones. He would snort like an angry horse and clench and grind his teeth, and it seemed that the breath coming out of his mouth was all red; then he would shout like a trumpet in battle, and whatever he had his teeth in or was gripping in his hands he would pull to pieces. In short, when he was in a rage, he had no sense or awareness of anything else, and this became apparent on many an occasion.[52]

When shortly after this the young Lancelot severely beats his tutor for offending him, threatening even to kill him if he can catch him outside the world controlled by the Lady of the Lake, she reacts with pleasure:

When the lady heard him react with such resolve, she was very pleased, as she realized that he could not fail to become a worthy knight; she was very pleased that, with God's help and hers, he would be a man of great valor.[53]

In many other cases – and even in this case – rational calculation can be seen to stand behind emotional outbursts and the consequences that followed. Wrath felt and vengeance taken in protection of honor formed a framework of thought and action for elite warriors; they did not need to decide on the spot whether to reconstruct it when some affront triggered a mini-crisis. It was how they thought. And it was how writers wanted to show them thinking. The emotions surrounding sacred honor need not be considered either as a mere mask hiding real motives (unstained by emotions) for action or as the sole generating force; in practice they must have worked so well together that even those swinging a sword or carrying a torch toward a dwelling could not separate them. Just as prowess seeking honor has proved essential to our understanding of chivalry in general, this closely linked pairing played a crucial role within the potent emotional set of anger, wrath, and a desire for vengeance. As we turn to omnipresent fear, we will encounter them again actively at work.

---

[52] *Lancelot-Grail*, II, 18.   [53] Ibid., II, 21.

FEAR AND ITS ANTIDOTES

Beyond the fear of shame and dishonor, did the men-at-arms experience sheer physical fear of combat and its consequences for life and limb? Finding from a distance of many centuries the active presence of such fear (perhaps through measures to lessen or erase its force) represents a daunting investigative enterprise. Yet the task is as important as it is challenging. If we could characterize these elite fighters either as fearless paragons or as craven boasters, analysis would be simple. In fact, a full range of meanings and behaviors will appear. Admonitions prescribing ideal behavior stand out prominently, but descriptions of observed behavior also reveal internal struggles and even record instances of flight from a battle in abject terror. Many sources only reluctantly yield such information, but by drawing generally on the entire range of evidence we can construct a broad view on physical fear. This requires finding a way past what Andrew Taylor has incisively termed "the code of silence, never once acknowledging fear." This code operated through "role-playing and self-censorship" in which "noble speeches served to maintain the knight's public status, to hearten his friends and to intimidate his enemies, and they also became his memorial."[54]

Of course at the ideal end of the scale, heroic knights appear unblemished by fear, and lesser mortals are urged to pattern themselves on such attitudes and actions. In *The Book of the Order of Chivalry*, his often-translated and widely circulated treatise, Ramon Llull made the case uncompromisingly:

Since nobility of courage cannot be vanquished or overcome by one man or by all the men that exist, and yet one body can be vanquished and seized by one other, the malfeasant knight who fears more desperately for the strength of his body when he flees from battle and forsakes his lord does not practice the office of the knight because of the villainy and weakness of his courage, nor does he serve or obey the honoured Order of Chivalry that had its beginning in nobility of courage.[55]

---

[54] Andrew Taylor, "Chivalric Conversation and the Denial of Male Fear," in *Conflicted Identities and Multiple Masculinities: Men in the Medieval West*, ed. Jacqueline Murray (New York: Garland, 1999), 176, 178. Taylor notes (179) the two components of this code: "understatement and aggressive vaunting or abuse, one repressive, the other expressive."

[55] Noel Fallows, trans., Llull, *Book of the Order of Chivalry* (Woodbridge, Suffolk: Boydell, 2013), 48–49. Fallows rightly claims this is "the first modern English

The term "fearless" is regularly coupled in romance with other virtuous labels: every hero is "a worthy and fearless fighter" or "a faithful and fearless knight."[56] A foretelling of the coming of the perfect knight Galahad in the *Lancelot* within the Vulgate Cycle includes, among his defining qualities, that he will know no fear.[57] His father, Lancelot, was taught basic ideals of chivalry, while young, by the mysterious and magical Lady of the Lake who, in a famous conversation, insists, "A knight must not, out of fear of death, do anything that might bring him dishonor or even a hint of it, but must fear a shameful act more than death."[58] His response redoubled the message: "I will not let fear of any kind stop me from receiving the high order of knighthood."[59] This basic message glows with religious valorization in the *Quest of the Holy Grail* when a Worthy Man tells Percival that God "would ... test you and see whether you are ... as loyal a knight as those who follow the order of chivalry... Nothing should diminish your courage, whether fear or earthly danger... If he succumbs to fear, he's not a true knight."[60]

Such passages bear comparison with other statements in the famous treatise by Ramon Llull that employs similar terms and standards for the ideal knight:

It behooves the squire who desires knighthood to understand the great burden of Chivalry and the great perils that await those who wish to uphold Chivalry for the knight should hesitate more before the vituperation of the people than before death, and shame must cause greater suffering to his courage than hunger, thirst, heat, cold or any other suffering or hardship to his body. And therefore all these perils must be revealed and announced to the squire before he is dubbed a knight.[61]

The knights who ride through Thomas Malory's *Morte Darthur* often uphold ideal standards regarding fear. A common statement from one of these great fighters carefully and boldly explains that some course of action they are following has no link to the debased motive of fear.[62] Of course they cause considerable fear in their enemies. Tristram causes great fear in a terrifying giant. Even the mention of

translation derived directly from the original work composed in medieval Catalan" (31).

[56] *Lancelot-Grail*, I, *Story of Merlin*, 239, 247.   [57] Ibid., II, 253.   [58] Ibid., II, 59.

[59] Ibid., II, 61.   [60] Ibid., IV, 33.

[61] Fallows, trans., Llull, *Book of the Order of Chivalry*, 59–60.

[62] Examples can be found in Vinaver, *Malory: Works*, 198, 276, 281, 296, 343–344, 347, 366, 508, 612, 618, 693.

Lancelot causes fear in King Mark; and Malory admits that two knights who put fear into the Red City ride along with a sense of great "bobbaunce[boasting] and pryde."[63]

Such high standards – of avoiding fear but causing it in others – likewise appear in chivalric biographies and vernacular manuals. Fear is never attributed to William Marshal, though he assuredly caused a good deal in others. Not long after this biography was written, the Flemish court poet Baudoin de Conde, in a didactic poem entitled "Le Bacheler," sternly warned knights to avoid avarice, which causes "fear that . . . draws back from many a deed of prowess."[64] Charny's *Book of Chivalry* represents an extended hymn to bold prowess with admonitions for knights to fear only shame.[65] The great Scots heroes who stride through *Barbour's Bruce* could match their literary counterparts. Robert Bruce inspires his men with exemplary bravery and prowess, and Sir James Douglas is said never to have known fear, no matter how strenuously he was assaulted.[66] Díaz de Gamez's biography of Don Pero Niño opens with an elaborate origins myth for chivalry, with the dilemma being to find the best men to be knights in an imagined past; the select group emerges as the body of men who demonstrate their capacity to "give good blows, and bear fear well, and have no qualms about death."[67] Woodworkers are strong and butchers are inured to blood, but the men who become elite fighters fear shame and conquer fear of battle as no others could. Díaz de Gamez insists that his hero cared so much for honor that he feared no danger that beset him.[68] Confronted by the fears of his crew before an impending sea fight, Pero Niño tersely responded, "He who has fear, let him flee."[69] Such sentiments likewise appear in the biography of a great Burgundian knight, Louis de la Tremoille, written in 1527. During the French campaign in Italy, he exhorts the men who are transporting the French king's artillery through the Alps, saying that

---

[63] Vinaver, *Malory: Works*, 307, 361, and 437, respectively.
[64] Archives Nationale, Paris, ms Fr 428, lines 140–145 of "Le Bacheler," as translated by Elspeth Kennedy (unpublished).
[65] Kaeuper and Kennedy, *Book of Chivalry*, passim.
[66] *Barbour's Bruce* praises the bravery of the Bruce regularly; on Douglas, see bk. 19, lines 595–598, "he that na tyme was effrayit."
[67] Díaz de Gamez, Carriazo, *El victorial*, 5–6; Evans, *Unconquered Knight*, 4–6.
[68] Díaz de Gamez, Carriazo, *El victorial*, 110; Evans, *Unconquered Knight*, 65.
[69] Díaz de Gamez, Carriazo, *El victorial*, 255; Evans, *Unconquered Knight*, 163.

the King, our sovereign Lord, prays you through my mouth that, bearing all these things in mind, you will march your honor before the fear for your lives, and that, your courageous hearts not converted to soft wool, you will show him in effect of your noble will to move his artillery through these hard mountains. To men of little courage, such a thing would seem impossible, but to men of honor this is but a game.[70]

Of course some of the many forms that fear could take are openly acknowledged and accepted in romance, treatise, and biography; for fear may imply only sensible caution or prudence. Fear of God joins love of God in a perfect, pious fusion; a prudent man fears thunder and lightning in the natural world, as he fears treachery and treason in the political and military world. Magical events that alter the expected order of the world may cause even a great hero such as Lancelot to tremble.[71] While on campaign, caution or fear of ambush or encirclement is only prudent, and a wise leader will take appropriate steps to protect himself and secure his advance toward victory.[72]

Yet one species of fear haunted chivalry, circling utterly beyond formal toleration. This was the fear felt in active practice of knighthood when a man-at-arms was expected to perform the deeds of arms that win honor. Such disabling fear was easily equated with cowardice; it eviscerated needed prowess and bonded with shame; it denied knightly function and derogated elite status. A knight could feel fear *for* someone he loves, but must not feel fear *of* an enemy he must confront. Repeatedly in the *Lancelot-Grail* cycle and even more frequently in Malory's *Morte Darthur*, as a speaker takes some prudent course of action, he carefully specifies that he is *not* acting out of fear.[73] Even the Marshal's biographer, telling how his hero left the court of Henry II because of ruptured relations with the Young King, adds, "He did not look like a man in flight or one who feared another

---

[70] "Panegyrique de Louis de la Tremoille", in *Collection complèt des mémoires relatifs a l'histoire de France*, vol. XV (1820), trans. Daniel McDonald (unpublished), 69–70. I am grateful to Mr. McDonald for making this translation for use in my seminar.

[71] E.g., Lancelot feels fear when the ground suddenly moves beneath him. Vinaver, ed., *Malory: Works*.

[72] E.g., *Lancelot-Grail*, I, 407 (ambush), *Lancelot-Grail*, II, 189–190 (treachery), *Lancelot-Grail*, IV, 40 (fear and love of God), *Lancelot-Grail*, I, 229 (thunder and lightning).

[73] E.g., in *Lancelot-Grail*, IV, 190, 253, 260, 271, 300; *Lancelot-Grail*, V, 127–128, 132, 139, 140. Examples in Malory are too numerous to cite, but see Vinaver, *Malory: Works*, 276, 347.

knight."[74] Similarly, a knight pictured in *The Merlin Continuation*, when called upon to yield in a fight and save his life, voices the creed with equal clarity:

Ill health to anyone who does that while he has life in his body! For after I myself had acknowledged my cowardice, I would never have honor. Certainly, I'd rather die a hundred times, if that were possible, than one single time to say or do something that looked like cowardice... never for fear of death will I do or say anything that might turn to my shame.[75]

Nearly all arms bearers knew that this absolute standard stated the ideal, even if they also knew the human tendency to react in line with imperatives of self-preservation and calculation of gain and loss. Ideal standards sometimes actually determined action, even if it meant self-destruction. Giles d'Argentaine was long remembered among the Scots no less than his English comrades for scorning the general flight as the battle of Bannockburn went against the English, who began to seek safety in flight; he chose, instead, to ride determinedly to his death against waiting Scots' spears.[76] Chivalric courts must also have buzzed with talk when they heard accounts of the blind king of Bohemia's consciously suicidal charge at the battle of Crécy, where he was guided against enemy ranks by squires willing to join him in the fatal charge, touching armored elbows to guide him to death with honor. Interestingly, as Craig Taylor has noted, few modern readers realize that he was repairing a gaping hole in his honor caused by leaving the field of battle at Vottern.[77] The ideal and the actual stand paired in the incidents, a clear and likely not uncommon failure being

---

[74] *History of William Marshal*, I, lines 6842–6843. William did, however, travel under royal safe conduct.

[75] *Lancelot-Grail*, IV, 235. For a discussion of an earlier period, see Richard Abels, "Cowardice and Duty in Anglo-Saxon England," *Journal of Medieval Military History* 4 (2006), 29–38.

[76] Seymour Philips, *Edward II* (New Haven: Yale University Press, 2010), and *Barbour's Bruce*, bk. 13, lines 320–323; *Vita Edwardi Secundi*, ed. N. Denholm-Young (Oxford: Oxford University Press, 1957), 53–54; Sir Thomas Gray, *Scalacronica 1275–1363*, ed., trans. Andy King (Surtees Society, vol. 209) (Rochester: Boydell & Brewer Press, 2005), 76–77: "After saving the king from dismounted Scottish knights, Giles says, 'I am not accustomed to fleeing, and I don't wish to go any further; I commend you to God.' He put his spurs to his horse, and went back to fight, where he was killed."

[77] Craig Taylor, *Chivalry and the Ideals of Knighthood in France during the Hundred Years War*, 133, citing sources. Sir Thomas Gray, *Scalacronica*, trans. Andy King (Surtees Society), 76–77.

redeemed by heroic action. In honor culture, as in calculations of royal favor within the English political orbit, good practice of violence wiped out a debt incurred by bad practice of violence. The blind king's case can stand for many other instances that could be added in which concern for honor drove out all fear, including the fear of death. Naomi Hurnard has argued that in England the general policy of pardon for homicide granted in return for military service evolved after 1294 when Edward I "made pardon available to every able-bodied male criminal who cared to earn it by military service."[78]

No count of acts of fearlessness would accurately measure flight versus bravery or self-sacrifice, and questions will stubbornly remain. Could rational men truly be, in the ideal chivalric sense, fearless, or could they, perhaps, best be brave without being truly fearless? However these questions are answered, the existence of a chivalric ideal retains its importance, forming a backdrop against which more prosaic calculations were made. It becomes a factor we must recognize, realizing that if we are to understand chivalry in action we must analyze what was thought as well as what was done. The gold standard for knightly action would ever have been lodged in most medieval minds, even if we know such a standard may not have routinely determined actions. In modern parallels, belief in business competition may coexist alongside preference for monopoly, protective tariff policies, or even lavish government subsidies. Likewise – at the other end of the political scale – "Brussels carpet progressives" may staunchly believe in equality, so long as it touches them very little. Elite medieval arms bearers were likely no more – and no less – driven by a combination of ideals and self-interest than are people today.

Delving below the surface of medieval sources, we can find recognition of the reality of fear among practicing knights, confirming that no simple framing of the issue remains satisfactory. Alongside didactic portraits of fearless heroes, most texts at some point detail abject physical fear, often leading to plainly cowardly actions in contrast to thought and practice of great heroes, real or imagined. Limitations of

---

[78] Naomi Hurnard, *The King's Pardon for Homicide before ad 1307* (Oxford University Press, 1969), 248. Cf. J. Andrew Villalon, "'Taking the King's Shilling' to Avoid 'the Wages of Sin': English Royal Pardons for Military Malefactors during the Hundred Years War," in *The Hundred Years War, Part III: Further Considerations*, eds. J. Andrew Villalon and Donald J. Kagay (Leiden: Brill, 2013), 357–436.

human nature are at least indirectly acknowledged. Men who embarked on rugged and dangerous military campaigns, and who anticipated and experienced physical combat conducted with honed weaponry amid buzzing flights of bolts and arrows, would not have been human had they not known fear. Many authors represent such natural fear almost as frequently as they praise ideal fearlessness.[79]

Plain and almost casual speaking about fear may be a means of emphasizing how tough and even deadly the fight was for hardy heroes. In a society in which a good end made all the difference for eternity, the warriors knew they needed to have settled spiritual accounts; fear would thus be especially potent if the arms bearers were thrust suddenly into combat when they had not recently or fully confessed their heavy burden of sin.[80] Saying the enemy died without confession gives particular pleasure to Jean le Bel, but deep sorrow affects any writer if friends die thus.[81] Prudent warriors are shown communing themselves with three blades of grass or symbolically recognizing their mortality by kneeling and thrusting a bit of soil into their lips.[82]

Disaster could drop upon them unexpectedly. Far from standing resolutely against the approaching enemy, whole armies suddenly break formation in accounts written into both chronicle and imaginative literature; the warriors flee in panic, abandoning their leaders in their fear[83] and forgetting in the rush for supposed safety that the

---

[79] E.g., *Lancelot-Grail*, I, 419, and *History of William Marshal*, I, line 3940 as examples selected almost at random from accounts that could be cited.

[80] E.g., *Lancelot-Grail*, II, 219.

[81] *The True Chronicles of Jean le Bel*, 185, on the death of the duke of Normandy's cousin, the count of Alecon, and uncle, Count Louis of Blois.

[82] E.g., Kay, *Raoul de Cambrai*, laisse 120.

[83] E.g., *Lancelot-Grail*, II, 195, 201; *Barbour's Bruce* is replete with instances of men fleeing in fear, though such behavior is usually attributed to the English. Chronicles of the Hundred Years War also narrate flight from many battlefields, as any reading of Froissart, Jean le Bel, or Geoffrey le Baker will reveal. Jean le Bel, *True Chronicles*, notes and emphasizes when men-at-arms and knights resolutely take a stand against superior forces during a retreat: e.g. (91) a contingent of the Bishop of Liege's men, led by Connars de Lonchiens, "dismounted to make a stand, preferring to die than flee" when surrounded by more than seventy Hainaulters; two cannons and a squire along with Connars "mounted such a valiant defense that they earned great honour." Cf. Geoffrey le Baker, *Chronicle*, 77–78, commends both sides during the battle of Neville's Cross (1346), for being willing to die rather than flee; but he blames the Scottish marshal, Earl Patrick, in command of their rear guard, for precipitating the Scottish rout, and he reports

real killing will soon begin as they are hunted down as scattered individuals or small groups, or are drowned in the inconvenient river that bordered so many battlefields. The fawning biographer of Louis de la Tremoille, a great Burgundian knight killed in the early sixteenth century, gives him a speech, no less frank than uplifting, delivered to his troops awaiting battle:

Let us then deploy our hands, open our hearts, raise our spirits, heat our blood, and defy fear, that our young King's love so benign, lenient, gracious, and generous guides us, and that none turns to flee, for those who do shall be hanged. It is better to die defending yourself than to live as a fugitive; for life saved through fleeing is a life surrounded by death.[84]

One way of emphasizing the rigor of a battle was to say no combatant could be so bold as to declare he was not filled with fear.[85] When the *History of William Marshal* declares a battle was fought "neither side fearing the other in the least," the unusual claim seems intended as hyperbolic complement, rather than realistic description.[86] In fact, in a sober moment the poet/biographer writes that, at one point, Henry II and his men, fearing a large French army moving toward them, had early morning Masses sung.[87] Men engaged in combat are shown sometimes to quake or tremble with fear, to fall down upon the ground, and to beg for mercy, acknowledging defeat so that their lives and limbs will be spared.[88] One unfortunate fighter in a *chanson* loses bowel control and soils his saddle.[89] Panic may even come upon armies on the eve of battle like an unexpected mist.[90] Flemish troops who were attacked while enthusiastically looting Saint-Omer fled in

---

that Lord Percy presciently mentioned before the battle, "The cowardice of that traitor, who has never dared to meet us on an open field, will profit us more than a thousand Scots could harm it." The earl's cowardice and shameful behavior is contrasted with the loyalty of those who chose "a fair death before a shameful life" protecting their king. Often a set of negative moral qualities is used to describe those higher-ranked knights and men-at-arms who retreat.

[84] *Panegyric de Louis de la Tremoille* (unpublished), trans. Daniel McDonald.
[85] *Lancelot-Grail*, III, 306. [86] *History of William Marshal*, I, line 6061.
[87] Ibid., I, lines 8518–8519.
[88] Examples provided in R. W. Kaeuper, "Vengeance and Mercy."
[89] Michael Newth, trans., *Song of William*, in Newth, *Heroes of the French Epic*, lines 343–348, a reference to the fearful Count Thibaut.
[90] An excellent case involving both sides in the Anglo-Norman invasion of Ireland appears in *The Deeds of the Normans in Ireland (La Geste des Engleis en Yrlande)*, trans., ed., Evelyn Mullally (Dublin: Four Courts Press, 2002).

such panic that they later "could not explain how or why it had happened than if they'd been enchanted."[91]

Even the great cannot keep a secure footing atop their pedestals of ideal fearlessness. We may not experience surprise that morally doubtful kings opposed to the Arthurian court such as Rion and Claudas may be said to suffer from fear or to find their armies melting away on a battlefield;[92] Claudas, who is lauded because he "feared a life of shame more than a decent death,"[93] nonetheless fears having his head cut off in combat.[94] Yet even King Arthur, who can be characterized as "not a man who wished for any fear of death to behave like a coward," in fact knows fear when the dread giant of Mont-Saint-Michel raises his huge cudgel to strike.[95] Many Arthurian heroes join the queue of fearful realists. The King of a Hundred Knights fears a disabling sword blow; news of a Saxon invasion makes the assembled barons' flesh crawl from fear.[96] In their fight, Gawain and Segurade seem evenly matched, yet "neither was so brave that he was not fearful of losing his life and his honor forevermore."[97] In the climactic fight against Mordred as Camelot crumbles, Yvain is said to know fear for the first time in his life.[98] Similarly, Balain, earlier praised as the best knight, feels fear in his heart late in his troubled life.[99]

These men are pictured fighting quotidian battles, but what of crusaders? Crusade chronicles may sometimes picture militant saints joining the fight against Muslim armies, but they can also frankly record sheer panic among the merely worldly warriors. Writing of the crusade of Richard Lion-Heart, one chronicler, for example, may contrast Western arms bearers who fear no danger to perfidious Greeks who are debilitated by needless fears, but repeatedly he comments on abject fear within Western Christian ranks as well.[100] He seems to have encountered enough fear to muse about it abstractly:

Fear, in its anxiety, gives all things, however uncertain, an appearance of probability; and when a confused state of affairs comes to the knowledge of

---

[91] Bryant, *The True Chronicles of Jean le Bel*, 88–89.
[92] *Lancelot-Grail*, I, 296–297, 314.   [93] Ibid., II, 49.   [94] Ibid., I, 314.
[95] Ibid., I, *Story of Arthur*, 293, 404.   [96] *Lancelot-Grail*, I, 233, 235.
[97] Ibid., I, 162.   [98] Ibid., IV, 151.   [99] Ibid., IV, 218.
[100] Shaw, ed., trans., *Chronicles of the Crusades* (London: Bohn, 1848), 109, 122, 130, 168, 210, 236.

others, they are themselves disturbed, and their minds are apt to be alarmed lest everything should turn out disturbed.[101]

Joinville is even more personal as he narrates a crisis during the first crusade of Louis IX. As capture loomed, one of his domestic servants suggested they all accept martyrdom, since it would lead to paradise. Such advice could almost come from a sermon exemplum. Opting rather for capture and a chance to live, Joinville tersely reports, "we none of us took his advice."[102]

The many sources that acknowledge fear are willing to offer some degree of understanding to the fearful, even if the author formally praises heroes who are fearlessly courageous. *Barbour's Bruce* grants that some men who otherwise fight bravely will tremble with fear under sudden attack.[103] Such generalization turns specific when he notes of Earl John of Atholl that "His hart began to faile all-out" seeing the setbacks of the Bruce, the number of enemies he faced, and troubles and fears all around; given constant hunger and alarms, the earl said, he reckoned his life not worth a straw.[104] Even more dramatic, the constable holding out against an assault on the keep at Roxburgh maintained a sturdy defense as "a man off gret valour," Barbour says, until he was struck by an arrow in the face; fearing for his life, he then arranged surrender.[105]

The fear at issue in fighting men was, of course, generated by other fighting men, and without restraint authors sing the praises of this capacity to instill fear in others; if a good knight should ideally not feel or at least not show fear, he should assuredly instill fear in others. Feeling fear (however human) can bring the taint of timidity that inflicts dishonor; inducing fear in opponents, on the other hand, proves dominance, provides protection for honor, and elevates status. The author of the panegyric written for the Burgundian family of Louis de la Tremoille in 1527 recalls roots of the family tree going back into the thirteenth century and says with enthusiasm that some of these forebears "for their noble arms, were feared and dreaded, because they were rich, valiant and wise in the ways of war."[106] Often enough stated to be considered a maxim, the best knight will be the knight most feared – and loved. Meritorious capacity to inspire fear

[101] Ibid., 273.   [102] Ibid., 243.   [103] *Barbour's Bruce*, bk. 2, lines 298–299.
[104] *Barbour's Bruce*, bk. 3, lines 307–312, 314–320.
[105] *Barbour's Bruce*, bk. 10, 474–485.
[106] *Panegyric de Louis de la Tremoille* (unpublished), trans. Daniel McDonald, 2.

surfaces regularly in imaginative chivalric literature. "Tristan was an exceptionally good knight, feared by all."[107] Claudas, a great knight, if not a moral exemplar, is feared by all his neighbors.[108] Of course, collectively, Camelot is "feared and respected."[109] Like an Arthurian hero, the historical Robert Bruce was admired for overcoming his enemies and cleaving the head of a major opponent.[110] He regularly fought so resolutely throughout the wars of independence that his biographer is sure all his enemies feared him.[111] At one critical point, in order to protect his retreating forces, he stands alone at a narrow ford (with only God to aid him, he insisted); he killed fourteen attackers one by one – Barbour claims that the attacking force numbered more than two hundred men – until the rest fled in fear.[112] In fact, all the heroes in *Barbour's Bruce* are said to inspire fear through their prowess. Robert Bruce's stalwart coadjutor, James Douglas, had avenged his father so well that all Englishmen feared him, and the terror he caused became a leitmotif in Barbour's account.[113] He was as dreaded as "the fell devil of hell," in fact, and his name was used to frighten disobedient children.[114]

Even Ramon Llull's idealistic treatise on chivalry emphasizes the knightly duty to induce fear and establish dominance within a kingdom – rather than among competing knights from beyond its borders. The warriors act, that is, to restrain and overawe the mass of men they considered subordinate beings. In other words, the Order of Chivalry secures proper order in society:

> Just as clerics, through an honest life, good example and learning, profess the Order and office of inclining people to devotion and a good life, so knights, by upholding the Order of Chivalry through nobility of courage and force of arms, profess the Order to which they belong so that they may incline the people to fear and they will in turn be afraid of committing offenses against each other.[115]

---

[107] *Lancelot-Grail*, V, 249.   [108] Ibid., II, 15.   [109] Ibid., V, 214.

[110] E.g., *Barbour's Bruce*, bk. 13, 50–56.

[111] E.g., *Barbour's Bruce*, bk. 3, lines 147–152, 180–182, for fear on the part of the lord of Lorne and a quotation from one of his retainers. Percy is said to be in dread of Robert (bk. 5, lines 185–191 and 220).

[112] *Barbour's Bruce*, bk. 6, lines 129–180.

[113] *Barbour's Bruce*, bk. 1, lines 291–295 (avenging his father); for later statements, see bk. 4, lines 412–418. Douglas is at least once said to fear the might of Englishmen (bk. 5, lines 440–441; bk. 8, lines 67–70; bk. 15, lines 551–562).

[114] *Barbour's Bruce*, bk. 15, lines 551–562.

[115] Noel Fallows, trans., Llull, *The Book of the Order of Chivalry* (Woodbridge, Suffolk: Boydell, 2013), 42. Fallows rightly claims this is "the first modern

In a later chapter he is even more specific, insisting that needed labor on the land is secured only by fear of the knights:

It is the office of the knight to maintain the land, for out of the dread that the people have of the knights they hesitate to destroy lands, and out of fear of the knights, kings and princes hesitate to proceed against each other. But the malfeasant knight who does not come to the aid of his temporal, natural lord, against another prince is a knight without office, and he is the same as faith without works, and he is the same as miscreance, which is against faith.[116]

Clear male superiority is equally important in Llull's classically misogynistic view:

Since man possesses more common sense and understanding and is of a naturally stronger disposition than woman, this enables him to be better than a woman, for if he were not so capable of being good like a woman it would follow that goodness and the force of nature would be contrary to goodness of courage and good works. Thus, just as man, because of his nature, is more disposed than woman to have noble courage and be good, so man is more disposed to be treacherous than woman, for it he were not he would not be worthy of having greater nobility of courage and a greater advantage for being good than woman.[117]

Divine endowments enable men to create proper fear in society generally and more particularly in all women, even as they achieve priceless honor through fearless combat.

Our sources show that emphasis, in general, falls on men who can cause other men to quake. On any particular battlefield the hero enacts his enemies' worst fears as he clears his own path with a deadly and destructive sword; often he finds his enemies falling back before him in fear and dread. Such capacity is regularly admired in William Marshal no less than in Lancelot. The historical figure and the imaginative chivalric creation are described in similar terms.[118] Here is the Marshal in action. He

> proved himself as a valiant knight:
> having broken his lance,
> he drew forthwith his sword
> and went right into the fray to lay about him.

English translation derived directly from the original work composed in medieval Catalan" (31).
[116] Ibid., 47.   [117] Ibid., 41.
[118] R. W. Kaeuper, "William Marshal and Lancelot: The Issue of Chivalric Identity," *Essays in Medieval Studies* 22 (2005, online and in print), ed. Anita R. Riedinger, 8–17.

Anyone watching him would not have thought that he still had to learn about fighting.

> He had to give and receive many a blow
> before retiring from that fight;
> and he had no desire to leave the field
> before making his accomplishments plain for all to see.
> What a deadly companion they found him to be
> as he cut a swath through the throng.
> Many he found who let him through,
> for the blows he dealt were so violent that
> they were greatly feared
> coming as they did with such force behind them.[119]

One knight hit by William was so terrified by the blow that he slid off his horse and hid in an upper room in abject fear.[120] Lancelot is similarly imagined to clear a path as even his boldest opponents find themselves seized with fear.[121] His own view, by contrast, is resolute: "As long as we dare . . . fear doesn't matter."[122] He later specifically links fear with cowardice.[123]

The formula of fearless heroes causing fear in others appears throughout Arthurian literature. Among such heroes, Gawain, following a standard incognito fight, lauds the young Hector in classic terms,

> "God help me," said Sir Gawain, "of all the knights of
> your age in the world, you're the one I would most
> reluctantly fight to the finish, both because you have served
> me and because there is plenty in you that one should
> fear."[124]

It is a high compliment. And Merlin similarly praises King Lot as "a valiant man and a good knight; one should fear him greatly."[125] Bors advises that an Arthurian battle plan includes a reserve force composed of "the most worthy men, the knights who most deserve to be feared in all the world."[126] Even minor figures are used to make the point: Canart, a follower of King Claudas in opposition to Camelot, is said to be "the man whose prowess and boldness most makes him most deserving to be feared in the world."[127] "Worthy" and "feared" are readily paired qualities.[128]

---

[119] *History of William Marshal*, I, lines 911–925.   [120] Ibid., II, lines 16686–16701.
[121] Ibid., II, 234, 257, 299.   [122] Ibid., II, 301.   [123] Ibid., III, 170.
[124] Ibid., II, 221.   [125] Ibid., IV, 195.   [126] Ibid., III, 310.   [127] Ibid., III, 307.
[128] Ibid., V, 127.

How could knights square the circle and reconcile bravery, fear, and the preservation of honor? Those who gathered in any hall, in any chivalric era, could clearly have found significant points of agreement, yet they might well have disagreed on the basic question of how openly fear should even be acknowledged. Should it not simply be denied? Geoffroi de Charny in his several treatises and Robert Bruce through his biographer point out a useful approach. Discussions in these works are especially valuable sources because they were written, in one case, in a period of crisis for the kingdom of France and, in the other case, as a retrospective account and analysis of the arduous Scottish struggle for independence. In each case fear had to be confronted as a force affecting the chivalry that provided crucially practical ideals and practices. Though both works laud fearless heroes, each grasps the nettle and deals with the fear closely linked to suffering endured or vividly anticipated. And, as argued previously in this book and at length elsewhere, these works are not outliers; we can find important elements of their approach widespread in chivalric literature.[129]

Charny in particular leans heavily in many passages toward idealistic dictates about bold prowess, obviously reinforced in his lifetime by the pressing need for heightened military vigor on the part of the French lay elite, faced with devastating incursions by the English and their allies. Yet fear, its management, and the consequences are necessarily on his mind as well. In his *Demandes*, which pose questions on military conduct, Charny steps off the dais from which he generally preaches militant virtue and poses frankly quotidian issues encountered in an active knight's life: under what conditions can a man-at-arms leave a losing battlefield?[130] What is the relationship between surrender and cowardice?[131] Can a lord himself decide without loss of honor to leave a losing fight and through a prudent retreat "save his war"?[132] Aware of a lost fight, should his men personally see their lord safely off the field and out of danger, or should they stoutly remain and simply send him to safety?[133] One of

---

[129] Argued in R. W. Kaeuper, *Holy Warriors*, 94–116, and previously in Chapter 9.

[130] Question 7 in Charny, *Demandes*, printed in original French in Michael Taylor, "Critical Edition," and in English translation in Muhlberger, *Charny's Men-at-Arms*.

[131] Question 78 in Charny, *Demandes*, ibid.   [132] Question 7, ibid.

[133] Questions 7 and 8 ask about the lord; Questions 37 and 39 ask about others leaving field of battle; Questions 79 and 88 discuss cowardice and surrender.

his final questions indirectly brings together honor and shame, fear, prudence, and valor: he wants a discussion on whether wisdom or prowess (*sen ou prouesce*) is more important to the elite arms bearers.[134] If the concern in the entire set of questions seems, in general, focused more on equitable distribution of pay, loot, and prisoners than on issues of bravery, fear, and tactics, all issues circling around fear register as important in his thinking and are present on his list of questions for discussion.

Though his *Book of Chivalry* shows high idealism, the very existence of fear is also recognized in its pages in two ways. First, it is roughly skewered as timidity by Charny's blunt wit. Vigor in arms is ceaselessly elevated, and fear of fighting is denounced as the emotion that could diminish essential prowess. Charny's visceral contempt overflows in discussing men who are fearful of much in life; they worry that blocks of masonry may fall upon them from buildings, or that bridges may collapse if they ride across them; even to see battle wounds would be simply too distressing. The puritanical streak in him emerges when he denounces the new fashion of short jackets and tights; men who show their backsides, he growls, will run in battle.[135]

Yet Charny is pragmatic; he knows that fear cannot be so readily brushed aside by ridicule, even if he enjoys trying. In effect, fear must be acknowledged, if with averted gaze and curled lip. The great need is to use and transform its emotional energy, enlisting it as an ally. His concise homily to arms bearers is not to think about what the enemy will do to them, but to concentrate on what they will do to their enemies.[136] The truly good men, he is sure, will manage to master fear, turning it into energy for campaigning and fighting. One factor making this possible is the powerful bonus on offer. As we have seen (in Chapter 9), he is certain that a warrior's reasonable fear counts as one of the many forms of sufferings that true men-at-arms endure meritoriously within the order of chivalry.[137] Suffering in the righteous and demanding role given to elite arms bearers by God brings spiritual merit, no less than a hope of victory on the field. A proud knight, Charny instinctively slashes with his pen at rank cowardice; but at a deeper level within his own psyche, he knows the reality of

---

[134] Question 90.   [135] Kaeuper and Kennedy, *Book of Chivalry*, 189.
[136] Ibid., 130–133.
[137] Ibid., passim, especially sections 40 and 41, discussed in Kaeuper, *Holy Warriors*, 96–104.

fear and the cost of overcoming it in order to perform great deeds of arms. In his verse treatise, *Livre Charny*, he vividly portrays the agony of waiting for the physical and psychological release of a cavalry charge over the field of battle: as the arms bearer waits in position atop his great warhorse, arrows and lances rain down on him; he sees the bloodied bodies of his friends sprawled on the ground around him; he is well mounted and could easily escape, but to flee would be a loss of sacred honor. His rhetorical question resonates: "Is he not a great martyr who puts himself to such work?"[138]

The soul-searing suffering of arms bearers may be a spawning ground for fear, but the honor at stake will be diminished or lost altogether unless stout men gain control of their emotions. Charny's message is as direct as his beloved cavalry charge: fear is real; but only the culpably timid allow it to overwhelm them; the good arms bearers persevere and with God-given endowments win earthly glory, divine favor, and heavenly joy at the close of a vigorous career. The formula is as clear to him as life itself.

In presenting the life of Robert Bruce, Barbour thinks along broadly similar lines of courage enacted by hard, virtuous action aided by divine grace. But he adds a term to this linked pair of valor and grace. Between the tough and meritorious warrior action and the blessings of divine grace he inserts the middle term of his era and place — Scottish independence. It enables courage almost as a collective species of salvation, or at least an achievement simultaneously granted by God and merited by the labors and hardships of combat. Where Charny argues that hard fighting and divine grace bring glory in this world and salvation in the next, Barbour argues for Scottish independence won through this bond, almost as a foretaste of the heavenly feast to come. If suffering causes fear — and we can recall Earl John of Atholl declaring that hardships endured rendered his life not worth a straw — God rewarded the Scots, as he had rewarded the ancient Maccabees they read about in holy writ; divine blessing descended on such just and hard-won struggles, bringing achievement despite fear. These were men,

> ... yat war in gret distress
> And assayit full gret hardyness
> Or yai mycht cum till yar entent,

---

[138] *Livre Charny*, lines 363–593, in Taylor, ed., "Critical Edition," quotation at 457–458. For other references to martyrdom, see lines 130ff, 863.

> Bot syne our Lord sic grace yaim sent
> Yat yai syne throw yat gret valour
> Come till gret hycht & till honour,
> Magre yar fayis euerilkane
> Yat war so fele yat ay till ane
> Off yaim yai war weill a thowsand,
> Bot wuhar God helpys quhat may withstnand.[139]
> [who were under great stress
> And tested their truly great stoutness
> Before they might achieve their goal.
> But later our Lord sent them his grace
> That tjey hrough great valor
> Came to hight renown and honor
> Despite each and every foe
> Who were so numerous that for each loyal man
> There were a thousand foemen.
> But where God helps foes maybe withstood.]

The text is suffused with accounts of the virtuous Scots' endless pain, travails, and sufferings; and for all his high talk of fearless men inspiring dread in powerful enemies, Barbour shows Robert Bruce rationally fearful in specific settings, as when foiling attempts on his life by assassins.[140] Though Bruce dreaded treason and trusted men only after he knew them well, "whatever dread he had, he showed his men a cheerful countenance."[141] Barbour pointedly tells the story of Tydeus, a hero of Greek mythology, who was "sundele affrayit" (somewhat afraid) when he was ambushed, but quickly recovered his full spirits, moved by his "gentle [i.e., noble] and worthy heart."[142] Thus does an able man triumph over fear. And thus did Charny and Barbour – drawing upon ideas that permeated chivalric literature – square the circle: they enthusiastically revered fearlessness, pragmatically accepted the fact of fear, and wholeheartedly praised the committed men who mastered fear in order to enact the hard profession that earned not only what Malory would term worship on earth, but divine favor and eternal bliss.

CONCLUSION

The practicality of chivalry, stressed throughout this book, was well served by employment of anger, wrath, and the keen desire for

---

[139] *Barbour's Bruce*, bk. I, lines 445–456.   [140] Ibid., bk. 5, lines 636–641.
[141] Ibid., bk. 3, lines 671–676.   [142] Ibid., bk. 6, lines 222–227.

revenge. Deeply felt, these emotions were readily put to work as the watchdogs of sacred honor and enviable status. Nonknightly or subknightly people, it may be assumed, felt some of the same emotional surges, but the lay elite were certain they were especially entitled to such affective components of personality, and they could channel remarkable energy and manpower into their use and expression. They thought of themselves as the supreme possessors of honor; they were privileged fighters in the divine plan and were ready and willing to fight to preserve the honor this afforded them.

Fear in the dread guise of timidity should ideally be laughed out of court and courage brought forward. Did it not secure glory and telling glances from ladies in the present life, and help secure passage to heavenly life? Yet the reality of fear was not lost on any man who had impatiently – even fearfully – awaited the trumpet call for a life-or-death cavalry charge or who had put a shaky ladder against the stone wall of a besieged town and started the climb. Fear had to be made grist for the mill of courage, though all men-at-arms knew the grinding would be fine, indeed.

REFLECTIONS

REFLECTIONS

Genuine understanding of roughly half a millennium of early European history will falter without an effort to analyze the phenomenon of chivalry, for the ideals and practices of chivalry formed an essential component of society and civilization throughout those generations. Its voice was prominent whether the inquiring listener focuses on the practice of violence and war, governance, social and cultural life, the framework of religion, the process of getting and spending, or the bonds of friendship and ideal and actual gender relations. The ideals and actions of elite arms bearers always put them in a prominent position, ever playing a crucial role. Since the close engagement of chivalry with such basic issues of life makes it an inescapably important subject, we do the topic and ourselves a disservice if we relegate chivalry to the slight category of fanciful escapism or imagine it to be some ideal system in a long-ago fairyland.

Of course the forms in which chivalry was expressed were indeed impressively colorful and could take on a superficial playfulness of speech, action, or attire; and in their bright hues and utter quaintness, chivalric displays have proved continuing attractions to modern audiences for whom the contemporary world may seem a bit drab and tirelessly pragmatic. Much publication about medieval chivalry seems intended to meet this need, which is likely felt by many a writer or picture-book compiler, as it is certainly felt by the filmmakers. In all such presentations, chivalry intrudes few questions into the minds of consumers of print, film, or video game, nor does it raise problems for analysis that could engage scholarship. If brave men in shining armor fought evil, if muscular men protected the weak and unfailingly honored all females, if they humbly practiced the piety taught to them, then surely all was well.

The medieval evidence we have examined, likely to have caused surprise by its abundance no less than its themes, presents a much more complex and vastly more interesting chivalric world – one that, however colorful, was built not simply on easy agreement but on conflicts, contradictions, and paradoxes. In studying these complexities, we learn about real people, about multiple sets of ideals in dialogue and often in contention, and about the role of governing institutions with power emerging to match their claims.

One guideline for utilizing evidence in this book has emerged from a conviction that multiple types of sources must be employed, and that care must be taken to read each for its specific usefulness. The hunt has stretched across centuries and across Europe. Such a search and effort at understanding has required use of chronicles, vernacular treatises and handbooks, biographies, and the great mass of imaginative literature. Obviously, many of these works confidently celebrated and flattered their elite patrons and those sitting proudly near them on the dais in a hall. And one of the functions of these works was surely to instruct the next generation in broadly accepted lessons on how to act and speak if they would advance and prosper. Yet these works often also reveal debate and conflict of ideas, increasing our awareness of what any type of source does and does not tell us. Few sources that historians use convey simply and exactly what happened in the distant past; and establishing event and chronology form only the beginning of historical inquiry in any case. Some of our most informative sources, in fact, hold importance precisely because they are idealist or imaginative. They point to problems perceived at the time, and they may offer solutions or debate choices among possible solutions. Of course intense discussion and debate were features of the medieval schools, but were scarcely limited to academic halls.

Reading our full range of evidence has quickly brought to the surface contention about exactly what chivalry should be, who should form its ranks, and how these chivalrous men should act. In company with medieval writers, who never tired of quoting the maxim from Saint Paul, we can happily assert, "For everything that was written in the past was written to teach us."[1] How easy our task

---

[1] Romans 15:4.

would be if we could – blind to all evidence to the contrary – hold that the knights and men-at-arms in these centuries uniformly accepted an Augustinian view of violence, or if we could conclude that chivalry as conceived in the minds of arms bearers and as always enacted in their world was a direct projection of the prescriptive views offered by Ramon Llull or Honoré Bonet.[2]

Instead, the essential task remains, as this book has argued, the search for working ideals and assumptions among knights and men-at-arms. To reach such common assumptions, we must draw on all available evidence and accept some contention and much purely prescriptive idealism among writers, and especially among those who were not practicing knights and likely not even very close to them. For early chivalric centuries, this group encompasses almost all writers, though by later centuries we can hear the voices of the knights themselves more clearly. These knights were assuredly not scholars or abstract philosophers, yet we have regularly seen that they cherished ideals to justify and guide their hard profession and to bolster their elite status. In addition to their obvious schooling through experience and the precepts of practical mentors, they borrowed selectively from a range of writings and adapted what they needed with confidence in their right so to do. Finding the operative sets of ideas and practices that resulted from this process has been in this book, and remains for future inquiry, the daunting challenge. Only thus can chivalry be understood as a remarkably active, undoubtedly necessary, and equally dangerous force in its society.

The framework created for chivalry necessarily rested on foundations that incorporated paradox and contradiction. These tensions, appearing both within ideals and behavior and between ideals and behavior, were important and have proved instructive. We have seen that they long served as sources of great strength rather than elements of debilitating weakness. Far from impairing or limiting the power and spread of chivalry, these seemingly contradictory dimensions actually animated a construct as complex as any Gothic vault, which also relied on constant pressures or tensions among component parts, often operating at a great height. Major issues stemming from

---

[2] Of course a careful reading of Llull's treatise shows what Noel Fallows has termed its combination of praise and admonition, its paradoxes and near schizophrenia: Fallows, Llull, *The Book of the Order of Chivalry*, 10. This text is often read as though it were purely and uncritically admiring of chivalry.

the elite use of armed force in medieval society, that is, did not simply disappear or dissolve within chivalry, all strains eliminated in easy agreement. Rather, these tensions remained actively at work in operating frameworks of ideas and behavior that gave chivalry much of its strength.

One set of forces existing in active tension paired knighthood with agencies of governance that were significantly expanding their power. A proud sense of independence informed one side of this dyad. Most knights throughout this period cherished rights to licit violence and also proudly exercised some degree of jurisdiction over a great mass of subordinate people; elite arms bearers indeed carried and used swords and in many cases could gaze with considerable satisfaction on the gaunt gallows on which their full judicial power was demonstrated. Possessing these highly practical rights assuredly enhanced their keen sense of sacred honor. Potential conflicts with the broadening claims of king, great prince (lay or ecclesiastical), or urban councils easily materialized. Yet, for all their proud sense of independence linked to a truly touchy sense of honor, the chivalrous ranks significantly came to serve royal and other governing agencies (some of them ecclesiastical or urban).

The process took time to come to completion and seldom proceeded without struggles, but the crown provided cherished leadership in war that was thought glorious and was expected to be profitable. Kings in time accepted knighthood as one of their personal distinctions, and the crown likewise generally became a great sponsor of tournaments, edging away from simple regulation or stern attempts at prohibition. The flow of royal patronage in general was expected and appreciated as lands, stipends, and rich heiresses were distributed. And if laws, law courts, and judicial personnel could be intrusive and tedious, especially when operated by little people without background, their usefulness likewise became increasingly apparent; even the chivalrous would sometimes rather sue than fight. Stout resistance to authorities who intruded into private spheres was real; the entire body of romance literature stands as witness to a fanciful yet powerful wish that in an ideal world kings would essentially play the part of vigorous leaders of successful war bands, not that of heads of an administration that regulated and taxed. Eventually the power of some form of the state dominated this world; significantly, however, the ranks of knighthood learned that they could accept the result, with some grumbling, granted, reverberating for a long time.

The relationship of chivalry with the governing power of medieval Christianity provides a special case in point. In many aspects of their lives, elite arms bearers practiced the piety that all Christians were taught and were expected to exercise; and to that extent they can be considered faithful sons of Holy Mother Church. Yet their independence where social status and military profession were concerned is obvious. They knew they were not ordinary members of the flock of the faithful, and their undoubted piety (joined to elite status) covered them like armor as they purposefully selected or quietly rejected clerical dictates on sensitive matters such as tournament, sexuality, or crucial dimensions of warfare. They joyously took part in tournaments, blithely conducted love affairs, and fought fellow Christians by brutal methods likely to produce victory, even as they prominently attended Mass, went on pilgrimage (and the armed pilgrimage of crusade), gave alms, and endowed ecclesiastical establishments. Their relationship with clerics was respectful to the full extent that they thought it could be; quotidian anticlericalism was ever present, but never an issue crippling piety; the crucial line for them was always, rather, the fit of their status and honor-producing prowess within all-surrounding religion.

Another set of tensions seemed to divide a mental framework of formal courtesy from a practice of violent self-help. The courtesy has long been recognized and emphasized by scholars; but perhaps these academics have shied away in distaste from the bloody vengeance, violence, and widespread destruction that can also be plentifully documented. Both were, in fact, easily present in the same medieval figures. Along a single axis of honor, knights could play the refined courtier (complete with at least occasional reticence and blushes in the presence of beautiful women) and also enact joyous conquest or hot-blooded revenge against individuals or entire regions, singing about the virtues of righteous wrath afterward, goblets brimming with clear wine. In fact, courtesy was not the polar opposite of violence, and the arms bearers were certain of the benefits of each dimension of their lives in its rightful place. Medieval Europe does not represent the only violent society to expect and practice a highly formalized set of social customs under the mantle of courtesy. Honor, it is useful to remember, was inscribed on a social rather than a moral slate.

A variant on this theme appears in the knightly claim to stand as protectors of women, the poor, and the defenseless. The question too infrequently posed, of course, is against whom their ideal or supposed protection was needed and offered. Arms bearers actually left in the wake of their campaigns widows, orphans, and destitute families amid looted and smoldering towns and villages surrounded by devastated or blackened fields once bearing crops. Whatever later romantics wanted to believe about them, these warriors avidly ravaged enemy land, amassing booty that sustained status and enabled the great virtue of largesse. The protection of ladies was only a slightly more secure feature of their profession. Famously, ladies were to be honored and protected, but mere women of no status were so often treated as sexual prey. And even the elite ladies, who are generally pictured as unvarying adherents of the system of values by which elite males lived, could in truth face dangers. Though they may be pictured captivated by accounts of prowess and willing to be won as tournament prizes, ladies knew that abduction and rape were far from unknown. Some recoverable female voices, such as that of Marie de France, sprinkled vitriol over the male obsession with showy prowess and the ideal faithfulness of those in armor to females they adored.

Yet another layer of tension pitted automatic entitlements of birth against some form of actual achievement in a fiercely competitive world. The achievement usually meant deeds of arms, or (in time) the rendering of mere administrative service or possession and skillful dispensing of acquired wealth. The intertwined and evolving story of knighthood and nobility stands in witness to this tension, with stalwart individuals or groups of highly effective warriors seeking and often gaining elevated status. If the highly born originally thought chivalric status insufficiently grand, they came finally to think of newcomers as likely insufficiently entitled to be included among the knighthood.

Perhaps the fundamental set of chivalric forces in complex relationship with their world appears in the tension and attraction between the practice of chivalric piety and religious prescriptions. As ideally and abstractly formulated, many principles of Christianity could only with difficulty be incorporated into a chivalric ethos that did not feature humility, forbearance, and forgiveness of enemies. Yet as mediated for knightly lives and professional careers, the circle was roughly squared. With the essential help of clerical allies, hard military careers could be transformed into penitential exercises reducing the vast debt for sin, while the knights envisioned themselves as close followers of Christ who could be considered both a valiant warrior defeating sin and the Devil, and a sacrificial lamb offering up his body on the cross. They exposed their bodies to pain and suffering in necessary penitential payment for their inevitable sins. Such creative manipulation of ideas asserted within bounds of orthodox piety best shows the resourcefulness of their thought. It likewise registers the effective power of their social position, working in tandem with their military role.

Writing about the sheer dominance of the aristocracy throughout medieval centuries, Timothy Reuter frankly asserted that the fundamental question ought to be: "How did they get away with it?"[3] Any full response to such a question would be demanding, but we might profitably apply his probing question to the knighthood in the centuries under study. It seems at least significant that even a quick review of basic areas of tension and paradox within chivalric ideals and practices leads to a realization that elite arms bearers could always have it both ways; they could with confidence claim one dimension of reigning belief in their lifetime, and practice or turn to its near opposite, if that proved more convenient. They could, that is, stoutly oppose regulation by major governing agencies, except when it was in their interest to cooperate, stress loyalty, and reap benefit; they could display refined courtly manners that emphasized social superiority and pose as protectors of those in need, but campaign brutally in lands that were not (or only were becoming) their own; they could transform their hard profession of arms into the following of Christ, earning penitential credits to offset their sins by the suffering that a warrior life entailed. A justification was always available, even a glowing source of praise and valorization.

A control over paradoxes surrounding key issues thus empowered chivalry. Yet alongside all these sets of alternate possibilities the medieval knighthood also possessed a lodestone for guidance. This key to justifying action lay in a set of core beliefs ever providing directions, as clearly as the passage of the sun overhead. Achieving and maintaining honor remained the great goal, and superb displays of prowess offered the great means to advance it. The formula

---

[3] Timothy Reuter, *Medieval Polities and Modern Mentalities* (Cambridge University Press, 2006), 113, and "Nobles and Others: The Social and Cultural Expression of Power Relations in the Middle Ages," in *Nobles and Nobility in Medieval Europe: Concepts, Origins, Transformations*, ed. Anne Duggan (Woodbridge: Boydell, 2000), 86.

became a mantra. Religious piety, at least as appropriated by the arms bearers, significantly blessed the process. It may be worth emphasizing, as Pitt-Rivers observed some time ago, that honor presents a social more than a moral goal.[4] Perhaps that distinction blurred for knights. Riding resolutely forward, arms bearers could make any of the particular choices within the entire range of issues we have noted, confident that their thought and action were righteous and no less certain that they should possess each cherished assertion and right as fully merited. That an elite military group resolutely occupying a towering social peak would construct such a system can cause little surprise. The surprise may rather come from the relative lack of scholarly attention devoted to its widespread and consequential framework. If this book encourages such discussion, it will have succeeded in its aims.

---

[4] Julian Pitt-Rivers, "Honour and Social Status," in *Honour and Shame: The Values of Mediterranean Society*, ed. J. G. Peristiany (London: Weidenfeld and Nicolson, 1965).

PRINTED PRIMARY SOURCES

Actes du Parlement de Paris, 1st ser., 1254–1328, edited by E. Boutaric, 2 vols.
(Paris, 1863–1867); 2nd ser., 1328–1350, I (1328–1342), edited by
Henri Furgeot (Paris, 1920).

Adam Murimuth. *Adae Murimuth Continuatio Chronicarum; Robertus de
Avesbury de Gestis Mirabilibus Regis Edwardi Tertii*. Rolls Series 93.
Edited by Edward Maunde Thompson. London: Eyre and
Spottiswoode, 1889.

Ambroise: The Crusade of Richard Lion-Heart, 2 vols. Edited by John L. La
Monte and translated by M. J. Hubert. New York: Columbia
University Press, 1941.

"Annales Londonienses." In *Chronicles of the Reigns of Edward I and Edward II*.
Rolls Series 76. Edited by William Stubbs. London: Longman, 1882–1883.

Andrew the Chaplain. *The Art of Courtly Love*. Translated by John Jay Parry
and edited and abridged by Frederick W. Locke. New York: Frederick
Ungar, 1957.

Ayala, Pero Lopez de. "Cronica del Rey don Pedro." *Biblioteca de Autores
Espanoles*. ed. M. Rivadenyra. Madrid: Impresores de Camara de S.M.,
1877.

Barbour's Bruce, 3 vols. Edited by M. P. McDiarmid and J. A. C. Stevenson.
Edinburgh: Scottish Text Society, vols. 12 (1980), 13 (1981), 15 (1985).

Bayerische Chroniken des XIV Jahrhunderts (Chronicae Bavaricae saeculi XIV).
Edited by Georg Leidinger. M.G.H. SrG 19. Hannover, 1918.

Benton, John F., ed. *Self and Society in Medieval France: The Memoirs of Abbot
Guibert of Nogent*. Toronto: University of Toronto Press, 1985.

Bertram de Born. *The Poems of the Troubadour Bertram de Born*. Edited by
William D. Paden, Jr., Tilde Sankovitch, and Patricia H. Stäblein.
Berkeley: University of California Press, 1986.

Biblioteca de Autores Españoles. Madrid: Ediciones Atlas, 1846–1880.

Bibliotheca rerum Germanicarum, vol. 5. Edited by Philipp Jaffé. Berlin: Weidmann, 1869.

Bracton, Henry de. *On the Laws and Customs of England*, 4 vols. Edited and translated by Samuel Thorne. Cambridge, MA: Belknap Press of Harvard University Press, 1968.

Bromyard, John. *Summa Praedicantium*. Venice: Donimicum Nicolinum, 1586.

Brunetto Latini. *The Book of the Treasure (Li Livres dou Tresor)*. Translated by Paul Barrette and Spurgeon Baldwin. New York and London: Garland, 1993.

Bryant, Nigel, trans. *The High Book of the Grail: A Translation of the Thirteenth Century Romance of the Grail*. Ipswich: Brewer, 1978.

trans. *Merlin and the Grail: Joseph of Arimathea, Merlin, Perceval: The Trilogy of Prose Romances Attributed to Robert de Boron*. Woodbridge, Suffolk: Boydell & Brewer, 2001.

trans. *Perceforest: The Pre-History of King Arthur's Britain*. Woodbridge, Suffolk: Brewer, 2011.

trans. *The True Chronicles of Jean le Bel, 1290–1360*. Woodbridge, Suffolk: Boydell, 2011.

Cabaret d'Orville, Jean. *La Chronique de le bon duc Loys de Bourbon*. Edited by A. M. Chazaud. Paris: S. H. F., 1976.

Caesarius of Heisterbach. *Dialogue on Miracles*. Translated by H. von F. Scott and C. C. Swindon. London: Routledge, 1929.

Calendar of the Close Rolls. HMSO (1892–1954).

Calendar of the Patent Rolls. HMSO (1901–1909).

Cantar de Mio Cid. 4th edition. Edited by R. Menedez Pidal. Madrid: Espasa-Calpe, S.A., 1964.

Catalogue of Seals in the Department of Manuscripts in the British Museum, 6 vols. Edited by Walter de Gray Birch. London, 1887–1900.

Chanson d'Aspremont. Edited by Louis Brandin. Paris: Champion, 1970.

Chanson de Guillaume: Texte établi, traduit et annoté. Edited by Francois Suard. Paris: Bordas, 1991.

Chastellain, Georges. "Le livre des faits du bon chevalier Messire Jacques de Lalang." In *Oeuvres de Georges Chastellain*. Edited by Kervyn de Lettenhove. Brussels: Heussner, 1866.

Chevalier au Barisel: Conte pieuse du XIIIe *siècle*. Edited by Félix Lecoy. Paris: Champion, 1955.

Chrétien de Troyes. *Erec and Enide*. Edited and translated by Carleton W. Carroll. New York: Garland, 1987.

Lancelot: The Knight of the Cart. Translated by Burton Raffel. New Haven: Yale University Press, 1997.

Yvain, the Knight with the Lion. Translated by Ruth Harwood Cline. Athens, GA: University of Georgia Press, 1975.

Chronicas de los reyes de castilla, 3 vols. Edited by Cayetan Rosell. Madrid: M. Rivadeneyra, 1975–1978.

Chronicle of Adam de Salimbene. Edited and translated by Joseph L. Baird, Giuseppe Baglivi, and John Robert Kane. Binghamton, NY: Medieval & Renaissance Texts & Studies, 1986.

Chronicle of Duke Erik. Translated by Erik Carlquist and Peter C. Hogg. Lund: Norse Academic Press, 2012.

The Chronicle of Geoffrey le Baker. Translated by David Preest, with introduction and notes by Richard Barber. Woodbridge, Suffolk: Boydell Press, 2012.

Chronicle of John de Venette. Translated by Jean Birdsall. New York: Columbia University Press, 1953.

Chronicles and Memorials of Great Britain and Ireland during the Middle Ages, 51 vols. Edited by William Stubbs et al. London, 1858–1911.

Chronicles of the Crusades: Contemporary Narratives of the Crusade of the Richard Coeur de Lion by Richard of Devizes and Geoffrey de Vinsauf and of the Crusade of Saint Louis by Lord John de Joinville. Edited and translated by Margaret Renee Shaw. London: George Bell and Sons, 1903.

Chronique de Jean le Bel, publiée pour la Société de l'histoire de France. Edited by Jules Viard and Eugene Déprez. Paris: Renouard, 1904.

Chronique normande du XIVe *siècle*. Edited by Auguste Molinier and Émile Molinier. Paris: Librairie Renouard, 1882.

Chroniques des quatre premiers Valois. Edited by Simeon Luce. Paris: V.J. Renouard, 1862.

Cloetta, Wilhelm, ed. *Moniage Guillaume: Les deux redactions en vers du Moniage Guillaume*. Paris: Firmin-Didot, 1906.

Collection des ordonnances des rois de France, 22 vols. Paris, 1723–1849.

Collections for the History of Staffordshire, vol. 10. Edited by G. Wrottesley. London: Harrison and Sons, 1889.

La Couronnement de Louis: Chanson de geste du XIIe *siecle*. Edited by Ernest Langlois. Paris: Champion, 1969.

The Coutumes de Beauvaisis de Philippe de Beaumanoir. Translated by F. R. P. Akehurst. Philadelphia: University of Pennsylvania Press, 1992.

Deeds of the Normans in Ireland: La Geste des Engleis en Yrlande. Translated and edited by Evelyn Mullally. Dublin: Four Courts Press, 2002.

Dialogus de Scaccario. Edited and translated by Charles Johnson. Oxford: Oxford University Press, 1955.

Díaz de Gamez, Gutierre. *El victorial, crónica de Don Pero Niño, conde de Buelna*. Edited by Rafael Beltran Llavador. Salamanca: Universidad de Salamanca, 1997.

    El victorial, crónica de don Pero Niña, conde de Buelna, por su alf'eraz Gutierre Díez de Games. Edited by Juan de Mata Carriazo. Madrid: Espasa-Calpe, 1940.

The Unconquered Knight: A Chronicle of the Deeds of Don Pero Niño, Count of Buelna. Edited and translated by Joan Evans. 1928, reprinted Cambridge: Medieval Castilian Series, 2000, and Rochester: Boydell Press, 2004.

Ecclesiastical History of Orderic Vitalis, 6 vols. Edited and translated by Marjorie Chibnall. Oxford: Clarendon, 1968–1980.

Etablissements de Saint Louis: Thirteenth-Century Law Texts from Tours, Orleans, and Paris. Edited and translated by F. R. P. Akehurst. Philadelphia: University of Pennsylvania Press, 1996.

Euvres de Rigord et de Guillaume le Breton, historiens de Phillipe-Auguste: Chroniques de Rigord et de Guillaume le Breton. Edited by H. Francois Delaborde. vol. 1. Paris: Renouard, 1882.

Froissart, Jean. *Oeuvres de Froissart*, 26 vols. Edited by Kervyn de Lettenhove. Paris: Bruxelles, V. Devaux et cie, 1867–1877.

Gamez, Gutierre Diaz. *El victorial, cronica de Don Pero Nino, conde de Buelna.* Edited by Juan de Mata Carriazo. Madrid: Espasa-Calpe, S.A., 1940.

Gardner, John, trans. *The Alliterative Morte Arthure: The Owl and the Nightingale and Five Other Middle English Poems in a Modernized Version, with Comments on the Poems.* Carbondale: Southern Illinois University Press, 1973.

Geoffrey of Monmouth. *The Historia regum Britanniae of Geoffrey of Monmouth*, 5 vols. Edited and translated by Neil Wright. Cambridge: Cambridge University Press, 1984–1991.

"A Gest of Robyn Hod." In *Robin Hood and Other Outlaw Tales.* Edited by Stephen Knight and Thomas Ohlgren, 80–168. Kalamazoo, MI: Medieval Institute Publications, 1997.

Gray, Sir Thomas. *Scalacronica 1275–1363.* Edited and translated by Andy King. Surtees Society, vol. 209. Rochester: Boydell & Brewer, 2005.

Gray Birch, Walter de. *Catalogue of Seals in the Department of Manuscripts in the British Museum*, 6 vols. London: Longmans, 1887–1900.

The Great Tournament Roll of Westminster: A Collotype Reproduction of the Manuscript, 2 vols. Edited by Sydney Anglo. Oxford: Clarendon Press, 1968.

Guillelmus Duranti, Rationale divinorum officiorum I–IV; V–VI; VII–VIII. Corpus Christianorum Continuatio Mediaevalis 140, 140A, 140B. Edited by Anselme Davril, O.S.B. and Timothy M. Thibodeau. Turnhout: Brepols, 1995, 1998, 2000.

Haut Livre du Graal: Perlesvaus. Edited by William Nitze and T. A. Jenkins. Chicago: University of Chicago Press, 1932.

Henry of Lancaster. *Livre de seyntz medicines.* Edited by E. J. Arnould. New York: Oxford University Press, 1994.

Heroes of the French Epic: A Selection of Chansons de Geste. Translated by Michael Newth. Rochester: Boydell & Brewer Press, 2005.

Histoire de Guillaume le Marechal: History of William Marshal. Edited by
    A. J. Holden, S. Gregory, and D. Crouch and translated by
    S. Gregory. London: Anglo-Norman Text Society, 2002–2006.
Italian Literature II: Tristano Riccardiano (Arthurian Archives). Edited and trans-
    lated by F. Regina Psaki. Cambridge: D.S. Brewer, 2006.
Kaeuper, Richard W., and Elspeth Kennedy. *The Book of Chivalry of Geoffroi
    de Charny.* Philadelphia: University of Pennsylvania Press, 1996.
The Lais of Marie de France. Translated by Robert Hanning and Joan Ferrante.
    Durham, NC: Labyrinth Press, 1978.
Lancelot, 8 vols. Edited by Alexandre Micha. Geneva: Droz, 1978–1983.
*Lancelot-Grail: The Old French Arthurian Vulgate and Post-Vulgate in
    Translation,* 5 vols. Edited by Norris J. Lacy et al. New York:
    Garland, 1993–1995.
Lancelot of the Lake. Translated by Corin Corley with an introduction by
    Elspeth Kennedy. New York: Oxford University Press, 1989.
Langlois, Monique, and Yvonne Lanhers. *Confessions et jugements de criminels
    au parlement de Paris (1319–1350).* Paris: S.E.V.P.E.N., 1971.
Le Jouvencel par Jean le Bueil. Edited by Camille Favre and Léon Lecestre. 2
    vols. Paris: Renouard, 1887.
Leuwis, Hencricus de (Dionysius Cartusianus). *Opuscula insigniora.* Cologne:
    Birckmann, 1559.
The Liber Poenitentialis of Robert of Flamborough. Edited by J. Frances Firth.
    Toronto: Pontifical Institute, 1971.
Llull, Ramon. *The Book of the Order of Chivalry.* Translated by Noel Fallows.
    Woodbridge, Suffolk: Boydell, 2013.
Malory, Thomas. *Works.* Edited by Eugène Vinaver. New York and
    Oxford: Oxford University Press, 1971.
Matthew Paris. *Matthew Paris: Chronica Majora.* Rolls Series, 7 vols. Edited by
    H. R. Luard. London: Longman, 1872–1884.
The Memoirs of Philippe de Commynes. Edited by Samuel Kinser and translated
    by Isabelle Cazeaux. Columbia: University of South Carolina Press,
    1969.
Merlin. Edited by Alexandre Micha. Geneva: Droz, 1979.
Metrical Chronicle of Robert of Gloucester, vol. 2. Edited by W. A. Wright.
    London: Eyre and Spottiswoode, 1887.
Migne, Jacques-Paul. *Patrologia Latina,* 217 vols. Paris: 1845 (CD Patrick
    Healey).
Mignon, Robert. *Leopold Delisle, Inventaire d'Anciens Comptes Royaux Dresse.*
    Paris: Imprimerie Nationale, 1899.
Monumenta Erphesfurtensia saec. XII. XIII. XIV. Edited by O. Holder-Egger
    . M.G.H., Script. rer. Germ., 42. 1899.
Muhlberger, Steven, ed., trans. *Charny's Men-at-Arms: Questions
    Concerning the Joust, Tournament and War.* Wheaton, IL: Freelance
    Press, 2014.

Jousts and Tournaments: Charny and the Rules for Chivalric Sport in Fourteenth-Century France. Translated by Steven Muhlberger. Union City, CA: Chivalry Bookshelf, 2002.

The Murder of Charles the Good. Translated by James Bruce Ross. New York: Columbia University Press, 1967.

Les Olim ou registres des arrêts rendus par la cour du roi sous les règnes de Saint Louis de Philippe le Hardi, de Philippe le Bel, de Louis le Hutin, et de Philippe le Long. Edited by Arthur Beugnot, 3 vols. in 4. Paris, 1839–1848.

Panegyrique de Louis de la Tremoille. In *Collection complèt des mémoires relatifs a l'histoire de France*, vol. 15. Paris: Foucault, 1820.

Parzival. Translated by Helen M. Mustard and Charles E. Passage. New York: Vintage, 1961.

Perceforest: The Prehistory of King Arthur's Britain. Translated by Nigel Bryant. New York: Boydell & Brewer, 2011.

Perlesvaus. Rochester, NY: D.S. Brewer, 1996.

Placitorum in domo capitulari Westmonasteriensi asservatorum abbrevatio: Temporiubs regum Ric. I., Johann., Johann., Henr. III., Edw. I., Edw. II. Edited by George Rose. 1811.

Posse, Otto. *Das Siegelwesen der deutschen Kaiser und Könige von 751 bis 1913*. Dresden: Wilhelm und Bertha v. Baensch Stiftung, 1913.

Powell, James M. *The Liber Augustalis; or, Constitutions of Melfi Promulgated by the Emperor Frederick II for the Kingdom of Sicily in 1231*. Syracuse: Syracuse University Press, 1970.

Price, Glanville et al., trans. *William of Orange: Four Old French Epics*. London: Dent, 1975.

Priest Konrad's Song of Roland. Translated by J. W. Thomas. Columbia, SC: Camden House, 1994.

Raoul de Cambrai. Translated by Sarah Kay. New York: Oxford University Press, 1992.

The Rationale Divinorum Officiorum of William Durand of Mende: A New Translation of the Prologue and Book One. Translated by Timothy M. Thibodeau. New York: Columbia University Press, 2007.

Recueil des actes des ducs de Normandie de 911 à 1066. Edited by Lucien Musset. Caen: Société des Impresions Caron, 1961.

Recueil des historiens des Gaules et de la France. Paris: Bibliotheque Nationale de France, 1738–1904.

René d'Anjou. *Traité de la Forme et Devis d'un Tournoi*. Edited by Edmund Pognon. Paris: Verve, 1946.

Rerum Italicarum Scriptores, II edition, 34 vols. Bologna: Nicola Zanichelli, 1900–1975.

Reynard the Fox. Translated by Patricia Terry. Berkeley: University of California Press, 1993.

Richard of Devizes. *Chronicles of the Reigns of Stephen, Henry II, and Richard*. Rolls Series, 3 vols. Edited by Richard Howlett. London: Longman, 1886.

Robert of Flamborough. *Liber Poenitentialis of Robert of Flamborough.* Edited by J. Frances Firth. Toronto: Pontifical Institute, 1971.

Robertus de Avesbury de Gestis Mirabilibus Regis Edwardi Tertii. Edited by Edward Maude Thompson. New York: Cambridge University Press, 1889.

Roger of Hoveden. *Gesta Regis Henrici Secundi et Gesta Regis Ricardi Benedicti Abbatis.* Rolls Series, 2 vols. Edited by William Stubbs. London: Longman, 1867.

Roger of Wendover. *Rogeri de Wendover Liber Qui Dicitur Flores Historiarum ab Anno Domini,* 2 vols. Edited by Henry Gay Hewlett. London: Longman, 1887.

Rotuli Parliamentorum; ut et Petitiones, et Placita in Parliamento. London, 1767–1777.

Rymer, Thomas. *Foedera, conventiones, liter,* 17 vols. London: A. and J. Churchill, 1704–1717.

The Saxon Mirror: A Sachsenspiegel of the Fourteenth Century, by Eike von Repgow. Translated by Maria Dobozy. Philadelphia: University of Pennsylvania Press, 1999.

Select Cases in the Court of King's Bench under Edward II, vol. 4. Edited with introduction and translation by G. O. Sayles. London: Bernard Quaritch, 1957.

Siete Partidas, 5 vols. Translated by Samuel Parsons Scott and edited by Robert I. Burns. Philadelphia: University of Pennsylvania Press, 2001.

The Song of Aspremont (La chanson d'Aspremont). Edited and translated by Michael Newth. New York: Garland, 1989.

The Song of Girart de Vienne by Bertrand de Bar-Sur Aube. Translated by Michael A. Newth. Tempe: Arizona Center for Medieval and Renaissance Studies, 1999.

The Song of Roland. Translated by Frederick Golden. New York: W.W. Norton, 1978.

The Song of Roland. Translated by Dorothy L. Sayers. Baltimore: Penguin Books, 1966.

The Song of Roland: An Analytical Edition, 1: Introduction and Commentary; 2: Oxford Text and English Translation. Edited by Gerard J. Brault. University Park: Pennsylvania State University Press, 1978.

South Lancashire in the Reign of Edward II as Illustrated by the Pleas at Wigan Recorded in Coram Rege Roll 254. Edited by G. H. Tupling. Chetham Society 3rd ser. 1, 1949.

The Statutes of the Realm, vol. 1 (1235–1377). London, 1810.

The Story of Merlin, Lancelot-Grail Cycle. vol. 2. Translated by Rupert T. Pickens and edited by Norris J. Lacy. Cambridge: D.S. Brewer, 2010.

Stephenson, Carl, and F. G. Marcham. Sources of English Constitutional History: A Selection of Documents from A.D. 600 to the Present. New York: Harper & Row, 1937.

Suger. *The Deeds of Louis the Fat*. Edited and translated by Richard C. Cusimano and John C. Moorhead. Washington, DC: Catholic University of America Press, 1992.

Taylor, Michael. "A Critical Edition of Geoffroy de Charny's *Livre Charny* and the *Demandes pour la joute, les tournois et la guerre*." PhD dissertation, University of North Carolina, Chapel Hill, 1977.

Victoria County History of Lancashire, vol. 2. Edited by William Farrer and J. Brownbill. London: Archibald Constable and Company, 1908.

Vie du Prince Noir by Chandos Herald. Edited by Diana B. Tyson. Tübingen: M. Niemeyer, 1975.

Villani, Giovanni. *Nuova Cronica*. Edited by G. Porta. Parma: Letteratura Italiana Einaudi, 1991.

Vita Edwardi Secundi: The Life of Edward the Second. Edited by Wendy R. Childs based on the translation of N. Denholm-Young. New York: Oxford University Press, 2005.

Vulgate Version of the Arthurian Romances, 6 vols. Edited by H. Oskar Sommer. Washington, DC: Carnegie Institution of Washington, 1909–1913.

William Count of Orange: Four Old French Epics. Edited by Glanville Price with an introduction by Lynette Muir. Translated by Glanville Price, Lynette Muir, and David Hogan. Totowa, NJ: Rowman and Littlefield, 1975.

Wolfram von Eschenbach. *Willehalm*. Translated by Marion Gibbs and Sidney Johnson. New York: Penguin, 1984.

SECONDARY SOURCES

Abels, Richard. "Cowardice and Duty in Anglo-Saxon England." *Journal of Medieval Military History* 4 (2006): 29–48.

———. "Cultural Representations of Warfare in the High Middle Ages: The Morgan Picture Bible." In *Crusading and Warfare in the Middle Ages: Realities and Representations; Essays in Honour of John France*. Edited by Simon John and Nicholas Morton. Aldershot: Ashgate, 2014.

Aberth, John. "Crime and Justice under Edward III: The Case of Thomas De Lisle." *English Historical Review* 107 (1992): 283–301.

Adams, Henry. *Mont-Saint-Michel and Chartres*. New York: Penguin, 1986.

Adams, James Eli. *A History of Victorian Literature*. Malden: Blackwell Publishing, 2012.

Adams, Jeremy Duquesne. "Modern Views of Medieval Chivalry." In *The Study of Chivalry: Resources and Approaches*. Edited by Howell Chickering and Thomas H. Seiler, 41–89. Kalamazoo, MI: Medieval Institute Publications, 1988.

Adams, Noël, John Cherry, and James Robinson, eds. *Good Impressions: Image and Authority in Medieval Seals*. London: British Museum, 2008.

Ailes, Adrian. "The Knight's Alter Ego: From Equestrian to Armorial Seal." In *Good Impressions: Image and Authority in Medieval Seals.* Edited by Noël Adams, John Cherry, and James Robinson, 8–11. London: British Museum Press, 2008.

Alexander, Michael. *Medievalism: The Middle Ages in Modern England.* New Haven: Yale University Press, 2007.

Allmand, C. T. *The De re militari of Vegetius: The Reception, Transmission and Legacy of a Roman Text in the Middle Ages.* Cambridge: Cambridge University Press, 2011.

——. *Society at War: The Experience of England and France during the Hundred Years War.* Rochester: Boydell & Brewer, 1998.

——. "The War and the Non-Combatant." In *The Hundred Years War.* Edited by Kenneth A. Fowler, 163–183. London: Macmillan, 1971.

Amodio, Marquis de. "Le Château de Verteuil." In *Memoires de la Société Archéologique et Historique de la Charente* (1958), 1–20.

Arnade, Peter. *Realms of Ritual: Burgundian Ceremony and Civil Life in Late Medieval Ghent.* Ithaca: Cornell University Press, 1996.

Arnold, Benjamin. *German Knighthood 1050–1300.* Oxford: Clarendon Press, 1985.

——. *Medieval Germany, 500–1300: A Political Interpretation.* Toronto: University of Toronto Press, 1997.

——. *Princes and Territories in Medieval Germany.* New York: Cambridge University Press, 1991.

Aznar, Agustín Bermúdez. *El Corregidor en Castilla durante la Baja Edad Media (1348–1474).* Murcia: Universidad de Murcia, 1970.

Bachrach, Bernard S. "Caballus et Caballarius in Medieval Warfare." In *The Study of Chivalry: Resources and Approaches.* Edited by Howell Chickering and Thomas H. Seiler, 173–211. Kalamazoo, MI: Medieval Institute Publications, 1988.

——. "Charles Martel, Mounted Shock Combat, the Stirrup, and Feudalism." *Studies in Medieval and Renaissance History* 7 (1970): 49–75.

——. "Medieval Siege Warfare: A Reconnaissance." *Journal of Military History* 58, no. 1 (1994): 119–133.

——. "The Milites and the Millennium." *Haskins Society Journal* 6 (1995): 85–95.

Bachrach, David. *Religion and the Conduct of War, c. 300–1215.* Woodbridge, Suffolk: Boydell Press, 2003.

——. *Warfare in Tenth-Century Germany.* Suffolk: Boydell Press, 2012.

Bagge, Sverre. *Cross and Scepter: The Rise of the Scandinavian Kingdoms from the Vikings to the Reformation.* Princeton: Princeton University Press, 2014.

Baldwin, John W. *Masters, Princes and Merchants: The Social Views of Peter the Chanter and His Circle.* Princeton: Princeton University Press, 1970.

——. *The Government of Philip Augustus: Foundations of French Royal Power in the Middle Ages.* Berkeley: University of California Press, 1986.

Balestracci, Duccio. *La festa in armi: Giostre, tornei e giochi del Medioevo.* Rome: Laterza, 2003.

Barber, Malcolm, and Keith Bate. *The Templars.* Manchester: Manchester University Press, 2002.

Barber, Richard. "Why Did Edward III Hold the Round Table? The Literary Background." In *Edward III's Round Table at Windsor: The House of the Round Table and the Windsor Festival of 1344.* Edited by Julian Munby, Richard Barber, and Richard Brown. Rochester: Boydell & Brewer, 2008.

Barber, Richard, and Juliet Barker. *Tournaments, Jousts, Chivalry and Pageants in the Middle Ages.* Woodbridge, Suffolk: Boydell, 1989.

Barker, Juliet R. V. *Tournament in England, 1100–1400.* Woodbridge, Suffolk: Boydell, 1986.

Barrow, G. W. S. *Robert Bruce and the Community of the Realm of Scotland.* Edinburgh: Edinburgh University Press, 2005.

Barthélemy, Dominique. "The Chivalric Transformation and the Origins of Tournament as Seen through Norman Chroniclers." *Haskin Society Journal* 20 (2008): 141–160.

"Les chroniques de la mutation chevaleresque en France (du Xe au XIIe siècle)." *Comptes redus de l'Academie des Inscriptions et Belles-Lettres* 151, no. 4 (2007): 1643–1665.

"L'Église et les premiers tournois (XIe et XIIe siècles)." In *Chevalerie et christianisme aux XIIe et XIIIe siècles.* Edited by Martin Aurell and Catalina Girbea, 139–148. Rennes: Presses Universitaires de Rennes, 2011.

"Encore le debat sur l'an mil!" *Revue historique de droit francais et etranger* 73 (1995): 349–360.

The Serf, the Knight, and the Historian. Ithaca: Cornell University Press, 2009.

Barton, Richard E. *Lordship in the County of Main, c. 890–1160.* Rochester: Boydell & Brewer, 2004.

Bastin, J., and E. Faral. *Onze poems de Rutebeuf concernant la Croisade.* Paris, 1946.

Bates, David. *William the Conqueror.* Gloucestershire: Tempus, 2001.

Bean, John Malcolm William. *From Lord to Patron: Lordship in Late Medieval England.* Manchester: Manchester University Press, 1989.

Bedos-Rezak, Brigitte. *Form and Order in Medieval France: Essays in Social and Quantitative Sigillography.* Great Yarmouth: Variorum, 1993.

"The Social Implication of the Art of Chivalry: The Sigillographic Evidence (France, 1050–1250)." In *Form and Order in Medieval France: Essays in Social and Quantitative Sigillography*, 1–31. Great Yarmouth: Variorum, 1993.

Bellamy, John G. *Crime and Public Order in England in the Later Middle Ages.* London: Routledge and Kegan Paul, 1973.

Bennett, Judith M., and Ruth Mazo Karras, eds. *The Oxford Handbook of Women and Gender in Medieval Europe*. New York: Oxford University Press, 2013.

Benson, Larry D. *King Arthur's Death, the Middle English Stanzaic Morte Arthur and Alliterative Morte Arthure*. Kalamazoo, MI: Medieval Institute Publications, 1994.

"Tournament in the Romances of Chrétien de Troyes and L'Histoire de Guillaume le Marechal." In *Chivalric Literature: Essays on Relations between Literature and Life in the Later Middle Ages*. Edited by Larry D. Benson and John Leyerle. Toronto: University of Toronto Press, 1976.

Biller, Peter, and Alastair J. Minnis. *Handling Sin: Confession in the Middle Ages*. Rochester: Boydell & Brewer, 1998.

Bisson, Thomas N. *The Crisis of the Twelfth Century: Power, Lordship, and the Origins of European Government*. Princeton: Princeton University Press, 2009.

"The 'Feudal Revolution.'" *Past & Present* 142 (1994): 6–42.

"The 'Feudal Revolution': Reply." *Past & Present* 155 (1997): 208–225.

Bliese, John R. E. "Aelred of Rievaulx's Rhetoric and Morale at the Battle of the Standard, 1138." *Albion: A Quarterly Journal Concerned with British Studies* 20, no. 4 (1988): 543–556.

Blockmans, William, and Antheun Janse, eds. *Showing Status: Representations of Social Position in the Later Middle Ages*. Turnhout: Brepols, 1999.

Boffa, Sergio. *Warfare in Medieval Brabant, 1356–1406*. New York: Boydell Press, 2004.

Bonet, Honoré. *The Tree of Battles*. Edited and translated by G. W. Coopland. Cambridge, MA: Harvard University Press, 1949.

Bosl, Karl. *Die Reichsministerialität der Salier und Staufer: ein Beitrag zur Geschichte des hochmittelalterlichen deutschen Volkes, Staates und Reiches*, 2 vols. Stuttgart: Hiersemann, 1950.

Bouchard, Constance. *Those of My Blood: Creating Noble Families in Medieval Francia*. Philadelphia: University of Pennsylvania Press, 2001.

Boulton, D' Arcy Jonathon Dacre. *The Knights of the Crown: The Monarchial Order of Knighthood in Later Medieval Europe, 1325–1520*. Rochester: Boydell & Brewer, 1987.

Brown, Elizabeth A. R. "The Tyranny of a Concept: Feudalism and Historians of Medieval Europe." *American Historical Review* 79, no. 4 (1974): 1063–1088.

Brown, Warren C. *Violence in Medieval Europe*. New York: Longman Press, 2011.

Brundage, James A. *Law, Sex, and Christian Society in Medieval Europe*. Chicago: University of Chicago Press, 2009.

The Medieval Origins of the Legal Profession. Chicago: University of Chicago Press, 2008.

Bull, Marcus. *Knightly Piety and the Lay Response to the First Crusade.* Oxford: Oxford University Press, 1993.

Bullough, D. A. "Europae Pater: Charlemagne and His Achievement in the Light of Recent Scholarship." *English Historical Review* 85, no. 334 (1970): 59–105.

Bumke, Joachim. *Courtly Culture: Literature and Society in the High Middle Ages.* Translated by Thomas Dunlap. Berkeley: University of California Press, 1991.

The Concept of Knighthood in the Middle Ages. Translated by W. T. H. Jackson. New York: AMS Press, 1982.

Caferro, William. *John Hawkwood: An English Mercenary in Fourteenth-Century Italy.* Baltimore: Johns Hopkins University Press, 2006.

Mercenary Companies and the Decline of Siena. Baltimore: Johns Hopkins University Press, 1998.

Cameron, Sonja. "Chivalry and Warfare in Barbour's Bruce." In *Armies, Chivalry and Warfare in Medieval Britain and France: Proceedings of the 1995 Harlaxaton Symposium.* Edited by Matthew Strickland. Stamford: Paul Watkins, 1998.

Campbell, James. *Essays in Anglo-Saxon History.* New York: Bloomsbury Publishing, 1995.

Cantimpratanus, Thomas. *Bonum universale de apibus.* Edited by Georgius Colvenerius. Douai, 1597.

Cazelles, Raymond. *Société politique, noblesse et couronne sous Jean le Bon et Charles V.* Paris: Librairie Droz, 1982.

Chandler, Alice. *A Dream of Order: The Medieval Ideal in Nineteenth-Century English Literature.* Lincoln: University of Nebraska Press, 1970.

Cheyette, F. L. "The Royal Safeguard in Medieval France." In *Post Scripta: Studies in Honor of Gaines Post (Studia Gratiana 15),* 631–652. Rome, 1972.

Chibnall, Marjorie. *World of Orderic Vitalis: Norman Monks and Norman Knights.* Woodbridge, Suffolk: Boydell & Brewer, 1996.

Clanchy, Michael T. *From Memory to Written Record.* London: Arnold, 1979.

Classen, Albrecht. "Self-Enactment of Late Medieval Chivalry: Performance and Self-Representation in Ulrich von Liechtenstein's *Frauendienst.*" *Seminar – A Journal of Germanic Studies* 39 (May 2003): 93–103.

Sexual Violence and Rape in the Middle Ages: A Critical Discourse in Premodern German and European Literature. Boston: Walter de Gruyter, 2011.

Contamine, Philippe. "Geoffroy de Charny (début du xive siècle–1356), 'Le plus prudhomme et le plus vaillant de tous les autres.'" In *Histoire et Société: Melanges Georges Duby, Vol. II: Le tenancier, le fidèle et le citoyen,* 107–121. Aix-en-Provence: Publications de l'Université de Provence, 1992.

La Noblesse au royaume de France. Paris: Presses Universitaires de France, 1997.

War in the Middle Ages. Translated by Michael Jones. New York: Wiley-Blackwell, 1990.

Coopland, G.W., ed. *Letter to King Richard II.* New York: Barnes and Noble, 1976.

Coss, Peter R. "Bastard Feudalism Revised." *Past & Present* 125 (1989): 27–64.

"Knighthood, Heraldry, and Social Exclusion." In *Heraldry, Pageantry and Social Display in Medieval England.* Edited by Peter R. Coss and Maurice Hugh Keen, 39–68. Rochester: Boydell & Brewer, 2002.

Lordship, Knighthood and Locality: A Study in English Society. New York: Cambridge University Press, 1991.

Courtiers and Warriors: Comparative Historical Perspectives on Ruling Authority and Civilization. Edited by Kasaya Kazuhiko. Kyoto: International Research Center for Japanese Studies, 2004.

Cox, Rory. "A Law of War? English Protection and Destruction of Ecclesiastical Property during the Fourteenth Century." *English Historical Review* 128 (2013): 1381–1417.

Crouch, David. *The Birth of Nobility: Constructing Aristocracy in England and France 900–1300.* New York: Pearson/Longman, 2005.

Tournament. New York: Bloomsbury Academic Group, 2006.

William Marshall: Knighthood, War, and Chivalry, 1147–1219. New York: Longman, 2002.

Crozet-Pavan, Elizabeth. *La derision au Moyen Age.* Paris: Sorbonne, 2003.

The Crusades, 4 vols. Edited by Andrew Jotischky. Routledge Critical Concepts in Historical Studies. Routledge, 2008.

Curry, Anne. "Disciplinary Ordinances for English and Franco-Scottish Armies in 1385: An International Code?" *Journal of Medieval History* 37 (2011): 269–294.

"The Military Ordinances of Henry V: Texts and Contexts." In *War, Government and Aristocracy in the British Isles, c. 1150–1500: Essays in Honour of Michael Prestwich.* Edited by C. Given-Wilson, A. Kettle, and L. Scales, 214–249. Woodbridge, Suffolk: Boydell, 2008.

Curta, Florin. "*Furor Teutonicus*: A Note on Ethnic Stereotypes in Suger's *Deeds of Louis the Fat.*" *Haskins Society Journal* 16 (2005): 62–76.

Davis, R. H. C. "A Norman Charter." *British Museum Quarterly* 25 (1962): 75–79.

Demoy, Germain. *Inventaire des sceaux de la Flandre: recueillis dans les dépôts d'archives, musées et collections particulières du Département du Nord,* 2 vols. Paris: Imprimerie Nationale, 1873.

Dingman, Paul. "Ethics and Emotions: A Cultural History of Chivalric Friendship in Medieval/Early Modern Times." PhD dissertation, University of Rochester, 2012.

Duby, Georges. *The Chivalrous Society*. Translated by Cynthia Postan. Berkeley: University of California Press, 1980.

La société aux xie et xiie siècles dans la région mâconnaise. Paris: Armand Colin, 1953.

"Les sociétés médiévales: une approche d'ensemble." *Annales. Economie, societe, civilization* I (1971): 1–13.

William Marshal, Flower of Chivalry. Translated by R. Howard. New York: Pantheon, 1985.

Duggan, Lawrence G. *Armsbearing and the Clergy in the History and Canon Law of Western Christianity*. Rochester: Boydell & Brewer, 2013.

Dykema, Peter A., and Heiko Oberman, eds. *Anti-Clericalism in Late Medieval and Early Modern Europe*. Leiden: Brill, 1993.

Edwards, John. *Christian Córdoba: The City and Its Regions in the Late Middle Ages*. Cambridge: Cambridge University Press, 1982.

Ehrstein, Stephen. "Gentry Behavior in Fourteenth-Century Lancashire." Master's thesis, University of Rochester, 1996.

Elias, Norbert. *Über den Prozess der Zivilisation*. Basel: Verlag Haus zum Falken, 1939. English translation by Edmund Jephcott. *The Civilizing Process: Sociogenetic and Psychogenetic Investigations*. New York: Urizen Books, 1978.

Erdman, Carl. *The Origin of the Idea of Crusade*. Translated by Marshall W. Baldwin and Walter Goffart. Princeton: Princeton University Press, 1977.

Fallows, Noel. *Jousting in Medieval and Renaissance Iberia*. Woodbridge, Suffolk: Boydell, 2010.

Feral, E. "Le Proces d'Enguerran de Coucy." *Revue d'Histoire du Droit francais et etranger* 4, no. 26 (1948): 213–258.

Fernández, Emilio Mitre. *La extensión del regimen de corregidores en el reinado de Enrique III de Castilla*. Valladolid: Gráf. Andrés Martín, S.A., 1969.

Firnhaber-Baker, Justine. "From God's Peace to the King's Order: Late Medieval Limitations on Non-Royal Warfare." *Essays in Medieval Studies* 23 (2006): 19–30.

"*Guerram pub lice et palam faciendo*: Local War and Royal Authority in Late Medieval Southern France." PhD dissertation, Harvard University, 2007.

"Seigneurial War and Royal Power in Later Medieval Southern France." *Past & Present* 208 (2010): 37–76.

Violence and the State in Languedoc, 1250–1400. Cambridge: Cambridge University Press, 2014.

Fleming, Donald. "Landholding by *Milites* in Domesday Book: A Revision." In *Anglo-Norman Studies* XIII. Edited by Marjorie Chibnall, 83–94. Rochester: Boydell & Brewer, 1990.

Flori, Jean. *Chevaliers et chevalerie au moyen âge*. Paris: Hachette, 1998.

L'essor de la chevalerie, 11ème et 12ème siècles. Geneva: Droz, 1986.

L'idéologie du glaive: préhistoire de la chevalerie. Geneva: Droz, 1983.

"Ideology and Motivation in the First Crusade." In *Palgrave Advances in the Crusades.* Edited by Helen J. Nicholson, 15–36. Basingstoke: Palgrave Macmillan, 2005.

"Knightly Society." In *New Cambridge Medieval History* iv, Part 1. Edited by Daniel Luscombe and Jonathan Riley-Smith, 148–184. New York: Cambridge University Press, 2004.

Richard Coeur de Lion: Le roi-chevalier. Paris: Payot, 1999.

Richard the Lionheart: King and Knight. Translated by Jean Birrell. Edinburgh: Edinburgh University Press, 2006.

Foran, Susan. "A Great Romance: Chivalry and War in Barbour's Bruce." In *Fourteenth Century England*, vol. 6. Edited by Chris Given-Wilson, 1–26. Rochester: Boydell & Brewer, 2010.

Fossier, Robert. "Fortunes et infortunes paysanes au Cambrésis a la fin du XIIIe siècle." In *Economies et sociétés au moyen âge*, 171–182. Paris, 1973.

Foster, R. F., ed. *Oxford Illustrated History of Ireland.* New York: Oxford University Press, 1989.

Fowler, Kenneth. "Froissart, Chronicler of Chivalry," *History Today* 36, no. 5 (1986).

Medieval Mercenaries. Oxford: Blackwell, 2001.

Frantzen, Allen J. *Bloody Good: Chivalry, Sacrifice, and the Great War.* Chicago: University of Chicago Press, 2004.

Frappier, Jean. *Étude sur "La Mort le Roi Artu."* Geneva: Droz, 1961.

Freed, John B. *Noble Bondsmen: Ministerial Marriages in the Archdiocese of Salzburg, 1100–1343.* Ithaca: Cornell University Press, 1995.

"The Creation of the Codex Falkensteinensis (1166): Self-Representation and Reality." In *Representations of Power in Medieval Germany 800–1500.* Edited by Björn Weiler, 189–210. Turnhout: Brepols, 2006.

Freedman, Paul. "Peasant Anger in the Later Medieval Ages." In *Anger's Past: The Social Uses of an Emotion in the Middle Ages.* Edited by Barbara H. Rosenwein, 171–190. Ithaca: Cornell University Press, 1998.

Friedman, John Block. *Realms of Ritual: Burgundian Ceremony and Civil Life in Late Medieval Ghent.* Ithaca: Cornell University Press, 1996.

"Robin Hood and the Social Context of Late Medieval Archery." In *Robin Hood in Greenwood Stood.* Edited by Stephen White, 68–85. Turnhout: Brepols, 2011.

Fryde, E. B. *Michael de la Pole: Merchant and King's Banker (d. 1366).* London: Hambleton, 1988.

Fryde, Natalie. "A Medieval Robber Baron: Sir John Molyns of Stoke Poges, Buckinghamshire." In *Medieval Legal Records.* Edited by R. F. Hunnisett and J. B. Post, 197–221. London: Her Majesty's Stationery Office, 1978.

Fuchs, Barbara. *Exotic Nation: Maurophilia and the Construction of Early Modern Spain*. Philadelphia: University of Pennsylvania Press, 2009.

Fuhrman, Horst. *Einladung ins Mittelalter*. München: C.H. Beck, 2000.

Furber, E. C. *Essex Sessions of the Peace, 1351, 1377–1379*. Colchester: Essex Archaeological Society, 1953.

Gaignières, François-Roger de. "Les Tombeaux de la collection Gaignières: Desains d'archéologie du xviie siècle." *Gazette des Beaux Arts* 84. Edited by Jean Adhemar (1974): 1–192.

Gautier, Léon. *La Chevalerie*. Paris: Victor Palmé, 1884.

  Chivalry. Edited by Jacques Lavron and translated by D. C. Dunning. New York: Barnes and Noble, 1965.

Gentry, Francis G. "Key Concepts in the Niebelungenlied." In *A Companion to the Niebelungenlied*. Edited by Winder McConnell, 66–78. Rochester: Camden House/Boydell, 1998.

Gillingham, John. "1066 and the Introduction of Chivalry into England." In *Law and Government in Medieval England and Normandy*. Edited by George Garrett and John Hudson, 31–55. Cambridge: Cambridge University Press, 1994.

  "Christian Warriors and the Enslavement of Fellow Christians." In *Chevalerie et christianisme aux xiie et xiiie siècles*. Edited by M. Aurell and C. Girbea, 237–256. Rennes: Presses Universitaires de Rennes, 2011.

  "Conquering the Barbarians: War and Chivalry in Twelfth-Century Britain and Ireland." In *The English in the Twelfth Century: Imperialism, National Identity, and Political Values*. Edited by John Gillingham, 41–58. Rochester: Boydell & Brewer, 2000.

  The English in the Twelfth Century: Imperialism, National Identity and Political Values. Woodbridge, Suffolk: Boydell, 2000.

  "Fontenoy and After: Pursuing Enemies to Death in France between the Ninth and Eleventh Centuries." In *Frankland: The Franks and the World of the Early Middle Ages*. Edited by Paul Fouracre and David Ganz, 242–265. Manchester: Manchester University Press, 2008.

  "Holding to the Rules of War *(Bellica Iura Tenentes)*: Right Conduct before, during, and after Battle in North-Western Europe in the Eleventh Century." In *Anglo-Norman Studies* 29. Edited by C. P. Lewis, 1–15. Rochester: Boydell & Brewer, 2006.

  "Killing and Mutilating Political Enemies in the British Isles from the Late Twelfth to the Early Fourteenth Century: A Comparative Study." In *Britain and Ireland, 900–1300: Insular Responses to Medieval European Change*. Edited by Brendan Smith. New York: Cambridge University Press, 1999.

  Richard I. New Haven: Yale University Press, 2002.

  "Women, Children and the Profits of War." In *Gender and Historiography: Studies in the Earlier Middle Ages in Honour of Pauline Stafford*. Edited by

Janet L. Nelson, Susan Reynolds, and Susan M. Johns, 61–74. London: Institute of Historical Research, 2012.

Girouard, Mark. *The Return to Camelot: Chivalry and the English Gentleman.* New Haven: Yale University Press, 1981.

Good Impressions: Image and Authority in Medieval Seals. Edited by Noël Adams, John Cherry, and James Robinson. London: British Museum, 2008.

Gorlon, Daniel. *Citizens without Sovereignty.* Princeton: Princeton University Press, 1994.

Gravdal, Kathryn. *Ravishing Maidens: Writing Rape in Medieval French Literature and Law.* Philadelphia: University of Pennsylvania Press, 2011.

Guyol, Christopher. "Benedictine Sermons and Coercive Violence in Late Medieval England." In *Prowess, Piety, and Public Order in Medieval Society: Studies in Honor of Richard W. Kaeuper.* Edited by Daniel Franke and Craig Nakashian. Leiden: Brill, forthcoming.

English Monasticism and Royal Governance in the Fourteenth and Fifteenth Centuries. PhD dissertation, University of Rochester, 2013.

"'Let Them Realize What God Can Do': Chivalry in the St Albans Chronicle." In *Fourteenth Century England* IX. Edited by J. S. Boswell and Gwilym Dodd. Forthcoming.

Guzman, Fernan Perez de. "Crónica del serenísimo príncipe Don Juan, segundo rey deste nombre en castilla y en leon." In *Biblioteca de Autores Españoles* 68. Edited by M. Rivadeneyra. Madrid: Impresores de Camara de S.M., 1877.

Hahn, Thomas, ed. *Sir Gawain: Eleven Romances and Tales.* Kalamazoo, MI: TEAMS, 1995.

Hall, Bert. "Lynn White's *Medieval Technology and Social Change* after Thirty Years." In *Technological Change: Methods and Themes in the History of Technology.* Edited by Robert Fox, 58–101. New York: Routledge, 1996.

Halsall, Guy. *Warfare and Society in the Barbarian West, 450–900.* New York: Routledge, 2003.

Haren, Michael. *Sin and Society in Fourteenth-Century England: A Study of the Memoriale Presbiterorum.* New York: Oxford University Press, 2000.

Harvey, P. D. A., and Andrew McGuinness. *A Guide to British Medieval Seals.* London: British Library, 1996.

Hascher-Burger, Ulrica. *Between Lay Piety and Academic Theology.* Leiden: Brill, 2011.

Hathaway, Stephanie. *Saracens and Conversion: Chivalric Ideals in Aliscans and Wolfram's Willehalm.* Oxford: Peter Lang, 2012.

Havercamp, Eva. *Medieval Germany, 1056–1273.* 2nd ed. Oxford: Oxford University Press, 1992.

Henneman, John Bell. *Olivier de Clisson and Political Society in France under Charles V and Charles VI.* Philadelphia: University of Pennsylvania Press, 1996.

"The Age of Charles V." In *Froissart: Historian*, edited by J. J. N. Palmer, 36–49. Woodbridge, Suffolk: Boydell Press, 1981.

Hewitt, H. J. *Organization of War under Edward III: 1338–62*. Manchester: Manchester University Press, 1966.

   The Black Prince's Expedition. Manchester: Manchester University Press, 1958.

Hicks, Michael. *Bastard Feudalism*. New York: Routledge, 1995.

Hillgarth, J. *The Spanish Kingdoms*. Oxford: Oxford University Press, 1976.

Holt, J. C. *Magna Carta*. New York: Cambridge University Press, 1965.

   Robin Hood. New York: Thames and Hudson, 1982.

Homans, Margaret. *Royal Representations: Queen Victoria and British Culture, 1837–1876*. Chicago: University of Chicago Press, 1998.

House, Adrian. *Francis of Assisi*. London: Chatto and Windus, 2000.

Housley, Norman. *Contesting the Crusades*. Malden, MA: Blackwell, 2006.

Huizinga, Johan. *Men and Ideas: History, the Middle Ages, the Renaissance*. Translated by James S. Holmes and Hans van Marle. New York: Meridian Books, 1959.

   The Autumn of the Middle Ages. Translated by Rodney J. Payton and Ulrich Mammitzsch. Chicago: University of Chicago Press, 1997.

Hurnard, Naomi D. The King's Pardon for Homicide before AD 1307. New York: Oxford University Press, 1969.

Hunt, Alan. *Governance of the Consuming Passion*. New York: St. Martin's Press, 1996.

Hunt, Janin, with Ursula Carson. *Mercenaries in Medieval and Renaissance Europe*. Jefferson, NC: McFarland, 2013.

Hurtig, Judith W. *The Armored Gisant before 1400*. New York: Garland, 1979.

Hyams, Paul R. "Henry II and Ganelon." *Syracuse Scholar* 4 (1983): 23–35.

Imsen, Steinar, ed. *The Norwegian Domination and the Norse World, c. 1100–c.1400*. Bergen: Fagbokforlaget, 2010.

Jaeger, C. Stephen. *Ennobling Love: In Search of Lost Possibilities*. Philadelphia: University of Pennsylvania Press, 1999.

   Scholars and Courtiers: Intellectuals and Society in the Medieval West. Burlington, VT: Ashgate, 2002.

James, Mervyn. "English Politics and the Concept of Honour." In *Society, Politics and Culture: Studies in Early Modern England, 1485–1642*. Oxford: Past and Present Society, 1978.

   Society, Politics and Culture: Studies in Early Modern England. New York: Cambridge University Press, 1988.

Jamison, Evelyn Mary. *The Norman Administration of Apulia and Capua: More Especially under Roger II and William I, 1127–1166*. Dulles: David Brown Book Company, 1987.

   "The Norman Administration of Apulia and Capua: More Especially under Roger II. and William I. 1127–1166." *Papers of the British School at Rome* 6, no. 6 (1913): 211–481.

Jocelin de Brakelonde, "Chronica." In *Memorials of St. Edmund's Abbey*, vol. II. Edited by Thomas Arnold. London: Eyre and Spottiswoode, 1890.

Johnston, Mark D. *Evangelical Rhetoric of Ramon Llull: Lay Learning and Piety in the Christian West around 1300*. New York: Oxford University Press, 1996.

Jolliffe, J. E. A. *Angevin Kingship*. London: A. and C. Black, 1955.

Jones, Chris. "Middle Ages." In *Encyclopedia of the Romantic Era, 1760–1850*. Edited by Christopher John Murray, 743–744. New York: Routledge, 2013.

Jones, Martin H., and Timothy McFarland, eds. *Wolfram's Willehalm: Fifteen Essays*. Woodbridge, Suffolk: Boydell & Brewer, 2002.

Jordan, William Chester. *Louis IX and the Challenge of Crusade*. Princeton: Princeton University Press, 1979.

Kaeuper, Richard W. "Chivalry and the 'Civilizing Process.'" In *Violence in Medieval Society*. Edited by Richard W. Kaeuper. Woodbridge, Suffolk: Boydell & Brewer, 2000).

    Chivalry and Violence in Medieval Europe. Oxford: Oxford University Press, 1999.

    "Chivalry in Barbour's *Bruce*." In *Kings, Knights and Bankers: Collected Essays*. Edited by Christopher Guyol. Leiden: Brill, 2015.

    "An Historian's Reading of the Tale of Gamelyn." *Medium Aevum* 52 (1983): 51–62.

    Holy Warriors: The Religious Ideology of Chivalry. Philadelphia: University of Pennsylvania Press, 2009.

    "The King and the Fox: Reaction to the Role of Kingship in Tales of Reynard the Fox." In *Expectations of the Law*, ed. Anthony Musson, 9–21. Rochester: Boydell & Brewer Press, 2001.

    "Literature as the Key to Chivalric Ideology." *Journal of Medieval Military History* IV. Edited by Clifford J. Rogers, Kelly DeVries, and John France, 1–15. Rochester: Boydell & Brewer, 2006.

    "Revenge and Mercy in Chivalric Thought." In *Peace and Protection in Medieval Europe*. Edited by T. B. Lambert and D. Rollason, 168–180. Toronto: Pontifical Institute of Mediaeval Studies, 2009.

    "The Social Meaning of Chivalry in Romance." In *Cambridge Companion to Medieval Romance*. Edited by Robert L. Krueger, 97–114. Cambridge: Cambridge University Press, 2000.

    "Vengeance and Mercy in Chivalric *Mentalité*." In *Peace and Protection in the Middle Ages*. Edited by David W. Rollason and T. B. Lambert, 168–180. Toronto: Pontifical Institute of Mediaeval Studies, 2009.

    War, Justice and Public Order. Oxford: Oxford University Press, 1988.

    "William Marshal and Lancelot: The Issue of Chivalric Identity." *Essays in Medieval Studies* 22 (2005), edited by Anita R. Riedinger, 1–19.

Kaeuper, Richard W., and Elspeth Kennedy. *The Book of Chivalry of Geoffroi de Charny: Text, Context, and Translation*. Philadelphia: University of Pennsylvania Press, 1996.

A Knight's Own Book of Chivalry. Philadelphia: University of Pennsylvania Press, 2005.

Karras, Ruth Mazo. *From Boys to Men: Formation of Masculinity in Late Medieval Europe*. Philadelphia: University of Pennsylvania Press, 2003.

Keegan, John. *The Face of Battle*. New York: Penguin, 1978.

Keen, Maurice. *Chivalry*. New Haven: Yale University Press, 1984.

"Chivalry and Courtly Love." In *Nobles, Knights and Men-at-Arms in the Middle Ages*, 21–42. London: Hambledon Press, 1996.

The Laws of War in the Late Middle Ages. London: Routledge, 1965.

Nobles, Knights and Men-at-Arms in the Middle Ages. London: Hambledon Press, 1996.

Kelsey, Harry. *Sir Francis Drake: The Queen's Pirate*. New Haven: Yale University Press, 1998.

Kennedy, Angus. "The Hermit's Role in French Arthurian Romance." *Romania* 95 (1974): 54–83.

Kennedy, Elspeth. "The Quest for Identity and the Importance of Lineage in Thirteenth-Century Prose Romance." In *The Ideals and Practices of Medieval Knighthood* II. Edited by Christopher Harper-Bill and Ruth Harvey, 70–86. Woodbridge, Suffolk: Boydell Press, 1988.

Keupp, Jan. *Dienst und Verdienst: Die Ministerialen Friedrich Barbarossas und Heinrichs VI; Mono-graphien zur Geschichte des Mittelalters 48*. Stuttgart: Hiersemann, 2002.

Killarby, Catherine Kovessi. *Sumptuary Laws in Italy 1200–1500*. New York: Oxford University Press, 2002.

King, Andy. "Treason, Feud and the Growth of State Violence." In *War, Government and Aristocracy in the British Isles, c. 1150–1500*. Edited by Chris Given-Wilson, Ann J. Kettle, and Len Scales, 84–113. Rochester: Boydell & Brewer, 2008.

"War and Peace: A Knight's Tale; The Ethics of War in Sir Thomas Gray's Scalacronica." In *War, Government and Aristocracy in the British Isles*. Edited by Chris Given-Wilson, Ann Kettle, and Len Scales, 148–162. Rochester: Boydell & Brewer Press, 2008.

Knight, Stephen, trans. "The Tale of Gamelyn." In *Medieval Outlaws: Twelve Tales in Modern English Translation*. Edited by Thomas H. Ohlgren, 264–289. West Lafayette: Parlor Press, 2005.

Knight, Stephen, and Thomas Ohlgren, eds. *Robin Hood and Other Outlaw Tales*. Kalamazoo, MI: Medieval Institute Publications, 1997.

La Jan, Regine. "Continuity and Change in Tenth-Century Nobility." In *Nobles and Nobility in Medieval Europe: Concepts, Origins, and Transformations*. Edited by Anne Duggan. Rochester: Boydell & Brewer, 2000.

Leclerc, Jean. "Un document sur le debuts des Templiers." In *Receuil d'études sur Saint Bernard: Rome, Apud Curiam Generalem Sacri Ordinis Cesterciansis* 2 (1966): 87–99.

Lerner, Robert E. *The Heresy of the Free Spirit in the Later Middle Ages.* Berkeley: University of California Press, 1972.

Leyser, Karl. "Early Canon Law and the Beginnings of Knighthood." In *Communications and Power in Medieval Europe: The Carolingian and Ottonian Centuries.* Edited by Timothy Reuter. London: Hambledon Press, 1994.

"Frederick Barbarossa: Court and Country." In *Communications and Power in Medieval Europe: The Gregorian Revolution and Beyond.* Edited by Timothy Reuter, 143–156. London: Hambledon Press, 1994.

Lieberman, Max. "A New Approach to the Knighting Ritual." *Speculum: A Journal of Medieval Studies* 90 (2015): 391–423.

Lucas, Robert H. "Ennoblement in Late Medieval France." *Medieval Studies* 39 (1977): 240–260.

MacDonald, Alastair J. *Border Bloodshed: Scotland, England and France at War, 1369–1403.* Edinburgh: Birlinn, 2009.

Maddicott, J. R. *Origins of the English Parliament, 924–1327.* New York: Oxford University Press, 2010.

Simon de Montfort. New York: Cambridge University Press, 1994.

Maier, Christoph T. *Crusade Propaganda and Ideology: Model Sermons for the Preaching of the Cross.* New York: Cambridge University Press, 2000.

Maitland, F. W. *Roman Canon Law in the Church of England.* London: Methuen, 1889.

Manteyer, Georges de. *Memoires de la société nationale des antiquaries.* Paris, 1890.

Marvin, Laurence R. "Atrocity and Massacre in the High and Late Middle Ages." In *Theatres of Violence: Massacre, Mass Killing and Atrocity throughout History,* 50–62. New York: Berghahn Books, 2012.

McCoy, Richard C. *Rites of Knighthood: The Literature and Politics of Elizabethan Chivalry.* Berkeley: University of California Press, 1989.

McEwan, John, and Elizabeth A. New, with Susan M. Johns and Phillipp R. Schofield. *Seals in Context: Medieval Wales and the Welsh Marches/ Seliau yn eu Cyd-destun: Cymru a'r Mers yn yr Oesoedd Canol.* Aberystwyth: Cambrian Printers/Canolfan Astudiaeth Addysg, 2012.

McFarlane, K. B. "Bastard Feudalism." *BIHR* 20 (1947): 161–180.

McNab, Bruce. "Obligations of the Church in English Society: Military Arrays of the Clergy, 1369–1418." In *Order and Innovation in the Middle Ages: Essays in Honor of Joseph R. Strayer.* Edited by William C. Jordan, Bruce McNab, and Teofilo F. Ruiz, 293–315. Princeton: Princeton University Press, 1976.

Mickel, Emanuel J. *Ganelon, Treason, and the "Chanson de Roland."* University Park: Pennsylvania State University Press, 1989.

Moore, R. I. *The Formation of a Persecuting Society: Authority and Deviance in Western Europe, 950–1250.* Malden, MA: Blackwell, 2007.

Morillo, Steven. "Milites, Knights and Samurai: Military Terminology, Comparative History, and the Problem of Translation." In *The Normans and Their Adversaries at War: Essays in Honor of C. Warren Hollister.* Edited by B. Bachrach and R. Abels, 167–184. Woodbridge, UK: Boydell & Brewer, 2001.

Murphy, David. *Condottiere 1300–1500: Infamous Medieval Mercenaries.* Oxford: Osprey Publishing, 2007.

Mulberger, Steven. *Charny's Men-at-Arms.* Wheaton: Freelance, 2014.

Musset, Lucien. *The Bayeux Tapestry.* Translated by Richard Rex. Rochester: Boydell & Brewer, 2005.

Nakashian, Craig. "A New Kind of Monster . . . Part-Monk, Part-Knight: The Paradox of Clerical Militarism in the Middle Ages." PhD dissertation, University of Rochester, 2009.

Norma, Edward R., ed. *The Victorian Christian Socialists.* New York: Cambridge University Press, 1987.

O'Callaghan, Joseph F. *Reconquest and Crusade in Medieval Spain.* Philadelphia: University of Pennsylvania Press, 2003.

Ormrod, Mark. *Edward III.* New Haven: Yale University Press, 2011.

Orrman, Eljas. "Rural Conditions." In *The Cambridge History of Scandinavia.* Edited by Knut Helle, 250–312. New York: Cambridge University Press, 2003.

Painter, Sidney. *French Chivalry.* Ithaca: Cornell University Press, 1957.
William Marshal. Baltimore: Johns Hopkins University Press, 1933.

Phelps, Dayton. *Beguines of Medieval Strassbourg.* Stanford: Stanford University Press, 1995.

Philips, Seymour. *Edward III.* New Haven: Yale University Press, 2010.

Pitt-Rivers, J. A. "Honour and Social Status." In *Honour and Shame: The Values of Mediterranean Society.* Edited by J. G. Peristiany. London: Weidenfeld and Nicolson, 1965.

Pizan, Christine de. *The Book of Deeds of Arms and of Chivalry.* Edited by Charity Cannon Willard and translated by Summer Willard. Philadelphia: University of Pennsylvania Press, 1999.
The Book of Peace by Christine de Pizan. Edited and translated by Karen Green. University Park: Pennsylvania State University Press, 2008.

Plucknett, T. F. T. *Legislation of Edward I.* Oxford: Oxford University Press, 1949.

Pollard, A. J. *Imagining Robin Hood: The Late Medieval Stories in Historical Context.* Abingdon: Routledge, 2004.

Powell, James M. *The Liber Augustalis or, Constitutions of Melfi Promulgated by the Emperor Frederick II for the Kingdom of Sicily in 1231.* Syracuse: Syracuse University Press, 1970.

Poly, Jean-Pierre, and Eric Bournazel. *The Feudal Transformation, 900–1200.* Translated by Caroline Higgitt. New York: Holmes & Meier, 1983.

"Que Faut-il Preferer au 'Mutationnisme'? Ou le Probleme du Changement Social." In *Revue historique de droit francais et etranger* 72 (1994): 401–412.

Posse, Otto. *Das Siegelwesen der deutschen Kaiser und Konige con 751 bin 1913.* Dresden: Wilhelm and Bertha v. Baensch Stiftung, 1913.

Powell, James F. *A Society Organized for War.* Berkeley: University of California Press, 1988.

Powicke, Michael R. "Distraint of Knighthood and Military Obligation under Henry III." *Speculum* 25 (1950): 457–470.

Prestwich, Michael. *Edward I.* Berkeley: University of California Press, 1988.

Puff, Helmut. "Same-Sex Possibilities." In *Oxford Handbook of Women and Gender in Medieval Europe.* Edited by Judith Bennett and Ruth Karras, 382–384. New York: Oxford University Press, 2013.

Raso, María Quintanilla Concepción. *Nobleza y caballería en la Edad Media.* Madrid: Arcos Libros, S.A., 1996.

Reuter, Timothy, ed. "Early Canon Law and the Beginnings of Knighthood." Reprinted in *Communications and Power in Medieval Europe: The Carolingian and Ottonian Centuries.* London: Hambledon Press, 1994.

   Germany in the Early Middle Ages. New York: Longman, 1991.

   Medieval Polities and Modern Mentalities. Edited by Janet L. Nelson. Cambridge: Cambridge University Press, 2006.

   "Nobles and Others: The Social and Cultural Expression of Power Relations in the Middle Ages." In *Nobles and Nobility in Medieval Europe: Concepts, Origins, Transformations.* Edited by Anne Duggan, 85–100. Rochester: Boydell & Brewer, 2000.

Reynolds, Susan. *Fiefs and Vassals: The Medieval Evidence Reinterpreted.* New York: Oxford University Press, 1996.

Riley-Smith, Jonathan. *The First Crusade and the Idea of Crusading.* Philadelphia: University of Pennsylvania Press, 1991; 2nd revised edition, Continuum, 2009.

Rittgers, Ronald K. *The Reformation of Suffering: Pastoral Theology and Lay Piety in Late Medieval and Early Modern Germany.* New York: Oxford University Press, 2012.

Rivard, Derek. *Blessing the World: Ritual and Lay Piety in Medieval Religion.* Washington, DC: Catholic University of America Press, 2009.

Rodríguez-Velasco, Jesús D. *El debate sobre la caballería en el siglo XV.* Salamanca: Junta de Castilla y León, 1996.

   Order and Chivalry. Translated by Eunice Rodríguez Ferguson. Philadelphia: University of Pennsylvania Press, 2010.

Rogers, Clifford J. "Bellum Hostile and 'Civilians' in the Hundred Years' War." In *Civilians in the Path of War.* Edited by

Mark Grimsley and Clifford J. Rogers, 33–77. Lincoln: University of Nebraska Press, 2002.

Soldiers' Lives through History: The Middle Ages. Portsmouth: Greenwood, 2007.

War Cruel and Sharp: English Strategy under Edward III, 1327–1360. Woodbridge, Suffolk: Boydell & Brewer, 2000.

Roland, Alex. "Once More into the Stirrups: Lynn White Jr., *Medieval Technology and Social Change*." *Technology and Culture* 44, no. 3 (2003): 574–585.

Rosenwein, Barbara. "De Cluny à Auxerre, par la voie des 'émotions': Un parcours d'historienne du Moyen Age." http://cem.revues.org/12520.

"Worrying about Emotions in History." *AHR* 107 (2002): 821–845.

Ross, D. J. A. "Pleine sa hanste." *Medium Aevum* 20 (1951): 1–10.

Round, Nicholas. *The Greatest Man Uncrowned: A Study of the Fall of Don Alvaro de Luna*. London: Tamesis Books, 1986.

Ruiz, Teofilo F. *From Heaven to Earth*. Princeton: Princeton University Press, 2004.

Sociedad y poder real en Castilla: Burgos en la baja Edad Media. Barcelona: Ariel, 1981.

Spain's Centuries of Crisis: 1300–1474. Malden, MA: Blackwell, 2011.

Saul, Nigel. *English Church Monuments in the Middle Ages, History and Representation*. New York: Oxford University Press, 2009.

Sawyer, P. H. "Technical Determinism: The Stirrup and the Plough." *Past & Present* 24 (1963): 90–100.

Scaglione, Aldo. *Knights at Court: Courtliness, Chivalry and Courtesy from the Ottonian Court to the Italian Renaissance*. Berkeley: University of California Press, 1991.

Scales, Len. "War and German Identity in the Later Middle Ages." *Past & Present* 180 (2003): 41–82.

Shadis, Miriam. *The Queen's Hand: Power and Authority in the Reign of Berenguela of Castile*. Philadelphia: University of Pennsylvania Press, 2012.

Sloan, John. "The Stirrup Controversy." medieval@ukanym.cc.ukans.edu, October 1994.

Smail, Daniel Lord. "Common Violence: Vengeance and Inquisition in Fourteenth-Century Marseille." *Past & Present* 151 (May 1996): 28–59.

The Consumption of Justice: Emotions, Publicity, and Legal Culture in Marseille, 1264–1423. Ithaca: Cornell University Press, 2003.

"Enmity and the Distraint of Goods in Late Medieval Marseille." In *Emotions and Material Culture*. Edited by Gerhard Jaritz, 17–30. Forschungen des Instituts für Realienkunde des Mittelalters und der Fruhen Neuzeit. Diskussionen und Materialien, no. 7. Vienna: Der Österreichischen Akademie der Wissenschaften, 2003.

"Faction and Feud in Fourteenth-Century Marseille." In *Feud in Medieval and Early Modern Europe.* Edited by Jeppe Büchert Netterstrøm and Bjørn Poulsen, 113–132. Aarhus: Aarhus University Press, 2007.

"Hatred as a Social Institution in Late-Medieval Society." *Speculum* 76 (2001): 90–126.

Southern, R. W. "Medieval Humanism." In *Medieval Humanism and Other Studies,* 29–60. New York: Harper & Row, 1970.

Western Society and the Church. New York: Penguin, 1990.

Sposato, Peter. "Chivalry and Honor-Violence in Late Medieval Florence." In *Prowess, Piety, and Public Order in Medieval Society: Studies in Honor of Richard W. Kaeuper.* Edited by Daniel Franke and Craig Nakashian. Leiden: Brill, forthcoming.

"Nobility, Honor and Violence: Knighthood and Chivalry in Florentine Tuscany, 1200–1450." PhD dissertation, University of Rochester, 2014.

"Reforming the Chivalric Elite in Thirteenth Century Florence: The Evidence of Brunetto Latini's Il Tesoretto." *Viator: Medieval and Renaissance Studies* 46, no. 1 (2015).

Stabler, Tanya. *Beguines of Medieval Paris.* Philadelphia: University of Pennsylvania Press, 2014.

Stephenson, Carl, and Frederick George Marcham. *Sources of English Constitutional History.* New York: Harper & Brothers, 1937.

Stone, Lawrence. "The Inflation of Honours 1558–1641." *Past & Present* 14 (1958): 45–70.

Strayer, J. R. "The Costs and Profits of War: The Anglo-French Conflict of 1294–1303." In *The Medieval City.* Edited by H. A. Miskimin et al., 269–292. New Haven: Yale University Press, 1977.

On the Medieval Origins of the Modern State. Princeton: Princeton University Press, 1970.

The Reign of Philip the Fair. Princeton: Princeton University Press, 1980.

Strickland, Matthew. "Mise a mort ou clemence? Killing or Clemency? Changing Attitudes to Conduct in War in Eleventh and Twelfth-Century Britain and France." In *Krieg im Mittelalter.* Edited by H. H. Kortüm, 93–122. Berlin: Akademie Verlag, 2001.

"Rules of War or War without Rules? – Some Reflections on Conduct and the Treatment of Non-Combatants in Medieval Transcultural Wars." In *Transcultural Wars from the Middle Ages to the 21st Century.* Edited by H. H. Kortüm, 107–140. Berlin: Akademie Verlag, 2006.

"Treason, Feud and the Growth of State Violence: Edward I and the 'War of the Earl of Carrick,' 1306–7." In *War, Government and Aristocracy in the British Isles, c. 1150–1500: Essays in Honour of Michael Prestwich.* Edited by Chris Given-Wilson, Ann J. Kettle, and Len Scales, 84–113. Rochester: Boydell & Brewer, 2008.

"The Vanquished Body: Some Comparisons and Conclusions." In *El Cuerpo Derrotado: Cómo Trataban Musulmanes y Cristianos a los Enemigos Vencidos: Península Ibérica, ss. VIII–XIII.* Edited by Maribel Fierro and Francisco Garcia Fitz, 531–570. Madrid: Editorial CSIC – CSIC Press, 2008.

War and Chivalry: The Conduct and Perception of War in England and Normandy, 1066–1217. New York: Cambridge University Press, 1996.

Takayama, Hiroshi. *The Administration of the Norman Kingdom of Sicily.* Leiden: Brill, 1992.

Tardiff, J. "Le Proces d'Enguerran de Coucy." *Bibliotheque de l'Ecole des Chartes* 79 and 80. Paris, 1918.

Taylor, Andrew. "Chivalric Conversation and the Denial of Male Fear." In *Conflicted Identities and Multiple Masculinities: Men in the Medieval West.* Edited by Jacqueline Murray, 169–188. New York: Garland, 1999.

Taylor, Craig. *Chivalry and the Ideals of Knighthood in France during the Hundred Years War.* New York: Cambridge University Press, 2013.

Taylor, Michael. "A Critical Edition of Geoffroy de Charny's *Livre Charny* and the *Damandes pour la joute, les tournois et la guerre.*" PhD dissertation. Chapel Hill: University of North Carolina. 1977.

Tegnér, Gören. "The Oldest Equestrian Seals in Sweden." In *Good Impressions: Images and Authority in Medieval Seals.* Edited by Noël Adams, John Cherry, and James Robinson, 66–70. London: British Museum Press, 2008.

Thorne, Samuel, ed., trans. *On the Laws and Customs of England.* 4 vols. Cambridge: Published in association with the Selden Society [by] the Belknap Press of Harvard University Press, 1968.

Throop, Susanna A. *Crusading as an Act of Vengeance 1095–1216.* Aldershot: Ashgate, 2011.

Tout, T. F. *Chapters in the Administrative History of Medieval England,* 6 vols. Manchester: Manchester University Press, 1920–1933.

Tracy, Larissa. *Torture and Brutality in Medieval Literature: Negotiations of National Identity.* Rochester: Boydell & Brewer, 2011.

Turner, Ralph V. *Men Raised from the Dust: Administrative Service and Mobility in Angevin England.* Philadelphia: University of Pennsylvania Press, 1988.

Turner, Ralph V., and Richard R. Heiser. *The Reign of Richard Lionheart: Ruler of the Angevin Empire, 1189–1199.* New York: Routledge, 2013.

Tyerman, Christopher. *God's War: A New History of the Crusades.* Cambridge: Belknap Press of Harvard University Press, 2006.

The Debate on the Crusades, 1099–2010. Manchester: Manchester University Press, 2011.

Utz, Richard, and Tom Shippey, eds. *Medievalism and the Modern World.* Turnhout: Brepols, 1998.

Vale, Malcolm. *Piety, Charity, and Literacy among the Yorkshire Gentry.* Borthwick Papers 50. York: St. Anthony's Press, 1976.

War and Chivalry: Warfare and Aristocratic Culture in England, France, and Burgundy at the End of the Middle Ages. Athens, GA: University of Georgia Press, 1981.

Van Engen, John H. *Sisters and Brothers of the Common Life: The Devotio Moderna and the World of the Later Middle Ages.* Philadelphia: University of Pennsylvania Press, 2008.

Van Winter, Johanna Maria. "The Ministerial and Knightly Classes in Guelders and Zutphen." In *Acta Historica Neerlandica*, 171–187. Leiden: Brill, 1966.

Vauchez, Andre. "La notion de Miles christi dans la spiritualité occidentale aux XIIe et XIIIe siècles." In *Chevalerie et christianisme aux XIIe et XIIIe siècles.* Edited by Martin Aurell and Catalina Girbea, 67–77. Rennes: Presses Universitaires de Rennes, 2011.

The Laity in the Middle Ages: Religious Beliefs and Devotional Practices. Edited by Daniel E. Bornstein and translated by Margery J. Schneider. Notre Dame, IN: University of Notre Dame Press, 1993.

The Spirituality of the Medieval West: From the Eighth to the Twelfth Century. Translated by Colette Friedlander. Kalamazoo, MI: Cistercian Publications, 1993.

Vaughan, Richard. *Philip the Bold: The Formation of the Burgundian State.* London: Longman, 1962; new edition, Woodbridge, Suffolk: Boydell, 2002.

Philip the Good: The Apogee of Burgundy. London: Longman, 1970; new edition, Woodbridge, Suffolk: Boydell, 2002.

Veitz, Mark A. "Shoot Them All: Chivalry, Honour and the Confederate Army Officer Corps." In *The Chivalric Ethos and the Development of Military Professionalism.* Edited by D. J. Trim, 321–347. Leiden: Brill, 2003.

Ventrone, Paola. "Feste, apparati, spettacoli." In *Comuni e Signorie.* Edited by F. Cardini, 393–412. Florence: Casa Editrice Le Monnier, 2000.

Verbruggen, J. F. "The Role of the Cavalry in Medieval Warfare." Translated by Kelly DeVries. In *Journal of Medieval Military History* III. Edited by Clifford J. Rogers and Kelly DeVries, 46–71. Rochester: Boydell & Brewer, 2005.

Villalon, L. J. Andrew. "'Cut Off Their Heads, or I'll Cut Off Yours': Castilian Strategy and Tactics in the War of the Two Pedros and the Supporting Evidence from Murcia." In *The Hundred Years War*, Part II. Edited by L. J. Andrew Villalon and Donald J. Kagay, 153–184. Leiden: Brill, 2008.

"'Taking the King's Shilling' to Avoid 'the Wages of Sin': English Royal Pardons for Military Malefactors during the Hundred Years War." In *The Hundred Years War, Part III: Further Considerations.* Edited by L. J. Andrew Villalon and Donald J. Kagay, 357–436. Leiden: Brill, 2013.

Vollrath, Hanna. "Ideal and Reality in Twelfth-Century Germany." In *England and Germany in the High Middle Ages*. Edited by Alfred Haverkamp and Hanna Vollrath, 93–104. New York: Oxford University Press, 1996.

Warren, W. L. *Henry II*. Berkeley: University of California Press, 1977.

Weiler, Bjorn. *Kingship, Rebellion and Political Culture: England and Germany, c. 1215–c. 1250*. Basingstroke: Palgrave Macmillan, 2007.

Weinfurter, Stefan. *The Salian Century*. Translated by Barbara M. Bowlus. Philadelphia: University of Pennsylvania Press, 1999.

West, Charles. *Reframing the Feudal Revolution: Political and Social Transformation between Marne and Moselle, c.800–c.1100*. New York: Cambridge University Press, 2013.

Whetham, David. *Just Wars and Moral Victories: Surprise, Deception and the Normative Framework of European War in the Later Middle Ages*. Leiden: Brill, 2009.

White, Lynn, Jr. *Medieval Technology and Social Change*. New York: Oxford University Press, 1964.

White, Stephen D. "The Ambiguity of Treason in Anglo-Norman-French Law, c. 1150–c. 1250." In *Law and the Illicit in Medieval Europe*. Edited by Ruth Mazo Karras, Joel Kaye, and E. Ann Matte, 89–102. Philadelphia: University of Pennsylvania Press, 2010.

"The 'Feudal Revolution.'" *Past & Present* 152 (1996): 196–223.

"The Politics of Anger." In *Anger's Past: The Social Uses of an Emotion in the Middle Ages*. Edited by Barbara H. Rosenwein, 127–152. Ithaca: Cornell University Press, 1998.

Whitteridge, Gweneth. "The Identity of Sir Thomas Malory, Knight-Prisoner." *Review of English Studies* 24, no. 95 (1973): 257–265.

Wickham, Chris. "The 'Feudal Revolution.'" *Past & Present* 155 (1997): 177–208.

Winroth, Anders. *The Conversion of Scandinavia*. New Haven: Yale University Press, 2012.

Wright, Nicholas. *Knights and Peasants: The Hundred Years War in the French Countryside*. Rochester: Boydell & Brewer, 1998.

Wyatt, David. *Slaves and Warriors in Medieval Britain and Ireland: 800–1200*. Leiden: Brill, 2009.

Young, Alan. *Tudor and Jacobean Tournaments*. Dobbs Ferry: Sheridan House, 1986.

Zink, M. *Froissart et le temps*. Paris: Presses Universitaires de France, 1998.

INDEX